I0819266

CROSSROADS

CROSSROADS

A MEMOIR *in* BASEBALL AND LIFE

DUSTY BAKER

WITH STEVE KETTMANN

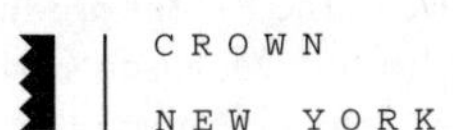

CROWN
An imprint of the Crown Publishing Group
A division of Penguin Random House LLC
1745 Broadway
New York, NY 10019
crownpublishing.com
penguinrandomhouse.com

Library of Congress Cataloging-in-Publication Data
Names: Baker, Dusty, 1949- author. Title: Crossroads: a memoir in baseball and life / Dusty Baker. Identifiers: LCCN 2025050923 (print) | LCCN 2025050924 (ebook) | ISBN 9780593800430 hardcover | ISBN 9780593800447 ebook |
Subjects: LCSH: Baker, Dusty, 1949- | Baseball players—United States | Baseball managers—United States | LCGFT: Autobiographies
Classification: LCC GV865.B237 A3 2026 (print) | LCC GV865.B237 (ebook)
LC record available at https://lccn.loc.gov/2025050923
LC ebook record available at https://lccn.loc.gov/2025050924

Editor: Kevin Doughten
Editorial assistant: Jessica Jean Scott
Production editor: Natalie Blachere
Text designer: Andrea Lau
Production: Christopher Andrus
Copy editor: Ethan Campbell
Proofreaders: Rob Sternitzky and Miriam Taveras
Publicist: Tammy Blake
Marketer: Mason Eng

Manufactured in the United States of America

1st Printing

First Edition

The authorized representative in the EU for product safety and compliance is Penguin Random House Ireland, Morrison Chambers, 32 Nassau Street, Dublin D02 YH68, Ireland, https://eu-contact.penguin.ie.

I'd like to thank God for everything in my life and
for the many blessings that have been bestowed on me and my family.
I pray for the strength to be a better man, and I pray for all of us.
I dedicate this book to my mom and dad, along with all my family and
friends and everyone else along the way who inspired me.

CONTENTS

CHAPTER 1

Mom and Dad Gave Us Our Strength

I was raised to give everyone a chance. Or at least to try. My parents taught us to keep our eyes open and to trust our feelings about people. If you did that, you could trust that person enough to let them show you who they are. You might end up being disappointed, but more often than not, you would see the good in people. That core conviction has turned into a lifelong philosophy of mine. The Devil might show up to lead some people astray, but most people have a lot of good in them, so why not look for the good?

Mom and Dad were both strong personalities. They gave me a strong moral foundation. From the time I could first crawl, my parents made sure to build up in me a sense of responsibility and a sense of possibility. I was the oldest of five, and my younger siblings and I would know the difference between right and wrong. My dad instilled tremendous common sense into me from an early age, and my mom always wanted to expose me to book-learning and intelligence, which I associated with her side of the family. It was a basic contrast between the two of them. I'm a combination of both. Thanks to Mom, all of us siblings would take our educations as far as we could. The emphasis on education came from my mom, but my dad was the enforcer. Dad led by example. He encouraged us to always be aware of our surroundings and be ready for whatever came along.

We were raised to be open to life and open to people—to what

Dr. King called "the content of their character." Here's the thing about growing up Black in America: You have to see more. You have to notice more. You have to think more about getting along with white people than they ever have to think about getting along with *you*. There's no sense being bitter or angry about that. It's just reality.

Every time you meet someone new, it represents a crossroads. To set aside your fears and your self-doubt, to shut down your overactive mind that sometimes throws too many thoughts at you—that can be challenging. Do I keep my heart open to that person? Do I trust in my faith in God and my faith in the basic good in people? Do I keep looking out at the world with the spirit of a child? I'm still working on that.

— — — —

I was born Johnnie B. Baker Jr. in June 1949, four years after World War II. I look back now and see that if I hadn't been raised the way I was, if I hadn't been taught by both parents to be responsible, I probably would have wound up in trouble later in life. I came of age in the 1960s, when the Vietnam War was raging and tearing the country apart. You had the Civil Rights Movement and then the Black Power Movement, hippies, and free love. It was a confusing but beautiful time all at once.

We hosted National Association for the Advancement of Colored People (NAACP) meetings at our house, usually about twenty-five or thirty people, a few white or Mexican American but mostly Black. My dad built that house with a big picture window in the living room, where everyone gathered on Saturday evening, since both my parents worked all week and Sunday was reserved for church activities. I was in the Junior NAACP from the time I was twelve or so, and I listened closely when my mom talked about the importance of voting. I learned young about the unfairness of hiring practices and discrepancies in pay structure, and how there was no governing body to which one could appeal. I first realized in those years that some racism can be triggered by your parents' economic success. I found out that before the Black Power Movement came along and united us, there was a separation of dark skin and light skin within our race. I only made one all-star team in youth baseball, when I was twelve, and never made another one until I got to the big leagues. But I noticed kids making that all-star team who just happened to have the same last name as the sponsor on the back of their uniform. The world was not always fair.

My parents were always trying to find a way to help me see and know more. As the firstborn, I was forced to notice more because I was subjected to more, and more was asked of me. At the time, I didn't always take too kindly to that. Usually I just wanted to forget myself playing outside, which was how I came to be called "Dusty."

In my family, there was only one Johnnie B., and that was my dad. He never let anybody call me "Junior." There was a dispute in the family over who first gave me my name. My dad would say he did, but my mom and her sister, my Aunt Loreena, were just sure it was one of them.

Loreena was my cool aunt. She was my mom's older sister, and she taught me a lot. I learned from her about forgiveness. She gave me books to read and opened me up to spiritual things that went way beyond what I learned as a junior deacon in church. My Aunt Loreena was my spiritual leader. She was an entertainer, lived in Oakland, and always drove a big new Lincoln or Cadillac. When I was old enough, she let me drive her car and cruise around with my buddies. Aunt Loreena said she first gave me the name "Dusty," and I wasn't going to argue. I was always out in the yard playing and couldn't keep my clothes clean for more than half an hour.

But my mom said she was the one to give me the name. She claimed she started calling me "Dusty" because I used to like to eat dirt. She said dirt-eating ran in the family. She had an aunt who also liked to eat dirt, she insisted. Something about the elements, iron or whatever else, which the body needed for nutrition. "Boy, what you *doing* eating dirt?" my mom would cry out into the yard. My mom was a very intelligent woman who spoke with clarity and precision and would later serve as my agent in early negotiations with the Atlanta Braves. Hear me when I say ain't no way I'm challenging her word on that—and I put it that way knowing full well how much my mom hated the word "ain't."

I grew up in the small city of Riverside, California, which doubled in size from 50,000 to 100,000 when I was still a kid, but I was raised country all the way. My dad would not have had it any other way. That was how he had been raised back in Florida, and what was good for him was good for us. We might as well have been living in the South, like my dad as a boy. We had a chicken coop, and it was my job to collect the eggs most mornings—and ever since I dropped one, I can't eat eggs over easy with yolk running all over. We hunted and we fished, and we did both to put food on the table. My dad could flat-out shoot. He would pull out his single-shot shotgun and empty a chamber at a rabbit or bird and then load that thing up again, all as fast as you could fire an automatic. He could shoot, but he couldn't run, not with that bad leg of his. So I was his hunting dog. Dad shot the birds and I went and got them. It was a good way to learn. If you think like a hunting dog, you're always going to have an edge as a hunter. That turned me into a lifelong hunter, the way that gardening and tending our fruit trees as a boy inspired in me a lifelong passion. Anytime I'm at home in Sacramento, I love to work in my garden and tend to my fruit trees.

You look back at your childhood and ask yourself questions about how you turned out. Was I always destined to become me? From the time I was a baby? Or was I shaped by my environment to grow up into the man I would become? I was very fortunate to have the parents I did and to grow up where I did, an hour east of L.A., where at the time we had total integration, in sports and in school, Blacks and whites and Mexicans and Asians.

I was raised in the church, and that was where I was instilled with my fundamentals and my outlook on life that shaped the man I am today. I can thank the church for steering me away from the pool hall. In fact, to this day, I have never learned to shoot pool, because the pool hall was right across the street from Park Avenue Baptist Church. I knew I better not dare to be caught coming out of that pool hall. Someone was always watching. They would tell on you in a heartbeat. They would reprimand you and send you home, and then you'd get a whipping. You were reminded to never embarrass the family name. Consequently, very few of us got into any kind of trouble. That was the epitome of a village raising a child, Neighborhood Watch in the true sense, before Neighborhood Watch ever existed.

We always ate as a family and said grace every night when we sat down to dinner. On Sundays, we went to church all day. I was a junior deacon and my dad was a deacon. I also sang in the junior choir, and my mom and dad were both in the choir. Sunday school started at nine-thirty A.M., then you had the regular service from eleven A.M. to one P.M., then you went home to eat lunch as a family and play ball out in the yard and eat dinner. We went back to church at night for Baptist Training Union, which was where I played piano recitals for the church. I wanted to play the boogie-woogie or Jerry Lee Lewis, but instead I had to perform "The Blue Danube" followed by "Hungarian Rhapsody." I had to bow, and all my buddies were there, snickering as I banged my way through. I was so embarrassed, man. It wasn't always easy being my mom's son, the way she was always focused on giving us class and culture.

We always had music playing at home when I was growing up. My mom woke us up every morning with Lou Rawls, her favorite. We knew it was time to get up out of bed when we heard "Tobacco Road." My mom loved a good melody and wanted music that she could sing along to like Johnny Mathis or anything out of Motown. She liked a big, booming, soulful voice. My momma, she *loved* Mahalia Jackson. My dad was the straightest man in the world, but he was *into* Miles Davis. I didn't understand Miles. I really didn't. But I *liked* Miles and I picked up an attraction to him and to jazz from my dad. He had some friends who were musicians, like Blinky Allen, the jazz and R&B drummer, whose son Kim played on my brother Rob's Little League team, and later for the Seattle Mariners. My dad was also into the blues—that was his favorite, and you knew he was home from working his two or three jobs when blues started filling up the house. I didn't understand the message of the blues, but I liked the melody of it and the rhythmic sounds. I didn't know they were often singing about oppression. I could tell something was wrong, I just didn't know what.

My mom pushed me to take piano lessons because she thought that would be a good grounding in music for me. I was always infatuated with the guitar and wanted to learn that, but my mother said no way. I also loved the saxophone, so in eighth grade I signed up for a music course at school and the teacher told me no. She said I could not play the sax because I had the wrong lips. What was she talking about? Wrong lips? I went home that night and stared at myself in the mirror, trying to figure it out. "Man," I'd ask myself in the mirror, "what's wrong with my lips? They ain't too big and they're not too skinny. I see people playing sax with all kinds of lips. And that teacher told me I had the wrong lips?"

My mom would make us go to classical concerts in an outdoor venue one town over in San Bernardino, where she and my dad worked at Norton Air Force Base. She was just sure I loved those classical concerts, because I would usually be smiling and nodding my head. She didn't know I was smiling because I kept a transistor radio in my pocket with an earpiece snaking up into my ear on the other side from where my mom was sitting. I would be listening to Vin Scully calling Dodger games.

I figured if I was going to learn the piano, I'd learn to play like Little Richard, loud and with feeling. Then I saw Jerry Lee Lewis play "Great Balls of Fire" live on television. I always thought it was *The Ed Sullivan Show,* but I guess it had to have been *The Dick Clark Show* on February 14, 1958 (thanks to our copy editor for looking that one up!). Smoke or fire was coming out of the piano. I loved everything about that cat's style. He was the one I was going to emulate. One day when my mother came home, I had my feet up on top of the piano and was pounding away. When my mother saw that, she had a fit.

"Have you lost your mind?" she asked me. "Get your feet off that piano!"

"Mama! Jerry Lee Lewis!"

"You're Dusty Baker! You're no Jerry Lee Lewis!"

— — — —

My dad never cursed and he never drank. He expected us to listen and listen good when he spoke. It was always "Yes, sir," or "No, sir" and "Yes, ma'am" or "No, ma'am" to my parents and my elders. Everybody in town, they loved my dad, but they feared him, too. He was a kind man but big, built like the football player Jim Brown. He never actually did anything for them to fear him, it was just the thought of what he could do. My dad was fair but strict. He always told us to be firm but fair, which was how I've always managed. My dad didn't spare the rod, but now that I look back, I never got a switch or a belt that I didn't deserve. Even when I did bad, I knew what to do. But being bad was fun, too. It was more fun being bad than being good.

I could never lie to my dad because he could see right through the lie every time. I couldn't get away with nothing. I got so tired of being under his discipline that I tried to run away from home when I was about nine years old. My dad parked at the grocery store and went shopping. I was supposed to wait in the car, but instead I took off. I was walking as fast as I could, no idea where I was going, when I saw him pull up next to me.

"Get in the car," he said.

I was a runaway for two blocks. That was how long that lasted. I got a good whipping and never tried that one again. Now that I've been a dad myself for years, it really hits me that we teach our children through how we handle certain moments. They give us an opportunity to communicate and to share values, especially if those moments are memorable enough. Once, my sister snitched on me to my dad and told him I'd been hiding dice inside my pillowcase. My dad took the dice, walked out to the driveway, and used a hammer to pound them into dust! I never forgot it.

I knew not to steal, but temptation will sneak up on you. I swiped a Mr. Goodbar candy bar from Mr. Carlos's little neighborhood market, but Mr. Carlos saw me and called my dad. When I got home, my dad asked me to crack a smile. I couldn't lie with chocolate all between my teeth. He knew I didn't have any money to be buying chocolate bars. I had to go to my piggy bank and get a nickel to pay back Mr. Carlos. I had to walk back down to his store and apologize—and then come home and get a whipping.

Those lessons stayed with me and helped prepare me for other, more important lessons that would come later on in life. "No son of mine is going to be a liar, a thief, or a gambler," my dad would say. And from that time on, I never stole anything or made an illegal penny in my life. "Oh, my aching back," my dad would always say after I got busted doing something wrong, or he would just shake his head and say, "This is going to hurt me more than it hurts you."

I mostly got all As and Bs, but one time I got a D in conduct. Rather than show that to my dad, I smudged it, and wrote in a C instead. I thought I was pretty smart, but I didn't fool my dad for a second. He gave me a week to confess. When I did, I got the belt.

"You lied to me, and no son of mine is going to be the class clown," he told me.

I was always a little wild. Not too wild, but just wild enough to find ways to have my fun, though I never went too far off the rails. I was never afraid of anybody, but I was afraid of what my dad would do if I got in trouble. He held me to high standards. "Don't embarrass the family name," he would always tell me, and I was always aware of that.

Both of my parents worked at Norton Air Force Base. My dad did whatever he did, which he said was top secret—and never told us more than that. Mom worked at Norton as a secretary. In those years, the government offered some of the best jobs that African Americans and other minority people could get. The pay was decent. The benefits were good, especially the health insurance. Back in the day, many Black people worked for the post office because it was a government job.

When I was growing up, I never knew the love of grandparents, which other kids would tell me about. That's why I'm so happy to have grandchildren now. Both my mom's parents died before I was even born, and my dad's parents were across the country in Florida and died when I was young. My dad, the youngest of six, was born in rural southeast Georgia in 1925, but he grew up in Lakeland, Florida. He remembered catching fly balls during Detroit Tigers spring training games in the 1930s and selling the balls back for a nickel each. That was deep into the Depression, and money was tight. He said he saw Babe Ruth play in Lakeland his last season as a Yankee, 1934. I heard that my dad would have been a great ballplayer, but he hurt his knee, and it had to be fused, so he always had a stiff leg and walked with a noticeable limp. But he never complained.

In March 1943, he enlisted in the Navy and saw duty in the Pacific as a gunner's mate in the Black Navy. That was before the U.S. Navy was desegregated in 1947. He was based in the Philippines and never told us much about what that was like, though one time he did show me a picture of himself with some beautiful girls he'd met there. I took a look, and he was right—those girls were beautiful. Years later, I married a beautiful Filipino girl, who my dad liked a lot.

After the war, my dad took a civilian job at Norton, where he started out as a sheet metal technician and ended up with an office job. He didn't want to pick fruit, which was what a lot of Blacks in Florida ended up doing, picking oranges or grapefruits. In California, he met Freddie Christine Russell, soon to be my mom. Her family had moved from Oklahoma to Indio, California, out in the high desert, where they picked dates before moving to Riverside.

Growing up, I was very close to my Uncle Floyd, my mom's youngest brother, who came to live with us after my grandparents passed. Her youngest sister, my Aunt Eva, went to live with relatives in Oklahoma. Her older sisters were my Aunt Loreena, the singer, and my Aunt Ana Mae, who worked for Martin Luther King Jr. Uncle Floyd was eleven years older than me, and he was like my big brother. He played the congas, and he showed me how to box. He also taught me how to play basketball, which he knew well as a player for the Junior Globetrotters. Floyd always had a word of advice for me. He left right after he finished high school and enlisted in the Navy when I was seven or eight.

My job every Saturday evening was to polish my dad's shoes. If I missed a spot, even just one little spot, I could polish them all over again. To this day, you will not see a scuff mark on my shoes. Once I finished polishing my dad's shoes, it was also my responsibility—along with my brother Rob—to wash and polish my dad's 1956 Oldsmobile Super 88, a stylin' car with three hundred horsepower and chrome all over the place that Rob and I had to buff and shine. That car was an important sign of affluence in the Black community. It was a car that turned your head. My dad always had nice cars, and then he had his old panel-sided Fred Sanford pickup truck, which Rob and I also had to wash, which he used for his work as a handyman and for gardening jobs. My mom always had a nice car, too. To this day, I always keep my cars clean—and always own a truck—and people call me a neat freak.

My dad was always working at odd jobs when he wasn't at the Air Force base, and I was usually there with him, picking up his strong work ethic and an entrepreneurial spirit. (I even started a business setting mousetraps around the house, and my dad gave me a nickel for every mouse I caught.) My dad and I would tack the seats at the movie theater in town. Once when he dropped the magnetic hammer on the floor by accident and asked me to pick it up, I leaned down and I could hear rats scurrying around. I picked that hammer up as fast as I could.

Sometimes we tarred roofs or poured cement or did carpentry work. We would head right over the Victoria Bridge from our new house that my dad had built to the wealthy neighborhood where my dad would mow lawns or whatever else needed doing. They talk about the "other side of the tracks." Past Victoria Bridge, less than half a mile from our house, that was the "other side of the bridge." I went to elementary school and junior high school with kids who lived there, but it was a different world.

One weekend I was working with my dad on a gardening job near Victoria Country Club at the house of some rich kid in my school, the kind of kid who would make the all-star team in place of me, just because of who his dad was. Money talks, I learned that one early. Or as we said in the '60s: *Money talks, bullshit walks.* I didn't like that rich kid. I guess he didn't like me much either, since he knew I was a better player than he was in any sport he chose. My dad and I were working in the front yard, and this rich kid called me over.

"Pick up that piece of paper," he ordered me.

For a guy who was always quick with a smile, I also had a quick temper. I went from zero to sixty faster than my dad's Super 88.

"Hey, man," I said in a low, surprised voice, not even a threat, more like a warning. "I'll kick your butt."

"Son," my dad called out, and I walked over to him.

"You go over there and you pick up that piece of paper," he told me. "We need this job. You hear me?"

I didn't say a thing. There was no talking back to my dad. Not then. Not ever.

"Then on Monday, when you're back at school, and they're playing flag football, well, you'll be playing tackle," my dad said in a strong, low voice. "You just run right over him."

"Yes, sir," I said.

I picked up that piece of paper, and the next week I took out my frustration on that rich kid. Oh man, he didn't know what hit him.

My dad taught me a lot when he made me pick up that piece of paper. No one controls your own emotions but you, not unless you let them. My dad was one of the coolest dudes I ever met. He could control his emotions as well as anyone I ever saw—except when it came to me. My dad explained something important to me at the time, which it took years for me to understand, which was the difference between what he called *outer dignity* and *inner dignity* and the importance of knowing which was which. The outer dignity is what you'll do to keep your job and feed your family. There has to be room for that to stretch a little sometimes. Your inner dignity is different. Your inner dignity involves fixed points that cannot be moved. No man should intrude on your inner dignity. You can't let that happen. But everybody's inner dignity and outer dignity are a little different. Along the way, you have to learn for yourself what you will take and what you will not take. You must be more determined and have more character. You have to find a way to pull strength from some of the negatives. That was never easy, then or now, but I see some of those same characteristics now in my own son, the inner strength and dignity. When a person intrudes on your inner dignity, then you have to say, "Screw this job," stand up for your rights, and hope that God will provide for you. I've always been taken care of when I guarded my inner dignity.

I saw my dad and mom struggle at times with anger, trying not to let it eat them up. They would come home, and I could tell from one look at them that something had gone wrong at work. They had endured some indignity. My dad never shared that with us. He kept it bottled up. But my mom sometimes would give us a deeper glimpse of what she went through. She'd graduated from high school and tried to find a job as a secretary, but for some reason those jobs kept going to white women who my mom knew were less qualified. She was an excellent typist and went to a special school to learn shorthand. Then she was hired and learned the job. Before long, they would have her training a new secretary. The next thing she knew, the new secretary would get a promotion and be her boss, even though my mom had trained her. I would see her crying about that kind of injustice.

For her second job, she decided she wanted to be a model. She sewed her own clothes, as women did back then, using a Singer sewing machine. She applied to a modeling school in Riverside, but was rebuffed. They thought she sounded white on the phone, but when she showed up and they saw she was Black, she was turned away. White girls who walked in would get accepted promptly. (Years later, I thought of my mom when I was with the Dodgers, trying to rent a spring training condo in Vero Beach, and was told, "No vacancies." I found out that some of my white teammates went in after me, and for them, there were plenty of vacancies.)

I remember my mom crying over being rejected by that modeling school, but she wasn't about to put up with that kind of disrespect. Her inner dignity did not allow it. Instead of quitting, she sued—and won. That was my mom. She would sue in a minute. After that, she founded her own charm school. I used to work there, starting at about ten or eleven, checking in all the girls when they arrived. That was one job I liked.

My mom prepared me for life in so many ways I did not appreciate at the time. She had me setting the table and washing dishes and ironing and sewing my own clothes from an early age. She taught me to cook. To this day, I don't like to hear cursing around women, because in our house, there was none of that. My mom absolutely did not go for that. You were trained to open the door for women. I can remember getting out of the car and her just sitting there, not moving.

"Mom, what's wrong?" I asked.

"Open the door, or pull out a chair and wait," she said.

So much happened when I was growing up in the 1960s that was shocking, it's hard to believe it was all squeezed into one decade. Then, as now, often you didn't even want to know what was in the news because it was a constant reminder of the real world. Then, as now, racism was like a fever that was spreading. It was a confusing time then, and it's a confusing time now. You feel progress being made, like when you watch TV and see commercials featuring interracial couples, but you don't know what to make of it. Is that just marketing? Is racism as real as ever?

My parents were determined to give me the tools to think for myself about what was happening and never be afraid to stand up for what was right. My dad was big on Jackie Robinson, who broke baseball's color barrier with the Dodgers only two years before I was born, and also gravitated to Martin Luther King Jr. and his vision and leadership ideals, because as a breadwinner he had to be more tolerant. My mom by comparison was drawn more to Malcolm X, whose picture she had on the wall, and the Nation of Islam. I was a combination of both and would later go through a period at about age fifteen where I wanted to change my name to Dusty X. When my dad found out what I wanted to do, his answer was an emphatic no. "Your name is Johnnie B. Baker Jr.," he told me. "And if you change your name—I brought you into this world, and I'll take you out of it."

A lot was going on and in my family we were always up on it. Civil rights was big in my house, for both my mom and my dad. My dad would make us watch the evening news together. We subscribed to *Ebony* magazine, which was like *Life* magazine for Black people, and *Jet,* a news magazine small enough to fit into your pocket, and also *Sepia* magazine, similar to *Ebony,* which every year had a spread on all the Black baseball players and some Latino players as well. I loved the Dodgers, especially Tommy Davis. I always had an affinity for the Braves as well, because of Hank Aaron and also Félix Mantilla, a second baseman from Puerto Rico, and Billy Bruton, a center fielder who hit line drives and could run like the wind. Years later when the Braves signed me, Hank Aaron paid me a compliment when he said I reminded him of Billy Bruton.

My mom was determined to give us culture, starting with me as the oldest of five. She wanted us to have the kind of exposure she herself never had growing up in Indio at a time before the Civil Rights Movement. She made sure to expose us to great books, like *Go Tell It on the Mountain* by James Baldwin and Langston Hughes's *The Panther and the Lash.* Not many kids are crazy about reading, but she figured if those books were lying around the house, along with others by Frederick Douglass, W. E. B. Du Bois, and Marcus Garvey, sooner or later we would give them a chance. (Later I studied journalism at college because I wanted to be a writer.) And we couldn't help but absorb some perspective and pride and maybe a little attitude. My mom always told me I was going to have culture whether I wanted it or not. Love is discipline, and I had plenty of both.

In our Riverside neighborhood, we lived racial tolerance every day. To us, it wasn't "tolerance," it was just life. You didn't think about it most of the time. Every once in a while, you would get reminded about racial intolerance, but that was the exception. So many of my closest friends back in Riverside were Mexican Americans that I would call myself the Black Mexican. To this day, soul food for me might be collard greens and fried catfish, or it might be tamales and tacos. My Uncle Floyd married my Auntie Maria after he came out of the Navy, and half their family was Mexican, so my cousins were half Black and half Mexican. We would go visit them in Tijuana, and later my uncle moved his family to San Diego. One time when I was with the Dodgers, some of my homeboys came to San Diego to watch me play, and one of them, Chile, called out to me from the stands, "Hey Mexican!" I said, "I ain't no Mexican," and he said, "Well I ain't no brother, and you always hollering, 'What's up, brother?' " So I started answering to "Mexican."

– – – –

For us growing up, sports was everything. To us, if you didn't play ball, man, you were just a little punk, you know what I'm saying? We did it for entertainment. It was how we tested ourselves and how we proved ourselves. I was lucky to have my dad as my coach. I don't know how he found the time. He would come home from his day job at the Air Force base, take a nap for about twenty minutes, and then go to another job, but somehow he never missed one of my games.

My dad hated complainers. He never got sick and he never, ever complained. To this day, I can't stand chocolate, because growing up I learned to hate the chocolate taste of Ex-Lax. It never failed. If I told my dad my back hurt, he would tell me, "Go get the Ex-Lax." If I said my knee was throbbing, it was "Go get the Ex-Lax." I had enough. I could be half dead and I wouldn't tell my dad. I said to myself, *Damn, what's Ex-Lax got to do with it? Why I got to run to the toilet every time I'm hurting?* I learned never to complain.

All year long, we moved from one sport to another. I loved every sport, but what I really wanted to do was box. I'd seen pictures of my dad boxing in the Navy, and I wanted to be like him. He had big strong hands. We used to watch Friday night fights on *Gillette Cavalcade of Sports* on NBC every week. My brother Rob and I would box and act like we were the Brown Bomber, Joe Louis, or Floyd Patterson or Archie Moore. Those guys were all heroes in the Black community, and they were always my heroes, like Jesse Owens, the star of the 1936 Olympics in Berlin. I boxed a little at the YMCA. I won some bouts, but then one kid punched me right in the nose, and after that I'd had enough. I hung up my boxing gloves. It was fun when I was doing the hitting, but getting hit was no fun at all. That was good news to my mom, who from the very beginning was against me boxing.

My parents were both working and wanted us to stay busy, so we always had summer school, and after school we took swimming lessons. My parents did everything they could to get away from racial stereotypes. My dad swam, my mom was a strong swimmer, and we swam together all the time all summer. When I wanted a skateboard, my dad built me a skateboard. When I wanted a ten-speed bike, he went to the dump and put some ten-speed handlebars on my bike and told me, "You don't need all those gears. All you need is start and stop." The man had a point. It's easy to get "need" and "want" confused. We didn't have everything we wanted, but we had everything we needed.

My dad liked having us play at home. If I was hanging around with a new friend, he wanted to see for himself what that kid was like. If he didn't like the looks of someone, I'd hear about it fast, and he would tell me he did not want that kid over at the house no more. We had a big backyard, and friends would all come over for football and baseball games. One of the best things that happened was when my dad made me a basketball rim and backboard from materials he found at the dump, and put up lights on the garage so I could play until midnight. The neighbors would yell at me to stop bouncing that basketball so they could get some sleep, until later, when I got good, and they all said, "That's my neighbor."

Rob and I used to play a game called strikeout. All we needed was a bat and a dirty old tennis ball, and we would pitch to each other against the garage door, even as the light of day was fading and the ball was harder and harder to see. I would do everything I could to strike Rob out, since the next day when we started again he would be batting, but somehow the little sucker always found a way to tip off the ball and stay alive. He was about eighteen months younger, but he was as good at ten as I was at twelve.

All the guys in town had been coached at one time or another by my dad and his friend and assistant coach, Roy Hale, who was white. My dad was always coaching Little League teams, before I was old enough to play, and one of his star players was future big-leaguer Bobby Bonds, part of a great family of athletes. It was a big deal for us in Riverside in August 1964 when Bobby's older sister Rosie, who used to babysit me for five bucks, won the Olympic qualifier for eighty-meter hurdles and competed in the Summer Olympics in Tokyo. She won her heat in Tokyo in her first race, finishing in 10.6, as fast as anyone ran that day, but in the final she hit the second hurdle and finished last. Rosie was the American record holder.

Bobby Bonds, four years older than me, was as good an athlete as I'd ever seen anywhere. I'd never seen anyone move the way he moved, smooth and lightning quick. He was the fastest, the strongest, and the best built. You couldn't take your eyes off him, because he was always doing something spectacular. To me, he was everything you wanted to be. If he could compete in four sports, football, basketball, track, and baseball, and be the best in all of them, then it was up to me, when my turn came, to show I could do the same. I could put up points on the basketball court like Bobby, and I had my moves as a running back in football, and I could always hit a fastball, but at that age I never had the power and strength to hit home runs the way Bobby did. I hit some triples—I would drive the ball and then use my speed to fly around the bases—but I only hit two homers playing youth baseball in Riverside. Bobby was a kid who pitched a no-hitter and hit two homers in one game.

It wasn't always easy having my own dad as my coach. He would tell me I had a bad attitude and had some hard lessons to learn. As much as I didn't want to hear it at the time, he turned out to be right. One time, I threw my glove down in frustration, and my dad cut me from the team, so I was sent to the minors and played on a team his friend coached. The next year, I was back on my dad's team, but he cut me for throwing my bat against the wall after I struck out. Believe it or not, I played for him again the next year—and again he cut me, and I ended up back in the minors playing for his buddy. I tried to quit so I could make some money with a paper route, and he wouldn't let me. The way he saw it, he had too much invested in me, buying me a Ted Williams–autographed baseball glove from Sears for $9.99, for me to quit and squander that investment. "No son of mine is going to quit anything," he said.

Sometimes my dad taught me by saying nothing at all. I remember the time my only all-star team in Little League was playing El Centro, and the whole season was on the line. If we could beat these guys, we would advance all the way to the sectional finals. Late in the game, we had a lead. But my dad, as my coach, had put me in right field, and I hated being in right field. We always thought right field was where you stashed the weakest fielder on your team. (Leaving aside the fact that Hank Aaron, Roberto Clemente, Frank Robinson, Rocky Colavito, and Al Kaline all played right.)

So I was out there pouting, pissed off at my dad for making me look bad. El Centro loaded the bases, threatening to take the lead. Still I was distracted and sulking. Then an El Centro kid drilled a ball to me in right field. I got a late break, because of all that pouting. By the time I reached for the ball, near the fence, it bounced off my glove and over the fence for a grand-slam home run. We lost, all because I let that ball pop out of my mitt. All my teammates came up to me afterward to tell me it was okay, it wasn't my fault, but I knew it was. My dad, he didn't say a word. He didn't have to. I knew. I had cost my team, all because I wasn't ready to make a play. I hated that feeling so much, I vowed then and there to never let anything like that happen again. And it didn't. From that day on, I was determined to be the best outfielder I could. There might be three or four times in your whole life when you mess up and can never forget. That for me was one of them.

— — — —

Looking back, it starts to feel like the crossroads you come to are life's way of teaching you different lessons. I was blessed to have a family like I did and to have so many people along the way take an interest. In my family, we were always there for each other, each our own way, even when we weren't talking about all we were going through. I got so mad at my dad for being so hard on me all the time. I seriously thought he was just being mean. I loved him, but I couldn't understand why he was so hard on me. Now I see he was just trying to raise me to be a good man.

Life is full of moments that test you and save you. You go through the hard stuff. You wrestle with your choices when you come onto another crossroads. You pray on it. Then you know you made the best decision you could, and you don't look back. And you lean into what's next and let a new day flood you with fresh joy or whatever else is in store for you.

If you put off hard decisions, sometimes life decides for you, and you kick yourself later. I have some regrets, everybody does, but I don't have many. You learn to get better at accepting what's coming. So much of life is about acceptance. You have to be aware of your opportunities and that makes you ready for whatever comes—since you can control some things, but most of it is out of your control. My cousin Troy, my Uncle Floyd's son, took to calling me The Planner, because I always had a plan. But most of the time, my plans didn't quite work. The plans that were made for me were the ones that worked best.

I learned young the importance of practice and hard work. If I saw my hero Elgin Baylor pull some new move on the basketball floor when I was in seventh or eighth grade, I'd work on that move over and over again until it was *my* move. Same with Sam Jones's bank shot. I didn't even like the Celtics, because they used to beat the Lakers all the time, but I respected them, and I spent hours trying to copy Sam Jones's shot. In football, I'd watch Lenny Moore and later Gale Sayers and learn whatever I could from them. I wore high-top shoes because my dad made me, so I wouldn't hurt my ankles, and he told me I looked just like Lenny Moore. (I wore his Number 24 like I'd later wear 40 for Gale Sayers.) If Tommy Davis or another player on the Dodgers did something at the plate, I would try to emulate him and practice that move over and over and over. I was always a stickler for practice.

Above all, I learned to be natural, as Ted Williams wrote in his book *The Science of Hitting,* which I studied all the time when I was in the minor leagues, so much so that the book became my baseball bible. Ted was far ahead of his time. Nowadays you'll often see graphics go up during baseball games giving a detailed breakdown on what a given hitter bats when a pitch is thrown a particular place. Ted had a graphic like that in his book, which was published in 1971. "My first rule of hitting was to get a good ball to hit," Ted wrote. "I learned down to percentage points where those good balls were. The box shows my particular preferences, from what I considered my 'happy zone'—where I could hit .400 or better—to the low outside corner—where the most I could hope to bat was .230. Only when the situation demands it should a hitter go for the low-percentage pitch." Like if you've got two strikes on you and have to swing.

Baseball and other sports happen in the real world, bounce by bounce. The only way to understand at a deeper level is to learn to look closer. Riverside Poly High and Riverside City College shared a stadium. We would go watch football games there every Friday night, and all the Black dudes in town used to sit up on top of this hill, like you were at the movies. You could see most of the field, except for one end zone. My dad didn't want to pay for us to sit in the stands, but we had just as much fun up on the hill. On the basketball side, I used to go to RCC to watch Bobby Rule, who went on to play for the 76ers, and the coach was Jerry Tarkanian. Rule was a left-handed power forward and center, six foot nine and strong, and he led RCC to a 35–0 record and the state title in 1964. Rule used to bring me with him to practice when I was twelve or thirteen, just to soak up what I could, and I was the only little kid who was allowed to watch practice, because I'd just be quiet and watch and learn.

If I flip through the pictures of my youth sports teams or in my old school yearbooks, I see Black and brown and white faces all side by side, like in the 1965 yearbook for Polytechnic High School in Riverside, which came out in June '65 at the end of my sophomore year. I turned sixteen that month and felt like I was coming into my own at school, playing football and basketball and baseball. That yearbook had two pictures of me playing football, flashing some speed, including one with a caption reading: "Casually waving as he flies past Santa Ana's 'B' player, Dusty Baker forges through the line toward the goal." I thought I looked like my hero Lenny Moore, the great Baltimore Colt they called "Lightning Lenny." Most of all, I was always trying to be like Bobby Bonds, one of a group of great Black athletes in our area who were a little older than me, also including Marshall Anderson and Art Gilmore, all multi-sport athletes who ended up in the Riverside Sport Hall of Fame, and Dell Roberts and Mike Davis and Bobby's older brother Robert, who played football at San Jose State and in 1965 was drafted by the Kansas City

Chiefs. Another was Tommy Hall, aka The Blade, who went on to play for the Cincinnati Reds. My dad's buddies would all come over to our house and put on music until late at night, some of them playing a card game like pinochle, and it was fun for me to hear them talk and absorb how they thought about things, pretending to be asleep so I could eavesdrop.

Up until 1965 in my family, our lives revolved around a few fixed points, our home and our church and the ball fields where we played and watched our sports, and Norton Air Force Base, where my dad had worked for as long as I could remember. Suddenly that spring we found out the base was being downscaled. Dad's job was discontinued. He was given two other options. He could take a new job in either Ogden, Utah, or Sacramento, California. For me, Utah was intriguing, since my friend Big Mike Davis played football at Utah State and loved it. He wanted me to go there. His brother Stan Davis, Bobby Bonds's best friend, later pitched in the St. Louis Cardinals' organization. My dad chose Northern California, working at McClellan Air Force Base twenty minutes northeast of Sacramento. We never asked him why he picked Northern California over Utah. There were some things we didn't ask.

My dad went up on his own to find us a new house. A real estate agent wanted to show him houses only in Black neighborhoods, so my dad found a house he liked in the nearby community of Carmichael. The house was two miles from Del Campo High School, which, as we would find out soon enough, was all white. It was a major adjustment, to say the least, but moving up there taught me some life lessons that would stay with me.

The timing of our drive north from our old life in Riverside to a new life in Northern California couldn't have been much more dramatic. This was August 1965. Six months earlier, Malcolm X had been assassinated at the Audubon Ballroom in New York City under strange circumstances, with three Nation of Islam members charged in the shooting. Two weeks later, on March 7, tragedy unfolded in Alabama during the Selma to Montgomery march, when John Lewis and others were savagely beaten by police, though they eventually reached Montgomery on March 25.

All around the country that summer, the tension was rising along with the heat. In Los Angeles that August, it was combustion time. Anger over racism was the flashpoint. A questionable arrest of a young Black man drew a crowd that soon turned ugly. For a week, the Watts neighborhood was like a war zone with thirty-four deaths and up to 14,000 National Guard called out to enforce order. I knew right then I never wanted to be in the National Guard, clubbing my own people.

We had an aunt living in Los Angeles and had planned to see her on our drive from Riverside up north. When we got there, we couldn't believe our eyes, looking out the car window and seeing looting and fires being set by angry crowds. It was just an explosion of outrage at police. I was so young, I didn't know what to think, but I didn't feel any fear. I didn't worry that something was going to happen to us. I figured my mom and dad could handle anything.

It was only a four-hundred-mile drive up to Carmichael, near Sacramento, six or seven hours packed into the car, but after those glimpses of the Watts riots and hours of passing by wide open farm land, our new home felt millions of miles removed from our old lives. It felt like landing on another planet. My dad set it up that way, thinking we would have a better quality of life and a brighter future if we went to Del Campo High, a brand-new school with new buildings and a new pool and new language labs and new equipment, all the most modern of everything. My new school had good teachers and good facilities. It just didn't have any Black students.

Our first day, for some reason I didn't walk to our new school with my brother Rob. He walked the two miles by himself. People were so shocked to see a Black person. It got ugly, Rob told me. More than one driver screamed "Nigger!" out the window at Rob as he walked down the sidewalk. Rob told me he was scared to death, but at the same time, he could see how scared they were of him. And what was he doing to harm them in any way? Nothing at all. He knew no one at the school, but a friendly looking kid he'd never met saw what was happening and walked over to him.

"Are you okay?" he asked Rob.

Paul Fisher was his name, and he was Jewish. That small act of courage and decency, reaching out to my brother, helped Rob get through that day—and Paul and Rob became lifelong friends. It was the same way I met Dennis and Brad, who are my friends to this day. Dennis and his sister Patti and Brad and his mom, Mamma Johnson, were always there for me. My first day at school, Dennis and I had three classes together. I saw him checking me out.

"Hey, man, you looking for trouble?" I said to him at football practice.

"No, brother, I like your style," he said.

"Really?"

"I'm new at this school," he said.

"I am, too."

He told me his mom had just died and he'd transferred from Del Paso Heights, a predominately Black area of Sacramento.

"Man, I'm looking for a friend," I said.

"I am, too," he said, and from then on we were great friends.

I found my brother Rob at lunch that first day at Del Campo. He was in the lower wing, with the freshmen and sophomores, and I was in the upper wing with the juniors and seniors.

"Have you seen any other Black people?" I asked him.

"Yeah, you," he said. "What about you?"

"Just you," I told him. "We're it."

CHAPTER 2

Please God, Not the South

We left a lot behind in Riverside, including the best days of my parents' marriage, as it turned out. I didn't see that until later, but it was the plain truth. Moving to Sacramento was hard on my mom. She was homesick for Riverside and missed her family and friends—and the racial diversity of the community we'd left behind. By the year after we settled into our new house in Carmichael, my parents weren't together anymore. I can't really say what all went into them growing apart. As a kid, you only know so much. My mom had been so young when I was born, just three months past her eighteenth birthday, she never got to do much before adult responsibilities took her life over. She was looking for more freedom to do things like go back to school and travel.

My mom was more of a free spirit than my dad. That was why she had to see the world and also why she let me subscribe to *National Geographic,* which was expensive—it sold for $1 per issue in 1965. Not many people at that time could afford to subscribe to that magazine, which helped me develop my curiosity about other places and other people. Anyone who was a kid in the 1960s knows what I'm talking about. I loved *National Geographic* because I felt like I was seeing the world without having to go farther than our living room. I loved photography and nature. You flipped through the thick glossy pages of that magazine with its sharp color pictures of leopards or gorillas or maybe an African village, and you felt like you'd actually been to those places. My mom loved travel so much, she later worked as a travel agent and truly got to see the world.

Moving up to Sacramento rounded me out in a lot of ways that I didn't even know I was being rounded. Southern California was hot weather, it was faster paced, and it was much more diverse, at least where we came from in Riverside. Northern California was more rain and colder winters. Life in the Sacramento area had a different rhythm. You took the time to go fish or hunt because all of that was readily available right down the street. In Riverside, you would have to drive miles to get to rivers and forest, but now it was right there. The two things I liked most about Northern California were being able to fish almost anytime I wanted and, given the climate, my allergies didn't kick up as much, so I was able to breathe better. And I started to grow.

My dream was always to be a professional athlete. I didn't care which sport, just so long as I made it. I was always battling to gain weight and strength. My brother Rob would lift weights and blow up like Superman. Not me. I would get stronger, but I wouldn't show it. I was skinny no matter what I did. I wore ankle weights walking to school and walking around to build up leg strength because that was what athletes did. I heard that Jumpin' Johnny Green said he could jump high because he always jumped rope. Jumpin' Johnny was a great rebounder who set a New York Knicks rookie record with twenty-five rebounds in a February 1960 game against the Philadelphia Warriors. I wanted to jump like him, and took to jumping rope all the time. I was always doing something to get stronger.

I don't know how I would ever have made the transition to a new school if I didn't have sports. Not only was I the only Black kid at Del Campo, besides my brother Rob, but I was going into my junior year of high school with kids who all knew each other from the year before. They didn't know much about me, except that I was from Southern California—and I was fast. We moved into our new house in Carmichael in August 1965, and within a week or two, I pulled on football pads and was practicing with the team.

Very quickly I opened some eyes, just doing what I loved. I always had such a fire burning beneath the smile I showed the world. That fire had burned in me going back to when I first watched Bobby Bonds and saw that he was the best in every sport he did. I burned with a competitive fire to be the best at everything I did. In one of our first games that season, I sliced my way through the Washington High defense for a thirty-eight-yard touchdown run, and we won 18–6. *The Sacramento Bee* took to calling me "the workhorse of the Cougar brigade." It might have felt great, except I didn't feel great. Something was wrong. I could feel my heart beating in my chest, and it was not right. It kind of hurt.

My dad took me down to see a doctor to get checked out. The doctor asked me a lot of questions, like if I'd ever had something called rheumatic fever. What was *that*? Why would he think I had it? The doctor said I had an irregular heartbeat and they needed to shut me down for a month to find out if playing sports was making the problem worse.

One month! I couldn't believe it. I had other things I cared about, my family and my friends, church and music and chasing girls, but sports brought it all together. Now this doctor was telling me to take a one-month break from sports—I couldn't even participate in PE! It was awful. I had to watch our football games from the sidelines in my street clothes. Sports felt like the only thing connecting me with others at my school. Now I felt cast out.

After a month, I went back to the same doctor, and again he pulled out a stethoscope and listened to my heartbeat. Still the irregular heartbeat.

"The kid, he'll never play sports again," the doctor pronounced.

I felt like my life had been ripped away from me. I was in total disbelief. My dad was as skeptical as I was. He wasn't about to take the word of that one doctor, so he decided to find a specialist for a second opinion, the best we could find. He drove me two hours into Oakland to see the specialist in one of those two tall silver Kaiser buildings near Lake Merritt. It was Halloween, and for me it was like the ultimate "Trick or treat," the kind of crossroads that feels like a scary movie.

"He's a normal growing boy," the Kaiser specialist in Oakland said.

"He'll grow out of his heart murmur. I see no reason why he shouldn't compete in sports."

I was so happy, I thought I was going to bounce off the ceiling. Back home in Carmichael that night, I was like a young racehorse that had been in the corral for a month. My whole game was speed and balance, and for a month I hadn't been able to do anything. It tore me up to be inactive all those weeks, like in that song by John Lee Hooker (who years later became a good friend): "It's in him and it got to come out."

"Dad, can I run?" I asked.

"Where are you going to run to?" he wanted to know.

"Dad, I just want to run."

I was out the door and flying down the sidewalk in nothing flat. By the second week of November 1965, I was begging the football coach to put me back in the lineup for the final game of the season on November 13. Finally, he agreed. I was out of shape and it was cold and rainy and muddy. We got our butts kicked, but I didn't care. I was so happy to be out there on the field playing football again. That felt to me like the greatest night even though we had a terrible game.

The day after my first football season at Del Campo, I turned to basketball, which was my first true love in sports. I was lucky to be playing for Eli McCullough, then just twenty-eight, a young coach who tried hard to understand me. He had been a great multi-sport athlete growing up in Santa Fe, New Mexico, playing sports with a lot of kids from the Native American reservation. He was in just his third year as Del Campo basketball coach when I arrived for my junior year after moving from Riverside. He was sitting in his office one day when his assistant, Ken Smith, rushed in out of breath.

"Coach, you've got to see who's in the gym," he said.

I kept hitting jump shots from all around the floor, and he thought to himself, *Lord, you've listened to my prayers.* Less than a month after our last football game, I was the high scorer for Del Campo in a basketball game against Washington High that we lost 54–40. In a game against La Sierra on January 11, I scored twenty-one points, and we still lost. Then in our home gym on January 21, I led us with nineteen points and fifteen rebounds against San Juan, and we finally won a game, 52–47. That snapped a streak of losing sixteen straight league games.

Coach McCullough was hard on me at times because he knew I needed that. He loved my dad because he never meddled and never told him what to do with me. If Coach had to discipline me, my dad backed him 100 percent.

I loved basketball practice, but one thing I loved more was fishing, especially when the salmon and steelhead were running. One time during basketball season, I heard that the salmon were running on the American River, right down the street from my house, and I wasn't going to miss that, even for a Saturday practice. I called Coach McCullough and kind of coughed into the phone and told him I wasn't feeling too great. I felt like it was worth it until I showed up at school on Monday.

"How are you feeling?" Coach McCullough asked, playing it cool.

"I'm okay, feeling a lot better, Mr. McCullough," I said.

"And how many fish did you catch?" he asked.

My track coach, John Kimball, had spotted me out in the middle of the river, trying to hook a salmon. There weren't too many Black kids around. I was hard to miss.

The one thing Coach McCullough had always told me was "Don't lie to me." And I had lied to him. As punishment, he benched me. That was torture for me, having to sit on the bench, out of the action, unable to do anything to help my team. I learned a valuable lesson from that: Telling the truth to your coaches and honoring your commitments always has to come first. For years to come, I told my own players, "Tell me the truth."

That year was my introduction to Del Campo, and it was not easy. Brad Johnson, the second friend I made after Dennis Kludt, told me I ought to talk to this one girl, Linda, a Russian girl in the school. He said she thought I was cute and liked me. That turned out to be a good tip. Linda ended up being my first girlfriend, which caused an uproar at the school. Some dudes cornered me in the bathroom. I quickly saw the true colors of some of my teammates on the football team. Some of them wouldn't even block for me, which pissed me off a lot. Coach John Eaton, who had been in the same backfield in college as Dick Bass, and who later played for the Rams, had to call a team meeting.

My dad went out on a limb to get me track shoes, football shoes, and basketball shoes. I had to have those shoes, and he came through for me. He was also working a second job at Sears by then and found a way to pay for me to attend the Squaw Valley Warriors Basketball Camp in the summer of 1966 after my junior year of high school. This was a high-altitude camp held at the site of the 1960 Winter Olympics, near Lake Tahoe. I always loved the mountains, a paradise for anyone who loves to fish and hunt.

I was in awe of the Warriors of the NBA, still the San Francisco Warriors then, or sometimes just "The City" Warriors. I met Rick Barry at that Squaw Valley camp, one of the greatest shooters ever, and he helped me on positioning and thinking the game. I got to play a little with him, and what I noticed was the way he moved. Rick Barry was as fast at six foot eight as I was at five eleven. That was what really amazed me. I'd never seen that kind of quickness in a big guy.

It was at that camp that I first met Al Attles, a point guard for the Warriors then who would later become a great coach. He was twelve and a half years older than I was, and the first thing you noticed was his voice, deep and strong, but kind. Al loved California, but talking to him, you knew he was from the East Coast. Al was actually born in New Jersey then drafted by the Philadelphia Warriors in 1960. He was with the team when it moved west in 1962.

Al noticed right away that I could be better. He helped me with my jump shot, adjusting my release point so the ball came off my hand straighter. Suddenly I could see the basket a lot better. My shot felt great. I ended up being named Most Valuable Player of that camp and developed a lifelong friendship with Al. Up until the time he died in 2024, even when he was deep in dementia, anytime he saw me he would always ask, "How's your jump shot?" He always said it with a twinkle in his eye.

As a senior, I was ready to have a big year in all my sports. But it turned out to be a rough one for me in a lot of ways. My parents were both such strong presences in our lives, like fixed points, it was a painful step forward into the unknown for all five of us kids when they split up. My mom took a trip with her sister, my Aunt Ana Mae, and when she came back something was different between my parents. Before that time, we had never seen them argue in front of us. Now all of a sudden, their marriage was over. My dad went to work one day and didn't come back. He rented a place over near American River College. I used to complain about my dad being real strict with me, but the truth was, I deserved it—and I missed him not being there all the time. Neither of my parents explained to us what had changed between them. I only know nothing happens overnight. Their divorce became official in October 1966, barely a year after we'd moved from Riverside.

Up until the divorce, we always had hot meals every morning, or breakfast cereal, and we always had dinner. On Fridays, sometimes we'd get a special treat to go to a drive-in, get some hamburgers from A&W Root Beer, and watch the movie. My dad liked Westerns, and my mom liked drama. That all changed. We were all shocked. It was hardest on my younger brother Vic and my younger sister Taria. As the oldest, I tried to be strong, but it was a confusing time. You don't think your dad is capable of being hurt. You know your mom can be hurt. You see the signs.

I tried to channel my confused emotions into my competitive fire in sports. I was in the middle of a good season playing football for Del Campo, high-stepping my way through tackles. I ran for more than 100 yards in a game and caught three passes for 160 yards with two touchdowns and also had an interception on defense. By the end of that month, *The Bee* did an article about how I "did almost everything" in another game we lost, running the ball for 217 yards, and also passed for a long touchdown and had another interception. They were writing about me having "the greatest moves of any back" ever to play in the area, which might have made me feel good if I hadn't been so distracted by our family issues. Inside, I was still reeling over my sudden transformation into the man of the house with my dad now living elsewhere.

We played Stockton in basketball that December, and I scored twenty-seven points with nineteen rebounds—"Do-It-All Dusty Baker," they called me—but we still didn't win and I felt like I was losing my own private struggle. Back in those days, you didn't talk about things like divorce. I bottled it all up and got madder at life. The worse I felt, the less I tried to control my fists, especially if I was called the wrong names. If someone wanted a piece of me, I was ready to go. I never knew where my short temper came from. People still wonder how I can be so cool one minute and then, if I'm provoked, lose my temper. It's just how I am. Always have been.

I loved being a part of a team and never wanted to be singled out too much. The papers kept focusing on me, with headlines like "BAKER FROSTS COUGAR CAKE AS SPARTANS FALTER." Coach McCullough asked me if I'd seen the clips, and I told him I had—and wasn't happy. "You call that sports department and ask them never to use my name in a headline," I told Coach. "The *team* wins or the *team* loses."

I learned about being a good teammate, which was keeping in mind that you don't have to score all the points and you want to give others chances to score a bucket and feel better about themselves. Like back in Riverside, when I was a team leader and we were choosing up teams, I made a point of picking that kid who always got chosen last.

When Del Campo played some of the inner-city schools in Sacramento, I felt very comfortable, because for me it was like Riverside. There were a lot more Black guys and a few Mexicans and Asians. Some of the Black guys from downtown Sacramento resented me since they thought I was making a name for myself just because I played against a lot of white kids. When we'd go play one of the rich-kid schools in the district, white kids were calling me a bunch of names just because I was Black. Then we would play one of the mostly Black schools from Sacramento and they saw me playing with all these white guys and called me "white boy."

"Dude, I'm from Riverside," I'd say. "I ain't from Carmichael."

On Saturdays, I would sometimes go play basketball at Grant Union High, on Grand Avenue in Sacramento, and hone my skills by playing against older dudes, most of them Black guys. They didn't make it easy on me, I'll tell you that. Which was good for me.

"Come on in," they'd taunt me. "You ain't over there with those white dudes any more. Come on in and get a lesson!"

I loved it. I more than held my own and probably gave some lessons of my own. And made some new friends from Grant, like Leron Lee, who came from Del Paso Heights and ended up in the Sacramento Sports Hall of Fame after he played eight years in the big leagues and then eleven more in Japan, kind of blazing a trail for guys to go play over there. Other Grant friends included Curtis Brown, his brother Leon (my roommate later when I went to Mexico to play baseball), Bill Crenshaw, and Big Larry Brown, who wanted to recruit me to Gonzaga, where he went to school. All those guys went on to careers as educators and wound up as principals. They gave me an education, all right. On weekends, we would play cards and dominoes, and that introduced me to a whole culture, similar to what my dad and his buddies did back in Riverside. Those Grant brothers schooled me pretty good and talked a lot of shit while doing it.

I played basketball whenever I could. I couldn't get enough. Sometimes I wanted to play because I had a new move I was working on, and sometimes it was just a physical compulsion to get out there and move. One weekend, we had a school dance at Del Campo, and I knew I might want to shoot around the next day, so I put some spitwads in the door. When it closed, it sounded like it was locked, but it really wasn't. The Saturday morning after that dance, I came back. I hit the door and boom, sure enough, it opened right up. I couldn't turn all the lights on, I wasn't going to take the chance of someone seeing the lights and busting me, but that didn't slow me down much. I could work on my jump shot even if it was dark in there. But Coach McCullough happened to be stopping by his office and heard the ball bouncing.

"How did you get in?" he asked me.

I loved Coach McCullough, but I didn't want to get myself into more trouble. I was afraid to say anything.

"Don't lie to me," he reminded me.

I had lied to him once about going fishing for salmon. I wasn't going to lie to him again. I explained what I'd done to fix the door. He gave me a quick look, then reached into his drawer.

"Here," he said. "If you want to play basketball that bad, here's a key. Practice whenever you want." He trusted me that much, which meant a lot to me. It was a big responsibility. I was suddenly a big hero with a key to a state-of-the-art gym, and would bring my Grant friends over to run some games and work on our skills.

We only had the one gym at Del Campo, and our basketball practices ran from seven to nine P.M. As the season rolled on, Coach noticed I wasn't myself. I was missing free throws. I was missing layups. Which just wasn't me. Coach thought I seemed distracted and withdrawn. He would ask me what was wrong and I would say, "Nothing," but he could see right through that. I'd stay after practice a lot and we'd talk, sometimes until midnight. He knew I was sensitive. He could see how hard what I was going through was for me. Finally, after many of those talks, this man I respected and trusted told me to keep in mind that my parents' divorce was not my fault. I never thought of it that way, but he sure gave me something to think about. I needed to accept that so I could be there to support each of my parents and also my brothers and sisters.

— — —

My mom always had me aiming high in my education. She wanted us to expand our minds, anytime we could. She set the goals, and my dad was the enforcer making sure we did the work. At Del Campo, under the direction of my mom, I was taking algebra, geometry, biology, extra Spanish, and Advanced English. I wasn't really too worried about my grades, to be honest. I figured I'd get an athletic scholarship to a good college and find a way to focus more on schoolwork later. I remember getting a report card back, and it was not a very good one. I said to my mom, "I can't just take English? I have to take *Advanced* English?" It was always understood that I had to push myself to make my mind better, to make my whole self better.

That's what my mom was doing for herself at that time. First she went back to school in Riverside, taking some night classes, then when she came up to Northern California, she started going to American River College at night after work. She had a job at the U.S. Bureau of Reclamation, which managed water and other natural resources, and that was when I was really getting into the outdoors. From American River, she went to Sacramento State College, where she majored in sociology and minored in ethnic studies. She maintained a B average and graduated in 1970, then went to graduate school at Sac State in Black History. As part of her studies, she did research trips to Ghana, Kenya, Uganda, and Spain, and also visited London and Paris.

When I think about it, my mom was responsible for helping me be how I am now. I remember one time back in the third or fourth grade, my mom came to school to get me, and I had to be excused to go home and make up my bed. All the kids were laughing at me. My mom had been warning me to make my bed, telling me, "One more time, and I'm going to come to school and embarrass you." She never had to do that again. She taught me how to cook, sew, and iron. I had to iron my own clothes starting in the eighth grade, and she didn't like them wrinkled. She also didn't like holes in clothes. If she saw a hole in my pants or a shirt I was wearing, I had to iron a patch on there. To this day, I can't stand to have dishes lying in the sink. In our house when I was growing up, you had to clean up your room and make up your bed, no ifs, ands, or buts about it.

Later on, after the divorce, I would sometimes complain to my dad about my mom, and he would say, "I don't want to hear that, son. That's your momma." My mom sometimes talked bad about my dad, but my dad never talked bad about my mom. My dad was softer on the girls than he was on me and my brothers, and my mom was softer on the boys than she was on my sisters. I think that's pretty natural. I could get away with stuff with my mom that I wouldn't dare try with my dad. You couldn't fool my dad too much. My mom was more understanding, except she didn't like me staying out late at night. On the one hand, I really missed my dad and missed him being in charge, because I didn't want to be in charge. But on the other hand, I had more freedom than I'd ever had.

I was always lucky to have older people seeing potential in me and trying to help. During my senior year of high school, my mom had me meet a young politician named Willie Brown. She'd met him through her work with the NAACP and as an activist. Brown, a young California State Assemblyman from San Francisco, always had style and was always smart. He'd just been elected to the Assembly in 1964, but he was making a name for himself. He would rise to become Speaker of the California Assembly and then be elected as San Francisco's first Black mayor, but back then I just thought he was cool and knew how to carry himself. What really impressed was the way he dressed—later he was famous for wearing only Wilkes Bashford suits and for the articulate way he always spoke. I used to go see Willie at the State Capitol when I was in high school. My mom made me go see him. She thought it would be good for my education, and it was. He had a big influence on me and taught me how to carry myself and be myself no matter who I was around.

My dad always liked the idea of me going to Santa Clara University, a Jesuit school in what would later be known as Silicon Valley, where he was sure I'd get a good education. I was being recruited by a young assistant coach there named Carroll Williams, himself once a star athlete at Lincoln High in San Jose and then San Jose State. We connected right away, and he was very understanding about my parents' divorce. We had fishing in common, and I'd tell him about spots I knew in the Sierra mountains where I loved to go fishing.

One night in May 1967, a month before baseball's amateur draft, Coach Williams came to a game of mine so he could drive me to Santa Clara afterward for a weekend recruiting visit. It was late by the time we hit the road. The highway was deserted and dark. About an hour into the drive, a deer ran in front of us, near Hercules after we'd crossed the Carquinez Bridge on Interstate 80. Coach Williams tried to swerve to avoid the animal, but it was too late and the deer slammed into the side of the bumper. He stopped the car so we could take a look, but the deer was dead. We were both shaken up by that. It made me think of having a guardian angel always looking out for me.

I liked the Santa Clara campus. I stayed in the dorms for the weekend, and Terry O'Brien, a sophomore guard, showed me around and introduced me to the guys, like Bud Ogden, a six-foot-six forward who set a school record that year with fifty-five points in a game, and his younger brother Ralph. I'd seen Ralph Ogden play at the Tournament of Champions at American River College the year before and thought he was one of the best basketball players I'd ever seen. That team also had a good center in six-foot-ten Dennis Awtrey, who went on to play in the NBA, which shows you how good a team it was.

I also got to hang out with some of the guys on the baseball team, including the only two Black guys, Albert and Alvin Strane, twins from Oakland who played shortstop and second base, and first baseman Big Bob Spence, from San Diego, who was later chosen in the first round of the 1967 baseball draft by the Chicago White Sox. I was impressed with Santa Clara, which was sunny and beautiful that weekend. I even got to see Jefferson Airplane and Cal Tjader perform at an afternoon benefit concert. But I didn't think I wanted to go to another predominantly white school, like Del Campo, even if my dad wanted me to. Also, my tryout with the baseball team did not go well. The Santa Clara baseball coach, Sal Taormina, was not sure about me. "He's okay," he told Carroll Williams. "He needs a little seasoning. He doesn't go back on the ball well."

You can imagine what I thought of that. My senior baseball season at Del Campo had been disappointing. I knew the major-league scouts were there to see what I could do. I figured they wanted to see me hit home runs, so I was trying to hit a home run every time up, even though that was not my game. I was a speed guy, skinny and underdeveloped at that age. I tried to be something I wasn't and had a bad season. We won the league anyway, helped by my homeboys Dennis Kludt and Gary Woodrell. At the same time I was playing baseball, I was running track, trying to be like Bobby Bonds. I'd show up at track meets in my baseball uniform, like Bobby Bonds, and I went to the state track meet at Balboa Stadium in San Diego, like Bobby Bonds.

At the insistence of my dad, I signed a letter of intent to play for Santa Clara starting in the fall of 1967. I had scholarship offers in basketball, football, and track from schools in multiple states, but none in baseball, which did not surprise me at all after the baseball season I had my senior year of high school. The baseball draft was coming up on June 6, and I had no idea whether I would be selected. You didn't enter the draft. You just waited to see if a team had chosen you.

I loved basketball and football and wanted to play one or both in college. It was the 1960s, man! There was a lot going down, but college campuses were an exciting place to be and I wanted to go to San Jose State or Arizona State. *Playboy* magazine had done an article on the top party schools in America and rated San Jose State and Arizona right at the top. The dad of a friend of mine had the magazine, and of course we pulled out the centerfold and had a look at the girls, but then we read that article. I told my dad I wanted to go to one of those two colleges.

"Oh no, boy!" he told me. "You ain't going to those schools. Those are the one-two party schools in the country!"

I didn't have the nerve to ask my dad if he'd been reading *Playboy* and saw the same article I had. I kept quiet.

I had adult responsibilities now as the man of the house. With my dad now having to pay $300 a month in rent on his own apartment, the economic spokes of the wheel were now out of balance for our family. I didn't want to be a burden on my family, even if I was on an athletic scholarship. My mom was in college, and my brother Rob would soon be going to college, and two years after him my sister Tonya. I had to make some money, which meant I'd have to give serious thought to playing baseball if a team drafted me.

What I dreaded more than anything was the possibility of the Atlanta Braves drafting me and having to go to the South to play baseball. For years, my parents had us watch the evening news with them, and I'd seen footage of the Freedom Riders being sprayed with fire hoses and attacked by dogs in the South. The night before the draft, I prayed, *Please, God, anywhere but the South.* I wasn't chosen by any team in the early rounds, probably because of the off year I'd had as a senior and doubts about whether I would play baseball. They were right to have doubts. A lot of scouts had been at my games, showing some interest, but my dad had told teams not to waste a pick on me because there was no way I'd be signing. Still, I was hoping to be drafted, even if I was going to tell them no.

The baseball draft was not televised back then. You waited for a phone call, basically. The first day of the 1967 baseball draft came and went without a phone call. That was not a big surprise, but it was still disappointing. Finally, on the last day of the draft, my phone rang. It was the Atlanta Braves. They'd taken me in the twenty-sixth round—I was bummed to go that low, but I also understood I was fortunate to be drafted at all, given my senior year. Atlanta was the last city I wanted to select me. It was the worst possible thing, having my only path forward in baseball run through the South—except, in another example of how you come to crossroads in life, it turned out to be the best thing for me.

- - - -

My mom came through that year with one of the best birthday presents ever. I'd been raised to love music, and she knew how much I wanted to go to the Monterey International Pop Festival that month, three days of hanging out and grooving and catching most of the hottest new rock acts. Our local paper had an article announcing that on Friday night, June 16, performers would include Lou Rawls, a favorite of my mom's, our wakeup music for years with "Tobacco Road," and also the Jimi Hendrix Experience, featuring a young left-handed guitarist from the Pacific Northwest who played upside down and backwards. The Monterey Pop Festival, about a three-hour drive away, would go down in the books as Woodstock before Woodstock, one of those cultural happenings of the 1960s no one wanted to miss. One thing I knew: If my dad was still in the house, he would never have said yes. I wouldn't have even asked.

My mom's gift to me was two tickets and twenty bucks, plus she gave me her white station wagon, an AMC Rambler Classic, to drive down to Monterey for the weekend, if it would make it that far. I couldn't wait to tell my best friend Dennis I'd scored tickets and we could go together, but Dennis had to work at the gravel pit and was a no-go. That meant my other great high school friend, my neighbor Gary Woodrell, lucked out. My mom liked Gary and figured he'd keep me out of trouble.

All over America, young people were hitchhiking or driving to the San Francisco Bay Area that month to be part of the scene. A new song had just come out about how if you were going to San Francisco, be sure to wear some flowers in your hair. A month earlier, the Sacramento paper had an article about how 100,000 of these flower children were expected for what they were calling the "Summer of Love" in San Francisco.

The music I heard that weekend blew my mind. When some intense rock-and-rollers from England called the Who knocked out an anthem about our generation, and sang, "I hope I die before I get old!" in Monterey, a lot of us sang along. Janis Joplin sang her heart out, and her voice had a way of picking you up and knocking you down all at once, like when she sang "Ball and Chain" at Monterey and Big Mama Cass was a row or two in front of us, shaking her head "Wow." Gary and I slept in the car and took it all in, the music and the scene and the girls—oh man, there were a lot of fine-looking girls there. There was so much reefer in the air, I'd never seen anything like it, but Gary and I said no to marijuana, as committed athletes.

I'd have been thrilled to hear any one of the bands that performed that weekend in Monterey. They were all that good, and all that different. Seeing all of them was as much fun as I'd ever had in my life. I still can't believe the lineup: T-Bone Walker, one of my dad's favorites and John Lee Hooker's mentor; Jefferson Airplane; Country Joe and the Fish; Canned Heat. A lot of musicians I'd never heard before that weekend turned into some of my favorites for years to come, none more so than Jimi Hendrix, whose intense guitar playing both frightened and attracted me to his music all at once. Hendrix was cool. When he set his guitar on fire during his Monterey set, we all knew we'd seen something that changed our lives.

- - - -

American Legion ball was where you really got to play against the best competition. Each team was a combination of three schools, so guys you had played against ended up as your teammates. Those were the biggest games around Sacramento, other than winter ball at Renfree Park, which was a tradition I didn't like, because for me it was too cold in winter to play baseball. If I'm cold, I want to be playing football or playing basketball in a gym. I don't want to be cold playing baseball. For me, it was all seasonal. One thing I liked about Northern California was that you almost had four seasons, which I wasn't used to. I'm a trees man, not a desert cactus guy. I love trees. I love watching them turn. My favorite time of the year is the fall when everything is changing all around you. You know it's going to rain and the wind is going to blow and knock all the leaves off the trees. Then you have a bunch of leaves to pick up, and you start the process all over again. I loved the fall, but it was always too short.

I was lucky to have American Legion baseball to redeem myself. Playing American Legion ball that summer, after I was drafted by the Braves, I got on a roll. I loved my coach, Spider Jorgensen, who was the perfect coach for me at that time. He was soft-spoken and low-key and never told us what to do. He coached us through what sounded like suggestions. Spider never made anything more complicated than it needed to be, but he got me focused to give every game—and every at bat—my full attention. Spider had us doing pro drills that were so good, I used them as a coach and manager for years to come.

Given that the Braves hadn't drafted me until the twenty-sixth round, I had my doubts whether they'd be willing to pay me much of a signing bonus. My American Legion play pushed them to up their offers. Generally speaking, the first-rounders made pretty good money and maybe into the second round, but after that you couldn't expect much. You'd think as a twenty-sixth-rounder, I was an afterthought for the Braves, but their scout, Bill Wight, had made up his mind that he saw a big future for me. The Braves had concluded that if I could channel all my ability into one sport, baseball, instead of playing different sports all year long, they'd have a good ballplayer to develop. Mr. Wight kept coming by the house to talk to me and my mom and lure me away from basketball. My dad didn't live there anymore and had two jobs, but he had a way of showing up anytime Mr. Wight came by.

My first weekend back in Sacramento after the Monterey concert, I had three hits in a game for my American Legion team, Fair Oaks. We kept playing well and earned a best-of-three playoff with Charles Eggen, the team we tied, and kept advancing. I was swinging the bat well and having fun and playing my game, and people were noticing. Going into the playoffs, I was hitting .382, after hitting .229 that high school season trying to hit home runs to impress the scouts. In one American Legion game, I scored our first run by reaching base on a fielder's choice, then stealing second, stealing third—and sprinting home on a wild pitch. We won the division and advanced.

I learned a lesson in our first game at the state championships in Yountville. In the second inning, we were up a run and the other team's second baseman walked. When the next hitter smoked a deep fly to me in center, I was surprised the runner was trying to tag and advance to second—and he beat my throw. That was one I wanted back, but in baseball, as in life, there aren't too many you get back. We lost that game, but bounced back in a game against South Torrance on August 13. We were facing Bart Johnson, a future Chicago White Sox pitcher, but had a 2–0 lead going into the eighth. Then our catcher, Lynn Mason, lost a pop-up in the sun, the ball hit him in the head, and South Torrance came back to win. Lynn was so ticked off with himself, he went in after the game and ripped a sink right off the wall of the bathroom. It was a tough game to lose, but I loved playing on that team. That was the most fun I had playing baseball in my whole life, and I answered any questions the Braves had about me. They'd been asking, "Does he love baseball? Or does he love football and basketball?" That question was answered when I turned down a trip to Mexico with basketball all-stars to stay with my American Legion team.

Their first bonus offer to me was around $6,000. Carroll Williams of Santa Clara drove up to Yountville to watch that game with South Torrance, and he had some good advice. "If you get a large bonus, you should sign," he told me. "If not, you should come to college."

The Braves came up from their first offer—a lot. Eight times, they made me a new, sweeter offer, and each time I got a little closer to being ready to sign, but I wasn't there yet. My dad had not wavered one iota. He was dead set against my signing with the Braves since he wanted me to have an education. He wanted all of us kids to attend and graduate from college and prepare for our futures. Looking back, my dad was right: I was giving up my strongest sport, basketball, and giving up a scholarship, to take a chance on trying to make it as a big-league baseball player without understanding what long odds I faced. Back then, if you were a pro in one sport, you were a pro in all sports. You couldn't go back to play college basketball after playing pro baseball. That made the decision even more momentous.

My mom was handling my negotiations. She was nobody's fool, and she was going to look out for me. Bill Wight kept stopping by to see her with a fresh offer. The Braves wanted to fly my mom and me down to Los Angeles on August 18 when the Braves were in town to work me out one more time and get a look at me. Bill Wight was advocating for me with the team, but the Braves' general manager, Paul Richards, was making the trip to L.A., too. He was eager to see me play with his own eyes, rather than going only on Bill Wight's recommendation.

I didn't think much about what it would be like to meet great Braves players I'd been hearing about for years. I was nervous, but mostly nervous about making the right choice. It weighed on me, that decision. I knew that if I signed with the Braves, it would upset my dad, and the situation was already contentious enough.

They put us up at the team hotel, and I rode on the bus to go work out with the team before the game on a Saturday afternoon. I was a Dodger fan, and my hero on the Dodgers was Tommy Davis, a batting champion in '62 and '63, so I was thrilled to go to Dodger Stadium with the Braves. I was even more thrilled when they suited me up and I went out and took batting practice. There I was, looking about fifteen years old, and they'd given me a uniform with no name on the back—so some of the fans there for BP were kind of giving it to me.

"Hey, no-number!" one called out.

"That guy doesn't even have a number!" someone else yelled, and they all laughed.

I didn't care! I was on the field. They were watching me, I wasn't watching them. That was like an out-of-body experience, standing on the grass at Dodger Stadium and looking up. I'd never seen anything like that view. The only time I'd been to Dodger Stadium was when I'd gone as a fan and sat in the upper deck. Now I was looking up at that upper deck from field level.

I was a nobody to these Braves players. I could have been any kid to them. I met Joe Torre, who was friendly enough, but like the rest of the team, he was focused on beating the Dodgers, not talking to an unsigned kid they'd never heard of before. I met Felipe Alou, who was exceptionally nice to me and gave me one of his bats, which my mom saved and gave me years later when Felipe was managing the San Francisco Giants, and I had him sign it.

On the bus ride back to the hotel, I sat next to Hank Aaron. I was raised to respect my elders and wait until they talked to me before I talked to them. I kept my mouth shut. It wasn't like we were shooting the breeze. How much does a kid talk to Hank Aaron? He asked me some questions about me and about our family.

"Are you going to sign?" he asked me.

"Mr. Aaron, I don't know," I said. "It's a big decision."

He gave me a long look. He had seen me work out with the team and sized me up as a ballplayer, and now he was sizing me up as a young man. He gave me the advice of a fellow ballplayer.

"If you have enough confidence that you'll be in the big leagues by the time your college class graduates, then go ahead and sign," he told me. "If not, then you go to school."

Confidence? That was something I had. I was sure that if I signed and joined the Braves organization, I would make it to the big leagues way before my college class was going to graduate four years later. I was sure because I knew I would find a way to make it happen, no matter what it took. I knew I had athletic talent, which was why they wanted to sign me. I could run. I was quick. I could jump. I could hit, and I could throw. And I felt I was smart enough to outthink most of them, too. But I had to develop more strength. I needed to work at it to get better at baseball, but I grew up thinking of hard work as a given. That came naturally to me. I could never have shrugged off my responsibilities like that. To me, those responsibilities were very real.

My mother wasn't a big baseball fan, but even she knew who Hank Aaron was. Everybody did. The week before I met him, Hammer hit his thirtieth home run of the season in a game against the Giants, giving him another season with thirty or more homers. My mama knew he was a great player, and she saw he was also a good man, sensitive and intelligent and mentally strong. He reminded me of somewhere between my dad and my uncles, and my mom took to him right away.

"Will you look out for my son, like he was your own son?" my mom asked Hank.

"Yes, I will, Mrs. Baker," Hank said.

He was not a man to waste words. He didn't say more than he needed to say. But when he gave his word, you could count on it.

Back at the hotel after the game, my mom and I went up to Mr. Richards's suite. That was some big suite. Mr. Richards said he was taking a shower before he went out to dinner and left my mom and me sitting there watching his TV. I started looking around the room. There on top of the TV he had left a big wad of bills wrapped up in a rubber band. It was such a big wad of cash it needed a rubber band to hold it all together! Paul Richards was no fool. He knew what would get my attention. I still didn't know what I would do, but the idea of signing was growing on me.

This was one of the biggest decisions of my life, and I felt the weight of it pushing down on me. Before I went to sleep in our room at the Braves' team hotel in L.A., I prayed on that decision. I was direct in my prayers, as I often was, and prayed to wake up the next morning with a sense of clarity. That prayer was answered. Waking up the next day, I knew what I needed to do. My mom and I signed the contract with the Braves, which included incentive bonuses and also a provision that the team would pay for my college education. I owed it to my family to do what I could to bring in money to help pay the family mortgage and send them to college.

I promised my mom I would go to college anyway, I'd find a way to do both, and I did. I could work my baseball schedule around my schedule at American River College, not the other way around. There was a war raging in Vietnam, and I wanted nothing to do with it. To avoid being drafted, you had to stay in school. You had to carry a full load, fifteen units, and if you got an F or had to take an incomplete, that was it. Your status was changed, and you were eligible to be drafted.

I admired Muhammad Ali and others who took a strong stand against the war. Ali had been drafted—and refused to go. That June, just a few days after I caught Hendrix in Monterey, a jury in Houston, Texas, needed only twenty-one minutes of deliberation to decide unanimously to convict Ali, then twenty-five, who was sentenced to five years in jail for refusing to fight in what he saw as an unjust war. (The U.S. Supreme Court overturned the ruling years later.) Ali was a great boxer, maybe the greatest ever, but he was also a man who thought for himself and a man who made sense, a hero to young Black people all over the country. Ali once said, "The only man I idolize more than myself is Henry Aaron." When Ali told his draft board in Louisville in 1966, "I got no quarrel with them Vietcong," he was making a point for a lot of us. Why should young Americans go die face down in the jungle trying to kill North Vietnamese? This wasn't like World War II, a war that was easier to understand. It wasn't just dissent over the U.S. war in Vietnam, it was all tied up together, the clash between police and young people in the alternative scene, the war. At Monterey, I heard Stephen Stills sing, "There's battle lines being drawn / Nobody's right if everybody's wrong / Young people speaking their minds / Getting so much resistance from behind." He wrote that song about a clash with police outside an L.A. music club, but it applied to everything that was going on. It was a time of real confusion.

My mom and I flew home from L.A., to Sacramento that Sunday. I packed up, and on Monday morning, Dennis and Brad took me to the airport, all without my talking to my dad. I was not looking forward to that conversation.

By the time I signed with the Braves on August 21, 1967, it was too late in the 1967 season for the Braves to send me to A-ball, so they flew me down to Austin, Texas, to get my feet wet right away in Double-A, just two steps removed from the big leagues, and that was when I first met Ralph Garr and Cito Gaston. One day I was playing in front of all my friends for the American Legion championship of California, then I was in L.A. taking batting practice at Dodger Stadium, then in the blink of an eye I was in Texas, an eighteen-year-old kid among grown men.

CHAPTER 3

"Up Against the Wall, Boy"

We were just trying to go out for some Chinese food. This was July 1969, a month after my twentieth birthday, and I was with one of my older teammates on the Double-A Shreveport Braves, a white dude from L.A. named Ted Bashore. Ted was one deep cat. He always had his nose in a book, reading some far-out stuff, psychology or quantum physics or maybe a Dostoevsky novel. Ted's wife Penny worked as a model and she *looked* like a model, tall and slender and well dressed. She was in from California visiting Ted for couple of weeks, and they asked me to come to dinner at the one Chinese restaurant in Shreveport. Afterward I wanted to help with the check, but Ted said no way. That was the code. The older player picked up the check. Penny and I could meet him out front.

I started to walk outside with Penny and didn't get far. Once I hit the sidewalk, two cops in a squad car pulled over and were on me in nothing flat. They didn't like me standing out on the street with a white girl. They wouldn't listen when I tried to explain. Before I had any idea what was happening, I was up against the wall.

"Boy," a Shreveport cop told me, "don't you know it's against the law for a Black man to be on the streets after dark with a white woman? You hear me?"

I was afraid to keep talking, since I could see this was no time to fly off the handle. I was a young kid from California who could be a little headstrong, but I had seen news clips on TV in our living room back home showing what happened when a young Black man stood up to a white cop in the South. I knew it could be seriously detrimental to my health.

Just then I heard Ted's voice.

"It's cool, it's cool," Ted told the cop as soon as he got outside. "He's with me. We're both with the Shreveport Braves."

The cop looked from me to Ted and back to me.

"I don't care who he's with," the cop said. "He can't be on the street with a white girl."

"That white girl's my wife," Ted told him.

The cop finally let me go. We walked back to my car, a canary yellow Oldsmobile 4-4-2, my first car, which I loved as much as any car I've ever owned. Once we started driving, we talked over what had just happened. We were all shocked and stunned, but not exactly surprised. That was just how it was in 1969. By that point in my life, I'd played in the big leagues and served my country in the United States Marine Corps Reserve. My unit in Shreveport—headquartered right next to the ballpark—was an MP unit, as in, Military Police. None of that mattered to these Shreveport cops. I wasn't a person to them, just because of the color of my skin.

I realized I had a choice. Either I let them get inside my head or I didn't. I was going to feel angry. That was always going to be there. But I didn't have to show it. And I didn't have to let it eat me up. I didn't have to be afraid—not of anyone.

Looking back now, that wall in Shreveport was one of the hairier encounters I've had in a lifetime of getting out and about in the world and never worrying much about what might go down. I've found that generally in life, if you stay cool and keep your eyes open, alert to what's going on around you, then you're usually all right. No matter where I was, no matter how much I found myself moving around, from one team to another, one bus league to another, I always tried to keep a cool head. I've never had a problem with people. I can think of maybe a couple times total in my whole life, once in a Black neighborhood and once in a white neighborhood, where I started to have that feeling of *Damn, maybe I'm in the wrong place.* But it all worked out fine. So far, anyway.

Ted Bashore ended up becoming a lifelong friend. A first baseman with some power, he was just three years older than me, but he seemed worldly and wise. He'd grown up in L.A. and played both football and baseball at UCLA. Ted always seemed to know about any subject. Like if we were talking and I mentioned a book I'd read, like *Don Quixote* by Cervantes, not only had he read it, he'd taken a course on it at UCLA along with the star of the Bruins basketball team, Lew Alcindor (Kareem Abdul-Jabbar). Ted completed his UCLA degree in psychology that year and was on his way to graduate school. (He would earn his PhD in psychology, do cutting-edge research on brain wave patterns, and teach at multiple universities—then later work with my San Francisco Giants players as a sports psychologist.)

"Look out for Bashore," the Braves warned me when I joined the Shreveport team. "He's strange. He might even be some kind of California hippie."

California hippie? What were they talking about? Didn't they know I was from California? In some organizations, California guys didn't have a good reputation. They thought we were strange. They thought we were too freethinking. They thought Ted was a hippie because he had long hair, and they assumed he was smoking marijuana. They weren't going to convince me Ted was some kind of bad influence. One thing about me, then and always—I make up my own mind about people.

That summer, Ted was reading *Crime and Punishment.* We'd be on some long bus ride in Arkansas or Texas, and Ted would tell me about this crazy cat Raskolnikov. Ted had different ways about him, which I liked. Show me someone a little different, and I'll show you a chance to learn more about myself. He ate granola, which I'd never heard of back then, and drank coconut milk, all of which he called "health food." Ted got me thinking, I'll say that much.

I'm grateful for having that time in the South. The cops who had me up against that wall opened my eyes in a way I could never have done on my own. When your only option on the road in the minor leagues is staying in a one-room shanty behind Momma's Soul Food Kitchen while your teammates get put up in a nice hotel or live with host families, you never forget what that feels like. As bad as things were in the South, I still had a great time and learned a lot about myself and a lot about being Black and being a Black man. These are lessons that I would not trade with anybody. I'd even say I feel kind of sorry for anybody who *didn't* have those lessons, because they are lessons you can't really explain unless you've been there. That was the best thing that ever happened to me, being in the South for that period of time when I needed it, because I was at a crossroads over my anger at inequality. If you look at all my baseball cards when I was young, you won't find one that shows me smiling. I was angry. Hank Aaron used to get on me about being mad all the time. He told me, "You've got to rechannel that energy to do what you gotta do." He was right. Hank usually was. That anger would have eaten me up if I had let it.

My first month in the South was the hardest. One week I was at Dodger Stadium in L.A., trying to stay cool and not stare too much as I suited up and practiced with these Braves players I'd admired for years. Then after a quick trip home to enroll at American River College, I was on a flight to Austin, Texas. I was a young kid who came off to some as cocky and full of himself when half the time I was just scared. I was winging it and hoping it wasn't obvious how much I still had to learn.

The Austin Braves averaged nine hundred fans per game that season at Disch-Falk Field. It was Double-A baseball, but to me it felt like the big time. I might have been the youngest player in the league. My first game was on a Saturday in August 1967. I was the skinniest little dude on that team, and I felt even skinnier looking at some of these big, strong, fully grown men who were suddenly my teammates. Our left fielder, Dave Nicholson, was built like Mickey Mantle, six foot two, 215 pounds. My second game, Nicholson hit two homers. The man had easy power. Cito Gaston, soon to be one of my lifelong friends, was also on that team, and he was always big and strong, six foot three and 190. Everywhere I looked, I saw big, fully developed guys. I called back to my homeboys in California and told them the truth. It was great to be there and all, but I had some doubts. Had I done the right thing signing with the Braves to stake everything on making it as a baseball player?

"This is only Double-A, and these guys are *full-grown men,*" I said on the phone.

I had confidence in myself. I knew I would improve and I also knew that like all the men in my family I would be a late bloomer who grew into his strength over time. But I had to learn a kind of patience I'd never had. The guys I was going against were more powerful and more experienced than me. How was I ever going to make my way up to Triple-A, let alone the big leagues? I had a lot of work to do.

Luck goes a long way in life. I was lucky to have some great teammates in Austin, starting with Ralph Garr, who was three and a half years older than me, a gifted all-around athlete from the South who had graduated from Grambling College and became my lifelong brother. There was also Adrian and Wayne Garrett, two brothers from Florida, and Cito, a future big-league manager, who joined Hank Aaron in stepping up to be there for me when I needed someone to get my back. He taught me and kept an eye on me all at once.

I had not talked to my dad since I signed with the Braves. I knew he was not going to be happy with me, to say the least. It all happened so fast, there in L.A., then it was all about packing and flying off to Texas. I felt like I had to make an adult decision, and I made it. The family needed me to bring in more income, and this was my way to do that. I didn't like it. I would much rather have been showing up as big man on campus at one of those party schools loaded with coeds.

Here was what I did wrong with my dad: I had another man do my duty for me. My Austin Braves team took a bus from Austin to Albuquerque, New Mexico, on my first road trip, and I picked up three hits in one day, even if it took me ten at-bats over the course of a doubleheader. I went in to see our manager, Hub Kittle, and asked if he could call my dad for me. I guess I was thinking Hub could break the ice for me and I'd talk to my dad again later. So I sat there and listened as Hub called my dad, who was without doubt one of the proudest men I've ever known. Hub passed on to my dad as secondhand news that his son had signed and was now with the Austin Double-A club in the Texas League.

"Put my son on the phone," my dad told Hub, "because I don't need some stranger to tell me what my son has done."

Those words haunted me for years to come. My dad was a man of few words. For him to say what he said, it hit me like a punch. If I was man enough to make an adult decision without consulting my dad, I should have been man enough to tell him what I'd done. My dad was disappointed in me, and I knew he had reason to be. That was the last conversation we had for three years.

The bus ride to Little Rock, Arkansas, for our next two games had me nervous. I'd seen Little Rock on too many news programs over the years. Looking out the window of our bus, I stared out at swamps south of Little Rock, and my thoughts were racing. I'd never seen swamps like this with my own eyes before. I'd never seen trees growing out of the water like that. But I'd seen TV programs about lynchings of Black people in Arkansas and heard about them dumping the bodies in the swamp. The bus rolled past more swampland, and I started to feel the fear of what it would be like if it happened to you. Our team was playing in Little Rock exactly ten years after an Arkansas governor by the name of Orval Faubus mobilized the Arkansas National Guard just to keep nine Black kids from going to school at Little Rock Central High. That was how it was.

Somewhere on that nine-hour bus ride into Arkansas in 1967, the bus pulled over so we could get some food. I was hungry and jumped up to get off the bus when I felt a strong hand reach out and hold me in place. It was Cito Gaston. "No, man," he said. "Let the white dudes get our sandwiches. We're going to stay on this bus." I could tell by the tone of his voice and the look on his face how serious he was. I got it.

We got to Little Rock for that Friday night game and Hub wrote me into the leadoff spot. Maybe the organization wanted me to get as many at-bats as possible. Or maybe Hub knew I needed a lift given what I was going through with my dad. Or maybe he just wanted my speed at the top of the lineup. Leading off on the road is like being first in line. Everything starts with you. Since you're the first batter of the whole game, you set the tone.

That night in 1967 at Ray Winder Field in Little Rock, I reached base on an error to start the game and then came around to score. That opened the floodgates. We knocked that Little Rock pitcher around for five runs in the first inning and sent him to the showers. You might think our big lead would have quieted the home crowd in Little Rock, but instead they were all riled up. I ran out to right field to play my position in the bottom of the first only to find that a group of fans in the right-field bleachers were all over me. They were hooting on me from the beginning, calling me nigger, calling me watermelon eater, calling me jigaboo, and some racist terms I'd never even heard before. And this was before a ball ever came my way. I'd been heckled before, one or two dudes, but this was a crowd of twenty-five or more all screaming insults at me.

Playing the outfield at Ray Winder Field was no cakewalk. Right field sloped down so much, when you looked at home plate, you couldn't see the batter's feet. He looked like he was sinking into quicksand. I was so nervous, I wanted to run away and hide. Then a fly ball was hit to me, I thought I had it lined up, and—*clang!*—it bounced right out of my glove. I dropped the ball for an error. You should have heard those rowdy fans in the bleachers after that. They were riding me so hard, I started crying. I had to just stand there and take it. Only later did I find out that it was a tradition in Little Rock that every Friday night, the nearby Arkansas State Hospital for the mentally ill would bring a group of patients out to the bleachers and let them shout themselves hoarse, pouring out hate if that was what they wanted to do.

I called home to my mama and told her I wanted to come home. But it was too late for that. I'd signed a contract. Cito and Ralph were with me when I called. They were always there for me. Cito was five years older than me, and he'd seen the world. Growing up in Texas, he figured he would either end up a ballplayer or follow in his dad's footsteps and work as a long-haul truck driver. Cito told me he would take care of me like I was his little brother, which he did. He talked me down. It was way too late to reverse what I had done in choosing the Braves. I couldn't have gone home anyway, since there would have been nothing waiting for me there. I had no alternative to making it in baseball. I got a hit in the Saturday game in Little Rock, which we also lost, this time in extra innings, then we climbed into the bus for the drive back to Austin for the last two games of the season.

I made a lot of lifelong friends on that Austin team, especially my future Braves teammate Ralph Garr. On the day before my first game in Austin, Ralph slid hard into second base and sprained his ankle and was out for the rest of the season, but he stayed with the team, and we always had a lot to talk about. Ralph had kept his eyes open growing up in Ruston, Louisiana, where on weekends he shined shoes at the local barbershop. He earned twenty-five cents a shine, pretty good money if you were good at it, which Ralph said he was. And I believed him, since the man always wore shoes that had been buffed to a nice sheen.

I couldn't wait to get home to California. I wanted to see my mom and my brothers and sisters. I wanted to see my friends. I had only been back at the family house on Marble Way in Carmichael a couple weeks when I thought I heard someone knock on the door. I looked out the window and didn't see anybody, so I went back in. Then I heard another knock. Somebody was definitely out there. I opened the door and saw a small Black dude, maybe four feet tall, looking up at me.

"Are you Johnnie B. Baker Jr.?" he asked me.

No one ever called me that, but it was my name.

"You've been served," he said.

"Served to what?" I asked.

"Served to appear in court," he said.

That was how I found out my own dad was taking me to court. He had told me he was against me signing with the Braves, and he was true to his word: He was suing to try to void the contract my mother and I had signed with the Braves, and along with it my $15,000 signing bonus. The contract included an educational bonus to pay for college and incentive bonuses as I climbed up the ladder to Double-A, Triple-A, and eventually the big leagues.

Nowadays if you're eighteen years old, you're legally an adult in most U.S. states. Back then in California, you weren't legally an adult until you turned twenty-one. So my mom found a lawyer to represent us and chose a prominent Black man, William K. Morgan. (Governor Jerry Brown later appointed him to be a judge.) My mom and I went down to see Bill Morgan in his office on Broadway, and he had a large oil painting of his mom on the wall behind his desk. No surprise my mom liked him! Bill Morgan was a smart, interesting guy. He had actually worked previously as the owner of a funeral home in Sacramento. He got into the law a little later in life, after his mom passed. She didn't like lawyers. "She hated their guts," he once told a reporter from *The Bee.*

I was so mad at my dad, I couldn't stand to speak to him. We showed up in court, my mom and me sitting there with Bill Morgan, my dad across the way with his white lawyer. I didn't even want to look at him. I was mad at him because, like many kids that age, I felt independent and grown up, even though I wasn't.

My dad and his lawyer invoked something called the California Child Actor's Bill, also known as the Jackie Coogan Act, to argue that even if my mom was my legal guardian, the contract could be blocked since I wasn't an adult. Coogan was a child actor who earned millions after appearing alongside Charlie Chaplin in *The Kid* (1921), but he never saw more of it than a weekly allowance of $6.25. Six bucks. All week. That was all his parents ever gave him. Then after his dad was killed in a car accident driving home from Mexico, when Coogan was twenty, Coogan's mother married the family attorney, and the two of them announced they didn't plan to give Jackie "a cent" of his past earnings then got to work burning through millions of his dollars. Jackie sued, a famous case that prompted the California legislature to pass a law setting up a mechanism for the state to serve as trustee in the financial affairs of minors. (And I grew up watching Coogan on TV as Uncle Fester on *The Addams Family.*) I've got to give it to my dad, or his lawyer, that was creative of them to apply to my case a law set up to protect child actors.

By early October, the *Sacramento Legal Press* newspaper was publishing a notice naming the Atlanta Braves and me—"Johnnie B. Baker Jr"—in a case of "minor gdn/ship of; petn for appt of gdn of pers & est of minor." The long and short of it was: My dad won. I became a trustee of the State of California until my twenty-first birthday. I was allowed to keep some of my signing bonus, enough to buy my 4-4-2 (the Braves also bought my mom a car, an Oldsmobile Cutlass), but most of it was invested in stock, specifically, Standard Oil of California (now Chevron) and IBM.

I was really pissed off. I was home in Sacramento for nine months going to American River College—I needed to be enrolled to avoid being drafted. All that time, I froze my dad out of my life. I never once talked to him. Brad and Dennis and I got an apartment together across the street from American River College, which was near my dad's place, but I never saw him. If I was out with my brothers and sisters and I dropped them off at my dad's apartment, I would sit in my car on the street rather than go inside. All those years he'd worked so hard, two jobs or more, and I didn't even come in to see how he was. Years later, my dad told me how deeply it hurt him when I would drop the others off and refuse to see him at all. To me at that time, I'd have been amazed to hear that my dad felt that way. I really had no idea. The man seemed invulnerable. All those years in Riverside and then Sacramento, I never saw any signs of sorrow or pain from my dad.

Dennis and Brad and I drove my 4-4-2 to Freeborn Hall at UC Davis or to Berkeley or San Francisco whenever we could. I loved that two-hour drive into the city, but it was a long way to drive back, late at night, especially if you'd been out having a good time. Ever since I caught the Jimi Hendrix Experience the year before at Monterey and had my mind blown, I'd been talking to anyone who would listen about Hendrix. I knew every word to every song. If Hendrix put out a new album, I'd be among the first to buy it and wear out the turntable checking it out.

I caught so much great music at Freeborn Hall over the years, but that year back home some of the acts we saw there included Big Brother and the Holding Company, who we'd seen at Monterey, the Paul Butterfield Blues Band—featuring Butterfield on harp and vocals and a guitarist named Elvin Bishop, who would end up being one of my best fishing buddies—and, most important, one of Bob Marley's last concerts.

Jimi Hendrix and his band had been touring Europe, but in February 1968, he was back in California. We drove into San Francisco to catch Jimi at Winterland, and one cool thing was they honored the Beatles, whose last concert ever was just a year and a half earlier at Candlestick Park, where I would later go to work every day for years. When Jimi started singing, "It was twenty years ago today," the opening line of "Sgt. Pepper's Lonely Hearts Club Band," we all cheered. Then, a few days later, Hendrix came our way for a gig in the Sacramento State College gym, which was organized by Sac State students. Tickets cost us $2.75. The gym was packed with more than four thousand screaming fans, and it was another great Hendrix performance, starting with "Are You Experienced?" and "Fire" and moving on to "The Wind Cries Mary," where Jimi's guitar sounded like a howling wind, and "Manic Depression." We came out of that gym feeling as wound up as I ever did at a baseball game. Hendrix was a force of nature, an amazing natural talent who taught himself guitar and did things his own way, but if you saw him live you never forgot that he was powered by joy. Music was not just something that made me feel more alive, it also fueled me and gave me the tools to be who I needed to be.

I had a lot of fun those months as a college student, but I made sure to stay in shape. The American River College track coach, Al Baeta, let me work out with the track team every day, but I couldn't take part in competition—not in track, not in any sport, since I was a pro baseball player. It was hard on me. All I could do was sit up in the stands and watch football or go to the gym and watch basketball. I couldn't take part, but I was always playing on the side. I couldn't get it out of me. My mom would call Bill Wight of the Braves and tell on me that I was in the park playing basketball or football again, but I couldn't help myself. It was what I really, really loved.

The only baseball I played that spring was during our Easter break from college. The Braves flew me to West Palm Beach to get in one week of spring training. I was in great shape, but rusty baseball-wise. That was my first taste of spring training, and I'd have loved to have more time to hang out with Ralph and Cito and see Hank Aaron and the others. But if I hadn't gone back to college, I might have ended up in Vietnam, like a lot of my buddies did. I was there at the end of spring training, just before the Braves season started on April 10. Just after practice one day in West Palm Beach, we were given the terrible news that the Rev. Dr. Martin Luther King Jr. had been assassinated. That was the saddest news I'd heard since President Kennedy was killed in 1963, when I was in eighth grade, and Malcolm X was killed in 1965, when I was in tenth grade.

By the time I arrived in West Palm Beach for my first Florida State League game on June 17, 1968, I was in excellent shape. I hit the ball hard my first two at-bats for two quick hits. But we had so many rainouts, I couldn't wait to move on from that league. There were so many long bus rides, and it rained every day. By the end of that month, I was sent to Greenwood, South Carolina, in the Western Carolinas League, another A-ball league. The Greenwood manager, Lou Fitzgerald, and Eddie Haas, a coach, were both from the South, and it felt like they rescued me.

My first game with the Greenwood Braves, I tripled, doubled, and singled and scored four runs. In my second game, I singled and doubled. I batted .342 for Greenwood that season and become a fan favorite, which was more of an accomplishment than I realized at the time. "They cheer him every time he comes to bat," Charlie Evranian, the Greenville GM, told *The Sacramento Bee,* "and I guess you could say that's a little unusual in the South, the fans cheering a Negro boy."

I was thinking more about going back home and going to school than I was about getting called up to the big leagues. I really didn't know how the Braves felt about me. But at the end of August, Braves farm director Bill Lucas phoned me in Greenville to tell me I was being called up to the Braves along with Ralph Garr, who was coming from Double-A Shreveport. I couldn't believe I was going to the big leagues. I knew there were a lot of good ballplayers in the Braves system who were ahead of me, and some of them envied me for skipping ahead when I'd only played three months of pro ball. I called my mom from a pay phone—collect, of course—to give her the news. Then I called some of my homies in Sacramento to tell them.

The Braves flew me to Atlanta to join the team later that week, where I met Ralph. I was only nineteen, but I was a big-leaguer. Ralph and I were roommates, staying at the old Dinkler Plaza Hotel on Forsyth Street downtown. One night Clete Boyer and Bob Uecker decided to take us out. Those two always had a good time, and if you were around them, you always had a good time. Ueck was a cutup. He could make anyone laugh, especially Hank. We hit it off right away, and even to the end of his life, Ueck would always come visit me. Those guys taught us how to be big-leaguers. For years to come, throughout my whole career, I did my best to treat rookies right, the way those guys had treated me and Ralph. They taught me to have fun but also to know when it was time to go to work. In other words, they taught me how to be a pro.

First, they bought us suits, since that was what veterans did in those days. (A year or two later, Pete Rose took Ralph and me out for lunch in Cincinnati and then back to his house, just because he liked talking hitting with us, and brought out six suits to give us. They were leisure suits, a fad at the time. They fit Ralph great. For me, my arms and legs poked out so much, I looked like Li'l Abner.) Then we hit the town. Where do you think they took us that night in Atlanta? To the Playboy Club, which was just a few blocks away, on Luckie Street. I was a wide-eyed kid who couldn't believe my luck. I have a Polaroid of Ralph and me, with Clete and Ueck and two Playboy bunnies with their cotton tails and floppy ears and abundant cleavage. I'm smiling ear to ear in the picture. I sent that Polaroid home to my buddy Dennis along with a note reading "Man, this is the life, being in the big leagues, and this is where I want to be and where I belong." I was finding that life as a major-leaguer—so long as you could show you belonged—felt awfully good to me.

We were in Atlanta for a home stand against the Astros and the Giants, then flew to L.A. for a four-game series with the Dodgers. In one year, I'd gone from being "no-number" on a tryout with the Braves at Dodger Stadium to being back as Number 12—the same as Tommy Davis—on the Braves, back at Dodger Stadium in September 1968 as a big-leaguer. That was every kid's dream, and I was living it. I still hadn't gotten into any games, but I was soaking it all up. I'd wave to my friends in the stands who had come from Riverside. They couldn't believe I was out there on the field either.

Our next stop was Houston for three games at the Astrodome. For our first game, we'd be facing Mike Cuellar, who threw that screwball, and he shut us down. By the top of the sixth inning, we were behind 5–0, and our manager, Lum Harris, sent me up to pinch-hit for our pitcher, Pat Jarvis. I was just happy to get into a game. I went up there, full of adrenaline, and swung at one of his screwballs. I topped the ball, then took off for first base as fast as I could. My first big-league hit was a swinging bunt. I went to third on Felipe Alou's single, but watched from third as Cuellar retired both Félix Millán and Hank Aaron to strand me there.

Next up was San Francisco, and a three-game series against the Giants at Candlestick Park. I may never have been happier to be back in the Bay after flying with the Braves to SFO. I'd watched many games at Candlestick over the years on TV, but I'd never actually been there before that day. I was so excited, I couldn't stop smiling. I'm sure I was grinning when I walked up to the visiting locker room—and was turned away. Mike Murphy, then the visiting clubhouse attendant, later a good friend, took one look at me and saw an underage kid trying to sneak into the Braves locker room. Murph was having none of it.

"I'm on the team," I insisted.

"So am I," Murph told me. "Get lost, kid."

I looked around, trying to find a friendly face, and spotted Jim Busby, the Braves third base coach that year.

"Mr. Busby!" I called out.

"What are you doing out there?" he asked.

"This guy here won't let me in," I told him.

"This kid's on the team?" Murphy asked Mr. Busby, who nodded. "Man, he looks fifteen."

For me it was a trip just being on the same field as guys I'd watched on TV just a few months ago. Hank Aaron helped me with that. "Respect them," he told me, "but don't gawk at them and don't idolize them, because you're going to have to beat them."

For the first game of that series at Candlestick Park, we were facing Giants ace Juan Marichal (25–8). Marichal was some pitcher, and also a handsome dude who always carried himself with class and dignity. I watched him work from the dugout, that high leg kick, that sizzling fast ball, and in the ninth I was sent out to pinch-hit. We were losing 8–0. All I knew was I'd better get some wood on the ball and then run as fast as I could and hope for the best. That was just what I did. I squibbed an infield grounder that took a bad hop and I flew down the line, running so fast nothing could stop me. I was wiry strong, but at that age I wasn't man-strong yet. Speed was my thing. I ran right past first base and halfway down the right-field line. As of that moment, I was 2-for-2 in the big leagues.

It was all so new to me, I didn't know how special it was to be out on the field with so many great players. Over on the Giants side, besides Marichal, you had Willie Mays and Willie McCovey, as potent a three-four hitting combination as baseball has ever seen. They were bigger than life figures to me. Leading off, you had my personal hero in sports, Bobby Bonds, whom my dad had coached back in Riverside. That was big for me, when my friend Bobby got called up that season as a rookie. And then to be playing in the same game as him, both of us from Riverside—we were both thrilled. During batting practice, I went over to talk to Bobby and introduced him to Ralph, then Bobby introduced us to Willie Mays.

"I like your MacGregor glove, Mr. Mays," I told Willie. "That's a nice glove, kangaroo hide."

Willie took it off and gave it to me. I wish I still had it.

That Braves team included not only Hank Aaron but also his brother

Tommie, my friend from the big leagues and the minor leagues, and in center field Felipe Alou, another future Giants manager. Our catcher was Joe Torre, future Hall of Fame manager, and one of our outfielders was Tito Francona, whose son Terry would manage in Boston, Cleveland, and Cincinnati.

The Santa Clara basketball coach, my friend Carroll Williams, was listening to Russ Hodges and Lon Simmons call that Giants game on radio. This was just one year after Coach Williams had been recruiting me to play basketball for him. When I singled, he called up Sal Taormina, the Santa Clara baseball coach who had watched me practice and said I looked just "okay."

"You listening to the Giants game?" Williams asked Taormina. "Well that guy you said needed more seasoning just got a single off Juan Marichal."

I was hanging out with Hank Aaron and Tommie Aaron and Ralph and—unbelievable as it might sound—Satchel Paige, not only a great pitcher and future Hall of Famer but one of the great showmen ever. In one of the all-time classy moves in baseball, the Braves announced in August 1968 that they were signing Satch, who by then was sixty-two years old, though he kept everyone guessing about his age. I always admired Braves president Bill Bartholomay for making that move, so that Satch, whose forty-year baseball career was mostly in the Negro Leagues, could add a few months of service time to qualify for a Major League pension. Satch was listed as assistant trainer or something like that, and the Braves had him hold pitching exhibitions to big-leaguers before some games, to put on a show for the fans. He never actually reached the active roster, but you always felt like he could have any day, even at sixty-two.

For me, having grown up on stories my dad told me about Negro League stars, above all Cool Papa Bell, Josh Gibson, and Satchel Paige, meeting the man and getting to spend so much time with him was like a bridge connecting me to another time and place that I'd always wondered about. On the road late in the 1968 season, Ralph and I would go to Hank's hotel room with Satch or go to Satch's hotel room with Hank and all sit back and listen to Satch tell stories. When I say listen, I do mean listen. I didn't ask many questions. That was my place in the presence of these grown men. That was how I was raised. You didn't hardly talk; you showed your respect for your elders by keeping quiet. You couldn't blurt out anything. You just had to raise your hand, like you were in school. If you asked too many questions, that meant you were too much in the conversation.

Satch was one of the greatest storytellers I've ever met in my life, and I've met some good ones along the way, from John Lee Hooker and Elvin Bishop to Orlando Cepeda, Bob Uecker, Joe Black, and Jim Gilliam. Half of Satch's stories sounded embellished, which they probably were, but we didn't care if he was telling the truth or not, because all we did was laugh. He would kill Hank laughing. Satch was a character, and I loved him right away.

"My name's Dusty," I said when we first met.

"I know," he said. "Your name's Daffy."

Daffy? But after that, I was always "Daffy" to him. He never got my name right, not once. Everywhere we went, people would give Satch fishing rods, and it was my job to carry them. Back then, the bellman didn't take the bags to your room. Young players took care of that. We were their "caddies," and Ralph and I always carried Satch's bags. He always promised us that he was going to give us some of those fishing rods, but he never did. He did give us entertainment. And he liked having us around, or at least he didn't *dislike* having us around, which for us was just as good.

Satch would have me catch his bullpen sessions. He gave me a two-by-four he carried around and told me to set that up as his target so he could throw at it. I laid the two-by-four across the plate.

"No, Daffy," he said. "Not across the plate. Point it toward me on the edge of the plate."

That was how he got his control. He didn't ice afterward. He didn't believe in using ice. Instead, he would use heat. His advice to me was to stay out of the training room, and it was advice I followed—as long as I could.

One thing I learned fast from my first days in the big leagues was always to be close to the traveling secretaries, the trainers, and all the clubhouse personnel. I treated them like gold. One of the guys who schooled me about this when I first got to the big leagues was Donald Davidson, the Braves' traveling secretary going back to the team's years in Boston and Milwaukee. He stood all of four foot two, owing to some kind of childhood disease, but he was a tough guy. Davidson was great to me. Back then, sometimes you had to get an advance on your salary to make it, and he'd give you an advance when you needed it. He really taught me the ropes and took care of us, especially Ralph and me.

I would have loved to have another offseason home in Sacramento taking more classes at American River College and hanging out with Dennis and Brad, but the Braves had other ideas for me. I would only get a short break. Their argument was I'd progressed in my development and was ready to be a star in the big leagues, but I had to make the commitment to baseball and couldn't be missing spring training in 1969 because of college. I also couldn't risk being sent to Vietnam.

Bill Lucas, Hank Aaron's brother-in-law, had a talk with me. That year he was Assistant Director of the Braves minor-league farm system, but in 1976 he would be promoted to general manager, becoming the first Black GM in Major League Baseball history. Raised in Florida, he had served as an officer in the U.S. Army. He explained to me at the end of the 1968 season that I was going to need to enlist in the military reserve. The organization didn't want me drafted, but they also didn't want me to miss half the season again, the way I had for my first year of study at American River College.

I understood. Missing half the season watered down your baseball progress. Given the intense competition, you knew that meant somebody would pass you by. One year you're a prospect, and the next thing you know, you're a suspect. I couldn't afford to turn into a suspect. I *had* to make it in baseball. It was as simple as that. I had to make it, first of all, because being a professional athlete was my lifelong dream and I had given up all other sports to make it in baseball, so this was my one chance. I also had to make it because if I washed out, it would prove my dad—and other doubters—right. I couldn't have lived with that. I had given up so much, scholarships and educational opportunities and other sports I loved a lot more than baseball. My family needed the money, and I needed to know I'd chosen right in forfeiting my education, which would have set me up to get a job that could make me a lot of money.

Bill Lucas suggested that to avoid Vietnam I join the National Guard, the way a lot of ballplayers already had, but that wasn't for me. I had no problem with giving more to baseball, but I did have a problem with the idea of joining the National Guard. To that, I said no way—you were not going to find me called out in uniform to crack down on some rioters. My sentiments lay much more with the ones in the street protesting the establishment than with the establishment itself.

If I had to enlist to avoid getting drafted, I wanted to join the Air Force Reserve. I thought the Air Force would be the easiest, because from what I'd heard, you probably wouldn't go into combat. But I wasn't the only one with that idea. Everyone wanted the Air Force, and they were full up. I also thought of following in my dad's and Uncle Floyd's footsteps and joining the Navy, but if I chose the Navy Reserve, that would require enlisting for four years of service. That would negate the jump on my baseball career I'd gained by signing out of high school. My only real option, as I saw it, was enlisting in the Marine Corps Reserve, the way Roberto Clemente, Rick Monday, and Dave Duncan had before me.

I enlisted in Atlanta in October 1968, and on the last day of the month I was sent to boot camp at Parris Island, South Carolina. Standing in line to get my hair cut, I ran into Big Bob Spence, who had shown me around the Santa Clara campus. The Marine doctors checked me out and found I had high blood pressure. That almost led to me being released from military service right there. I didn't fully realize up until that time how much I was being affected by the pressure I felt in life to succeed no matter what.

I was on a mission in boot camp. They lined us up the first day and announced that one of us would win out over all the others and be chosen as "honor man." When it came time to graduate, everyone else would be in green, but the honor man would be in dress blue, looking cool. I had to smile at that. Who were they kidding? Of course that was going to be me. My dad taught me to hunt when I was a boy, and I could shoot a rifle with the best of them. I had that covered. And I could run better than anyone. They told me I broke Roberto Clemente's pull-up record. My friend Tom Stienstra would later say about me that there are two Dustys, and they don't even know each other—one is the smiling, friendly, open-minded and easygoing Dusty the world mostly sees, and the other is a "no-nonsense, hard-ass competitive mofo." Competitive Dusty took over at Parris Island. I knew I'd be honor man wearing the dress blue, and I was.

That challenge helped get me through those weeks. I didn't mind all the physical challenges, the pushups and the obstacle course and all that stuff. For a professional athlete, that was not something to fear or worry about. The hardest part was the humiliation they inflicted on you and the way they made you take orders no matter if they made any sense at all. That threw me. But then I came to understand how they kind of break you down to build you back up. I probably learned more about teamwork during my time in the Marines than I did even playing baseball. My unit was never called up. By then, the U.S. was well on its way to losing the war in Vietnam. A lot of the guys I trained with were being sent over, and a lot of them died.

You learn things about your body and preparation as a professional athlete. People think about boot camp and the hardcore training they put a Marine through and probably assume that prepares you for anything, but it's more complicated than that. I could always run, I was light and quick, and I felt a lifelong joy in running. As a Marine, they never had you sprint—they had you go on long runs wearing those big heavy Marine boots.

I was the guidon of my platoon and marched out in front carrying the platoon's flag with "Semper Fi!" written on it. I did not volunteer for that role, I was chosen for it. I could do three miles like nothing, but I lost my turbo speed. I gained at least fifteen pounds of muscle in the Marines, and I couldn't shift gears anymore. I just had my Long, Slow, Distance gear. That made it hard for me getting back to baseball when the time came. Unlike the year before, when I was working out with the track team at American River College every day and in really good shape, the Marines did not prepare you for baseball at all. My game was all speed and balance. Long marches didn't help with that.

Six of us in my platoon were reservists, and some of the other guys didn't like us and would try to mix it up. They were most likely headed for Vietnam, and we were most likely staying stateside. That was something that bothered me, especially as the only dress-blue honor man in my platoon, the fact that they went and I didn't. Looking back, I think I would have volunteered to go fight with them if I hadn't had the responsibilities I did, feeling I needed to be there for my family.

Enlisting turned out to be an important crossroads for me, a bad experience that turned into a good experience and taught me about being a man. The Marines made me an expert in pistol and rifle. There were some things they taught you in the Marines that stayed with you, like learning to make that bed right. When I came back from the military, everything had to be neat and clean and I had to be right on time. Before that, I was late to everything. That used to drive my dad crazy. If we were going fishing and hunting, and you were a minute late, he would leave you. My whole life ever since the Marines, I've been a very punctual person. Being on time is always better.

Being a Marine taught me discipline and respect for the chain of command. It also taught me lessons about teamwork, not just teamwork in the sense of being on a field with teammates and playing a game together, but living with each other day-to-day in close quarters and making that work. It turned out to be great preparation for the baseball life, day after day together, a lot of that time in clubhouses where everyone has their space and you *respect* that space. That was how it was in the barracks. You had your bunk and not much else. The space you did have to yourself was your own, and it felt sacred to you. You learned quickly not to take up the space of the man next to you. You respected his space, and he respected yours.

I got in a little trouble with the Marine Corps because I wouldn't do recruitment commercials. I also declined to do a clinic at the Clark,

Morris Brown, and Morehouse College football field to try to sign up some little brothers to go in the Marines. The way I saw it, it was fine for me to be there, but it went against my beliefs to be responsible for others. I was heavily influenced and wanted to follow in the footsteps of Muhammad Ali, but couldn't at the time.

Every summer, I had to take two weeks away from baseball to go be a Marine. In Shreveport, I was assigned to an MP unit at Camp Pendleton in Southern California, south of L.A., and they had me on guard duty. Rule one was don't talk to the prisoners, who were there in a kind of holding tank, on their way from Vietnam to Leavenworth.

"Hey, Baker," a dude said to me.

How did he know my name? I wasn't supposed to talk to those guys. But I knew him! He was my neighbor back in Riverside. He was like the class clown, so I knew he probably got into hot water messing around. Another guy from Riverside was locked up, too, and this guy was brilliant. He was the kind of dude who would go home, get his homework done fast because it was so easy for him, and then he would be after you to come out and play, even if you still had your own homework to do. *Damn this!* I thought to myself. *I ain't shootin' no homies. I ain't shootin' nobody.* I took the shotgun shells out of my gun after that.

- - - -

I wish I could describe all the great music I caught in those years. Jimi Hendrix was back in the Bay for three gigs at the Winterland Ballroom in the North Beach area of San Francisco starting on October 10, 1968, and I was home long enough to catch him. Dennis and I knew that was a night to be in the city, checking out the scene. We drove in with a couple other friends and got a room in one of those flophouse-style cheap hotels a block or two from the corner of Broadway and Columbus, which was the center of the action. We got up to the room and pulled the mattress off the bed and threw it on the floor. Then we flipped to see who got to sleep on the mattress and who slept on the box springs. I lost.

Before that year, I was serious about honoring the pact I made with my friends to devote myself to sports and never smoke weed. We were all serious about that pact—for a while. But this was 1968. If you weren't cool enough to be getting high now and then, you were probably missing a lot. So we started to make a few exceptions to the pact when the occasion called for it.

Our cheap hotel was just around the corner from the Condor Club, where Carol Doda became the most famous stripper in the country after taking silicon injections. It was the talk of the country when the Condor became the first bar in the U.S. to go topless and Doda was lowered from the ceiling on a grand piano wearing her monokini. We couldn't even get into the Condor because we were too young. We kept walking and spotted a couple of guys who had stepped off the sidewalk into a kind of nook in one building to fire up a joint.

"Man, that guy really looks like Jimi," Dennis said.

He wasn't lying. The guy looked just liked Hendrix.

"Come on," I said, and we walked over to get a better view. The closer we got, the more this guy looked like Jimi. It actually was Jimi Hendrix.

"Let's ask him if he wants to try some of what we got," someone suggested.

Why not? They sent me over to talk to Jimi and I didn't stop to think about it, just headed over and said, "Hey, what's happening?" or whatever came to mind. The next thing you knew I was smoking a joint with Jimi Hendrix. I can't say I remember that much of our conversation, but Jimi was cool, just a guy out having a good time like us.

Then we headed over to Winterland and saw Jimi and his band blow the doors off the place. To this day, I consider Jimi Hendrix one of the greatest musical geniuses ever to come along. There was an incredible sense of energy when he took the stage. I loved when Jimi put his stamp on a song by Bob Dylan, also one of my favorites, the way he did that night with "Like a Rolling Stone." I really liked "Hey Joe" and "Red House," too. I think they also played "Foxy Lady" and "Purple Haze" that night. It was wild.

My military service meant I never did get an offseason break and had no spring training in 1969. I started my season with Double-A Shreveport, then on June 2, Felipe Alou was hit by a pitch in St. Louis and split his finger. The Braves wasted no time getting me on a plane from Shreveport to St. Louis.

My first day back with the Braves, I started in center field on June 3, but I was 0-for-7 in three games for Atlanta. Next up was a trip to Richmond for the big-league Braves to play an exhibition against their Triple-A farm team, and in that game I went 3-for-4 with a double, but then I had to do a weekend with the Marines and the Braves called up infielder Darrell Evans. By June 13, the organization moved me again, this time to Triple-A Richmond, where I played twenty-three games that season. I was so exhausted from all the moving around, I ended up sick with a 102-degree temperature. I was miserable. Sam Ayoub, the Richmond trainer, saved me, staying with me all day and nursing me back to health. Sam became a lifelong friend.

I was sent back to Shreveport for the end of their season, and by then I was running on fumes. I had nothing left. The Braves summoned me back to Atlanta, telling me I could be called up, get some more big-league time, and help them win a game or two before going to the playoffs against the Miracle Mets of 1969. Then after that they wanted me to go to the Instructional League in Arizona. I told them no thank you. Seriously, I turned down a promotion to the big leagues. I knew what I needed: some downtime at home in Sacramento. The Braves were shocked, but they let me go.

The next year, 1970, Ralph Garr and I were together most of the season with Triple-A Richmond, and I batted .325, which was good compared to everyone else except Ralph. He finished that season with a .386 average, leading the league. When it came to hitting, I was trying to keep up with Ralph, but I could never do it.

On June 15, I celebrated my twenty-first birthday with a hit at home in Richmond against the Louisville Colonels. There were only 726 fans in the stands that night, the lowest turnout of the season, and I was ready to get out of there and celebrate with Ralph. Richmond offered a great education in street life. Ralph and I were roommates, staying at the Eggleston Hotel down on Third Street. The Eggleston was one of the few places where we Black players could stay since nowhere else in town would rent to us. We hung out down there with the prostitutes and the pushers and the numbers guys and the pimps. They were our buddies. They looked out for us and wouldn't let us get in any trouble. If the cops raided the speakeasy, they made me go down the back stairs. I learned a whole bunch about the streets from those guys. I would take the prostitutes home, but I didn't do nothing with them, I swear. They were my age, a few years older, but world-weary, and I would ask them questions about their lives.

In September, I earned another big-league call-up and joined the Braves in Houston on September 11. I got into a couple games as a pinch-runner. Once, I came in for Hank Aaron and then tried to score from third base on an infield grounder the Astros shortstop couldn't handle, but Joe Morgan collected the ball and made a strong throw home, and I was out. They kept using me as a pinch-runner, and in San Francisco on September 14, I pinch-ran for Rico Carty and then threw Bobby Bonds out at home plate with a relay from Clete Boyer. Back then, if you threw your homey out on the bases, that was bragging rights, and my mom and my brother Vic and my sisters Tonya and Taria were there to cheer me on. I didn't get to start a game until September 19 in Cincinnati, when I went 0-for-3 and Ralph went 3-for-5. At home in Atlanta three days later, I went 1-for-3, to get going a little, and on September 25, I started in left field and finally got hot, getting four hits and adding two more in a game two days later to lift my average to .292, which was how the season ended for me.

When I got home to Sacramento late in the year and sorted through my mail, I had one of those moments of sudden clarity that only happen a few times in life. Finally twenty-one, I was no longer a trustee of the State of California. I was a legal adult with control over my own financial affairs. Back during the lawsuit, I wasn't happy when I'd been told my money had been invested in shares of Standard Oil and IBM. Who cared about oil? Or business machines? Or computers, which we first started hearing about in those years, room-sized computers and within a few years the first personal computers? I didn't care about any of that then. But I did care about dollars and cents. Because I had stock, I paid attention to the stock market, which became a lifelong interest. Now, home from the 1970 season, I opened a statement showing how the value of my stock had grown—and legally, it was all my money.

That was when it hit me how wrong I had been to be mad at my dad for those last three years. I got it. I understood. This was not a bad thing for me. It was a *good* thing, maybe a great thing. The most painful and slow-developing crossroads of my life taught me that with a little sensible discipline, you could be a man, an adult, and think ahead. You could take charge of your own financial affairs and be ready to face whatever might come, even if it was crazy stuff you could never make up in a million years. Not only was my dad never against me, he had given me an education in being smart about money and investments.

I'd grown up with my dad as a huge presence in my life. His wisdom, his example, shaped me in countless ways. Then I had pushed him away. I was angry, proud, and confused. I thought he'd wronged me. I thought about all those times I'd dropped off my brothers and sisters at his apartment and refused to go inside to see him. Now I drove over to the same apartment and knocked on his door. Even before he opened, I could smell the chitlins he was cooking up.

"Dad, can I talk to you?" I asked him.

"Come on in."

I was so nervous, I couldn't tell you where I sat or who said what, I just know I looked my dad in the eye and told him how I felt.

"I'm sorry, Dad," I said. "Will you forgive me? I was wrong."

There were no tears. My dad didn't want no tears. My dad hugged me and told me he'd been waiting for three years for that moment. That was when he divulged to me that he was capable of hurt. That was when he told me how hard it was on him all those times I refused to come inside the apartment where we were sitting now. I'd found a way to build a bridge back to my dad. I admitted I was wrong. My dad was always my dad. Now I was his son again.

CHAPTER 4

Trust Your Feelings

All my years as a manager, I would try to get things through to young players and come across my own limitations. It's one thing to have an insight, whether about life or about hitting a baseball, and it's another to be able to put that insight into words that you feel bring alive the idea for someone else. You go through years of trial and error. Looking back, you see that sometimes you thought you were doing a better job than you really were of passing along that core truth. You can make the greatest inspirational speech in the history of sports before a World Series game, or private pep talk with your key player, and if it's not the right talk at the right time for that team or that player, and it fails to land, then that's on you. It's about your words—and the hand you put on a shoulder, the look in your eyes, the quick smile you flash when a smile takes you over—but it's also about trust, earning the trust of your players. It's about teaching trust, the way Hank Aaron taught me as a young player, even though it took me years to see what he was doing.

I always told people I was born as a ballplayer on the Braves. Hank Aaron was like my baseball dad. He schooled me, and it wasn't always easy. Hank didn't talk much about what he'd been through as a boy and young man, but I knew it was more than I could ever imagine. He grew up poor in the "Down the Bay" section of Mobile, Alabama, in the 1940s. He told me he worked on an ice truck when he was young and that hauling all that ice made him strong. All the guys did manual labor back then.

Hank also talked to me about what motivated him: Jackie. In spring 1948, Jackie Robinson's second year playing in the big leagues with the Brooklyn Dodgers, the team came to Mobile for an exhibition game. Hank had just turned fourteen years old, and his dad, Herbert, took him to the game. Hank vowed that night, "I'm going to be in the big leagues myself, Daddy, before Jackie Robinson is through playing." Jackie was more than an idol to Hank, and to all of us. He was pride and motivation and inspiration all at once. Hank lived up to his pledge to his dad, and in 1954, he broke into the big leagues with the Milwaukee Braves at age twenty. He hit .280 with thirteen homers that year after a spring training injury to Bobby Thomson opened a spot for him, and overlapped with Jackie, whose last season was 1956.

Hank had something like a PhD in hitting except much better than that. More than almost any player who ever played the game, he could pick up any differences between a fastball, a slider, a changeup, in a split second as the ball came out of a pitcher's hand. "Henry Aaron is the only ballplayer I have ever seen who goes to sleep at the plate," the pitcher Curt Simmons once said, "but trying to sneak a fastball past him is like trying to sneak the sunrise past a rooster."

All of us could pick up pitches, but not with the speed and consistency that Hank could. Hank had tremendous focus. He knew what was coming, almost every pitch. Sometimes he was wrong, but not very often. Most of us see the ball that well for a period of time, maybe a week, maybe a few days, before we lose it and have to get it back, but Hank could see it for an extended period of time, and when he faltered, he might need only two or three days to get right. That was all about preparation and extreme talent and having the mental discipline to let nothing into your head that you don't want there. When you can do that, you have the freedom to feel and see that pitch as it's coming with perfect instant clarity. It's almost like how it is in a concert hall with world-class acoustics where that first note, off John Lee Hooker's Gibson or Buddy Guy's Stratocaster, is *all* that you hear and feel.

It wasn't just hitting. Life around Hank was the most advanced course in the art of being a complete player and person you could ever hope to take. As Joe Torre once said, Hank Aaron never made a mistake. He always thought everything through. When the Braves were moving me around in the batting order, putting me in front of Hank, then behind him, I was getting frustrated, but Hank gave me great advice: *Dusty, what you do is: Don't strike out. Don't hit it into a double play. Hit as many singles and doubles as you can. They'll stop walking me. You become the best RBI man you can be, that's all the protection I'll need.*

My time with Hank on the Braves gave me the foundation for what to be and what not to be—as a ballplayer, as a father, and as a man. Being around Hank on a daily basis was so special an opportunity to learn and grow, I couldn't fully appreciate it at the time. I thought I grasped how lucky I was, but only later did I truly understand. To go to his room after games was to go to school. To sit and learn from this wise, brilliant man fifteen years older than me and to absorb from him a sense of what was even possible, if I could learn my lessons well—that was beyond priceless. Hank was like my own dad in that he might brag on me to others, but he would never pass any of that on to me directly. That was how that generation was. It was serious, but always fun and full of laughs. Hank loved to laugh. He would crack up, and it would crack me up.

I remember one of my first seasons, talking to Orlando Cepeda about all the tough pitchers we were facing, like Tom Seaver, Jerry Koosman, and Jon Matlack of the Mets, Fergie Jenkins and Bill Hands of the Cubs, Bob Gibson of the Cardinals, and Don Sutton of the Dodgers.

"When are we going to face someone who isn't as tough?" I asked Orlando.

"Hey, man, this is every day in the big leagues," he told me.

When I asked Hank who was the toughest pitcher he ever faced, he told me without hesitation that it was Sandy Koufax. (Later, when I played for the Dodgers, I was sitting out in the bullpen during spring training and had a chance to talk to Koufax, and I asked him who the toughest hitter he ever faced was. "Bad Henry," Koufax told me.) One time I asked Hank who he went to when he was struggling. Who motivates the motivator? Hank, again without hesitation, told me that when he was struggling, he would go to Stan "the Man" Musial. After that, of course, I wanted to meet Stan the Man, and Hank introduced us. I was very deferential and respectful, because my dad, a big Musial fan, would have wrung my neck if I was anything less.

I asked Mr. Musial his theory of hitting, and he told me he tried to stay out of center field in the air. I've used that ever since, and passed it on to young hitters, but I never mastered it like Musial did. Some guys, when I share that, say, "How do you do that?" It wasn't easy. I had plenty of fly balls to center that were nothing but long outs, but I was a line-drive hitter. Hank didn't believe in an uppercut swing. He believed in a level swing: You come down through the zone and put backspin on the ball instead of *lifting* the ball. I never saw Hank hit a tape-measure home run, not one. But Hank didn't miss it. That was what Roy Campanella always used to say—take a good whack at it and don't miss. You don't foul it off. You don't overswing. You don't miss it.

It took me years as a big-leaguer to really put to use what Hank Aaron taught me. I had to take what I learned and apply it through physical and mental practice, but that took time. It wasn't what you learned, it was what you truly retained and could put into practice. I can say now looking back that I didn't really get most of what Hank taught me at the time. It took me years to catch up to understanding more of what he passed on to me about making a complete and consuming commitment to excellence. You had to have your eyes wide open and notice everything, from a shortstop taking a half-step toward the hole just before the pitch to a pitcher's eyes looking in or out. You took it all in. Hank taught me to have total recall of all situations and pitches you might see, and then you trusted your feelings. You were more alert that way. You found more truth that way. You hit the ball harder and more often that way. Hank schooled me to retain what he was teaching, I learned that from him, so that later I would grow into understanding why it was all so important.

Hank wasn't one to waste any words. He said what he meant and meant what he said. You learned quickly to stay alert and pay attention if you were one of his pupils, like Ralph Garr and Darrell Evans and me. We were smart enough to soak up anything and everything Hank had to say. In a way, Hank's best lessons came without words, and I'm talking life lessons even more than baseball lessons. In that, again, he reminded me of my dad. Hank's lessons came through even in the way he carried himself and set an example of dignity and honor just as much as it did in the way he walked out to the plate with the all-business attitude of a man who knew he had done everything he could to prepare for that moment.

You had to have talent and competitive fire. You had to feel a need deep inside of you to win. You also had to have a need to get better, a need to put more into tapping all that you could tap within yourself. If you had all that, then in a way the key to hitting, as taught by Hank Aaron, was deceptively simple.

Trust your feelings. That was Hank's ultimate lesson to me. If you don't trust your feelings, you can never be a great hitter. If you feel it, it's probably true. That was what Hank taught us. If something tells you that pitcher is going to throw you an outside fastball, he's probably going to throw you an outside fastball. If you have a feeling you want to take a pitch, take a pitch. If Hank took a pitch, he always had a reason, whether it was to see the movement or the late break or whatever.

Trust your feelings. Some people reading those words might think I'm talking about a hunch. Or an inkling. Those are words people use when they don't trust their feelings. An honest feeling is much deeper than a hunch or inkling. Feelings are powerful. Feelings are true. Feelings sometimes can't be explained. They come from the inside, but it's an external power that gives you that feeling in the first place. It's similar to when you sense danger. You can't explain why, it just happens. And it happens for a reason. And how often do you have that sense of danger and look back later glad that you did? Until you reach that point of trusting your feelings, you'll find you're second-guessing yourself. As we get older, sometimes we lose that. As we get older, we want factual findings. Children tend to trust their feelings more than we do. They're sometimes better at knowing what they know.

To me, baseball, fishing, and life are very similar. You have to have faith and you have to have confidence, but you also have to be aware when that one pitch comes or when that one bite from a fish comes. You have to remain alert, and that's hard, especially if there's no action. You have to relax enough to keep that alertness constant. As the great Japanese slugger Sadaharu Oh taught me one spring training: *You have to have the coolness of mind to control the burning desire in your heart.* You have to clear out your thoughts to be quiet in the mind and ready to react as quickly and decisively as possible.

Hank instilled in me the importance of always exercising your mind, the way you exercise your body, always exercising your memory and your recall, so you stay sharp and get sharper. The lesson stayed with me so much that to this day, I hate to use navigation apps on my phone. I try whenever I can just to drive somewhere from memory, which usually I can, and almost never get lost.

Hank watched the game. Better than anybody, he saw the whole field. He never took his eyes off the field. And he took in all he saw and used it to think ahead, the way a great chess player does, seeing what was going to happen before anyone else did. One time, he told me, "I'm going to hit a single to left, and the left fielder drops his head before he throws, so I'm going to take second." And that was just what he did. You could learn every time you watched Hank. He would clench his fist and form a little circle he could see through, then look out at the pitcher to zero in on his release point. He'd look out at the pitcher as long as it took to see what he was looking for. Or sometimes he would look through a hole in his cap to take a close look. Everything he did he thought through carefully.

"Do you understand?" he would ask me.

"Yeah," I'd say, but I didn't understand half the time. And Hank *knew* I didn't understand.

"Look, boy, if you don't understand, at least retain what I'm telling you about, and someday you may see it," he always said.

I followed that advice. I remembered everything he said, or as much as I could, anyway. As the years went by, more and more of what he had taught me years earlier came into focus for me. He talked to me about keeping an eye on the shortstop, watching for any movement, to signal a particular pitch being on the way, and five years later, I understood. Decades later, I would use stories from Hank when I was trying to explain something to one of my players.

I learned from so many who came before me. Tony Pérez and Bob Watson talked to me about driving in runs in key situations. Ron Fairly spoke to me about two-strike hitting, and Big Bob Veale, a pitcher, taught me about zoning the plate, cutting it in half. All these guys taught me. Some of it I understood, and some of it I didn't at the time, but I came to understand it all. Some of this I've passed on to young hitters, but you have to be careful not to overload a twenty-two-year-old with everything you think you learned over fifty years in baseball. You just hope they will retain, the same way Hank taught me to retain, so that later they can put some things together.

Hank was a walking advanced seminar in the art of hitting. He had a different theory and philosophy for every pitcher he would face. If he was facing a tough lefty like Steve Carlton, he said, *If you recognize spin from the hips down, take the pitch. By the time it gets to the plate, it will be a ball.* Or against Tom Seaver, he told me, *If it's a fastball from the waist up, take it, because by the time it gets to you, it'll be up around your neck.* Back then, we were always being told that it was mathematically impossible for a pitch to rise. But I knew what I saw with my own eyes! Now pitchers are taught backspin to make the pitch rise.

Hank was a student of hitters as well as pitchers, and a student of base running. He always knew where the ball was going. I don't think I ever saw him dive. If Hank was on third base, ready to move toward home on contact, once he watched the bat through the strike zone, he would know what the ball was going to do, whether a ground ball or a line drive. It took me a while, watching him, to get it. On defense, he would move me around in the outfield, and I would go just where he told me. Then the ball would be hit right where he moved me. Back in those days, there were no organized scouting reports. That was where the total recall came in. Hank would know how a guy held his hands, high or low, in or out. He would know if he was going to be a pull hitter or opposite-field hitter. He would move us accordingly, much in the way I heard Willie Mays did with the Giants outfield.

Hammer worked harder than any of us, and he worked tirelessly. Before I fell under his example, I thought training meant finding some guys and running some full-court basketball for hours. Hank would run around the gym with a medicine ball the whole time we were playing basketball. He might have had the strongest wrists in baseball. Everyone knew that. We knew why. He always had hand grips and would work on those to make his hands and wrists and forearms stronger, which also explained why he was such a great handball and racquetball player.

There's baseball shape and there's physical shape, and they are two different things. You prepare for baseball by playing baseball. What amazed me most about Hank was his consistency and his ability to play with pain. That was what he taught me as much as everything. He had sciatic nerve problems and dealt with a lot of pain, but most people never knew. You would see him literally *thinking away* pain. And he had very little wasted motion in everything he did during a baseball game, which was another way of staying in the lineup and being consistent. *Stay off that disabled list,* he would school Ralph and me. *You've got to play with pain.* Probably the thing I'm most proud of when I look back on my baseball career is that I was never on the disabled list. I could have been, I probably *should* have been, but I never was.

Hank didn't overexplain. You watched and learned. Outwardly he was always stoic in the best sense, never boastful. Internally, I'm sure he was the most confident guy in the world, but you would never hear him brag. He didn't let us clown around to show up the opposition and didn't like showboating. One time in 1972, I threw my helmet down out of frustration, and I got an earful from Hank. "Don't throw that helmet, boy, put it back on the rack," he told me. "And don't throw that bat either. It's not the helmet's fault or the bat's fault that you struck out. Sit down and figure out how to get him next time."

Hank was only thrown out of a game one time in his twenty-year career. He struck out and threw his bat down, and it hit the home-plate umpire. Never again. He learned his lesson. Hank believed in quiet dignity, and he loved that quality in others. He was a big fan of Westerns like *The Man Who Shot Liberty Valance,* where a lot of the time you don't quite know who the hero is until you watch closely and see how the action plays out. To this day, I love Westerns. Once I'm done catching a game in the evening, a lot of times I'll turn on a Western until I fall asleep. The code of the Old West, quiet strength and fighting for what's right even when it's hard, those were values that Hank instilled in Ralph and me and others on the team.

Hank at that time stood for civil rights, but he also brought the racial sides together at a time where there was a lot of racial tension. You saw it in some of the older people on both sides, and especially the younger people. There were lines that separated Black and white in the country and especially the South, but they were actually closer in some strange ways. In the South, white people and Black people basically ate the same kind of food, and most practiced the same religion.

He was a proud Black man but showed everybody respect—if you showed him respect—and was loved by his teammates regardless of color, and he was ready to help anybody and everybody on our team. He commanded respect because he embraced essential values like working hard and being modest and thinking of others. The Braves' leader in home runs in '73 wasn't even Hank, it was our second baseman, Davey Johnson. One time in L.A. in the months leading up to his 715th home run, a white-haired woman in sneakers came up to Hank and asked if he was the home-run king of baseball. Without missing a beat, he told her, "No, ma'am, Dave Johnson is upstairs in his room."

— — — —

Like Hank, Ralph Garr had also grown up in the South, and he was always after me to keep in mind that there were lines I did not want to cross. He had a hard time getting that message through to me. Every year, back then, I would start my season by driving my Olds 4-4-2 two thousand miles to pick Ralph up in Louisiana. First I went south down I-5 to Los Angeles, and from there I drove out past Riverside into the high desert, Joshua Tree National Park, and Arizona. I don't know if I've ever loved anything as much as the feeling of being young in that 4-4-2 out on the road, feeling the power under the hood and feeling the wide-open road ahead, and the sense it gave me that anything was possible.

It was eight hundred miles on I-10 from L.A. to the West Texas border, and I always found some cheap little motel and stayed the night in El Paso, because that was the beginning of Texas. From there it was the interstate right across Texas, through Midland and Abilene and Fort Worth. If I got tired, I picked up a hitchhiker, usually a hippie, because I knew no hippie was ever going to turn violent on me—and he might even have some good tunes to share. Two things I did to keep myself awake: one was cranking up my Led Zeppelin cassette as loud as I could, the other was tuning into Wolfman Jack on the radio from Gatlinburg, Tennessee. You knew Wolf was coming on when he started howling in the middle of the night.

I would pass through Dallas and on to Ruston, Louisiana, where I picked up Ralph. After a few days hanging out there with Ralph and J. R. Richard, who I knew from the Instructional League, we would be on our way. We took I-20 East, and then up and over the Vicksburg Bridge across the Mississippi River from Louisiana and into Mississippi. This was Hinds County, Mississippi, near Jackson. Three years in a row, I got a ticket going across that bridge, either coming or going. It was like they were waiting for me there every year.

"Where you going, boy?" one Mississippi cop asked me, checking out the California plates on my canary yellow 4-4-2. "You drivin' mighty fast."

It was a good thing I had Ralph there.

I started to say, "I ain't gonna be no—" when Ralph hit me in the side, as if to say, *Keep cool, man! You don't want to start nothin'!* And he was right. I didn't. We didn't.

I had to write a letter and pay a fine to Judge Terry Hinds. "Do you think Judge Hinds is related to the Hinds of Hinds County?" I asked Ralph.

He couldn't believe how slow I was to get the idea.

"Baker, you in the South," he said. "Here, the district attorney is related to the judge. Everybody is probably in the family."

I went to spring training in 1971 with every intention of making the big-league club, but I'd seen Ralph go back to Triple-A after he'd led the league in hitting, so I was also realistic. On the last day of spring training, the Braves gave me the word before that day's game that I had made the team to start the season. I was thrilled. The moment was doubly sweet for me because, unlike in past years, when through my own stubbornness I never called my dad, now I could call him. I went over to a pay phone in the clubhouse and called California, collect, to give my dad the good news. He might not have let on, but I could tell from his voice how happy he was. I even made arrangements to have my 4-4-2 shipped from Florida to Atlanta for the season.

We were playing the Yankees that day and lost, but our only run came home when I was up in the ninth and hit a grounder in the infield that scored Guy Rose from third. Then I came back in after the game, and everyone was quiet. The Braves had changed their minds. I was going back to the minors.

It was a crushing blow. Only much later did I find out the real reason the Braves decided to send me down to Richmond: It was Hank. He told them that was the best move, because I needed the at-bats and the game experience. I never said a word about any of that to Hank. I was pissed off and confused. I was thinking about it financially, making more in the big leagues to help my mom and my family. Later I came to understand that he was right, but at the time, the move left me floored.

I decided to let my bat do the talking. Richmond had a two-game exhibition series with Atlanta before the regular season, and I could work out a little frustration. The Braves had gone over to new pinstripe uniforms then, and that meant the Richmond team got stuck with wool hand-me-downs. I doubled in our 6–0 win over the big team in the first game and homered in the second game. After the series, they brought me back in and said I was making them look bad, so they were promoting me to the big leagues again.

I was excited to join the Braves in Cincinnati for Opening Day, but I also felt bad for my friend Tommie Aaron, Hank's brother, who was sent down. One of my homeboys from Riverside, Tommy Hall, was pitching for the Reds that year. He was so skinny, they called him "The Blade," but ever since we were kids, he always threw hard. We were hanging out the day before Opening Day, watching *The Price Is Right* with Bob Barker on the TV in the hotel, and suddenly it looked like there was a double exposure in the picture on the TV. Behind Bob Barker I could see a tornado, right there on the TV. I turned around and went to the window and saw the same tornado across the river tearing up a trailer park. I felt like I was in *The Wizard of Oz,* wondering what the tornado would do next. Then it crossed the river and went back up into the sky over downtown Cincinnati.

- - - -

Hank's chase of Babe Ruth's home run record made him an important symbol of Black pride and Black achievement in the early 1970s. All the civic leaders respected Hank, who was very close to Andrew Young, the former pastor in Marion, Alabama, who worked with Dr. King and served as executive director of the Southern Christian Leadership Conference. I met Mr. Young at Hank's house and heard him talk to Hank about his desire to run for Congress. I was just a kid then, and I did a lot of listening without having much to add to the conversation. Through Hank, Ralph and I met people like Ralph Abernathy, another minister turned civil rights leader who was a mentor to Dr. King, and Maynard Jackson, elected mayor of Atlanta in 1974, becoming the first Black mayor of any city in the South; the Rev. Jesse Jackson, who was only eight years older than me, and who later gained a national profile as a presidential candidate and leader of the Rainbow Coalition; and Herman Russell, the first Black member of the Atlanta Chamber of Commerce, whom I worked for briefly in the offseason, selling insurance.

Among Hank's fans was the new governor of Georgia, Jimmy Carter, who took office in January 1971. As governor, Carter talked a lot about human rights; he did the same later as President of the United States. During his inaugural speech as governor in early 1971, he made a strong statement: "I say to you quite frankly that the time for racial discrimination is over. . . . No poor, rural, weak, or Black person should ever have to bear the additional burden of being deprived of the opportunity of an education, a job, or simple justice."

Carter was a man of deep and humble religious faith, like Hank and Ralph. My faith was important to me, as I'd been brought up going to church every Sunday, but in those years it often took reminders from Hank or Ralph to get me to go to church. That became a must for me for years to come, anytime I was in Atlanta, stopping by the Ebenezer Baptist Church, where Dr. King had been pastor until he was killed in 1968. Ralph and I became chapel leaders, and we ended up leading one of the first chapels in baseball. My teammates would kid me about that, always going out on Saturday night then coming to chapel on Sunday morning.

Jimmy Carter was also a big sports fan, something a lot of people don't know. He was even a fan of NASCAR racing, saving up so he and his wife could go to races at Daytona. In March 1971, while I was at spring training, Governor Carter showed up at an Atlanta Hawks game with the team ahead by one point, and his arrival set the Hawks off on a ten-point scoring run, and they won easily. I was there at Atlanta Stadium on Friday, April 9, 1971, when Governor Carter threw out the ceremonial first pitch for the first Braves home game of the season. All within about twenty-four hours, the governor rolled a pink ball to open the Women's International Bowling Congress in Atlanta, then attended several hours of the Masters golf tournament in Augusta, watching from the fifteenth green, before leaving early to come to our home opener. Over the coming years, Ralph and I often visited Governor Carter in his office at the Capitol on our way to games. I was proud to say that I was the favorite player of his mother, Mama Lillian. "I like that Dusty!" she would say.

— — — —

I really never knew what Hank saw in Ralph and me, and I guess in some ways I still don't. He promised my mom he would look after me, and he more than lived up to that promise. Hank must have seen some of himself in us. He knew we had the talent, and the question was: What would we do with it?

Only later did I understand how much Hank needed Ralph and me, how important it was that we could keep him loose, keep him distracted from the pressures of being Hank Aaron. He and his second wife, Billye, would have nearly fifty years together, but in 1972, Hank was going through a tough divorce. He had been together with his first wife, Barbara, eighteen years, and the divorce was hard on him. It hurt him deep. Barbara would cook for us all the time. I would be over there playing jacks and jumping rope with his girls, Gaile and Dorinda, and basketball with his boys, Lary and Hank Jr. When Hank started seeing Billye, a morning show host in Atlanta, some time after his divorce, he asked Ralph and me, "What do you think of her?" and then invited us to her house for dinner. Billye was a good-looking lady who made history as the first Black woman to host a morning TV show in that part of the country, *Today in Georgia,* starting in 1968. Later she had her own show, *Billye,* the way Oprah had her own show. Years later, Hank would tell people that having Ralph and me around to cheer him up helped him get through that divorce, which meant a lot to me. I was surprised to hear that. Ralph and I had no clue that we were helpful to Hank in that way.

There was nothing better than hanging out with Hank and Ralph, then going to the ballpark and being a part of the action. We were back at Candlestick Park on Saturday, May 8, 1971, looking bad against the Giants' tough left-hander, Ron Bryant, who shut us out through seven innings. Then Clete Boyer hit a pinch-hit homer, and I came up as lead-off hitter, reaching on an infield hit. Ralph came up and bunted for a single, bringing up Hank. His home run scored Ralph and me and made it a rout.

I had trouble getting on track with the Braves that season, just as Hank had thought I would. We were at home against the Expos on May 20, and I came into the game as a pinch-runner and got a hit in my one at-bat, but was still batting just .167 for the year. I'd never been to New York, and the team was packing up to go play the Mets at Shea Stadium. I was excited to visit New York City for the first time and was highly disappointed when manager Lum Harris called me into his office for twenty minutes to tell me why I was being sent down to Richmond again.

I took four days to join the Richmond team. I was busy pouting and wouldn't answer the phone in the apartment Ralph and I shared when they were looking for me. Finally, I drove to Richmond, where I was greeted by Tommie Aaron and all the familiar faces at the Eggleston Hotel. I started out cold. They wanted to move me to third base, an idea that I hated. They told me, "Put your chest in front of it and knock it down." I wanted to tell them, "I don't have no chest, I'm too skinny," but I kept quiet. That experiment lasted three games, and I returned to center field, where I had been an All-Star the year before.

I was so unhappy to be in the minors that the fans noticed. A little girl in Richmond wrote me a letter that really shook me up.

"What's wrong with you?" she wrote. "You're my favorite player, and if you're not the same Dusty Baker, then send the other one back."

When I read that, I figured I'd better stop feeling sorry for myself and start playing like myself again. I wanted to earn my way back to the big leagues.

— — — —

Hank was a former Boy Scout, and one of the big lessons he taught me was *Be Prepared.* Never think your way out of an opportunity, Hank told me. And never put yourself in a position to fail because you have not adequately prepared. It was a lesson I learned the hard way in 1972 when I didn't follow Hank's advice and lived to regret it. I would tell this story for years to come to players I managed, to remind them to always stay ready.

I came to Braves spring training camp that year excited for another shot at breaking through, but then I arrived and saw how many outfielders were ahead of me. Besides Hank, the Braves also had Ralph, Rico Carty, and Mike Lum to play outfield. It would be hard to break in. I'd batted .311 at Richmond in 1971, which was good, but not as good as the .325 I'd hit for Richmond one year earlier, and in my brief time with Atlanta in '71, I'd hit .226 in twenty-six games, compared to .292 in 1970 in just thirteen games. I was out of options, in baseball terminology, so the Braves would risk losing me if they sent me back to the minors, which wasn't what they wanted. I could have been claimed off waivers for a minimal price. As Hank knew, the team was high on me and saw big things. Lum Harris told a reporter in spring training that "every team" the Braves talked to about possible trades "wants Baker," but the Braves said, "No way." That spring Atlanta sports columnist Furman Bisher, sitting in the stands with a group of scouts, asked one which of the young Braves players he liked most? Was it Garr? The scout mentioned me. "In fact, we sit in the stands together a lot, me and other scouts, and we've talked about it," he said. "We're just about unanimous on Baker."

Just after spring training in 1972, the inevitable happened—we went on strike. Marvin Miller, the executive director of the Major League Baseball Players Association, was negotiating with owners to achieve some small basic gains for players, mostly having to do with player pensions. Miller had proposed turning to President Richard Nixon to mediate the disagreement, but that idea was rejected. Talks broke off at the end of the month, leaving us no choice but to strike. "The club owners are trying to grind the players in the dust," Miller said.

Most of the Braves players went back to Atlanta, and so did Ralph and I. We were told the strike would last maybe a couple days, so when we first got to town, Ralph and I booked ourselves into a nice suite in the Marriott downtown. Hank told us to come work out, but we didn't. We didn't do much besides hang out in the suite and have a good time fooling around. Then we ran out of money and went to sharing a single room. Then we ran out of money again and had to leave the hotel and stay with an Atlanta friend of ours, Joe Hand, who worked at the post office. Joe had a two-bedroom apartment, and Ralph and I flipped to see who got to sleep in the other bedroom. I lost and had to sleep on the couch, which was almost big enough for me.

"Come work out," Hank kept telling me.

"No, I'm the last guy on the team," I said. "I'm out of options, and I'm behind you, Orlando, Ralph, Mike Lum, and Rico Carty."

The strike ended suddenly. The owners backed down and agreed to pay a little more into the player pension fund. We showed up at Atlanta Stadium for an informal workout, and it was ragged. "Ralph Garr and

Adella and Harry Russell,
Mom's mom and dad,
my grandparents.

Arena Smith Baker,
Dad's mom and
my grandmother.

Dad in Florida with
Aunt Bert (sister) and
Amos (best friend).

Baker family by the sea, Rob, Dad, Tonay, Mom, Vic, and me (*left to right*).

Left to right: Aunt Anna Mae, Dr. King, and Ted Abernathy.
Working for Dr. King, Savannah, Georgia.

Aunt Loreena Russell, singer,
Mom's older sister and spiritual confidant.
(My TiTi, I was very close to her.)

Third-grade class at Riverside Laurel Elementary School (*second-to-last row, middle*).

Robie and me in front of our new house in Riverside before a Little League game. Dad's work truck in the background.

Riverside Little League, Bridgeport Brass Rockets. Dad (*upper right*); me (*middle row, third from right*).

Me, aka Dusty "B," playing team football, Riverside Poly, tenth grade, 1965.

My varsity football team, Del Campo High School, Sacramento, 1966 (*back row, middle*).

Del Campo High School varsity basketball team, 1967. Me (*back row, middle*), head coach Mr. McCullough (*far left, back row*), my future lawyer Randall Widman (*back row, far right*), and Dave Coleman (now a doctor at Princeton, *back row, second from right*).

Sacramento All Stars regional high school basketball team, while preparing for a tournament in Mexico. Darnell Hillman, aka Dr. Dunk and former ABA and NBA Pacers player (*back row, fourth from right*), and me (*front row, third from left*).

Playboy Club, 1968, rookies' night out (*left to right*):
Clete Boyer, Ralph Garr, me, and Bob Uecker.

Me and Dennis in West Palm Beach during spring training. Dennis drove across the country to see me after a long separation of not talking or writing.

In the Camp Lejeune barracks with Big Bob Spence (*far right*)—a friend from Santa Clara and later a player for the White Sox—and other Marines.

Honor Man in dress blues—the only recruit on graduation day, January 1969, Parris Island, South Carolina.

Me in college with my brother Vic, University of the Pacific, Stockton, California.

Left to right: Vic, me, and Rob in the Lake Tahoe mountains.

Me, Harriet, and Hank in 1973, shortly after being married.
William Herty Killian Jr.

Left to right: Ralph Garr, Ruby Garr, Larvell “Sugar Bear” Blanks, me, Hank Aaron, Rico Carty, Earl Williams, Oscar Brown, and Paul Casanova.
William Herty Killian Jr.

Hank and me in the on-deck circle studying the pitcher.
Courtesy of the Atlanta Braves

My job selling new cars at Walker Ford in Augusta, Georgia.

Left to right: Me, Tom House, Vic Correll, Maximino León, Monte Irvin, Hank Aaron, Satchel Paige, and Ralph Garr.

Dusty Baker, who both hit the ball well in the spring, looked like your grandmother," *The Atlanta Journal* reported. Three days later, we were taking the field in San Diego for the first game of the season on April 15. We might have had one real workout to prepare ourselves. I was out of shape but wasn't worried, since I was sure I had about as good a chance of getting into the game as one of the batboys.

Then in the first or second inning, Orlando hurt his knee. He had to come out of the game. Hank moved from right field to take over for Orlando at first.

"Grab your glove, Baker, and go to center field," Lum Harris called down to me.

"Me?" I asked. I couldn't believe it.

"Yeah," Lum said again.

I ran out onto the field, and I felt so unprepared, I was worried about what might happen. Hank had tried to warn me. He had pushed me to keep myself in shape. At the time, I just had too much of the kid still in me to get serious and see his words in a larger life context. A crossroads can be something that comes and goes and you make a choice and move on and don't think twice, and only later do you see that this was a decision you made or let be made for you that helped shape your life and who you are. My painful lesson the first month of the 1972 season was not that kind of thing. I was in a world of hurt, beating myself up over it. I knew I'd taken a wrong turn.

Unprepared as I was, I did get a hit that first Braves game of the season, a run-scoring single in the seventh, but I felt lost up there, physically and mentally. The next day, we had a doubleheader, and I played both games and didn't get a single hit. That makes for a long day: 0-for-3 in the first game and 0-for-4 in the second. We flew from San Diego back home to Atlanta, and I went 0-for-4 in back-to-back games against the Dodgers. Lum Harris gave me a day off to help me clear my head a little. I wasn't the only one waving at the ball. Hank and I were both in a 1-for-18 funk, though in his case everyone knew it was a fluke, and in my case people couldn't be sure. Ralph was in a 1-for-11 rut at that point, and Mike Lum not much better at 2-for-18.

I got back out there after the day off, really pressing for a hit, and went 0-for-4 again against the Dodgers. Lum Harris had seen enough. I was pulled from the starting lineup after that. I still had to stay ready, just in case, since he kept putting me in late in games as a pinch-runner or defensive replacement or pinch-hitter. I still couldn't get a hit, and my slump reached 1-for-23 (a .043 batting average).

"What do I do?" I asked Hank when Lum Harris benched me.

"I told you that you should have worked out," he said. And he was right. "Get to the cage. Go down there and you work your butt off. Just hit till your hands bleed."

I could see Hank was disappointed in me. The tiger cub with the big paws is going to trip over himself sometimes, and in that tripping comes the learning. In the tripping comes the movement forward. At the time, I didn't understand the high value the Braves placed in me as an up-and-coming talent. The Braves had protected both Ralph Garr and me during the expansion draft when Major League Baseball added four teams before the 1968 season: the Montreal Expos, San Diego Padres, Kansas City Royals, and Seattle Pilots. Since teams could only protect fifteen players, that said everything. Ralph and I were the only minor-leaguers the Braves protected. Hank couldn't tell me how highly esteemed I actually was in the eyes of the Braves front office. This information might have gone to my head, and not in a good way. But Hank knew. Hank was in on everything. All he could tell me was to get to work.

I hit, hit, hit, just the way Hank said I needed to do. And my hands hurt, just the way Hank thought they would. They didn't bleed, but it almost felt like they did. The work did not pay off immediately. I learned something I've passed on to many players since, which is that it takes the brain time, usually a couple days at least, to memorize a correct movement and gain that muscle memory. Some days I felt better. Some days I felt worse. In Pittsburgh on April 29, I finally got a chance to start a game and finally got a hit, and I liked that so much, I made it two, adding a double. The next morning, *The Pittsburgh Press* called me "weak-hitting Dusty Baker." Who were they calling "weak-hitting"? I never forgot those words, the rest of my career. I always tried to hit the ball hard, especially against Pittsburgh.

I kept taking extra batting practice, and kept riding the bench. I would go in late in games, and did have pinch-hits in back-to-back games at home against the Pirates at one point. That's the hardest thing for a young player to do, pinch-hit. But then the whole first half of May went by without me starting another game. It was rough.

It was a trip to the Astrodome of all things that woke me up. I'd been praying to have another opportunity, and Lum Harris finally wrote me into the lineup in Houston on May 15. I went 2-for-3 in the series opener, which we lost, then the next day I led off and *went* off, cranking a two-out solo shot in the third off my future Dodger teammate Jerry Reuss for the first home run of my big-league career. I finished the day 4-for-5 with a stolen base and finally felt like myself again. The next day I was 1-for-3 to give me a .636 batting average for the series and maybe my first real smile of the season.

After that, no one talked about me going anywhere. It turned into a dream of a season for me, and also for my buddy Ralph. We were two of the best young hitters in the league with the numbers to prove it. I stayed on a tear until mid-June, when I took a break to do two weeks of Marine Corps Reserve service. I was back with the team in time for our July 3 game at the Astrodome and picked up where I left off, going 3-for-5 with three RBIs. Once again, Ralph reminded me to pretend like I had never been away.

By then, Ralph and I were kind of accepted as two of the guys. Having that feeling was big for me. That was when I met and hung out with stars like Pete Rose, Willie Stargell, and Billy Williams. Rose and the Reds were in Atlanta in mid-August during the 1972 season for a four-day series, and in the first game, Ralph and I both went 2-for-5, and we won 7–5. The next day, Ralph had three hits and I had one, and we won again, 7–2. I had another hit the next day, and we won 9–4 behind Hank's twenty-fourth homer of the year.

The Reds veterans liked us, and during that series, they were having fun giving me a hard time on the field before the game. Rose, seeing me talking to a reporter, called out, "You've got to get a few good years up here, then you get the ink, Dusty!"

"Don't let 'em kid you, Johnnie B.!" Joe Morgan cried out, kinda defending me and kinda not. "You can do it all, Johnnie B.! Some of us can hit, some of us can only run! You can do it all, Johnnie B.! You're a big star!" You learn fast there is no way to defend yourself when the veterans start razzing you like that. In baseball, giving a guy a hard time is the sincerest form of praise.

After Billy Williams of the Cubs and I realized we had the same birthday, June 15, we became tight. He would come over to the little apartment I'd taken that season in Atlanta, next door to Ralph, or I went over to his house to eat. Back in those days, we all hung out at each other's places. If we were in Pittsburgh, we'd be with Stargell and Al Oliver and Gene Clines and Dock Ellis. Wherever we went, we hung out with the Black players on the other team. A lot of that was because of Hank, and some of it was because they thought Ralph and I could play.

The Braves had seen me deliver enough by then that they traded Rico Carty to make room for me. Ralph and I were both among the league leaders all season, pushing each other to do better. I cooled off a little in August, but got hot again in September, batting .391 over a sixteen-game stretch to put me second in the National League in hitting, at .325, behind only league leader Billy Williams (then at .335). "I figure I've got to go out and get two hits a game," I told the Associated Press with ten games left. "I've got to stay cool and capitalize. I've got to go catch Williams because he isn't going to come down to me."

I had that right. Williams finished the season at .333, but Ralph and I gave him a good run. On the last Saturday of the season, we were at Candlestick Park, and I doubled twice off Giants starter Jim Barr to lift my average to .326. The next day, we were going against Sudden Sam McDowell, and he had my number. I went 0-for-4 that day. We flew home to Atlanta for two final games, and Ralph and I both went 1-for-5. The stories in the papers were all about me trying to catch Billy, which I wanted to do so I could be like Al Kaline in Detroit, who won a batting title his rookie year. But mostly I was trying to catch Ralph. The last day of the season, we were up against Dodger left-hander Claude Osteen, who was going for his twentieth win. I got a hit and went 1-for-4, but Ralph was 3-for-4. I finished the season with a .321 average, third best in the National League, behind only Billy and Ralph, who finished at .325. Not bad for Ralph's second year and my first full season. We were proud of that, being roomies and coming up together.

- - - -

Ralph and I had become Hank Aaron's students. We had learned so many lessons from our teacher, starting with the need to do the work and prepare. Then we'd moved on to building up confidence by coming through when it mattered.

When people talk about confidence, the word can mean different things. Maybe it's a little like that inner dignity and outer dignity my dad taught me about when I was young, a lesson that has guided my life. You have the confidence you show to the world, some of us more than others, and you have the inner confidence that is really what sustains you and feeds you and lets you do what you want to do.

Inner confidence comes from your belief in yourself more than from what people have said about you. It has to do with what you'll need when times are bad. Those bad times can come from what other people say or do, but sometimes you bring them on yourself. Outer confidence can be faked. It can be played up, if that's your thing, though it was never mine. But inner confidence lives under the cold, hard eye of reality. You earn inner confidence by getting it done. Inner confidence comes from a succession of successes. You earn inner confidence by falling on your face and getting up and putting that behind you. You earn inner confidence by working hard to get better and then finding a groove and staying in that groove, as Don Baylor—who we called "Groove"—always used to say. You earn inner confidence by coming up when the pressure is at its most intense, like when the crowd is cheering against you so loud, your teeth hurt and you can hardly hear yourself think. But you do what you have to do. You find a quiet place in your mind where it's just you and the ball coming at you and the bat in your hands and that knowledge you have that the solid wood of that bat is going to barrel up and drive that ball to the gap or over a fence. Hank found a way to channel all those lessons to Ralph and me.

That November, I was in for a surprise. One year earlier, Hank had been honored as the "Brave of the Year" by the Atlanta chapter of the Baseball Writers' Association of America, and celebrated by hundreds of people gathered for a big dinner at a big hotel in the Atlanta area. Hammer was the Brave of the Year every year, the way we all saw it, but I guess they figured they had to mix it up. I got a call that November telling me that the Brave of the Year for 1972 was me. I was like, *Really?* On February 10, I would be honored at the Marriott Hotel in Atlanta with nearly a thousand people in attendance, along with that year's Cy Young Award winners, Gaylord Perry in the AL and Steve Carlton in the NL, and the MVPs, Johnny Bench and Dick Allen (who later became a good friend, and inspired me to hold out for fair pay).

I would have preferred being named National League Rookie of the Year, but I wasn't eligible. Going into 1972, I had ninety-eight big-league at-bats sprinkled over four seasons going back to 1968, which was nine at-bats too many, since the rules at the time said you could not have ninety or more at-bats and still be eligible. Ralph would have been Rookie of the Year in 1971, if he had not exceeded the ninety-at-bat rule, going into that year with 130 at-bats. Our teammate Big Earl Williams, who hit thirty-three homers that year, was selected instead, and no knock on Big Heavy, as we called him, but he batted .260 that year to Ralph's .343. The rules needed changing, and at the end of the 1972 season, the BBWAA met in Oakland and adjusted the rules so that, in 1973, so long as you didn't have more than 130 at-bats in previous seasons, you were still eligible. Too bad they didn't change the rules a couple years earlier. I would have loved to have had Ralph and myself as back-to-back NL Rookies of the Year. How cool would that have been?

Over the years, I've thought back and wondered: Would I have won the batting title in 1972, like Al Kaline did his rookie year, if I had listened to Hank Aaron's advice and worked out like he told me? I feel like I know the answer to that one. I probably would have. But the hard-won wisdom Hank was able to teach me was at least as valuable as any batting title or award.

CHAPTER 5

715

I don't think it makes a lot of sense to spend your life second-guessing the choices you've made. My parents just didn't raise me that way. It can eat you up, for one. And knowing you went the wrong way on a choice is enough. The pain of regret gives you that twinge that makes you remember and steers you another way the next time. I've heard it said, by someone else looking back years later, that in retrospect it almost feels like when you're in your twenties, it's your job to do stupid stuff you will come to regret. That's how you learn. That's how you move forward. That's how you become yourself, painful step by painful step.

Nothing about meeting Harriet felt like a mistake, I'll tell you that. One of my favorite parts of driving cross-country was the time I spent in Louisiana with Ralph and his family. The first time I visited the Grambling College campus, I felt like a kid in a candy store. Show me a pretty girl, a girl with a great smile or a great body or a great everything, white or Black or brown, and I'll probably be smiling. Let's just say I was smiling a lot on the Grambling campus, and they were all Black girls. That for me was like a step into a new world. Grambling wasn't just a historically Black university, it was a *historic* Black university, built from scratch in Louisiana by Black people for Black people starting in the late nineteenth century. I felt like I was breathing it all in, walking around that campus with Ralph—the history, the sense of others who had come there over the years, and what their time at Grambling had meant to them.

I had never seen so many pretty Black girls in one spot until I went to Grambling, and Harriet was one of the prettiest. She was the younger sister of Ralph's wife Ruby's roommate Theresa, and I fell for her before she fell for me. So it was my fault it went the way it did in the end. I should have known Harriet and I were just too different. She was from the South. I was from California. She was Catholic. I was Baptist. We just had different ideas and values. But that was part of the attraction.

Being from Louisiana, she turned me on to a world of music that was new to me, like Buckwheat Zydeco and Lazy Lester (who I met later and became a friend). I was always into discovering new music, and in those years Atlanta was the mecca of Black music, different from Motown, which I'd been listening to for years, with artists like Isaac Hayes, Al Green, and Gladys Knight. I saw them all. I went from digging Hendrix and the Airplane and the Mamas & the Papas to B.B. King and Bobby "Blue" Bland and Little Johnny Taylor. I had the best of both worlds. Ralph, being from the South, was more into the blues scene, which I got into. That helped me connect to the South, and it helped me become a man, especially a young Black man.

I fell hard for Harriet. I wanted to be with her. I was tired of squares telling me about what you had to do before you could live together. This was the 1970s. The Braves wouldn't let me bring Harriet to spring training, because they didn't even like me living with her. What business was that of theirs? I had to ask Hank about it.

"You don't do that in the South," Hank said.

"Hey, man," I said, "I ain't from the South. I'm from California."

I was holding out in 1973 for more money from the Braves when Harriet and I got married in Atlanta with Joe Hand as my best man. Since Harriet was Catholic, we had to produce birth certificates to show we were twenty-one. Ralph and Ruby lived in the apartment next door to us. Larvell "Sugar Bear" Blanks lived a couple doors down in that building, too, and his kids and Ralph's kids would always come over to our apartment and get some snacks.

Deep down, I knew I was too young to get married, but no one could tell me that at the time. One reason I wanted to get married was I thought it would settle me down. I was on a wild path. I knew it was wrong, but it was fun. I have a history of doing what I want to do, when I want to do it, and so I ran off and got married without telling my mom and my dad and without asking Harriet's mom. I was just twenty-three and Harriet was twenty-one. At least she and Ruby were close, and I knew Ruby would look out for her when I was on the road. She was a good girl, and I always prided myself on picking out the good girls. I got married because I was trying to do the right thing, and I thought getting married would keep me out of the streets, which I enjoyed. But it wasn't right.

— — — —

I never did change my name to Dusty X, the way I wanted to do when I was fifteen, but I did grow my hair out into an Afro after my time in the Marines. I wore it as a symbol of style and also of protest about a lot of things that just weren't right. To me, that was a symbol of being a part of the struggle, of identifying with the cause. As James Brown would say, "I'm Black and I'm proud." That didn't make me a radical. It made me a Black man alive in the 1970s. Where would it all lead? I would live to see a Black man elected President of the United States, a Black man who happened to be a friend of mine, and for me it would be a lot like how it was watching Hank Aaron going after home run number 715 all over again.

The more time I spent in the South from the late 1960s to the early 1970s, the more I felt called on to do what I could to represent Black people. Back in Southern California, where I'd lived until just after I turned sixteen, L.A. would have its first Black mayor, Tom Bradley, starting in 1973, and he would hold that office for twenty years. Times were changing. Through Hank I met so many bright, young Black civil rights leaders and future political leaders. I could see Hank's calm eye for talent, the same eye he turned on Ralph and me, taking in the mettle of these men. These men were at the top of the food chain. They were deep. They were thoughtful. They listened. They read. And yes, they dared to dream. These were figures who would go on to factor in the national story, and we all knew it. We were sure they would help usher in sweeping change. I felt pride in who they were and what they represented. I saw firsthand what my mom and dad had been talking about and trying to show me for years. I felt Black Pride, a pride that kept growing and ignited a fire inside of me.

With so much going on, it didn't feel like a great time to see the white friends I'd grown up with back in California, not even Dennis, my best friend of all, who spent so much time at our house he really was like part of the family. He lost his parents when he was young, and my whole family had always treated him like one of our own. Dennis was there with me in San Francisco the night we hit a J with Jimi Hendrix. We were connected for life, but by the spring of 1973, I just didn't know anymore if I could be friends with him the way I always had been. I felt more and more like we needed to have change, major change, in this country. Could I still have a white best friend? It wasn't about how I felt about Dennis or how he felt about me, but a reflection of the temperature of the country. I could put Dennis and me in a dangerous situation for both of us, just by being together. What if we were in the middle of a riot? What if Dennis and I were going to end up on different sides of the revolution? Seriously, man. One thing about revolution, any kind of revolution: You may think you see it coming, but you never know where it's going. I didn't know what to think, so I stopped calling Dennis, and I stopped writing. That was a big change for me. Going back to my first year in Sacramento when Dennis and I played football and baseball together on the Del Campo team and became buddies, he and I had always talked at least once a month. Now months went by and we had no contact.

One thing about being denied a place at the table: You set up your own table. And maybe your table turns out to be better anyway. A part of me would never stop being alarmed by Cito Gaston's hand on me on that bus from Little Rock, Arkansas, the hand and the voice and the message telling me: *Stop, you can't even be allowed to eat like any man.* In Florida every year for spring training, it wasn't quite like that, but it wasn't that different. We were better off, as Black people, gathering for cookouts, frying up fish we'd just caught, loading up on a batch of soul food cooked up by Ruby. She was from the small town of Lisbon, Louisiana, and she could cook anything. If we wanted our fish fried, she fried it up. If we preferred baked fish, then she baked it, along with black-eyed peas and collard greens, a good turkey spaghetti and hot-water cornbread, then some peach cobbler and banana pudding. As Ralph would say, she was a natural-born cook. I loved eating Ruby's food, and she loved watching me eat it. She would comment, "Dusty, you always eat strategically."

One afternoon during spring training in 1974, I was driving to a local shopping mall in my new blue Thunderbird just after practice when I felt eyes on me. We all know that feeling. My dad raised me to be aware of my surroundings at all times and to be alert. I've lived my whole life that way ever since. As much as I wanted to ignore the feeling of eyes on me that spring day, something made me look over. Sure enough, I turned, and the guy in the next car over was staring at me like he knew me. Because he *did* know me. It was Dennis. I looked over, and he looked back and just waved.

"Follow me," I said.

I was completely shocked. We drove to the little bungalow I was renting that spring on the West Palm Beach side of Lake Worth, and we both parked.

"You came all this way to see me?" I asked him after we hugged.

That was exactly what he had done. He made the trip having no idea what I'd say or do when I saw him there in Florida, but needing to find out. I wouldn't return his calls, so he drove cross-country to see what was up. He and his wife-to-be Yvonne, whom I'd introduced him to, loaded up his white '68 Mustang and hit the road, sleeping with friends along the way. I felt so much all at once, and I just couldn't believe it. Right then and there it was all clear: It was Dennis, my homeboy, and I was so happy to see him.

Dennis and Yvonne stayed in Florida another week and got to meet Harriet, my new bride. We would stay up late playing cards, Dennis and me, Ralph, and Paul Casanova, and after practice we would fish right out the back of our bungalow.

I called my dad to tell him what Dennis had done.

"He drove cross-country to see you?" my dad asked.

"Uh-huh," I said.

"Son, how many friends do you have, white or Black, that would do that?" my dad asked me.

— — — —

Pressure had been building on Hank for years, especially from the start of the 1973 season. By then he was in range of Babe Ruth's all-time home run record. That spring everyone was talking about how he only needed forty-two homers that year to reach 715 and break the record. "My breaking this record would be good for white and Black America," Hank said that summer. "For years baseball was a white man's game, and people said Blacks would never be able to play it because of the pressure. But here I am challenging the pearl of major-league baseball. You've got to be able to play and stand pressure to do that."

The closer Hank got to Ruth, the more his pursuit felt like it was about something much more than sports. He was going to break the record, and he was going to do it as a member of the Atlanta Braves at the height of the Civil Rights Movement. That was why civil rights leaders like Andrew Young, then serving in Congress, saw Hank's pursuit of the record as being so important. So did Maynard Jackson and young Jesse Jackson. I remember when we went to eat at Jesse's house in Chicago, Hank and Paul Casanova and Ralph and me, and the musicians Billy Preston and Ramsey Lewis were also there. We talked about everything that was going on—Hank's chase of the record and the times we were living through, college protests and women's lib and Vietnam and Watergate.

If anyone was worthy of the honor of home run king, it was Hank, and it wasn't just teammates and friends of his who thought that way. Governor Carter of Georgia was always in Hank's corner. "Everybody's for Hank Aaron," Milton Richman, Sports Editor of United Press International, wrote from our 1973 spring training in West Palm Beach. "He has almost as many people pulling for him to make it as Charles Lindbergh had forty-six years ago."

Hank received more mail than anyone that year, an incredible total of 900,000 letters, as the United States Postal Service later commemorated. Thousands arrived at Atlanta Stadium every week, most of them positive. One letter arrived with no address, only "The" and a picture of a hammer, followed by "Atlanta, Ga." Someone at the post office was a Braves fan. But this flood of letters came after Hank had spoken out about receiving hate mail—his words inspired a letter-writing campaign. Even then, he still received some ugly letters. Just imagine that: Here the man was, playing a sport and doing it as well as anyone ever had, on his way to a record that represented a triumph of the human spirit, something to make people feel good, and some people were so filled with hate and resentment that they felt compelled to pass their filth on to Hank?

Hank didn't show those letters to me or Ralph. It was like if your dad comes home from work pissed off about having to deal with some serious BS, and you say, "What's wrong?" and he says, "Nothing!" I could tell right away when Hank got a bad letter. He would crumple it up, those strong hands of his squeezing hard, and throw it down on the floor. Then when he left, Ralph and I—who had lockers on either side of his—would uncrumple the paper and read it.

The envelopes of some letters came scrawled with Ku Klux Klan hoods. Some made threats like "You will die in one of those games," and that one we forwarded to the FBI to investigate. Some threats were weirdly specific, like "A guy in a red jacket is going to shoot you," and then Ralph and I would be scanning the stands looking for someone in a red jacket. But Hank was unfazed. We were thinking about it more than he was.

It was tough, real tough. Hank responded by being even more focused. His concentration and focus during that period was unbelievable. He did not talk about how hard it was, but we could tell. He had to have a full-time bodyguard, Calvin, who was like our brother. The Braves gave Hank two rooms when we were on the road, one decoy room where he was registered, so that if anyone showed up looking for him, that was where they would go, and another room under another name where he actually slept. We were over at Hank's room every day, every night,

Ralph and me and Paul Casanova, doing our best to distract him or make him laugh if we could or just keep him company. On our team flights, Hank would make me sit next to him, with Ralph over on the other side. We clowned around a little, made him laugh, then he would fall asleep and Ralph and I would give each other a look and get up to go. Just then Hank would reach out those strong wrists, one on Ralph and one on me, and say, "Sit down," all without even opening his eyes. So we sat back down.

On the road, our manager Eddie Mathews would always check our rooms at curfew, calling in, "You two bastards in here?" We told him good night, waited half an hour, then snuck out, maybe to Hank's room. One time we were in Hank's room and Hank told us to get in the closet. Eddie came in and sat down, and he was in a mood to drink and talk. The whole time, for two hours, Ralph and I hid in the closet waiting for him to leave. That closet was as big as our room, and we fell asleep in there.

We were at home in Atlanta on the Fourth of July that season. Two uniformed policemen were stationed in the left-field stands to keep an eye on anyone taunting Hank or making threats. "They're on me every day," Hank told *Newsday* that week. "Yesterday, the day before, I just can't figure it." Who could figure it? Hank was quiet and dignified and worthy of nothing but respect. "I just want them to respect me like a man, the same way they respect any common white man," he said. "When I was a kid I realized that if your skin is black you're not going to be on equal terms. You have to fight a little harder when you're told you're second best. The Negro man has been the lowest creature on earth. Even a dog gets better treatment."

I learned so much about how to talk to reporters just watching Hank. He knew when to draw the line and when to say no to interview requests. But if he was going to talk, he talked. He showed us that all you had to do was be yourself and treat writers with dignity. You can't control what they write, and you can't always trust them to do the right thing, but if you start on the right note, they often reward your faith in them. Our next series was at Shea Stadium against the Mets, and New York

Daily News columnist Phil Pepe was there when Hank talked. "He sat there for about a half hour and answered every question patiently, honestly, directly," Pepe wrote. "He never refused to answer a question, never commented on the intelligence of a question, never showed annoyance or boredom with a question, although most of them he had answered before, many times. And when the interview ended, it was not Henry Aaron who terminated it, it was only when those who were interviewing him had no more questions to ask."

That Sunday, we faced our former teammate George Stone, Ralph's homeboy from Ruston, traded from the Braves to the Mets before that season. He got Hank out on a slow curve in the second, then I came next and homered off him. Hank's next time up, he knew Stone would try the slow curve on him again. Sure enough, he did, and Hank took him deep, earning a nice ovation from the crowd of 33,000. Hank got another shot at Stone in the sixth and this time beat him on a fastball away for career homer number 696.

It took him less than two weeks after 696 to reach 700. We were at home against the Phillies on a Saturday night, and Hank got all of a 1-1 pitch, sending it four hundred feet to left center for the milestone. The crowd roared as he rounded the bases and crossed home plate and kept cheering even after he made his way back into the dugout. They wouldn't stop cheering until Hank came back out of the dugout—twice. Pitcher Ken Brett, George's older brother, had been throwing Hank mostly breaking balls, but tried to get a fastball by him. "I wasn't going to pitch around him because of that guy behind him, Dusty Baker, I think he's one of the best hitters in baseball," Brett said afterward.

Hank hit another home run the next day to make it 701, three homers in three games, but then he hit only one over his next fifteen games, through our series at Wrigley Field in Chicago in mid-August. The day we arrived, the papers were carrying tributes to Babe Ruth, whose death had come exactly twenty-five years earlier. Nowhere else was like Wrigley, built in 1918, with fans in the outfield watching from their rooftops and ivy on the outfield wall. Some guys loved hitting there, but for me it was my worst-hitting ballpark, because I never saw the ball well.

We swept the Cubs in three games that series. In the eighth inning of the third game, Ralph and I started a rally by both walking, and Hank knocked a three-run homer to make it a rout—and give him 702. Then we flew to Canada for a series in Montreal, and Hank homered in each of his next two games, putting him within ten of tying Ruth.

Our eyes were on Hank to see how he was handling this whole thing and try to imagine how he was feeling. You don't think about history in the middle of living it. You think about it afterward. This was Hank's history. He was living it. I didn't want to do anything to distract from that. By the end of August, he was eight away, but we were at Candlestick Park. Hank didn't expect to hit any homers there and didn't. We headed next to San Diego, and by our first game against the Padres, Hank had two more homers, moving him within six of Ruth.

A week later, back in Atlanta, Hank hit career homer 710 against the Giants. Could he hit four more in our remaining thirteen games? Six games came and went with no more homers for Hank. Then he hit one at home against the Padres. Five days later at the Astrodome, he hit number 712 with a week left in the season.

Ralph and I were around Hank now more than ever. The closer he got to the record, the more tense it felt. We were more aware of possible danger. His bodyguard was more on edge. Everyone wanted a piece of Hank—they wanted to touch him, as if he wasn't real.

On the last Saturday of the season, at home against the Astros, Hank beat Jerry Reuss in the fifth inning for his fortieth homer of the season. That was number 713 of his career, putting him one behind tying the record, but it also made us the first team in history to have three players hit forty or more homers in a season: Hank, Darrell Evans (forty), and league leader Davey Johnson (forty-two).

I also homered that game to give me twenty-one for the season. That was the most home runs I'd ever hit in my life. I knew I was getting stronger or smarter or hopefully both. For that season, I finished with 99 RBIs and 101 runs scored—which would both hold up as the best of my career—and batted .288. I never felt so good playing baseball.

On the last day of the season, we had a crowd of more than 40,000 in

Atlanta, everyone wanting to see Hank make history, but he finished the day with three singles and no homers. The headline in the next day's *Atlanta Constitution* sports section said it all: "A WINTER TO WAIT." Hank told reporters—and us—"I'm just glad it's over for a while."

When I look back, I'm glad Hank didn't break the record that year. Waiting just added more drama, all through the offseason and spring training.

- - - -

When I was coming up in the big leagues, it was rare to have an agent. Babe Ruth basically had an agent, a PR guy named Christy Walsh, who looked out for Ruth's business deals, and Yogi Berra had an agent, a former Yankee traveling secretary who got fired and wound up working for him. By 1970, the Major League Baseball Players Association was negotiating the right of players to have sports agents looking out for them. The big change came after the 1974 season when A's owner Charlie Finley tried to renege on the details of a contract he'd signed with pitcher Catfish Hunter, a yearly twenty-game winner all through the early seventies and a Cy Young Award winner in '74. When Catfish's beef with Finley went to an arbitrator, the result was that his contract was thrown out, and he became baseball's first real free agent. When he signed a five-year deal with the Yankees worth more than $3 million, everything changed. Not until another round of rules changes the next year, following the Messersmith Decision, did the era of free agency really arrive.

Ralph made $55,000 in 1974 when he won the National League batting title and asked the Braves for a raise to $114,500 for the next season. The Braves countered with an offer of $85,000, so Ralph took his case to arbitration. The arbitrator sided with Ralph, awarding the "Road Runner" $114,500. Ralph, among the first to go to salary arbitration, became the first player to double his yearly pay that way.

I was lucky to find an agent who was a cool dude. I always liked hanging with Jerry Kapstein and talking to him about a lot of things, not just baseball. In the 1970s, Jerry was one of the top two or three agents in the business. I first met him in 1971, when he was a young graduate of Harvard and Boston College Law School just out of the Navy. He was only six years older than me, still in his twenties. Like a lot of young men, Jerry loved sports, and loved stats, and started doing stat work for radio broadcasts of Providence College basketball games when he was fifteen or sixteen. In the Navy, after law school, he worked on things like court martials, so when it came to negotiating with George Steinbrenner or Charlie Finley, there was no way Jerry was ever going to be intimidated.

At that time, a lot of guys avoided having an agent because the teams didn't like it and let you know it. That to me sounded like all the more reason to have one. Jerry worked as my agent starting in 1972, but that first season he worked basically for nothing. "If you don't like what I get for you, then you don't have to pay me nothing," he said. That first year, he might have got me triple the Major League minimum salary, at the time all of $13,500, which was why everybody worked in the offseason, myself included. I liked what he got me, so he became my agent. Then in 1973, the Braves tried to cut my salary, and I was glad to have Jerry in my corner. I held out and with Jerry's help earned a $5,000 raise. Jerry wasn't the type to yell, always polite, but he was firm in his tone and a fierce negotiator.

Not yet thirty, Jerry already represented athletes in all four major sports. To be an agent, you had to be a good scout, and he came down to our International League and built relationships with Don Baylor, Bobby Grich, Carlton Fisk, and me. His baseball clients also included Goose Gossage, Larry Bowa, and Garry Maddox. Jerry was all about being a good person and only wanted certain clients. "I want him to be a good person," he said of his ideal client at the time. "I want him to be loyal to me and to his ball club."

Other agents had pursued me, but Jerry stood out. He was relentless, but then so are most agents. Jerry was also one of the most honest guys I'd ever met. He was low-key, but he was a lion. That was how he thought of himself. He told me that he would eat raw meat before those negotiations in Conference Room 4B. He'd order rare steak, he said, since he was like the lion, and all animals, all the carnivorous animals, they get aggressive and need their protein. Jerry was great to me and my family. My dad loved him. My mom loved him. And I went to see him in Providence, Rhode Island, the first time I played in Boston, which was my first visit ever to the Northeast. I met his mom, and dad, and his brother and sisters. The thing about Jerry, above all else, was this: He was very loyal.

— — — —

The Braves opened the 1974 season on the road at Riverfront Stadium in Cincinnati. The one thing Hank made very clear to Ralph and me was that he wanted to get home run number 715 over with as soon as he could. It would be all business. Opening Day fell on April 4, a solemn date for us all. Just six years earlier on that day, the Rev. Martin Luther King Jr. had been assassinated. Jesse Jackson called Hank before our game that day and suggested he ask for a moment of silence before the start of the game, honoring Dr. King's memory. We never found out who said no to that. How could anyone turn down such a request? But they did. Hank was disappointed. We all were.

There were more than 52,000 fans packed into the stands that day, and they came alive right away. Hank came up in the first after Ralph walked, Mike Lum singled, and Darrell Evans flied out. Since I batted behind the Hammer in the lineup, I had a great view from the on-deck circle. I watched him take two balls from Reds starter Jack Billingham and then jump on a fastball that missed out over the plate. I watched Hank drive those strong wrists through the zone with metronomic efficiency and drive the ball just over the left-center fence to tie Babe Ruth's career home run record of 714. I got to be the first to congratulate him, pointing a finger at him as he crossed home plate.

He didn't say anything to me. That was Hank. He acted like it was just another homer, but knowing him the way I did, I could tell he was excited.

Hank announced he wanted to play again in the second game of the series, but when our manager Eddie Mathews noticed the chill in the air, he decided to give him a day off, no matter what the fans or the sportswriters or Commissioner Bowie Kuhn might have preferred. We lost again, but won the third game, even with Hank and Ralph both going hitless, and then flew back to Atlanta so that Hank could try to break the record at home against the Dodgers.

I felt the usual nervousness you feel before your home opener. It was very cold, and there was a tremendous amount of tension in the air. We were facing left-hander Al Downing, another future teammate, but first the Braves did their best to honor Hank before the game in the way he deserved to be honored. It looked like a parade out there, and why not? If anyone deserved a parade, it was Hank, for all he had done for the game of baseball, for all he had done for all of those who loved him, for all he had done for all Black people, but above all for all he had done for America.

We had a national TV audience tuned in, hoping to see some history, but the celebration hit a snag or two. They were going to release a thousand doves, which sounded cool to me and Ralph, but then came the announcement that the pregame dove display had been canceled because of "threatening weather." Morris Brown College sent its choir and Jonesboro High sent its school band, and we lined up on the basepaths for the ceremony. They had two rows of girls in shorts lined up on the infield, all of them holding up bats in tribute. "Should I walk through or should I run through?" Hank wondered.

For all Black people, celebrating Hank was celebrating ourselves. Sammy Davis Jr. was on hand. The great Pearl Bailey came out to sing the National Anthem, and when Pearl sang, she had everyone right with her. She sang with power and purpose and feeling, and when she belted out "rockets' red glare," you got chills. Pearl was emotional, too. It was not part of the program for her to speak, but she had to share what was in her heart. "If humanity could do just a little more of what we're doing here tonight—do a little more—we'd have it made," she said. "We're here out of love and seein' what's happenin'." She let those words sink in, then added: "Why not tomorrow, too? Don't tell me we can't."

We all wanted this over, the team, the city, the fans, and probably more than anyone, Hank and his family. We went in order in the first, and in the second, batting cleanup, Hank led off. When Al Downing walked him, the full crowd let loose with a loud round of boos. I was up next and doubled to left, scoring Hank. In the fourth, Darrell Evans's grounder to short took a tough hop and he ended up on first, bringing Hank up with a runner on.

Hank turned to me, in the on-deck circle, and told me, "I'm going to get it over with right now."

And I knew he would. I never doubted anything Hank said. It was a cold night, the coldest night I can remember for a game in Atlanta. Everyone was on their feet, cheering Hank, as he stepped into the batter's box. He looked calm and collected, as usual, taking a couple of easy half-swings, extending his wrists toward the pitcher, and waiting for the first pitch from Downing, which bounced. The wind-chilled crowd let loose with another round of booing.

The second pitch was a belt-high fastball. It was out over the plate where Hank could extend his arms and use his powerful wrists. He dropped the hammer, and the ball shot toward a billboard in left center reading "Think of it as money." The guys in the bullpen each chose their own section where they thought the homer would land. Tom House, given his academic mind, set up in left center field, because he didn't think Hank would try to pull it and take a chance of it going foul. Housy calculated right.

It was not a ticker-tape drive, but Hank always told me it's not how far, it's how many. They all count the same. We knew it was out the second Hank hit it. For me, watching from the on-deck circle, it felt like I'd hit it, that was how excited I was about the moment. For a minute, I was worried when a couple of dudes ran onto the field and ran around the bases with Hank, just fans, it seemed, but you never knew. Hank didn't seem too bothered. Davey Lopes, who would go on to be my teammate and godfather to my daughter, shook Hank's hand as he rounded second. At third base, Ron Cey, another future teammate, thought about shaking Hank's hand as he rounded the bag. "I was going to," the Penguin said afterward, "but I decided against it. I hated to disrupt Hank. It was his show. He earned it. He's Hank Aaron and I'm just another ballplayer."

I felt the same way. I watched it all from the on-deck circle, and I could have been the first at home plate, but I decided to hold back. This was Hank's moment. It was all about him. I didn't need to insert myself in that picture. It was wild, everyone rushing out. I was in the middle of the celebration, swarming Hank. I had the best view of anyone.

Hank hit the homer with Al Downing pitching, a Black man, and against the Dodgers, Jackie Robinson's team. Hank had told his father years before that he wanted to play in the big leagues against Jackie before he retired. All of this in Atlanta with the great Vin Scully making the call. "What a marvelous moment for baseball, what a marvelous moment for Atlanta and the state of Georgia, what a marvelous moment for the country and the world, a Black man is getting a standing ovation in the Deep South for breaking a record of an all-time baseball idol," Vin said. "And it is a great moment for all of us, and particularly for Henry Aaron, who was met at home plate not only by every member of the Atlanta Braves but by his father and mother."

Hank threw his arms around his dad. "Dad's really enjoying this," Hank said. Then as he started to walk away from home, his mom came running across the grass and held Hank close to her. To the national TV audience, it looked just like a proud mother, but what was really happening was that Hank's mom knew about all the death threats and wanted to protect her son using her own body as a shield.

I look back on that moment as one of the highlights of my career, and it was done by someone else. This was a world event. For years, Babe Ruth had epitomized America to the world. Who had more nicknames than Babe Ruth? He had his own candy bar! He was a bad boy that everyone loved. Even in the war movies, they would ask infiltrators about Babe Ruth, and if they didn't know how many home runs he'd hit, then they knew they weren't really Americans. Now Hank had eclipsed Babe Ruth. Hank's dad, who was from the country, like my dad, might have summed up the moment best. "A fox was chased by a hound all day, but at the end of the day he ran up a hill and looked back," Hank's dad said. "The fox saw the sunset and said, 'Hey, it don't matter if anyone catches me now—I've set the world on fire.' "

They stopped the game. When play started up again, I wanted to hit a home run for Hank but only managed a single.

— — — —

I always had trouble with the curve. (Clint Eastwood, who lived in Carmel, California, made a movie, *Trouble with the Curve*, and I was told I helped inspire the film. Eastwood played a scout, and in the movie he wears my custom-made Puma shoes.) Throw me a fastball and I was always happy, even if it was some serious cheese, but that breaking stuff gave me fits. The Braves first sent me to Mexico after the 1970 season to learn how to hit the curve in the Mexican Pacific League. One thing about Mexican pitchers, they can spin it, and in any count. It would be 3-1 and here comes a breaking ball for a strike. I played for the Yaquis de Ciudad Obregon in Sonora, which is in northern Mexico, across the Gulf of California from Baja. The last thing my mom told me before I left for Mexico was "Don't be the Ugly American," so I always tried to keep that in mind.

That was the toughest league I ever played in, but I loved Mexico. I loved Ciudad Obregon, I loved the food, I loved the people. I rode a Yamaha 250 motorcycle and had a good time exploring the area with my roommate, Leon Brown, also from Sacramento, who had his own Yamaha. The team got us the motorcycles. Our league included teams in Los Mochis, Guaymas, and Mazatlan, to name a few. The Hermosillo team, the Naranjeros, managed by Maury Wills, won the championship with one of the best hitters I've ever seen, Hector Espino. That was also when I first met Tony Oliva, already a big-leaguer and a great hitter. We also had John Lowenstein, who grew up in Riverside, and Hal Breeden, one of the finest hitters on our Richmond team, and Jan Dukes, from Santa Clara University, who taught me how to play the harmonica.

I was the only American on my team who could speak Spanish. I could order my own food, and, most important, I could talk to those pretty Mexican girls. One of our pitchers in Obregon was Vicente "Juevo" Romo, who had played in the big leagues. We were in Guaymas for a game in early January and it was so cold, there were almost no fans in the stadium. Seriously, the crowd was announced at seventy-two that day, which meant that less than a hundred people got to see Vicente pitch the first perfect game in league history. Leon Brown caught the final out. (When Leon and Dena got married in January 1973, a week after Roberto Clemente died trying to bring supplies to earthquake victims in Nicaragua, I was one of his groomsmen, and also agreed to be the wedding videographer, to save him a little money. That was the first and only time I ever did that for anyone. You should see all the nice shots of the floor and ceiling I recorded.)

I loved playing winter ball in Mexico, Puerto Rico, and Venezuela. It was integral to my career. Sometimes the road you don't take at one point becomes your road of the future. Back in high school, my mom and I had been excited about a trip to Mexico I'd been asked to join in the summer of 1967 with the basketball all-star team that included Darnell Hillman, Dr. Dunk, who played in the ABA, and other local stars. I wanted to see new places and meet new people and eat new food on that trip to Mexico, and use the Spanish I'd learned, because my mom was always after me to study my Spanish. It didn't happen then, because I couldn't let my American Legion baseball team down when it was going to the state championship. Staying helped decide my future for baseball, but years later, baseball gave me the chance to go.

After the 1971 season, Orlando Cepeda convinced me to join him and play for the Santurce Cangrejeros of the Puerto Rican winter league, which I also loved. Our manager was Rubén Gómez, the first Puerto Rican to pitch in the World Series. Don Baylor, my teammate, led the league with a .324 average, and Buck Martinez, my homeboy from Sacramento, was also on that team. Every Monday, we'd go surfing with him in the Atlantic. I didn't drink much at the time, but one night I had a few, and the next day were on a bus ride on a winding mountain road. My teammates Tony Pérez, who was Cuban, and pitcher Juan Pizarro, from Santurce, gave me mondongo, a soup, and I vomited that right out the window all over the side of the bus. After that, my nickname was Mondongo.

Early in the 1974 season, I had hurt my shoulder running into the outfield wall in Houston making a catch. I hit .256 that season, compared to .288 the year before, and went from ninety-nine RBIs to sixty-nine. I got a great idea going into the 1975 season. I could go play winter ball to get my stroke back together, but instead of Puerto Rico or the Dominican Republic, I could play for my Braves teammate Paul Casanova in Venezuela, along with Manny Trillo, who became a good friend after that.

I could also visit my sister Tonya, whom I hadn't seen in six years. Even though I was the oldest, she was kind of like the rock of the family. She was three years behind me at Del Campo High. She was freshman class president and a cheerleader, good at sports and good in her classes. She went to the University of California, Santa Barbara, and then her life took a direction that carried her far away from California. She was called by the Lord to do missionary work and ended up doing twelve years in Cartagena, Colombia, for Christians in Action. I figured if I was playing ball in Venezuela, the next country over, she could come see me, which was exactly what she did. Before Tonya got there, I was struggling. My team in La Guaira paid for her ticket, which I guess was a good investment since I hit a grand slam at the first game she attended, and we won. The team also arranged a celebration of Tonya's twenty-second birthday while she was visiting. For me, it was also a chance to explore my faith. I told her how much I missed her and asked when she was going to come home to California. She told me she had a boyfriend, Eduardo, whom she ended up marrying. I bought my dad a plane ticket so he could fly down and give her away at their wedding. They pastored together and eventually came home to California and started a bilingual church.

It's hard to convey the sense of camaraderie you develop with the guys you played with in the minor leagues and in winter ball and also the big leagues, especially among the minority guys. You stuck close to each other. I always got along great with my Latin American teammates and brothers. They took care of us, especially during the holidays, Christmas, New Year's, and Three Kings Day, with invites to their homes. Everyone was feeling homesick around the holidays, so that was important. That's why in later years as a manager I always made a concerted effort to make the Latin guys feel welcome and always felt comfortable managing them.

Hank Aaron was our protector and mentor and friend. He never told us he was thinking of moving on after the 1974 season. The team offered him a front office job but didn't want him back as a player, and that was when we found out. He'd made the decision to go back to Milwaukee, where he'd played the first twelve seasons of his career.

After Hank left, things weren't the same. It wasn't just me. Darrell Evans and Marty Perez and Ralph, everyone who loved Hank and depended on him to be our defender, we were all lost. After my numbers dropped when I hurt my shoulder, the Braves tried to cut my salary at the end of the 1974 season. What ate at me most was that I knew this Braves team was headed in the wrong direction. I grew weary of losing. In 1975, the Braves would finish 67–94. I also was homesick for California and my family. I wanted to go somewhere where I could start the season expecting to play October baseball and maybe win a World Series. So I went to Eddie Robinson, the Braves general manager, and talked to him, which he always made as easy for me as he could. He told me a number of times that I was his two sons' favorite player. I told Eddie I wanted to be traded.

"Have you ever been to Cleveland?" he asked me.

Cleveland? I told him no, I had not. That was in the American

League, and back then we didn't play American League teams except in the World Series. When I brought it up again with Eddie another time, again he asked me if I had ever been to Cleveland.

"Hey man, be quiet," Ralph scolded me when I told him what Mr. Robinson had said. "Quit asking to be traded! You'll get screwed!" Cleveland in those years was a perennial second division team. The Cleveland of those years was nothing like the Cleveland of today. They played in Cleveland Stadium, where Jim Brown had played for the Cleveland Browns, a stadium built on landfill next to Lake Erie, and it got really cold there. It was a tough place to play. I called Hank to get his advice.

"Man, how come every time I ask to be traded, they ask me have I ever been to Cleveland?" I asked him.

"You have to be patient," he said.

He set me straight. Years later, someone gave me a copy of the waiver-wire details for when the Braves had put me on waivers to see who had interest in me. I didn't even know at the time that I was on waivers. No one told me. If I'd have known I was on waivers back then, I would have taken it as a sign they wanted to move me, so maybe it's good I didn't know. I also didn't know yet that the Braves franchise was up for sale and the team leadership was intending to trade us all, which they eventually did.

Back then we all worked offseason jobs, and in the fall of 1973 I had worked at a dealership in Augusta, Georgia, selling new cars. For me, it came naturally because I've always liked talking to different people, and one of my favorite subjects, besides music or baseball or life on the road, has always been cars. I love everything about a fast, beautiful car from the look of it to the feel of it to the smell of it to the sound of it purring out in the fast line hitting twenty or thirty miles over the speed limit, which led to many tickets. I had to sell my original 4-4-2 after I got six speeding tickets in six months.

Working at that Augusta dealership, I was able to buy myself a nice 1974 Thunderbird, which I gave to Harriet's mother in Louisiana. So in November 1975, I told Eddie Robinson I was going home to California and wasn't coming back. Harriet and I set out driving, she in the Thunderbird for her mom and me in a Porsche 914 I bought for myself. There was so little room in that car, I had a little cloth box designed and installed it on the back of the rack. We spent some time with her mom and gave her the Thunderbird, then drove cross-country in my Porsche back to Sacramento.

That was some strange drive. At the time, there were a lot of headlines about UFO sightings in New Mexico, and it was all anyone was talking about. I stopped for gas somewhere in New Mexico, heading west, and heard people talking about how aliens had mutilated a bunch of cows and left no blood behind. It was like the panic when Orson Welles did *The War of the Worlds* on the radio—everybody was afraid of what these aliens might do to them.

I gassed up enough to drive right through New Mexico without stopping, but I was out in the middle of the desert in my Porsche on an ink-black night and my headlights started flickering on and off. That had never happened to me before. Now it was my turn to panic. Suddenly, I was sure all the UFO talk was true. *Oh Lord,* I said to myself, *please don't let nothing happen to Harriet and me.* I didn't want them taking us away in their flying saucers or whatever it is that aliens drive.

That was when I saw a motel up ahead. I wasted no time getting off the road and found a room for the night, feeling safe. We went to bed, and I had some music on and the TV going with the sound down. I wasn't paying much attention, trying to unwind from all that weirdness with my lights flashing, so I only half noticed at first when the screen started showing pictures of some different Los Angeles Dodgers players involved in some kind of major trade—Jim Wynn, Tom Paciorek, Lee Lacy, and Jerry Royster. *Man, that was a blockbuster trade,* I thought. *I wonder who they traded for?*

Then I saw myself on TV. I was the guy they traded for, along with Ed Goodson. That was how I found out.

I had grown up a Dodger fan listening to Vin Scully all the time and dreamed of playing for them and wearing number 12 like Tommy Davis.

But I was shocked. Eddie Robinson had never said anything about trading me to California. The first thing I did was call my dad, because we didn't have cellphones then, and no one knew where I was.

"Boy, they've been looking for you all day," he said.

Maybe those aliens making my car lights flash on and off had been trying to tell me something. I was forever grateful to Mr. Robinson for taking care of me and sending me to my favorite team as a boy. I was born on the Braves, and could now grow up to be a man on the Dodgers.

CHAPTER 6

High Five

You never quite get over your first love. It's always somewhere deep inside of you wanting to come back out. Even many years into my life as a big-league baseball player, I never forgot the joyous surge of love that I felt anytime I could get out in a gym somewhere and play some basketball. It was hard for me to quit playing basketball, really hard. Anytime I was back in Sacramento, I loved to go back to the Del Campo gym and mix it up, just like the old days. When I would bring in my homeboys from Grant High and run some games—Bill Crenshaw, Leon Brown, and his brother Curtis, and also Larry Brown (no relation), who'd tried to recruit me to Gonzaga—those games were just the pinnacle of joy.

Even in November 1975, back home in Sacramento the week after the Dodgers traded for me, that gym called to me, as it always had. My mama kept telling me not to play. But it was hard for me to listen to her, since I'd almost never been hurt. "Dusty, don't be hurting yourself playing basketball." She knew what that would mean at this point in my baseball career. Still, it felt so good to be back at the Del Campo gym, playing with Jerry Manuel and some of his boys and one or two of my brothers.

But pickup basketball is pickup basketball. Things happen. I went in for a slam dunk, right over someone. Weird how little things can matter so much. For some reason, the way the play developed, I pushed off my right foot, going up to slam the ball, instead of my usual left. I made the bucket, but then I came down wrong on my left foot, and I knew right away I hurt myself. I knew I screwed up big time.

I never got hurt. I used to brag on never getting hurt, which I shouldn't have done. Now my left knee was messed up. I felt terrible about what that meant for me. The Dodgers had just traded all these good players for Ed Goodson and me. I was trying to figure out how I was going to get out of this trouble, hoping the injury wasn't as serious as I had feared and would heal itself—and I'd never have to tell the Dodgers about it.

General manager Al Campanis flew up from L.A. in January 1976 to see me at a golf tournament at Haggin Oaks in Sacramento, not far from American River College. I remember talking to Al and just trying to be cool. (We never called him "Mr. Campanis," it was always "Al.") I knew my knee was hurt, but I didn't want to show it. Someone hit a golf ball past me, and I remember jogging very carefully, because I was scared Al would see I was damaged goods. I didn't know what to do or say. I thought I would somehow heal on my own, like Superman, because that was how it had always gone for me, but I was wrong, terribly wrong.

Spring training was coming up, and I knew I wasn't myself. I had lost what made me *me.* I had no balance. I couldn't stay on my front leg. I didn't have any power. All of a sudden for the first time in my life, I didn't have my speed, which I'd always counted on and depended on. Whether it was to get out of trouble, or grab an opportunity, I could always rely on my speed. I loved to run. I loved to race. To this day, if there is one thing I wish I could do, just for one day, it would be to run again.

— — — —

The trade that brought me to L.A. had a lot of symbolic power. The Braves were busy unloading talent, trying to look forward, not backward. The time of the Hank Aaron–led Braves was over. A team that defined an era had slipped into history. The trade was also a clear signal from the

Dodgers that second best was not good enough. They wanted to win and win now. The 1975 Dodgers won eighty-eight games. They were a good team. But they still finished twenty games behind the first-place Reds team (108–54) that went on to edge the Red Sox that year in one of the all-time great World Series ever played. Trading for me was a sign of the Dodgers being hungry to get better.

The flight back to Florida for spring training was rough. It had been my dream to play for the Dodgers, but now it felt like a bad dream. I always played exceptionally hard against the Dodgers so they would trade for me and I could wear Dodger blue. Now I was on my way to Dodgertown in Vero Beach, and I wasn't myself. Knowing it was all my fault was devastating. That was a big load to carry. It messed with my head, I ain't gonna lie. Jim Wynn, sent to the Braves as part of the trade that brought me to L.A., told a reporter that spring: "Dusty has all the tools to be a super player, but before he does, he has to get his mind together." Jimmy didn't know the half of it.

That first spring training with the Dodgers, I had lunch at the Dodger complex in Vero Beach and checked out the wall art. It was a mural extending down a long hallway that just blew my mind. I recognized Jackie Robinson in the mural, but then I spotted Spider Jorgensen tagging somebody out at third base. My American Legion coach Spider Jorgensen? Born in Folsom, California? What was he doing in the Dodgertown hallway? I called my dad as soon as I could.

"Dad, is this the same Spider Jorgensen?" I asked him.

"Yes, son, it is."

I couldn't believe it. Spider had never told me he played with Jackie. They made their big-league debuts together on April 15, 1947. And my dad never told me about Spider playing with Jackie, even though the whole time growing up, anytime my dad wanted to get my attention, he asked me: "What would Jackie do?"

One year after the 1972 strike, the owners had locked us out in 1973 and pushed back the start of spring training, but no games were lost. Now in 1976, the owners were scrambling again, trying to hold off free agency, but they were fighting a losing battle. Again we were locked out.

So I had more time to worry about my knee. There wasn't much I could do about it but hope it was merely a bad sprain and would heal quickly.

At least the lockout gave me a chance to get to know my new teammates. At first base in 1976 we had Steve Garvey, who was a good teammate and a great hitter, and who soon became a friend. The thing I noticed early on about Garv was how consistent he was. His personality was the same every day, and his hitting stroke was as reliable as they come. We had Davey Lopes and Bill Russell up the middle, also a solid one-two combination at the top of the order. Lopes, the team captain, was the most astute base runner I ever had as a teammate. Russell was steady at short and the guy you wanted batting in the clutch. Our third baseman Ron Cey, the Penguin, burned with competitiveness. That team was loaded with guys you knew would come through when it counted, always the sign of a good team.

Looking for a place to stay in Vero Beach during spring training, I called a nice condo complex across from the beach I'd heard about. They said no problem, come on over. Then when I arrived and they saw I was Black, all of a sudden no vacancy. Except that the day after I was there, I went to practice and found out a couple of my Dodgers teammates had gone in and the condo had vacancies again. It made me think of my mom, turned away from that modeling school in Riverside when she showed up and they saw she was Black. You can never really be prepared to deal with something like that, but in a way I was prepared. I learned through my mom's pain.

I was one of a few players who showed up one day early when spring training finally started on March 18, along with Garv, Lopes, Joe Ferguson, and pitcher Don Sutton. A few days into spring training, an Associated Press photographer captured an awkward moment. It was supposed to be a typical early spring picture of a manager welcoming two new players, and there was Dodger manager Walter Alston, grinning like a man holding all the cards, one hand on my shoulder and one hand on the shoulder of my teammate Ted Sizemore, a cool dude from Michigan. Walt Alston was smiling like he meant it, but not me. I was smiling, but I wasn't happy. I've seen pictures from those years where I looked angry and a lot where I'm joyful. In this one, I look like a man with a load on his mind. I look like a man who knows this could go either way.

Alston played his cards close to the vest. I had no idea what he was thinking. I didn't know him, but had been hearing about him since I was a kid. We didn't know this would be his last year managing the Dodgers after thirty-three seasons in Brooklyn and L.A. Most of the players who had come up in the Dodger system with Tommy Lasorda thought he might be in line for the job whenever Alston left.

I knew I was going to have a tough go of it. My knee just wasn't right. I was basically playing on one leg, meaning I was going to have trouble driving the ball. I went all spring without hitting a home run. Bill Buhler, the Dodger trainer, asked how I'd injured my knee.

"I hurt it running my dog," I told Dr. Bill.

He gave me a look that reminded me of my high school coach Eli McCullough. "Did your dog get an assist?" Dr. Bill asked me. Then he gave me that Coach McCullough look again. "Tell me the truth," he said.

Dr. Bill said if I was straight with him, I thought I could trust him not to sell me out to the Dodgers, so I told him what happened. We did everything to work on my knee and get me as ready as I could be, which helped me on Opening Day. We started our season at Candlestick Park against the Giants before 37,000, facing John "The Count" Montefusco. John liked to talk and promised a shutout that day. I turned on a Montefusco fastball in the first and homered to left. That ended the shutout talk then and there—but we lost the game, and that was my only hit of the day. Even hurt, I was excited to be a Dodger and to be playing for a team that had the talent to win.

I wouldn't hit another home run for more than three months. I had a seven-game hitting streak going in mid-April, then missed two games with a pulled hamstring. Before I hurt my knee, I never had a pulled muscle. Now I had a pulled hammy and then a pulled groin. Sometimes I was in pain and sometimes I wasn't, which kind of played tricks on my mind. But when I tried to hit, run, or throw, I always felt pain and knew something was wrong. It was like that old song "Dem Bones," the knee bone connected to the thigh bone and all that. It was all connected.

By early June, I was batting .249, hitting nothing but singles. Over one three-week period, I had only one extra-base hit. Alston commented to a reporter that if I couldn't do better, the Dodgers were "not going very far."

I was down-and-out. By August I was on the bench, used mostly as a pinch-hitter. I would wait to the last minute to go up and pinch-hit because the boos from the fans at Dodger Stadium would be so loud, I didn't want to hear it. This was where I had always wanted to play, for the Dodgers, and then I got my opportunity and blew it because I hurt myself playing basketball. But what could I do? Imagine the bad PR the Dodgers would have had, after trading all those guys for me, if they announced that I needed surgery. It would have made it look like they traded for a guy who was damaged goods, even though I didn't get hurt until the week after the trade.

I was miserable. That was the first time I heard so many negative things about myself. People kept saying I was a bust. It was the worst trade in history. And on and on. It got so I didn't even want to go out my door to the grocery store or go have a drink. That was when my strength really came in, the mental and spiritual strength my parents and family had helped build in me. Believe me, that year I needed all of it just to get through.

The Dodgers sent me to the team optometrist, Dr. Orlando Giraldi, at the start of August to see if my eyes had something to do with me not hitting. "I can help Dusty see, but I can't help him hit," Dr. Giraldi told the *L.A. Times.* Dr. Giraldi had also hooked up my idol Tommy Davis with contacts, so I was open to try, but those hard contact lenses made me feel like I had dirt in my eyes all the time. I saw *too much.* I started seeing beams of light coming out of lights.

The Dodgers wanted me to go see a psychiatrist, and I refused that. There was nothing wrong with my head. I knew where the pain was. Some guy named Bud Tucker wrote a column in the Long Beach *Press-Telegram* calling me a "traditional basket case." I'd never even heard the expression "basket case" before, and it pissed me off big time. From then on, I stopped reading the papers. Why should someone else's words be given the power to control my own self-esteem? But I was never going to be a ballplayer again unless something could be done about my knee.

It brought me some relief when the news finally came out in September that I needed to go under the knife, and the *L.A. Times* just tacked it on in a little note at the end of a game story, revealing that I was seeing limited action "because of a knee condition that has been an irritation for several seasons and will require surgery."

I was sticking with the dog story, even though I hated telling a lie. The *Press-Telegram* reported that month that I'd been playing on a bad left knee all season. "I haven't been able to run all year," I told the paper. "It's especially bad when I'm batting, trying to pivot on the knee. It was a freak thing that caused the injury. I was home running my dog."

Finally it came time to see Dr. Frank Jobe at the start of October. Dr. Jobe operated on Reggie Smith, Bill Russell, Bill Buckner, and me all on the same day. (The Dodgers traded for Reggie on my birthday, June 15, in 1976.) He told me when he opened up my knee he couldn't believe how much damage there was in there. It shouldn't even have been possible to play on it. Dr. Jobe put me in a cast from my hip to my ankle that I had to wear for eight weeks. That winter, the Dodgers dangled me as trade bait, offering me to the Chicago Cubs in a package to land Rick Monday. In the end, the Cubs preferred Bill Buckner, so the Dodgers traded him for Monday instead of me. I wasn't even good as bait.

I had a lot of work to do if I wanted to come back strong the next season. When they took the cast off, my left leg was so skinny, it had atrophied so much, that it never really came back to the strength of my right leg. To build up my leg strength again, I would run the stairwell at Dodger Stadium from the bottom to the top every morning with Bill Buhler. I hated that. When my leg got a little stronger, we started running outside. I could hardly breathe, let alone talk, and Bill would be talking to me the whole time, always a step or two ahead of me. I don't know how he did it. That was the start of a long, long road back. I started lifting weights to get my leg stronger, and I also built up my upper-body strength. I actually became a better hitter because I got stronger, but going into the start of the 1977 season, I knew I needed game action to see what I could do. That was when Tommy Lasorda, who did end up getting the job after Alston retired, went out on a limb to say I was his left fielder. That taught me as a manager not to be afraid to stick your neck out for a player if you believe in him. Here he was a rookie manager, and the sports talk shows and newspapers were on Tommy's ass for going with me after the year I'd had.

Just before Opening Day each year, the Dodgers had a Freeway Series of exhibition games with the Angels, just like the Giants played the Oakland A's before their seasons started. In 1977, the Freeway Series opened at Anaheim Stadium on Friday night, April 1. About an hour before the game, the Dodger PR guy, Steve Brener, came out of Tommy Lasorda's office looking for me.

"Tommy would like to see you," he told me.

An hour before the game? What was this? I walked into Tommy's office, and he was sitting at his desk with his head between his hands, like he was upset. He got right to the point.

"Man, I've got some bad news for you," Tommy told me.

"What is it?" I asked.

"Well," he said, "I talked to Al Campanis, and you've been traded to Cleveland."

"T, how can this be?" I asked him.

"I don't know how they could have done this to me, because I need you to play left field," he said.

I was shocked, but this was a tune I'd heard before. Back in Atlanta, general manager Eddie Robinson used to ask me, "Have you ever been to Cleveland?" The Braves didn't trade me to Cleveland. I'd gone to L.A. instead. But after the season I'd had my first year with the Dodgers, it was no stretch to think this time it had really happened.

"I don't understand why I've been traded," I told Tommy.

"I don't know either," he said. By then he had tears in his eyes. "Sometimes they don't consult the manager on these things."

"Man, why Cleveland?" I asked.

"I'm sorry, Dusty," he said.

Tommy turned to Dodger vice president Fred Claire, who was there in the office with us.

"Fred, when do you want to make the announcement?" Tommy asked.

"Well, it is April first," Claire said.

Tommy turned to me.

"Do you know what day it is?" he asked me.

"Hell yeah, I know what day it is," I said. "It's April first."

I still had no clue.

"If it's April first, it must be April Fools' Day," Tommy said, and then he couldn't stop laughing.

That was the best April Fools' Day gag anyone ever pulled on me my whole life—not even close. To this day, I'm always on guard on April first. They thought it was the funniest thing ever, but I was steamed!

I took that energy right into the game. I got my first at-bat in the second inning and hit a two-run homer off Angels starter Gary Ross—after going all spring training with no home runs. I also doubled and came around to score, and we won 5–0. My spring average stood at .333, showing I was back after the tough year before Dr. Jobe gave me back my leg. Tommy's joke seemed real, because I thought I had lost it all, I really did. I didn't love baseball the way I loved basketball until I got hurt and baseball was almost taken away from me. Only by learning to love baseball in a new way did I become a ballplayer again.

— — — —

It was an explosion of joy, basically. That was all it was, a shared moment of joy like thousands of others from my years in baseball.

But this one gets remembered. My teammate Glenn Burke and I made a random kind of history at the end of the 1977 season and gave the world what a lot of people call the first high five. For us at the time, it was just about living that moment. One thing about playing for Tommy Lasorda's Dodgers, you never shied away from celebrating how lucky you felt to be playing in a great city in great-looking uniforms in a great ballpark with great weather for a talented team that knew how to win and look good doing it. Lasorda had been after me for years while I was with the Braves to come to L.A. I would see him around the cage or on the field before games, and he'd be talking in my ear about how the Dodgers had the best-looking guys with the best bodies and the best uniforms. "Man, you got a good body, you need to be on the Dodgers," he would say in his years as third-base coach. "You damn right I do!" I would tell him, laughing. Tommy Lasorda could talk, that was for sure, but he was entertaining. And the man had a point: I *would* look good in a Dodger uniform.

Baseball is like life—it's all about ups and downs and how you deal with them. Impossible situations become possible. That was what kept me striving for a championship as a manager all those years. If I had gotten a championship ring early, I probably would have gone on and done something else. But you realize you're affecting a lot of people's lives, and what you do—or don't do—matters to them. You can never disappear. You always have to remain visible. And if you get knocked down, you've got to get back up, but you don't climb on nobody else to do that.

Baseball and life are all about how you bounce back. I had one dismal year where I could barely drive the ball, and now I was myself again, or at least a new version of me. I was scalding the ball and putting up numbers. Rick Monday dubbed me "Dr. Scald," and the name kind of stuck. I went into the last day of the season wanting to join the Thirty Homer Club. A week earlier, we had clinched at least a tie of the National League West, Steve Garvey hit his thirty-first homer, and Ron Cey and Reggie Smith both hit their thirtieth. That meant that if I could reach thirty, we would be the first team in history to have four guys hit thirty homers in a season.

We already knew that in two days we would be opening the National League Championship Series against Steve Carlton and the Phillies at home at Dodger Stadium. Reggie and the Penguin had a day off the last game of the season, at home against the Astros. Reggie told J. R. Richard at the start of the series that I was going to get my thirtieth off him that Sunday.

"Reggie!" I said. "He don't need no help getting me out."

J.R. was maybe the toughest pitcher I ever faced. I remember feeling tired that day, really tired. It had been a classic bounceback season, but it was a *long* season. I lifted my batting average from .242 the year before to .291 and doubled my RBI total from thirty-nine to eighty-six. I wanted that thirtieth home run. I wanted it bad.

"The good Lord did not intend to strand you at twenty-nine," Lasorda told me before the game. Ralph Garr always used to say, "Don't end on nines!" One year I ended up with ninety-nine RBIs with the Braves. I could hear Ralph talking to me when I was hitting .299 my last at-bat of the season in 1982, going against another nemesis of mine, Greg Minton of the Giants—and finished at .300. I've always said that to players: *Round your numbers up. Don't end on a nine.* I was real conscious of that, even though I did end on a lot of nines in my career. It's hard to avoid.

My first time up against J.R. in that Sunday game to end the 1977 regular season, I hit a line drive to left, but I didn't elevate it, and the ball fell for a single. I could see some guys behind the dugout at Dodger Stadium gambling on whether I'd get homer number thirty. The second time up, I foul-tipped a J.R. fastball into the catcher's mitt for strike three, one of fourteen strikeouts for J.R. that day. As I walked back to the dugout, I saw these guys behind the dugout exchanging cash. One guy was betting on me.

"Man, I ain't gonna get it," I said under my breath on the Dodger bench.

Tommy overheard me, which surprised me. I didn't intend for him to hear.

"You gotta believe!" Tommy told me. "The children of Israel were trapped by the Red Sea and they were delivered! If you get a home run, we go into the history books. Just go up there believing you're going to hit a home run."

"I believe!" I told Tommy, just to hush him up.

I got another shot at J.R. in the sixth. Manny Mota opened the inning with a pinch-hit homer to make it 2–1 Astros. J.R. threw me a fastball low and away, and I swear the ball looked like it stopped. It really did. To me, it looked like it was there on a tee for me to hit. I connected and sent it out to center field between the flagpoles. If it was in the ballpark, César Cedeño was going to catch it. When I saw CC in center give up on the ball, I knew it was out.

I could feel the big Dodger Stadium crowd rising to their feet and roaring. Our first-base coach, Jim Gilliam, gave me a low five as I rounded the bag. This was a taste of history, three teammates with thirty homers, and it made me think back to Hank's 715th home run. In a small way, I knew how Hank felt. By the time I rounded third, I could see those same dudes behind the dugout, the ones who were gambling. The one brother threw down his money and walked out; he must have lost. I crossed home plate, and my teammates swarmed me. Bill Russell gave me a hug, and Davey Lopes I think it was slapped me on the butt, then another hug from Tommy.

As I was walking to the dugout, I saw Glenn Burke, due up next. Glenn was also from California, a great basketball player at Berkeley High, and he was so excited he came toward me and threw up his hand in the air. What was I supposed to do? He was happy for me. He was thrilled. I wanted to continue the joy of the moment, so I just reached my hand up and hit his hand. I always say I didn't do anything, I just reacted to Glenn. Give him the credit. But it's cool to have been part of that moment. They call it the first high five—I guess because there are pictures of it. And what did Glenn do just after throwing that high five at me and jacking us both up? He went out to face James Rodney and connected for his own home run! That was one of only two home runs Glenn would hit in his four seasons in the big leagues.

— — — —

I loved playing on the Dodgers. We had a team full of stars, and we were Lasorda guys. Tommy bled Dodger blue. Like every man, Tommy had his faults, but most of the time his heart was in the right place. If he believed in you, he believed in you. Tommy made us believe that we were the best. That's a powerful thing I later kept in mind as a manager. As players, we're constantly being bombarded with negatives, so when someone really believes in you, that can give you a strength you don't even know you have. Another thing I adopted from Tommy was to always have good food around, because you can break down barriers through food. He always had famous people around, too, which always in its own way broke down barriers. Tommy made it like a family, being a Dodger. He knew all the wives and all the children, and would call them all by name, which made it all more personal and friendly.

That 1977 Dodgers team was well balanced, with good pitching and a powerful lineup. Garvey led our offense with thirty-three home runs and 115 RBIs. Ron Cey was right behind him with 110 RBIs. He drove in so many runs, by the time I got up, there weren't any RBIs left for me! Reggie Smith, a switch-hitter and excellent right fielder, led the way in average that season with .307. Reggie was better than all of us, a complete player who was the second best I ever played with behind Hank Aaron.

L.A. was without doubt the place to be at that time. In every sport, you had great athletes and great teams, pro and college. You could hang with Jim Brown and Fred "The Hammer" Williamson, who had both moved from football to acting, and actors like Scatman Crothers and Richard Roundtree, Shaft himself. The town was buzzing. There were superstars in different sports all in the same town. The Rams had Lawrence McCutcheon and then Eric Dickerson and Vince Ferragamo. Joe Namath was there at the end of his career. I would run into Joe at Dr. Frank Jobe's office, and now I see Joe every spring in Florida. The Angels were good, too. They had Rod Carew, Don Baylor, and Disco Dan Ford. Magic Johnson, Kareem, Norm Nixon, and Michael Cooper of the Lakers were out at Dodger Stadium as much as we were at the Forum. I went over to John Wooden's house for lunch, and that was when the great UCLA basketball coach gave me his Pyramid of Success, which I've tried to use throughout my life. O. J. Simpson was starting to act at the time, and Marcus Allen was at USC, to name a few. Mayor Tom Bradley and his wife Ethel were kind of the leaders of us all, and would bring us together.

Tommy had recommended me to play Jackie Robinson in a movie they were making, so I started taking acting lessons during the offseason. I even had a portfolio done for an agent to send around to the movie studios. I thought it was going to be fun, but those acting lessons were intense. It was similar to the military. They would tear you down and then build you back up. I almost walked out and took my money somewhere else.

In 1977, I was finally getting to play in the postseason. That was where I felt I belonged and where I'd always wanted to be. I'd never been in the playoffs, and after my dismal season in 1976, I bought myself a Porsche 911SC to celebrate my success in the '77 season. The excitement of the L.A. community, all of it, 1977 made up for everything that was negative in my career. What made it even cooler was having my dad and mom and my family and all my homeboys from Riverside and Sacramento there in the stadium.

We opened the National League Championship Series at home against the Phillies, two nights after I hit my thirtieth homer. The Phils got to Tommy John early and took a 4–0 lead. We could never catch them, even with a seventh-inning grand slam from the Penguin and three hits from Garv. But in Game 2, back at home one night later, Don Sutton gave us a complete-game, one-run gem, which was more than we needed thanks to one swing of my bat. Phillies manager Danny Ozark decided to walk Steve Garvey to get to me in the fourth inning. I thought at the time it was a sound move, even though it loaded the bases. I'd gone hitless in my last seven chances against their starter, Jim Lonborg, and hadn't homered against Philadelphia all season. I walked up to the plate, felt the roar of that crowd, and told myself, *Stay cool, stay cool. Don't try to hit it out of the park.* That was what Hank had always taught me: *If they walk someone to get to you, don't take it personally. Don't hit into a double play. Just hit a line drive.*

I did take it personally, despite what Hank drilled into me, but it didn't matter. Lonborg threw me a hanger, and I didn't miss. For some reason, he decided at that moment of all moments to drop down three-quarters and kind of half sidearm a breaking ball. (I talked to him many years later, and he said he had never dropped down like that.)

My first thought was that I'd hit the ball too hard. I drilled it, but the ball had so much topspin, it was sinking fast as it buzzed toward the fence. Some of our guys in the bullpen later told me they pushed the fence a little closer to home, so the ball would have a better shot at making it out. That grand slam felt like my gift to Los Angeles.

Then we went back to Philadelphia, a crowd of more than 60,000, and some of the rowdiest fans in sports. I liked going to Philly to play. They were knowledgeable fans and they were as hard on the home team as they were on us. Either they scared you or they fired you up. Personally, they fired me up. It was tied in the second when Steve Garvey singled off the Phillies' Larry Christenson and I doubled him home for the first run of the game, then came around to score on Steve Yeager's single. The fans weren't happy. They thought the umpires missed a call or two, and the noise really kicked up in the bottom of the second when things got weird. Our starter, Burt Hooton, lost his control. After a couple singles and a walk loaded the bases, the Phils' pitcher, Christenson, came up to bat. For a pitcher, he was a good hitter, and he had to pitch him carefully. Then Hooton walked in three straight batters to make it 3–2.

I came up in the fourth with a chance to tie it. Cey led off with a double to center, sprinting down to second that way he did, resembling a penguin. Garvey moved him up to third with a groundout. I jumped on the first pitch I saw, but popped it up to right field in foul territory and had to watch to see if Bake McBride could run it down. The ball bounced foul, and I was still alive. With the count 1-2, Christenson threw a nasty slider in the dirt, but I was able to lay off. I won the battle by fighting off a pitch and dropping it just in front of Bake McBride for a run-scoring single, and it was 3–3. That was my sixth RBI for the series, but I didn't think about that at the time. I was just trying to win.

Rick Monday, up next, scorched a ball right past me, and I had to kind of dance to avoid getting hit as I ran down to second. I took third on a passed ball, clapping my hands. Steve Yeager was walked intentionally.

Pitcher Rick Rhoden was up next. It didn't shock any of us that Tommy let him hit for himself. Rhoden was one of the best-hitting pitchers in baseball. He was the best golf player, the best free-throw shooter, the best ping-pong player, the best everything—he just couldn't run, because of a childhood injury. Rick hit a fly ball to shallow right, and I tagged up, but the throw easily beat me. My only play was to slam into Boone and try to knock the ball loose. Boone was like Johnny Bench—he was so strong, it was like sliding into a fire hydrant. He held on.

We were down by two runs going into the ninth, but somehow rallied with two outs, and went ahead on a hit by Clutch Man Billy, as we called our shortstop Bill Russell, and won. We had some clutch guys on our team. Davey Lopes was speed and power and the best base runner I ever played with, easy. The Phillies were squawking that Lopes was out on a key play at first in the ninth, but Lopes beat the throw. He usually did.

We had the momentum and wanted to strike first the next day in Game 4 to keep it going. I came up in the second with a runner on, facing their tough lefty Steve Carlton. I thought he would throw me a fastball with the count 2-0, and I got a fastball. I trusted my feelings, as Hank taught me. My homer gave us a 2–0 lead and made me the first player ever to drive in eight runs in a National League playoff series, breaking Hank's record of seven RBIs in a series in 1969. I only heard about that later—I wasn't paying attention to individual statistics, I just wanted to win. That was only the second time I'd had a winning season in pro ball. That was the only time I ever broke a Hank Aaron record, and I was proud of that.

In the fifth, I led off with a walk and came around to score from second on a wild pitch, and we won 4–1 to advance to the World Series. I was named Most Valuable Player of the NLCS, the first player so honored.

It was cool being the first one to win that award, but what I cared about was going to the World Series. Like any kid, I'd always dreamed of that. Back in Riverside, they'd gather us all up in the gym to watch the World Series together on a little black-and-white TV. Now I was on my way to Yankee Stadium to play in the World Series against the New York

Yankees, and I wondered how many kids would be out there watching me the way I used to watch.

The Yankees that year were managed by fiery Billy Martin, the former Berkeley High star. One year earlier, the Yankees had been swept by the Big Red Machine, and they were hungry. Ron Cey and Reggie Smith had been cold in the NLCS, since they'd been off a few days at the end of the season, but Steve Garvey and I had good playoffs. Then by the World Series, I was tired, but the Penguin and Reggie were hitting again. That taught me as a manager to rest guys, but at least give them a couple at-bats. Wild card teams knock off teams, because the teams that clinch early usually rest their players, and often they lose their swings.

Game 1 is always important psychologically. We scored two in the first inning to take an early lead, but the Yankees went up 3–2 going into the ninth. I was our first hitter up and singled off Yankee starter Don Gullett, with whom I was very familiar after facing him for many years when he was on the Cincinnati Reds. I came around to score to tie the game and push it into extra innings. We had our chances, but the Yankees won it in twelve. We bounced back to win the next day, but in L.A., the Yankees won two straight to take control and won the series in six games. Reggie Jackson had an unbelievable game, hitting homers in three straight at-bats to win Game 6 for New York.

Losing that World Series hurt, it really hurt. I thought we had the best team on earth.

– – – –

I had grown unhappy at home and was trying not to show it. When things are not right at home, no matter what profession you're in, things are probably not right at work either, and in 1978, I had an off year, batting .262 with eleven home runs. I remember one time late that season, coach Jim Gilliam gave me kind of a funny look and asked how I was doing. He wasn't asking about baseball. He was asking about me. He was asking if I had trouble at home—and I did, but I didn't want to talk to anyone about it, even Jim, whom I respected as much as anyone. But I ended up talking to him anyway, the way I'd talked to my high school coach Eli McCullough when my parents got divorced. Jim had been around. He had played in the Negro Leagues and been National League Rookie of the Year in 1953, and he'd seen a lot of life. Your manager is like your dad, and the coaches are more like your uncles. Sometimes you don't tell your dad everything, but you can tell your uncles. I could talk to Jim Gilliam about anything. I asked him once how to stay in the big leagues.

"If there's a hotshot young player in the minor leagues threatening to take your job, you send him back the minors," he told me, "the way Pee Wee Reese did with Maury Wills and Bob Lillis and Dick Tracewski and others."

"How do you do that?" I asked.

"By going out there, playing and performing."

I was trying. We finished the 1978 season with ninety-five wins and needed only four games to get past the Phillies in the NLCS to make it to our second World Series in two years. Again we were facing the Yankees, but under much sadder circumstances. Jim Gilliam had a brain hemorrhage that September and died just before the World Series. I couldn't believe it. How do you see a guy one day and the next he's gone? You're with a guy every day, and you depend on him, and then you come to the ballpark and never see him again? How can you process that? But you have to find a way to carry on.

We all wore black patches with number 19 for Jim and jumped out to an early lead in the Series, winning the first two games at Dodger Stadium. But after that, we lost four straight games and the Series. That was a tough blow, to be playing for Jim Gilliam and lose four in a row to drop another World Series to the Yankees. I was embarrassed to even go out in public for at least the next couple weeks.

Everything felt like a struggle. My home life had me messed up enough that during the 1978 playoffs in Philadelphia, my old friend and Shreveport teammate Ted Bashore came to see me in my hotel room. By this time, Ted had earned his PhD from the University of Pennsylvania and was working as a psychologist. He hypnotized me to help me concentrate and focus. I would not have trusted anyone else, but I trusted Ted, and it felt like he helped me out a lot. But it didn't make things any better with Harriet.

Early the next year, I went to see Jerry Kapstein to talk about whether I should admit my mistake and ask Harriet for a divorce. It was a rough talk, but I came away from it determined to take a painful step I was sure I needed to take.

"I got something to tell you," I told Harriet when I got home.

"No, let me tell you what I got to tell you," she said.

"What?" I asked her.

"I'm pregnant," she said.

We'd been having trouble getting pregnant, but now I was going to be a dad. That changed everything.

"What do you got to tell me?" she asked.

I shook my head.

"No, never mind," I told her.

I couldn't leave with a child on the way. That was not an option for me. So I hung in there. We tried to make it work. But I was probably making Harriet more miserable than she was making me. Mostly, it was my fault for asking her to marry me when I was only twenty-three and she was only twenty-one.

I became a dad for the first time in September 1979, and from the day Natosha was born, she and I have always had a tight bond. Even when she was a baby, I never talked baby talk to her. I just talked to her like she could understand me, and even from a very early age, I think she could. I knew how hard my parents' divorce was on me and my brothers and sisters. I stayed married for eight years thinking I was doing the right thing.

- - - -

We had an off year in 1979, but in 1980, we were in the hunt until the last day of the season. I had one of my best seasons at the plate, driving in ninety-seven runs, batting .294, and hitting twenty-nine home runs. Damn, there's that nine again! That September, the Dodgers gave a shot to Fernando Valenzuela, a young left-hander from Mexico, and he was dazzling, pitching seventeen innings and not giving up a single run scored. It was rare for anyone in the big leagues to throw a great screwball, a trick pitch that mostly lefties threw. For a lefty, it breaks down and away from a right-handed batter. Mike Cuellar, Jim Brewer, and Tug McGraw were all lefties who threw the screwball, and Mike Marshall, my teammate on the Dodgers, a Cy Young Award winner, was the rare right-hander.

I had learned back on the Braves that it's harder for a right-handed hitter to hit a left-handed screwball. Mike Lum was the only guy who could hit Jim Brewer, because he was a left-handed hitter and the ball broke in on him where he liked it. Not many guys could throw a screwball without hurting their arm. You need tremendous flexibility in your elbow to throw it. Fernando had the pitch mastered.

He didn't speak much English, but if you talked to him in Spanish, the way I did, he was funny and relaxed and smart. He called me "Estrella" and I called him "Estrella," and he was a star, no question. What a great story—growing up in the Sonoran Desert of northern Mexico in a town of barely a hundred people called Etchohuaquila, the youngest of twelve kids, living in a whitewashed adobe. Now here he was at age nineteen pitching in the big leagues like a veteran.

We finished the 1980 season with a three-game series at home against the Astros, who were three games ahead of us in the standings. We won the first two games, both by one run, to pull within one game of Houston for first place, then won again in the third game, 4–3, to tie the Astros. That meant the 1980 season would come down to a one-game playoff with Houston at the end of the regular season.

Steve Garvey and the other veterans and I talked to Tommy and begged him to start Fernando in the playoff, even though he was only nineteen years old, against Houston's veteran Joe Niekro. Nothing against anyone else, but Fernando was dealing—and the way we saw it, age was no factor. Tommy made the safe choice of going with the veteran, Dave Goltz. It turned out to be the wrong call. Goltz gave up eight hits in three innings, including a three-run homer to Art Howe, and we were never in the game. Our only run in a 7–1 rout came when I singled in the fourth, moved to second on an error, and scored on a single. I learned that day: Sometimes a manager has to go with the young, untested talent if his eyes tell him that's the right move. (Even if, as I later learned on the last day of the 1993 season, my move didn't work either.)

— — — —

I always wore sweatbands on my wrists going back to my time in the minor leagues. Playing in Shreveport and Richmond, you couldn't wear long sleeves, that would have been way too uncomfortable, and I had long skinny forearms and wanted to cover them up with something. My look kind of evolved over the years. In the minors, I wore very narrow wristbands, befitting the era. Then I took to wearing two of the little skinny ones. By the time I was a regular in Atlanta, I took to wearing wider sweatbands, which I liked more. It was hot in Georgia, and I liked being able to wipe my brow.

Then when I got to L.A., I took to wearing double wristbands custom-made by Mizuno, a Japanese company, which some people didn't like. It's a little hard to imagine, now that Japanese players are such an important part of Major League Baseball, but at the time I was traded to the Dodgers from Atlanta, it had only been thirty years since the end of World War II. For some veterans and their wives, the memories were too raw, and they protested ballplayers using gear from Japan. I actually received a number of letters.

Jim Darby, a Cal baseball coach in the 1970s, worked for Mizuno out of Burlingame, and a lot of us used Mizuno gloves, including Pete Rose, J. R. Richard, Burt Hooton, and about a hundred other big-leaguers. Jim would travel around with a Japanese guy named Takaharu Yano who was a wizard with a baseball glove. He could fix it, rebuild it, adjust it, whatever you needed—and all for free, because they were trying to expand their market share. They would show up at spring training in a Winnebago, Jim driving, and they would make your own glove right there. I helped design my own, and that was what I used in 1981 when I won the Golden Glove Award.

— — — —

L.A. in the 1970s and 1980s felt like a land of opportunity. There was always an opportunity to go out and explore the nightlife. There was always someone playing music in some part of town, you just had to find it. Only New York could parallel L.A. nightlife, because it stayed open later. I would go to the Forum or Hollywood Bowl to catch great R&B acts like Earth, Wind & Fire, Patrice Rushen, and Funkadelic, and jazz artists at the Roxy or Santa Monica Civic Auditorium like George Duke, Herbie Hancock, Ronnie Laws, Craig T. Cooper, and my favorite bass guitarist, Stanley Clarke. I always loved going down to the Troubadour on Santa Monica Boulevard in West Hollywood. The owner was a cat named Doug Weston, a six-foot-six dude in little Ben Franklin glasses, and he only booked acts he loved, or at least back then he did. So much went down at the Troubadour in the early seventies, you wouldn't believe it. It was a hip place and always smoky, because back then you were allowed to smoke indoors. Comics like Steve Martin and Cheech & Chong got their start there. I loved Cheech & Chong. They did what they wanted, and they were funny.

I caught the British blues man John Mayall at the Troubadour in the late seventies and also Tim Buckley, who had recorded a whole album called *Live at the Troubadour 1969.* Or I'd go to the Whisky a Go Go on the Sunset Strip, a cool spot that basically invented go-go dancers. Tom Petty and the Heartbreakers, who lived in town, played a lot of gigs there in 1977, but I didn't see him until they came up to San Francisco in early 1997 and played twenty nights at the Fillmore West.

I would talk music with anyone whenever I could, even at the barbershop—no, make that especially at the barbershop. In L.A., I used to get my hair cut at the same place as Miles Davis, my dad's favorite and Orlando Cepeda's favorite, one of the greatest musicians ever. I used to talk to Miles at the barbershop, which was across the street from Hamilton High School, where Sidney Wicks went before he played at UCLA and then for the Portland Trailblazers.

That was the first time I saw a man with hair extensions. Miles would look for me there at the barbershop, and I'd look for him. I would try to schedule my appointments just after his, and we'd talk baseball and music. I did most of the listening. I asked him a lot of questions. I was intrigued to talk about his music, which was out there. I could never figure out why my dad was so fascinated by his music, but later I came to see and appreciate his genius.

I always liked to have a good time, but I was never a big partier. There's a difference. Like a lot of kids who grew up in California in my generation, I smoked weed before I ever took my first drink. I didn't smoke much, since I was always a dedicated athlete, but there were times, like when we shared that joint with Jimi Hendrix. I couldn't stand the taste of beer. If I tried to drink rum and Coke, or bourbon and Coke, I'd get sick every time. To this day, I can't drink whiskey because it reminds me of those days when I was in American River College. I can't drink gin or vodka or tequila because they all make me want to fight. I found that out the hard way. Eventually I settled on Scotch as the one thing I could drink, but even then I realized that the thing that kept me straight and on the line was baseball—that and the fact that I had a conscience from going to church so much growing up, and all my life feeling a sense of responsibility to help provide for my family.

I was raised in baseball by Hank Aaron, and he drilled into me to remember that the game always came first. Money and having a good time came second, not the other way around. A lot of guys lost track of that. For them, it became first partying and second ball. That is never going to work, not for long, and it was never me. You've got to play ball and then party. Sleep was a good way to measure that. "You get eight hours sleep,"

Hank always told us. "From the time you go to bed, you get your eight hours sleep, no matter what time you go to bed." I always did my best to follow that, because that was what Hank had instilled in us.

Hank knew that I smoked a little weed. Orlando Cepeda knew, and my Uncle Floyd knew—and, as I found out thirty years later, my dad also knew. I tried to hide it. I'd go see my dad and sit way on the other end of the couch from my dad's chair, as still and quiet as I could. "I knew what you was doing, because you sat over there like a statue," my dad told me much later.

They all knew, but they also knew that I had direction. I tell young people now, you don't want to end up being a pothead. There's no difference between being a pothead and an alcoholic. One smokes all day and one drinks all day. That's no good, because you're not motivated. You lose sight of what's important. I want to be real clear here—that's especially a risk for young people, whose bodies and brains are still developing. Even as a responsible young adult with a strong sense of direction, I never saw any appeal in smoking until you just fell over. What good did that do? That was a waste of time. I hated the feeling of not being in control. That was never my thing. Guys would ask if I wanted to trip on hallucinogens, and I'd say, "No thank you." I've *seen* how you act on acid. A friend gave me some mescaline one time in Mexico. I tried one, and then flushed the rest down the toilet and prayed I'd never do that again.

CHAPTER 7

World Series Champs

You took two steps forward, and someone was always there wanting you to take a step back. I bounced back from my bad first year with the Dodgers and showed my value over the coming seasons. When I became a free agent after the 1980 season, Jerry Kapstein was determined to get me a contract that reflected that value. How valuable was I? That season, I finished fourth in voting for National League Most Valuable Player, behind only Mike Schmidt, Gary Carter, and Jose Cruz, some bad boys. I finished ahead of my teammate Steve Garvey and a lot of others in the voting. I had seventeen game-winning hits that year, best in the league except for Jack Clark's eighteen game-winners for the Giants, and I batted .294 with ninety-seven RBIs. I was ready to build on that season and try to keep getting better.

That summer, I asked my dad for advice.

"How much should I ask for?"

"The number is $800,000," he told me.

That was a lot of bread. I couldn't believe it. I asked Bob Welch, whom I'd also turned on to Jerry Kapstein, what he thought about the number my dad gave me. He just shook his head.

"There's no way the Dodgers are going to pay you that kind of money," he said.

I figured he was probably right. They started out low-balling me. They would come up on their early offers, then if I had a bad week, they'd drop down the offer again. Finally it all came to a head when the Dodgers made me an offer, $3.5 million over five years, which was almost there, but not quite. They were surprised when Jerry told them that wasn't enough to seal the deal. Jerry and I were ready to start negotiating with other teams if the Dodgers couldn't come up. I really thought I was gone. "I'm going to miss the team [and] the fans," I told UPI the first week of November. "I'm trying hard not to be emotional, but it's very disappointing to me." I meant every word. The San Bernardino paper wrote, "So long, Dr. Scald. Adios, Dusty. Bye, bye, Baker. Dusty Baker will almost surely never play another game as a Los Angeles Dodger."

This was the week Ronald Reagan, a former California governor, was elected President of the United States. It was a tense time. Our talks with the Dodgers went down to the wire. We had the outline of a deal, but there were some holdups, like the Dodgers wanted to add language to my contract banning me from surfing. Surfing? I wasn't surfing at the time. I'd surfed in Puerto Rico playing winter ball one offseason ten years earlier. I had to agree to no wood-chopping, since that was the only way they'd agree to let me keep hunting. No way I was giving up hunting. I wanted a four-year contract so I could be a free agent again, but the Dodgers insisted on five. Okay, if they insisted.

Jerry and I were sure the Dodgers would come back with a better offer before I officially became a free agent at midnight on November 10. That was midnight East Coast time, so for us in California nine P.M. At six P.M. that night, Jerry and I talked on the phone with the Dodgers from his office in San Diego. I agreed to a five-year, $4 million contract. We had a deal, but Jerry and I still had to drive from San Diego to the downtown L.A. office of the team's attorney, Bob Walker, to sign the paperwork by nine P.M. California time, or the whole thing would be null and void. This was an absolutely drop-dead deadline, and with Southern California freeways, you never knew.

But it was Monday night, and that meant *Monday Night Football,* and a great game at that. Jerry and I listened to the game on the radio as we drove, Ken Stabler and the Oilers taking on the Patriots. Nobody else was on the street. It felt like the way had been cleared for us to get there.

We made it with plenty of time to spare, I signed the contract, and I was happy as hell. And why not? My dad had said $800K was the number, and I was getting $800K. For context, I had just become one of only fifteen athletes in the entire world in any sport—any sport, you read that right—to make that much or more at that time. Moses Malone of the Houston Rockets in the NBA was reportedly making $800K then, and so was David Thompson of the Denver Nuggets. In baseball, Rod Carew, Garry Maddox, and J. R. Richard were also reported at $800K, and Pete Rose at $805K. The top-paid athletes were Dave Winfield, at a million-five, and Nolan Ryan, at $1.125 million, then Dr. J and Kareem in the NBA both at an even million, along with George Brett, Dave Parker, and Phil Niekro in baseball. The highest paid player in the NFL in 1980 was Sweetness, Walter Payton, and he made $450,000 that year. In the whole world at that time, only nine professional athletes had higher salaries than me.

The night I signed, I couldn't wait to drive my truck home and start celebrating. This was when we lived in Woodland Hills on a winding street across from a golf course with no parking in front of any of the houses on the narrow street, except the driveways. I had a dentist friend who lived across the street, and he had an extra parking spot next to his house he let me use. I parked my truck there and walked thirty yards or so toward home and saw that Harriet had left our garage door open. I was always on her about not leaving that door open, since you never knew who might come on in. As soon as I stepped into the garage, where I parked my Porsche and Harriet parked her Mercedes, two heads popped up. It was two dudes, one short and one tall and skinny. They were dressed up all in black like cat burglars, because they *were* cat burglars. They had been casing the joint. They wanted to steal my Porsche right out of my own garage. Once they spotted me, the little one was gone in nothing flat. He jumped the fence of my neighbor across the street, and *boom,* was gone across the golf course. The tall skinny guy, like six four or six five, tried running up the street, which was not the smartest move in the world.

It took me a block to catch him. He was trying to make it to a tow truck they had standing ready with an A-frame on the back with a big old bar they were going to use to make off with my Porsche. I loved that car, which I still own to this day! My dad couldn't stand thieves, and neither could I.

I beat the guy up and then dragged him back to my house, marched him up the stairs, and then beat him up some more. This was the second time I'd had my house burglarized, and I was really angry. The house had been broken into earlier that year when I was at spring training, and they took my speakers but left my stereo, which told me it was time to buy a new stereo.

I called up to Harriet.

"Bring my pistol down," I said.

"For what?" she said, all sleepy and dreamy, since by then it was almost midnight.

"No, bring my pistol down," I repeated firmly.

I frisked the tall thief, put him up against the wall, then called the cops and waited for them to arrive. The thief was crying, which infuriated me more, so I gave him a couple of body shots.

I was wearing a suit, a nice suit I'd put on to sign my contract. I was calling the police from my own home. I marched the thief with my pistol down to the street. We made it down there, and the cops pulled their guns—on me.

"Hey, man," I told the cops, making good eye contact and moving as slow as I could, "I'm putting the gun down right here."

It was real quiet.

"I live here," I said. I pointed to the burglar and added, "He's the bad guy."

Naturally, after I put the gun down, they were ready to listen. I realized then and there that you didn't have to be in the South for people to know that you were Black. In California, people were more subtle about some things, but the same problems were still there.

Not long after I signed that deal, my dad got a call from someone claiming to be from the KKK, who told him a Black man—except those weren't the words they used—had no business signing a contract for that kind of money. And they said they were going to burn a cross into my dad's front lawn.

"Come on over," my dad told the guy. "I'll be waiting for you."

I told my dad to call the cops.

"Son, I'm from the South," he said. "The cops could be one of them."

So my dad slept in his rocking chair for two weeks with his shotgun in his lap. He was ready in case the cowards showed. They never did.

There are other times when people surprise you—in a good way—and that includes some cops. One time when I was still a student at American River College, we had ourselves a nice little party going at someone's apartment and they raided the place, but the cops let me go. Then when I was playing in Richmond, I knew this cool speakeasy. From the outside, it looked like a wreck, like it had been condemned, but inside it was immaculate. My older buddy Sonny who owned the place ran numbers. I was in there one time when it got raided, but this one cop was cool—he recognized me from the Richmond Braves and knew I was a ballplayer, so he pulled the latch and let me make a getaway down the back fire escape.

Another time when I was with the Dodgers in Atlanta to play the Braves, I was driving along and some guy broadsided me. It was totally his fault, but the cops came and had to sort out the situation. The cop was more than understanding and had me go sit down over on the grass as he got a statement from the other driver, then let me go. I caught two breaks—one, I wasn't injured, and two, the cop recognized me and left me out of the police report.

- - - -

I loved playing for the Dodgers above all because I loved winning, and in 1981, I felt like we had the team to do that. I actually thought we had stronger teams the two other years we went to the World Series, but we were still good enough to play with anyone.

That was the year of Fernandomania. One time in spring training, Fernando was throwing BP in Vero Beach. He kept putting the ball right over the plate, and all the guys were hammering it. It turned into a joke, how far the balls were flying. The Latino guys started kidding Fernando about it. He seemed surprised. "No," he told them in Spanish, "I'm letting you do that."

Oh, really? Challenge on. Tommy Lasorda was right there and got a smile on his face. He came over to Pedro Guerrero, Reggie Smith, and me and told us to take our best cuts against Fernando. Then he turned to Fernando and told him to go after us. That was just what he did. It took him three pitches to strike out Reggie. I was up next and thought for sure I'd drive the ball, but I struck out on three pitches. So did Pedro. No one questioned Fernando on anything after that, except maybe all that bubble gum he chewed.

Fernando was always playing jokes on us. He would use twine to lasso the feet of a guy trying to walk by him in the dugout. He'd pull that old move of tapping someone on the shoulder from behind, then hiding before they could turn around to see who it was. Before Fernando joined us, I'd never met anyone who could kick a little beanbag up in the air again and again for fifteen minutes—a hacky sack—but he made it look easy and effortless. It was that way with a lot of things. He looked like a kid, and he acted like a kid, but he pitched like a man. Not just that, he pitched like a seasoned veteran who was smart and had total recall of every situation.

Fernando came to us like an angel at the time we needed him the most. At the start of the 1981 season, Jerry Reuss had to be scratched as Opening Day starter because of a calf injury. The rotation was set by late in spring training. Burt Hooten and Bobby Welch both had minor injuries as well. Dave Goltz and Rick Sutcliffe had just pitched and were unavailable. That left Fernando as the Dodgers' only option, even though he was twenty years old and still had never started a big-league game. No rookie had ever started for the Dodgers on Opening Day. Even Fernando didn't believe at first that Lasorda was asking him to do that.

Just before the game, some of us were wondering where Fernando was. Was the kid so nervous, he made himself sick? No, he was in the trainer's room taking a nap.

Fernando took the mound against the Astros and showed off that funky delivery of his, tilting his head to the sky just before he threw the ball, like he was looking to somebody up in heaven. I'd ask him, "Who you *looking* at up there?" They couldn't hit him. Fernando pitched a complete game shutout and Dodger Stadium was rocking. As I told reporters that month, "He closes out a game as well as anyone I've seen. You'd swear he thinks he's still in Mexico."

In every city we visited, thousands of people came out to see him—he inspired pride and joy in Latinos and a lot of other fans, too. The more people heard about Fernando, the more they liked his story. After Dodger scout Mike Brito signed him, the organization wanted him to learn a new pitch besides the fastball/curve combination he favored. Our teammate Bobby Castillo had somehow taught Fernando the screwball in one week during Arizona Instructional League the previous winter.

Fernando next took the mound on a cold Candlestick day, and this time he did give up a run, but still pitched a complete game and struck out ten Giants in a 7–1 win. Then he won again and again and again—throwing three consecutive complete-game shutouts to run his record to 5–0. On May 8, we were at Shea Stadium in New York facing the Mets, and Fernando took another shutout into the ninth inning. No one was better at putting the feeling of the moment into words than Vin Scully, who set the scene: "Once again, a large crowd has come out full of the question 'Is he for real?' And once again, the large crowd is one inning away from getting another shocking answer." Three outs later, Vin called out: "Fernando has his fifth shutout! Unbelievable! I can't believe it. It is the most puzzling, wonderful, rewarding thing I think we've seen in baseball in many, many years."

We were all thrilled for Fernando. He was baseball smart in a way only his teammates really understood, and he was a great teammate, fun to be around, one of the guys, always in on the joke. He got off to an 8–0 start and in June was even invited to the White House to meet President Reagan at a state luncheon for Mexican President José López Portillo at the White House. Asked about his "repertoire" of pitches, Fernando mentioned the curve and fastball and said he threw "two screwballs." Two? That gave National League hitters plenty to think about.

Fernando was hot, the team was hot, and I was hot. At the start of May, I was batting .346. I'd cooled down by June, but as of June 11, I was at .303 after going 3-for-4 with a double and stolen base. At the time, I was second in All-Star voting among all National League outfielders, behind only George Foster.

That turned out to be the last baseball we played for months. One year earlier, players had gone on strike to push the owners, but the strike lasted only a week at the end of spring training and did not disrupt the season. In June 1981, when players went on strike, it was clear the owners were going to take a much more combative approach. The issue was how teams would be compensated when they lost a player to free agency. "I would say if the owners back down now, we're dead," Royals owner Ewing Kauffman said.

I was having way too good a year to want to stop playing ball, but I had to follow those who preceded us and taught us the importance of solidarity. The cause meant more than the year I was having. I hated the forced break. But I had learned my lesson during the work stoppage of 1972 when Hank told me to stay ready and I didn't. This time, I kept my body and my mind ready. I did what I could to stay busy, including playing wiffle ball every single day with little Juan, Harriet's sister's son, then twelve years old, to keep my reflexes sharp. I thought I was wiffle ball champ, but Juan was tough to beat! I trained and lifted and sprinted and ran stairs at Pierce Junior College most days with Lee Lacy or with big Juan, Harriet's cousin. I also swam most every day and served as an instructor at youth baseball camps in Redondo Beach and Bakersfield. I advised the youngsters not to copy any one player—except maybe Pete Rose. "If you have to emulate somebody, emulate Pete Rose," I said. "He plays the game the way it's supposed to be played, with his heart. And he has a simple batting stance and approach."

I went back to Sacramento during the strike to see my family and one of my homies from Grant High, Milt Jackson, a former Tulsa cornerback, who had been the wide receivers coach for Bill Walsh's San Francisco 49ers. Milt asked me to come check out the 49ers minicamp at Sierra College in Rocklin that July. I always loved playing football, and it was an exciting time for the 49ers. That year they had one of the all-time great drafts, picking Ronnie Lott, Eric Wright, and Carlton Williamson in the first three rounds, three impact defensive backs. Instant secondary. Lott would end up in the Hall of Fame, and Eric Wright—the best cornerback ever, as Bill Walsh told me himself—is still one of my best friends.

I was standing on the sidelines in Rocklin watching them run sideline routes when Joe Montana threw an errant pass. It was coming right to me, so I reached up and caught it. Later, Milt asked me if I wanted to come meet Coach Walsh, whom I'd always respected. He always seemed prepared for every moment.

Milt brought me into Coach Walsh's office. "Do you know who this is?" he asked Walsh.

"I don't know," Walsh said. "The way he caught that pass, he looked like James Lofton."

Now, how did Coach Walsh know that James Lofton was my favorite wide receiver? Or maybe I just reminded him of James Lofton? Either way, Bill Walsh and I were cool after that. I've been around a lot of great teachers in my life, starting with my dad and my other dad, Hank Aaron, and a whole lot of uncles and aunts, but I don't know if anyone would ever teach me more than Bill Walsh did in the years ahead about coaching and leadership.

- - - -

When word finally came at the end of July 1981 that the strike was over, I had one thing and one thing only on my mind: playing baseball. That year was weird all around. The All-Star Game, instead of serving as a break, kicked off the second half of the season. I was a little disappointed to find out in the first week of August that I'd once again just missed being voted onto the All-Star team by fans, finishing in sixth place among outfielders. I had no choice but to take it in stride—and in a couple days I found out that National League manager Dallas Green had picked me to join the team as a reserve. It was my first All-Star game in the big leagues and my first All-Star game since Little League. I was excited, but I was rusty and I knew it. We went to Dodger Stadium for an exhibition game against our farm team the Albuquerque Dukes, and I went hitless. "We're human, man," I said. "Fifty days is a long time." No matter how much you work out, there's no substitute for game speed to keep you in baseball shape.

It was ironic that my first game in Cleveland was an All-Star game, given all the times Cleveland had been mentioned to me earlier in my career.

When I walked in the door to the clubhouse in Cleveland for the All-Star Game, Dallas Green and Pete Rose met me at the door.

"Baker, we haven't lost to the American League in ten years, and we're not going to lose now," Rose told me. "The reason we chose you is you're a winner."

Rose knew he would get my attention with that comment, and he did. I hate to lose, and I wasn't going to let my team lose that day if I could help it. In the sixth inning, my good friend Al Oliver, the former Pirate, lifted a little fly ball that carried over the head of our shortstop Ozzie Smith. If anyone had a shot at the ball, it was me. I sprinted all out to get over and had to dive to make the catch, but I hung on. That was seen as the defensive play of the game, keeping it close so we could come back to win—the National League's tenth straight win over the AL.

— — — —

1981 was the year of postseason comebacks. We won the first half of the season, prior to the strike, and Houston won the second half. The Reds had the best combined record in baseball that year but didn't win either half, so they went home. In the Division Series with Houston, we opened with two straight losses in the Astrodome and had to come home to Dodger Stadium facing elimination, but then we won three straight,

6–1, 2–1, and 4–0, to advance. We took the opener of the Championship Series against Montreal at Dodger Stadium, but then the Expos beat Fernando in L.A. and Jerry Reuss back in Montreal to put us one game from elimination in the best-of-five series. Games 4 and 5 would both be in Montreal, so if we were going to come back and win this thing, we'd have to do it on the road.

After our loss in Game 3, they told us to wear our travel clothes the next day, meaning a suit or a sports coat, and pack up our bags and bring them to Stade Olympique, so that if we lost we could go straight to the airport and fly home to L.A. I didn't like the sound of that at all. *If* we lost? It sounded to me like planning to lose. I prayed on what to do, sitting in my hotel in Montreal, and then picked up that Gideon's Bible they used to leave in every hotel room and looked up passages on faith. I found one I thought was fitting for the team. I liked it so much, I wrote it out to give it to Tommy Lasorda for our team meeting the next day. Hebrews 11:1: "Now faith is the assurance of things hoped for, the conviction of things not seen."

We arrived at the stadium for the game, and all my Dodger teammates were in suits and ties and had all packed up their suitcases—except me. I had on slacks and a shirt and sweater, since it was cold up in Montreal.

"Dude, you'll get us in trouble," they told me. "You're supposed to have a coat and tie on."

"Well, I'm not going back to L.A.," I said. "I'm going to New York. I'm going to the World Series."

I pulled Tommy aside and gave him that passage to read, but then added, "Don't tell nobody that it came from me."

Tommy called a team meeting. He got up and read that passage to the team and told them that I'd given him the quote. I couldn't believe he mentioned me after I'd very clearly asked him not to do that. But he had us believing.

Going into the third inning, it was still scoreless. The crowd of almost 55,000 had that antsy feel, ready for the Expos to make a move. They almost put us away one-two-three in the third, but Bill Russell reached on third baseman Larry Parrish's error, and I came up with a chance to bring him home. I lined one into the left-field corner for a double and we went up 1–0, but an inning later, Montreal tied it. The Expos were a talented team that had been good for years, and they were fighting for their first trip to the World Series.

That was where it stood in the eighth when Bill Russell struck out—a rarity for Clutch Man Billy—and I came up. I singled and watched from first as Steve Garvey got a fastball down the middle and launched it to left for a no-doubt-about-it two-run homer that made it 3–1. I stood at home plate after I'd scored and waited for Garv, and we did a double low five at home plate, then I slapped him on the helmet as we ran back to the dugout together. We were on our way. In the ninth, I bounced one back up the middle off Woodie Fryman for a single that brought in two more runs, and also came around to score myself on Reggie Smith's single. We won the game 7–1, and I went 3-for-4 with three RBIs. Tommy knew what he was doing reading that Bible passage on faith and saying it came from me, even though I asked him not to.

The deciding game was all about Fernando. He gave up a run in the first when Tim Raines led off with a double and came around to score, but then set down nine Expos in a row, putting up nothing but zeroes. Fernando could hit, and he came up in the fifth with runners at the corners after Rick Monday and Pedro Guerrero singled. Fernando made solid enough contact that his ground ball to second scored Monday to tie up the game 1–1. Fernando was unhittable after that, except for Lance Parrish's double in the seventh, and it was still 1–1 in the ninth. They brought in starter Steve Rogers in relief, an excellent pitcher, to face Rick Monday in the ninth, and Rick hit a home run to carry us to a 2–1 win. I was right. We *were* going to New York to face the Yankees in the World Series, starting the next day.

We were happy as hell, and celebrated in the visitors' clubhouse. I still had to go have my knee iced, the way I always did, especially after playing on that turf up there at Olympic Stadium, which was as hard on the knees as any surface in the league. I was always the last one out of the clubhouse, and I asked Tommy if I could ride with some friends to the airport. I walked out to the parking lot looking for my two little friends in Montreal, Alan and Mitch, who I knew from the time they were teenage fans. Alan and Mitch used to take me all over Montreal, and that day they were taking us to the airport.

As I came around a corner, it looked like Liz, Derrel Thomas's wife, had tripped or been pushed over, and the contents of her purse had started to spill out in the parking lot. A group of loud, drunk Canadian fans were accosting her. I confronted the fans, and things escalated fast. One guy threatened Darrel with a beer bottle. It was Ken Landreaux and his wife, Harriet and me, and Derrel and Liz, all fighting. We had ourselves a pretty good brawl there for a while until the security people showed up.

We got to the airport in time to make the team flight to New York. I settled into my seat, and all of a sudden my right hand started throbbing. It felt like I'd broken my hand, that was how much it hurt. I knew I had to tell Lasorda. I knew he'd be upset with me, and he was. We got to our hotel in New York late that night, and I called my dad and told him. He was upset with me as well.

"What did I tell you about fighting?" he said, just like my mom had said, "What did I tell you about playing basketball?" They both were right. What could I say?

The Dodgers found a hand specialist in New York I could see the next morning. He examined my hand and said it wasn't broken.

"You'll be okay in three or four weeks," he said.

"Three or four *weeks*?" I said. "I need to be okay in three or four *hours*."

I asked one of my teammates for some DMSO, a liniment they gave horses. I had my hand in that, stinking up the room. Then Manny Mota gave me one of those wraparound bowling sleeves, which I pulled on and tightened up to offer some protection.

"I can't play," I told Tommy. "I'm swinging one-handed."

"No, man, you got to play," he told me. "We're not the same team without you in the lineup."

I went out on the infield grass at Yankee Stadium for Game 1 wearing that bowling sleeve under my batting glove, even though it didn't help. I had on long sleeves and hoped it would take the Yankees awhile to catch on that I was hurt.

We were finally getting another shot at the Yankees in the World Series after losing to them in 1977 and 1978, but it didn't start well. We lost two games at Yankee Stadium before coming home to Dodger Stadium and getting a win behind Fernando. He wasn't his sharpest but hung in there for a complete-game victory, throwing 147 pitches and winning 5–4.

Friends of mine like Gary Matthews and Gary Maddox saw me in the first two games and called to ask what was up. "Man, you ain't swinging right," they said. "What's wrong with you?" They knew my swing and Tommy knew my swing and my teammates knew my swing, but the Yankees didn't know it. There was no interleague play back then and televised games were a rarity, like the "Game of the Week" that felt like an event, so the Yankees did not know my game. They just thought I was cold and slumping.

It was so hard to play hurt and not be able to produce. I was in tremendous pain anytime I put pressure on my hand, swinging the bat or doing anything else. A couple times I thought seriously about asking Tommy to pinch-hit for me, but I just couldn't do it. Hank always taught me to find a way to play through pain, but you could only take that so far. When I came up in the bottom of the fifth in Game 4, they flashed a graphic on screen showing my batting average. During the season it was .320, and so far during the World Series it stood at .083.

Game 4 offered some good examples of how this is a game of inches. We were down by a run when the Yankees' Willie Randolph led off the top of the sixth with a routine bouncer to short. Bill Russell's throw to first sailed on him, and Garv had to make an athletic play, coming off the bag to catch the ball then swipe-tagging Randolph before his outstretched foot could touch first base. He was called safe, even though replays seemed to show the tag getting made. That was one that might have gone either way with a quarter of an inch. Larry Milbourne, up next, tried to bunt him over, then swung away with two strikes and lifted a lazy little fly ball to me that was an easy play.

Dave Winfield, batting next, lifted a fly over my head that sent me running all the way to the wall. Again, inches: As I settled under it, I put my right hand out and tapped the top of the low outfield wall near the foul pole in left, just to know exactly how many inches away I was. I made the catch, and Willie moved up to second base on the tag. Next up was Oscar Gamble, another good friend going back to his days playing for the Cubs with Billy Williams. Oscar brought Willie home with a single to center, and that brought up Bob Watson, a great clutch hitter who taught me a lot about bringing in runs from third. He told me you want to get a ball up to hit a sac fly or a ball away that makes it hard for them to turn two. Bob took a ball that looked like strike three on the corner, but it was called a ball. Put it this way—it was a lot better pitch than the one to me an inning earlier that home-plate umpire Doug Harvey called strike three. Given new life, Watson tomahawked a sinking line drive toward the gap in left center, and I had to sprint over to the ball. I went flying as I extended the webbing of my glove to catch the ball just before it bounced, then tumbled to the ground and came up holding the ball high to show I'd caught it. But left-field umpire Nick Pelosi called it a trap. That was a big play in the game. I ran over to talk to Pelosi. Tommy Lasorda trotted out to join the debate. Back then, there was no replay review to sort it out. I'd have been vindicated, I firmly believe. Instead, a run scored on the play, and it was 6–3 Yankees.

We bounced back in the bottom of the inning to tie it, getting a break when Reggie Jackson lost a ball in the California sun. I led off the seventh and fouled two balls off to find myself down 0-2 again. I had a lot of respect for Jim Palmer, who was working the game broadcast as color man. He had seen me a lot and knew my game. He mentioned that I was falling behind early a lot. "He's a much better hitter than he's shown," he said.

I had two strikeouts on the day already and did not want to make it three. George Frazier, a tough reliever who could pitch every day, threw me a fastball just off the plate with the count 2-2, and it was a tough take, but I watched it go, and the count went full. I could feel that after the fastball away, he'd try to drop in a low breaking ball, which was what he did. It wasn't my best swing or anything, but I went down and got it and chopped a little bouncer toward short. It took a little bit of an awkward bounce, and I was gone. No way they were throwing me out on that ball, not even close. I went to third on a Rick Monday double that Bobby Brown in center missed by maybe an inch. Tommy John, my former Dodger teammate who signed with the Yankees as a free agent, came on in relief to face Steve Yeager, and I watched from third base as he warmed up. I wanted to do anything to help us win, happy to contribute any way I could in spite of my damaged hand. Yeager lofted a fly ball to right field, and I tagged up and scored to put us ahead to stay.

There are a lot of ways to help your team win. Back the next day for Game 5, I came up in the seventh inning against the Yankee ace, Ron Guidry, who struck me out with a nasty, late-breaking slider. He had a two-hit shutout going at that point. Pedro Guerrero was up next, standing in the on-deck circle, and Steve Yeager was coming out of the dugout to bat after him. On my way back to the dugout, I pulled them both aside.

"Look," I said, "Guidry's slider is breaking late. Move up in the box on him, but don't let the catcher see you. Then you can get to the ball before the break."

Guerrero nodded and headed up to the plate. Watching from the dugout, I could see Guerrero inching forward in the box. He took one strike and then stepped out. A moment later, Guidry threw the slider, but Guerrero got the ball before the sharp break. The ball shot off his bat and landed in the left-field bleachers for a solo homer, and just like that, the game was tied. The crowd at Dodger Stadium was rocking.

Yeager was up next. He also moved up in the box. Down 1-2, he turned on a slider and put it almost exactly where Guerrero had parked it a couple minutes earlier. We were up 2–1. That was all we needed. After that game, I was doubly happy. We had won the game, putting us one game away from a World Series championship, and my teammates had picked me up. On the flight back to New York, we knew we wanted to win Game 6 and not let the Yankees back up on their feet. The last thing we wanted was a Game 7 at Yankee Stadium.

My wrist felt a little better every day. Before Game 6 back in New York, Roy Campanella called me to remind me to just be patient and swing at strikes. Hearing from Campy was as good a pick-me-up as I could have had. Joe Black asked Reggie Smith to pass a message on to me as well, just reminding me to play my game.

I came up in the second inning of Game 6 against Tommy John, always a smart pitcher and tough competitor. Garvey and Cey had both singled, and I had a chance to put us on the board. I got ahead in the count, 2-0, and hit one sharply to the left side but foul. Then I tried to go with a low outside pitch but just got under it for a fly ball to Reggie Jackson in right field.

Willie Randolph, another future manager, homered off Burt Hooten in the bottom of the third to put the Yankees up 1–0, and then Jerry Mumphrey singled and Dave Winfield walked. That brought up Reggie Jackson, the Yankees' most dangerous hitter, with two men on base. Reggie hit the ball my way in left field, but it was an easy play, and I gloved it and ran back to the dugout.

It was such a tight game, we were determined to make something happen when I came up with one out in the fourth. The way my hand was feeling, really all I could try to do was hit it to right. Hank Aaron had hurt his hand one time pushing a car that was out of gas. After that, Hank had trouble with the high pitch and concentrated on hitting balls down in the zone. I thought about that and put it into action. I was also trying to follow Campy's advice and look for my pitch. Sometimes I took the first pitch, and sometimes I was up there ready to jump on it. This time, I jumped on it and lined the ball to right center for a single.

Then, with two outs, Rick Monday came up. With the count 2-2, I took off for second, and Monday whacked the ball right where I had just left for a single, giving us runners at first and second. Steve Yeager, next up, lined a ball between short and third into left field, and since I was running with two outs, I scored easily to tie up the game 1–1.

Tommy John was due up in the bottom of the inning, and I was as shocked as anyone to see Yankee manager Bob Lemon send up a pinch-hitter in his place. He was pulling John after just four innings. The cameras caught Tommy muttering in the dugout, “Un-fucking-believable.” We couldn’t believe it either. But man, were we happy to see him go, because having played with him, we knew how tough he could be. It was a relief.

With John out of the game, Davey Lopes led off the fifth for us with a single, and Bill Russell bunted him over to second. A batter later, Ron Cey chopped a ball up the middle that hit the seam of the grass and scooted into center for a single that scored Lopes. We had the lead. If we could keep it, the Series was ours.

The Yankee Stadium crowd was buzzing as I stepped up to bat. Having singled once already, I was feeling a little better. I watched a couple of breaking balls and then swung at a tough low pitch and fought it off enough to send a soft liner into shallow center. Willie Randolph ran back on from second base like maybe he had a play, but the ball floated just beyond his reach. I had myself another single. Now we had two runners on and a real chance to break the game open. Pedro Guererro scorched the first pitch he saw to left center for a triple. Cey scored and I followed, clapping my hands as I crossed home plate. We were up 4–1.

We never looked back. The Yankees put two runners on base in the bottom of the ninth, but it didn’t matter. Bob Watson flied out to center field to end the game and strand the runners.

We’d done it! We were World Series champions! The Yankee Stadium scoreboard read “Dodgers 9, Yankees 2,” and we didn’t have to hear “New York, New York” blaring on the speakers, which they always put on if they won. I hated hearing that song.

I was thrilled for my teammates and for Tommy Lasorda, and I so was happy for the people of L.A., who could finally celebrate a World Series win over the Yankees after two heartbreaking series in past years. For the first time in history, three players were named co-MVP—Roy Cey, Pedro Guerrero, and Steve Yeager—showing what a team effort the win had been.

For myself, I had mixed feelings. Mostly I was relieved. My teammates had picked me up in the ultimate way, carrying us across the finish line without me at full strength. I hit .320 that year, third in the league behind Bill Madlock (.341) and forty-year-old Pete Rose (.325), but in the World Series, I was not myself.

Baseball is a wicked teacher. I felt like Moses, who couldn't go to the Promised Land, but I had helped my team get there. If it's all about the team, and the team wins the World Series, then that's more important than how you performed individually. That was another crossroads, to accept that my best moment as a player was also, in the end, one of my lesser moments as a player. My wrist was never the same after that. Was it okay in three or four weeks? Not even close. I've had three hand operations over the years, and to this day, I still get trigger finger in that hand.

CHAPTER 8

Go Where You're Wanted

One of the best things about my years playing for the Dodgers was having my two brothers in L.A. with me. Rob, always brilliant, played some baseball for Cal Poly San Luis Obispo on a team with Ozzie Smith and Mike Krukow, before quitting to focus on school and earning his Master's in Education. He stayed with me in Woodland Hills and then found a place nearby in the Victoria Village complex. He took a job at Safeco Insurance and worked his way up to an executive position.

From me to my brother Rob to my brother Vic, it seemed like each brother was smarter—and stronger—than the last. Rob is smarter than me, by a lot I think, and Vic was brilliant, almost scary brilliant. He was also big and strong, six foot six and powerful. Vic played forward for four years at the University of the Pacific in Stockton, and was good enough to earn a tryout with the Golden State Warriors in 1977, but hurt his knee. He studied business at USC and American University in D.C., and his favorite courses were in statistics. Vic and I would talk stats all the time.

All three of us loved all sports, especially football and basketball, and we had so much fun going to games in those years. In January 1983, that year's Super Bowl was held at the Rose Bowl in Pasadena, the Redskins against the Dolphins. I was there with my brothers and cousin Juan and stopped off in the men's room. On my way out, I saw a group of cops had my brother Rob up against the wall.

"What the hell have I done?" Rob was demanding in a reasonable voice.

The cop said Rob fit the description of a pickpocket they were after.

"What's the description?" Rob asked.

"Five foot ten, 180 pounds, Black," the cop said.

Rob was really pissed off, and I didn't blame him. "You can damn near stop any Black man in this whole stadium for that," he told the cop. "And I'm six foot, 215 pounds," he added, because he was. Rob was strong.

By this point, we had a crowd around us, and Rob and Vic and I were all mad as hell.

"That's what's wrong with you people," the cop said. "You're always getting pissed off."

He seriously went there. He dropped a "you people" on us. We were seconds away from getting into a real scuffle when another cop showed up—and this cop was Black.

"Oh no," he said right away. He recognized me instantly and knew he needed to calm everyone down fast. As he was talking to the other cops, we heard a huge roar from the crowd. It was the fourth quarter. The Redskins were trailing and had a key fourth-down play. Their star running back, John Riggins, ran forty-three yards for a touchdown to turn the game around. We missed the play of the game because these cops wanted to hassle Rob and accuse him of being a pickpocket.

As I've said, I ran into some cops along the way who did right by me. But the thing is, you can't erase this stuff from your mind or from your heart. It stays with you, even when you want to forget it. So when Rob had to deal with a cop at the Rose Bowl dropping "you people" on us, it was like a flashback to other times other stuff had gone down—like back in the summer of 1968, when I left to play Single-A ball in Greenwood and Rob was in his bathrobe one morning driving our youngest sister Taria to summer school in my brand-new canary-yellow 442. On his way home, a cop followed him for about a mile, and Rob didn't like the feel of it at all. We'd seen this cop before. Rob stopped the car one or two doors down from our house, but when the cop stepped up and asked

Rob to get out of the car, something told Rob, *Don't do it!* He rolled up all the windows in the car and kept honking the horn until our mom came out of the house. She sized up the situation in no time. Mom gave that cop an earful. She went off on him and threatened to sue, and he could see she meant it. That was my mom. She was never afraid to take you to court. It didn't take long for that cop to get back in his car and drive off. We never saw him again.

When the San Diego Clippers NBA team moved to L.A. in 1984 and started playing downtown at the Memorial Sports Arena, I bought season tickets. One time, my Dodger teammate Bobby Welch was going to meet Rob and me out front, then we would go inside together and check out the game. I always said the white dudes from Michigan were cool, and Welchy was no exception. Welchy and I had been tight for years by then. Out front of the Sports Arena, I handed him his ticket, and the next thing you know, we were getting swarmed by cops.

"No scalping tickets," one cop told me.

No one was going to accuse me of being a ticket scalper. I never made a dishonest dime in my life.

"I ain't scalping no damn tickets," I told the cops. "What are you talking about? These are my fucking tickets."

"I told you, Negro, you can't read," the cop said.

When he said that, it infuriated me even more. There was a sign right there that read "NO SCALPING TICKETS." This fool was trying to tell me I couldn't read the sign.

"He ain't scalping no damn tickets, he's giving them to me," Welchy told the cop. "This is Dusty Baker."

Something clicked for the cop. He could see Welchy wasn't lying. Suddenly he switched gears totally and started trying to act all nice.

Another time, Reggie Smith's last season with the Dodgers, he and I were both leaving the parking lot after a game at Dodger Stadium. I'd parked in Lot 5 to go see my Uncle Floyd, and Reggie parked in right field. I was walking with Uncle Floyd when some kids I knew came running up to me. For years, I had all these young kids I would look after, the kind of young guys who could get into trouble if no one cared about them, but I took an interest. I would drive them into the games. They loved me and I loved them.

"Dusty, come, come, come!" they shouted at me. "They're killing Reggie."

"Oh no," I said, and we took off running together.

Reggie had been signing autographs, but he could only sign so many. When he said he had to go, one of the fans got mad at him, so mad that he threw a full beer bottle through the windshield of Reggie's car. When I got there, Reggie had little bits of glass all over the place in his Afro. He had one guy on the ground and was beating him up. The guy's friends were trying to jump Reggie. It was Reggie and me against at least four of these guys. I punched two or three of the others. We were kicking their asses when a car full of plainclothes cops came racing up. We were Dodgers, two of the stars of the team, and we were in the parking lot at Dodger Stadium, but when the car load of plainclothes cops arrived and rushed out of the car, they jumped *us.* We had to fight them, too. Why is it that when people see a fight and Black men are involved, they assume the Black men are the aggressors? They brought us all back to the office to sort it out.

"You can't be fighting the plainclothes," they kept saying.

"Hey, man, *they* jumped *us,*" I kept saying. "We didn't jump them."

Those are instances where all of a sudden, you know it doesn't matter what part of the country you're in. Some things don't change.

- - - -

Vic came and lived with me for a while, so we had all three brothers living near each other in Woodland Hills when we started Baker Brothers Partnership. That was why I'd talked Vic into studying business. We'd been saying since we were kids that we wanted to be the Richest Black Men in America some day, and in those years, we thought we were on our way.

We were involved in limited partnerships. We owned a bunch of buildings. We had helicopters. We had apartments, condos, shopping centers, all over the country from Maryland to North Carolina to Corpus Christi to Colorado Springs. We had fishing trawlers up in Seattle. We had oil transport boats in Brazil. We were part owners in Andersen's Split Pea Soup. It was exciting for a while, and no question Vic and his firm were brilliant in finding creative investments, but we were overextended.

We might have been all right if not for Black Monday, the stock market crash of October 1987. That made me realize that maybe in wanting to be the richest Black guy around, I was serving the wrong master for a while, because cash ain't king, God is the king that gives you the cash.

— — — —

Exits are hard in sports, like they are in life. By the end of 1983, it started to feel like I was going to be shown the door in L.A. when I wasn't ready to go. I batted .300 in 1982 with twenty-three homers and eighty-eight RBIs, but we finished a disappointing second that season. Before the 1983 season, Dr. Frank Jobe again performed knee surgery on me, this time on my right knee. I'd been telling him it was hurting for a long time, and sure enough, when he went in, he found torn cartilage and removed it, all through arthroscopic surgery. Dr. Jobe really saved my career. He was very good to me, and I tried to repay him by taking his kids fishing during spring training.

In 1983, we won our division again and played the Phillies in the NLCS. The Phillies had Pete Rose, Gary Mathews, Mike Schmidt, Joe Morgan, Greg Luzinski, and pitcher Steve Carlton. They were just better than us. We split the first two games of the series in L.A. and then lost both games in Philadelphia. I didn't know at the time it would be my last game as a Dodger, but even so, I went out swinging: 2-for-3 with a home run. I hit .357 in the NLCS to lead our offense, along with Derrel Thomas, who hit .444.

At baseball's winter meetings that December at the Opryland Hotel in Nashville, the talk in the hallways and bars was of how teams were looking to unload big contracts they'd signed with players who were beginning to tail off late in their careers. In the *L.A. Times,* Ross Newhan reported the Dodgers wanted to move me because I was thirty-four and still had two more years on my contract paying me $800,000 a year. As a ten-and-five man, ten years in the big leagues and five years with the same team, I couldn't be traded without my permission—which bewildered me, since it was the Dodgers who insisted I sign a five-year deal when I wanted to sign for four years.

Then came the headlines about how I had been traded to the A's—except that I hadn't been traded to the A's. That could only happen if I agreed. And I most definitely had not agreed to anything. "I said I would listen," I said. "I'm not doing the talking. The ball's in my court."

I was considering my options. I always had a lot of respect for Joe Morgan, both as a competitor and a man, and I knew he was from Oakland. He asked me to come see him at his house in Oakland to talk about the idea of joining the A's, and that was where I first met Sharon Jones and Earl Robinson, who both worked for the team. Sharon was the first African American woman hired to a high-level front office job in baseball. She was Special Assistant to the A's President, Roy Eisenhardt. Robinson, a former Dodger, had played both basketball and baseball at Cal and lived in the area and worked for the A's as Director of Special Projects, along with being a professor at Laney College. They all made a good case for playing in Oakland, but there were larger principles at stake. I had an ironclad no-trade contract that baseball was trying to break. It definitely seemed like the Major League Baseball powers that be were using my case to try to negate the ten-and-five rule that players had fought for.

It didn't matter where the Dodgers wanted to trade me, I wanted some say-so. That was my right. One year earlier, the Cardinals had traded Ted Simmons to the Brewers, and they had given him a bunch of money—well into the six figures, I heard—to waive his no-trade contract. In my anger, I didn't even give them a chance to get that far. That was a mistake on my part.

I told the A's general manager, Sandy Alderson, that I would only accept the trade if I had a chance to compete for playing time in the outfield, not just be used as a DH. The A's wanted me enough to send Alderson, manager Steve Boros, and Wally Haas, son of team owner

Walter Haas, down to meet me in San Diego at Jerry Kapstein's office. Alderson chose his words carefully. He said in Oakland, I'd be a two-way player "to the maximum extent possible."

Maybe I loved being a Dodger too much, or maybe I couldn't quite believe the team had really turned on me, even though that should not have come as such a shock. If Willie Mays, Hank Aaron, and Frank Robinson could all be traded, then anybody could be traded. So could I. But I just wasn't ready. I turned down the trade, surprising a lot of people and leaving open the question of why they wanted to trade me in the first place.

My thinking was simple. The Dodgers were a hell of a team and at the time I was stuck on that. To me the Dodgers were a team that could win and the A's at that time were not. The A's in 1984 would finish in fourth place, eight games under .500. Then again, the Dodgers in '84 would also finish in fourth place in their division. When I look back on it now, I cite my decision at the time as an example to players who ask me for advice. Should a guy accept a trade? I call upon my past to tell a guy: Hey, man, you go where you're wanted.

It was then, after I turned down the trade in early December 1983, that rumors about me picked up. What was going on? It had to do with drugs. I had smoked weed and tried mescaline one time in Mexico, but did not like it and prayed I'd never do it again, which I didn't. Cocaine was everywhere in those days. Almost anywhere in America at that time in the early 1980s, in whatever scene you were into, there was cocaine around. I tried some for a short period of time. I knew it was wrong and would have a bad outcome. And as a guy who had heart issues going back to high school, I knew I was playing Russian roulette with my life. But someone was pushing rumors in baseball about me. They were trying to make me out to be a cocaine addict or even some kind of drug pusher, which to me has always been the lowest thing on the block. As I said, I never made a dishonest dollar in all my life.

On February 8, 1984, the Dodgers invited Jerry Kapstein and me to a meeting with Al Campanis at team attorney Bob Walker's office. They called me in to give me the news that the Dodgers were releasing me. Al said I took it "wonderfully" when given the news. That just meant I didn't want them to know how I really felt. There was no point at that juncture. The decision had already been made.

Mark Heisler called it a "stunning move" in the *L.A. Times,* and openly questioned why the Dodgers would cast aside a team leader popular with teammates and writers valuable enough the previous season to bat third and rank second on the team in RBIs. I was pretty sure part of it was that I had some power and influence with other players. My brother Vic was advising six Dodgers on financial matters, and Jerry Kapstein represented five Dodgers. Heisler wrote in his article about how as recently as one spring earlier, Lasorda had asked me "to take a more overt leadership position," which was true. Then Heisler added, "Several Dodger officials say, however, that by midseason he had come to be regarded as a 'bad influence' by the front office. . . . And since his firing was announced, there have been published and broadcast innuendoes about possible drug involvement on Baker's part." That was the first time I'd ever heard anyone refer to me as any kind of "bad influence." I was always the good influence. I respected Mark. I understood he had a job to do, reporting on the allegations, even if they were unfair. To his credit, after he published that article, he wrote me a thoughtful letter apologizing for having written it.

My time as a Dodger had come to an end. All the joy I'd felt as a Dodger, all my years of loving my teammates and my team and my community, had come to being shown the door with rumors flying. I packed my gear and shook the hands of the reporters who covered the Dodgers one last time. On my way out, I told the reporters, "All I'm asking is that you guys be fair to me and stop all the drug crap. I've had enough."

I was frustrated, and said to one reporter, "I used to associate with Glenn Burke and nobody said I was gay. I associated with Bob Welch and nobody said I was an alcoholic. I associated with Steve Howe—and now everybody says I'm on drugs."

After the Dodgers released me, the San Francisco Giants were the first team to show serious interest. Frank Robinson, the Giants manager since 1981, called me to urge me to sign with the Giants. He told me I'd get playing time, including trying me at first base. A few days later, the Giants claimed me on waivers, and I had five days to decide what I wanted to do. I couldn't think about joining the Giants until I got things settled with the Dodgers, who suddenly seemed determined to rob me of money contractually owed to me. The Dodgers owed me $1.6 million. Full stop. No rumor could change that. I was due that money, whether I played for another team or not, since I had a guaranteed contract. It really did not seem all that complicated.

The Giants were appalled at me for not getting back to them. "We never had any idea what he's thinking," Frank Robinson said in late February. "I called Dusty the day we claimed him. His wife said he was out working, that she'd give him the message. Well, I still haven't heard from him."

What was I going to tell him? I thought something was rotten in Denmark. Why would the Giants claim me and pay my full salary or close to my full salary when all they had to do was wait twelve hours until after the waiver deadline and then pay me the minimum? It didn't make any sense, unless they were in cahoots.

The Dodgers stopped paying me. Which, again, made no sense. A contract was a contract. Jerry Kapstein and I filed a formal player grievance with the Dodgers. I felt like I was being set up. I kept my eyes open and paid attention. When I saw the same car following me, again and again, I knew I was under observation. (Years later, I met the guy who'd been following me and he confirmed he'd been assigned to follow me.)

Back in 1977, the Clash sang a cover of an old song that went "I fought the law and the law won." That might as well have been my theme song. I was getting tired of fighting the law. I didn't know how far to push it. I could take my case to arbitration, or I could try to settle. Major League Baseball wanted me to agree to drug testing and also to give away some salary—going from $800,000 a year to $600,000 with incentives, which I didn't like, since you never knew if you would get enough playing time to earn the incentive bonuses. Which I didn't.

The baseball protocol called for testing for marijuana, cocaine, heroin, and morphine, which made me wonder: "Who can play baseball taking those? You're going to be over there nodding off in the dugout."

I called my dad to ask for advice. Should I fight the law? Or let the law win?

"Son, you can only lose what's already yours, which would be all of your salary, if you lose an arbitration case," my dad told me. "The only way you can prove your innocence is on the field."

He had a point. And that was when Frank Robinson called again and told me, "You need to join us." That was really one of the best things that happened to me. I had no clue that my decision to join the Giants would end up being a precursor to my coaching and managing career, since I would get to know Bob Lurie, the team's owner. All I knew was I had to get back on the field and start playing baseball again.

The end of my time with the Dodgers came before the 1984 season started. Four decades later, I finally gained a little more insight into this period. I'd always gotten along well with Peter O'Malley, the Dodgers owner. All through my managing career, I would get one or two notes from Mr. O'Malley every year, just wishing me well. Then in 2024, I was in L.A. being honored as a former Dodger, and I saw Mr. O'Malley. We started talking, and he apologized. "Dusty, I'm sorry that I listened to what some people were saying to me about you back then," he told me. I thanked him, and it helped me put that painful period behind me.

By the time the Giants announced April 1 that they had reached a tentative agreement with me to play for them, I thought it was another April Fools' Day prank. But two days later, there I was, stuck in traffic at noon trying to get into Candlestick Park, just three hours after taking a physical at the Palo Alto Medical Clinic. By the seventh inning, I came out of the Giants dugout, wearing a Giants uniform and number 12, and got a standing ovation from the crowd of 54,000.

That was a tough start, especially after having to do my own spring training with no one to work out with but my nephew Juan. I arrived in San Francisco and had to find a place to stay. I rented a house in Hillsborough that Joe Montana and Dwight Clark had formerly rented.

I pulled my quad in Chicago in early May and never felt right the rest of the season, but I had a good time with the guys on the team. To this day, Mike Krukow and Duane Kuiper and I talk about that year. That was the first time I got to play with Al Oliver. And we also had talented young players like Jack Clark, Jeffrey Leonard, Bill Laskey, Manny Trillo—my good friend from winter ball in 1974 in Venezuela—and rookies Dan Gladden and Chili Davis. We had a good team—we just didn't win, and it was cold at Candlestick.

I learned a lot about managing from watching Frank Robinson. Frank not only had the background as one of the best right-handed hitters of his era, he'd also managed in winter ball and paid his dues. No one ever questioned Frank's leadership qualities or the man's intelligence. He was astute and shrewd. Playing against him, I had always thought he was a mean guy, but now that I was playing for him, I saw another side. One time, I didn't speak to him for about a week when I wasn't playing, and he didn't say anything. Then when we did speak, he said, "Oh, now you're talking to me again?" Frank didn't say much, but he didn't miss much. He knew some baseball, and he was about winning. I never saw a glimpse of that mean and nasty guy I had seen across the field and had a couple run-ins with.

I learned from every manager I played for—in some cases how to be, and in some cases how *not* to be. Both are equally valuable lessons. I felt Frank brought a lot of the Baltimore Oriole approach with him, emphasizing things like the importance of players dressing right and wearing a coat in the lobby. The players were not allowed in the hotel bar. Frank and Joe Torre dispelled the idea that good players couldn't make good managers, because supposedly they would have trouble teaching or explaining what came easily to them. Both were great players who went on to become great managers.

The Giants were in Atlanta in early August, and in the Friday night opener of the series, I doubled home a run in the fifth inning to give us a 1–0 lead, but the Braves came back to win 2–1 in extra innings. The next night, Frank was given the word that he was fired. We were in last place, 42–64, and Giants owner Bob Lurie felt he had to do something. "I know it's a tough situation," Frank told Lurie. "You have to do what you have to do." Frank came into the clubhouse to talk to the players and say his goodbyes. It was awkward. It didn't feel right. Frank had high standards and expected a lot out of all his players. I always liked that in a manager. He was not the reason we were a losing club.

Getting to know Bob Lurie, who I found I liked a lot, was a highlight of that year. He usually had a smile, even though we didn't give him that much to smile about on the field. For some reason, Mr. Lurie and I talked a lot that season, maybe more than I talked with Frank Robinson. Mr. Lurie never brought up my exit from the Dodgers, which I appreciated. He would invite me to stuff all the time, and whenever I could go, I did. I think he was genuinely interested in me. I had some good conversations with him and also with his wife Connie. I think they were curious to hear my perspective on various things. Mr. Lurie was always very pleasant, but one thing I noticed was he had stern eyes. Even when he was smiling, he had stern eyes.

I loved the fans in San Francisco, always one of my favorite cities, but I hated playing for a losing team. We finished that year 66–96. It all felt wrong to me. Danny Ozark finished out that season as Giants manager, and then in the offseason Jimmy Davenport was hired to take the job. He told reporters in January 1985 that he expected me to be his fourth outfielder, but I thought they would trade me rather than pay me $600,000. What I would never have guessed was that I would end up with the A's, the team that wanted me a year earlier and I'd nixed the trade.

This time, I was no longer a ten-and-five guy with a no-trade clause. And it was a bad time for me personally. I felt like both my marriage and my baseball career were spiraling down at the same time. I could hear Pete Rose talking to me about the baseball field being your only sanctuary from your personal troubles, which I repeated to myself many times, both in those years and many years into the future.

I had some soul-searching to do, and for guidance I turned to books that had been important to me over the years. One was *The Spook Who Sat by the Door* by Sam Greenlee, the story of the first Black CIA officer, which they ended up making into a movie. My mom made me read that book when I was nineteen, but only now did I really get it. Sometimes when you first read a book, it doesn't have relevance for you, but then later it's the right time. By 1985, it was the right time for Sam Greenlee to make sense to me. In that period, I looked in particular to the writings of Maya Angelou and James Baldwin to get me through. I also pulled out my copy of *The Art of War* by Sun Tzu, which would help guide my strategy to life and as a coach and manager in the years ahead.

For music, I was digging into Gil Scott-Heron, who made a name with a poem he read aloud to music, called "The Revolution Will Not be Televised." James Brown was singing, "I'm back!" in the song "Get Up Offa That Thing," and Marvin Gaye was singing "What's Going On?" When Hendrix used to sing about manic depression, I didn't understand what he was talking about, but I pulled Hendrix back out when my brother Vic was going through the same experience.

Music could either motivate me or soothe me or inspire me—or make me angry, which sometimes I needed to be. Music helped me see that I had no choice. I had to go where I was wanted. It was time for me to join the Oakland A's. What choice did I have, really, if I wanted to get on the field and get back the money I was owed?

The Oakland A's ownership at that time was unusual in the history of sports. I don't think I fully appreciated it until later, but the San Francisco family that ran the Levi Strauss blue jeans company, the Haases, were Giants fans who only bought the A's because they were persuaded to help the East Bay community by keeping the A's in town.

I'll say this for the A's: They traded for me in spring training because they knew I could help the team, and they had the good sense to ignore the drug rumors that still floated around. I joined the team for the 1985 season. As challenging as it was for me adjusting to a new role, there was a lot about that team I liked. When the trade came through, on March 24, all I had to do was go a couple miles from Giants spring training camp in Scottsdale, Arizona, to the A's camp in Phoenix. I didn't have much time and had to make the most of it. Hitting coach Jim Lefebvre threw me three or four extra BP sessions of a half hour each to get me ready.

When we got back to Oakland, I walked into Sandy Alderson's office and saw a picture of a Marine in dress uniform at attention.

"Who's that?" I asked him. I thought maybe it was his dad or brother. But it was Alderson himself. He was literally a poster boy for the Marine Corps. They'd used him in recruiting posters. His dad had been a pilot for the U.S. military in three wars.

"I'm also a Marine," I told him.

"I knew that," he said.

Alderson and I got along fine. He was the first GM I ever had who was not a former player, but he was actually pretty regular. He'd put together a team that was a mixture of veterans and young guys. My first season, we had a young muscular kid from Miami named Jose Canseco, who had a quick, powerful swing. He played most of the season in Triple-A then joined the A's in September and hit five home runs in twenty-nine games with a .302 average. Then the next year, 1986, he hit thirty-three homers with 117 RBIs and was voted American League Rookie of the Year and made the All-Star team. We had a good nucleus of young players that included Mike Gallego, Mike Davis, Stan Javier, Dwayne Murphy, Carney Lansford, Tony Phillips, Mickey Tettleton, and pitchers Curt Young and Steve McCatty, and the veteran Dave Kingman as DH. Late in 1986, we got a look at another young A's prospect, Mark McGwire, a big redhead, who came up in September—and the next year hit forty-nine homers as a rookie and was also named Rookie of the Year. The A's under Alderson and Eisenhardt ended up having the Rookie of the Year three straight years. (Walt Weiss was the other one.)

In May 1986, the Phillies released my good friend and former Dodger teammate Dave Stewart, who grew up in Oakland. Talented and tough, Stew had pitched well for us in L.A., but after trades to the Rangers and then the Phillies he was having trouble finding himself. I knew Stew had a lot more baseball left in him and deserved another chance. Stew thought so as well. "There were some people since Philadelphia who said I should just quit," he said afterward, "but I always thought better days were ahead."

I talked to our pitching coach, Wes Stock, and told him the A's should take a look at Stew.

"Does he have the stuff?" Wes asked me.

"Heck yeah," I said. "He just needs more grooming, a third pitch, and somebody to believe in him. He certainly believes in himself."

Stew had an intense look when he was on the mound, his cap pulled down low on his head. People talked about how menacing it made him look when he was staring in at the hitter. That was actually an old Dodger thing—in L.A., the pitchers were taught to wear their hats down low so hitters couldn't see their eyes and they would look more focused.

Stew drove down from Philly to throw for Wes while we were in Baltimore, and the A's signed him later that same month. I always thought I was directly responsible for bringing Stew to the A's, because I thought Wes Stock had agreed with me about him. Years later I found out Wes didn't listen to me at all. He advised the team to pass on Stew. Instead it was Sandy Alderson who pushed for it, partly because he had heard Bill Lajoie, a master baseball mind with the Tigers, also had interest.

We had started the 1986 season with Jackie Moore managing, and then before the All-Star break he was replaced by Jeff Newman, and the team looked for a longer-term replacement. Eisenhardt and Alderson liked that Tony La Russa, my teammate back on the 1971 Braves, was one of the first managers in baseball interested in computers. Midway through the season, the White Sox let Tony go and Alderson flew to Chicago to talk to him about joining the A's.

On July 1, we were in Oakland playing the Indians as the front office was wrapping up negotiations with La Russa to be the new manager of the team. Cleveland was ahead 7–0 when manager Pat Corrales had his catcher, Andy Allanson, steal second. Everyone on the A's bench was riled up about that. Stealing with a lead that big was seen as rubbing it in. Then in the seventh, Stew came on in relief and buzzed Julio Franco with a high, inside fastball. Before you knew it, Corrales was out on the field, swearing at Stew and trying to kick him. This was a huge mistake. Stew blocked the karate kick and countered with a right cross to Corrales's jaw.

As quickly as that, he was on the deck. It turned into a bench-clearing brawl that day that made the front page of the *San Francisco Examiner* with a big picture of me holding Stew back. These A's were going to be fiery, which was how I liked it.

Tony La Russa got the job, and a few days later, he called Stew to let him know he'd be starting against the Red Sox at Fenway Park the following Monday in Tony's managerial debut. That was the good news—Stew hadn't started a game since he'd been with Texas. "The bad news," Tony told Stew, "is that it's going to be a nationally televised game, and you're going to be pitching against Roger Clemens."

"Actually, that's all good news," Stew said. "I'm looking forward to it."

By then, Stew hadn't won a game in nearly two years, and Clemens had won fourteen straight before losing his last decision. Our record going into the game was 31–52, but we won the game. Canseco and Dave Kingman both homered, and Stew picked up the victory, on his way to a career 9–0 head-to-head matchup against Clemens.

It was great for Tony to get a win his first game out. Back then, he cut a much different figure than he would later on. He was always smart, but when he came to Oakland, he was carrying around the disappointment of having been fired in Chicago. You could tell that it bothered him because he had that kind of hurt look on his face. But he and I were always cool from the time we were teammates on the Braves.

I liked living in Northern California again. I loved L.A., but one could get in trouble there. Too much temptation in the streets: I liked women, and they liked me. I appreciated the laid-back attitude in Northern California, and I liked the weather, which was better for my sinuses and allowed me to breathe. I didn't function well in the arid climate down in Southern California. Up north, I found plenty of places to go bird hunting if I wanted, and fishing, which I'd always loved, going back to fishing with my dad as a kid. I still lived in L.A. in the offseason, so up north I was renting in Blackhawk, a gated community half an hour from the Oakland Coliseum. I spent a lot of time by myself that season. My daughter Tosh was in school in L.A. and she and Harriet would come up some weekends or when school was out. I would have visitors, like Ralph Garr Jr. and my nephew little Juan came to stay with me for a week or two. They were both teenagers. I would bring them to games and put them to work in the A's clubhouse.

One of the clubhouse attendants, little Jimmy, pulled me aside in August 1986. "Can I take them to a rap concert at Oakland Coliseum?" he asked me.

It was the Raising Hell Tour, Run-DMC with LL Cool J and some hip white kids from New York City called the Beastie Boys—they would all be famous soon enough. Tickets were fifteen dollars.

"Go ahead, man, as long as you bring them home by midnight," I said. "You need to take them while you still can, before rap music dies, because it ain't going to be around long." So much for my talent evaluation! Of course, I had a change of heart, and to this day I'm still listening to rap music and loving it. I took my son Darren to see Snoop Dogg twice, once when he was eight or nine and then again in 2025 when he was twenty-five.

One hip thing I did while playing for the A's was start wearing wristbands with original art on them. Back in L.A., I was friends with James Mims, a teenager whose dad had worked for the Dodgers for years and was the usher for the Vin Scully Press Box. I think I first met Mr. Mims, as we always called him, through Jim Gilliam, as their families were close. When James was at USC, he and I started talking about making custom wristbands with an image of my autograph on there. He had a better idea.

"Let's put your face on it," he said.

James got to work and hand-stitched my face on some wristbands, and then drove down to Palm Springs to show me when we were playing the Angels in spring training in 1986. I loved what he had done.

"Whoa, maybe you got something here," I told him.

Jeffrey Leonard had the idea to put "Say No to Drugs" on there, which he did. Once I started wearing them, other guys wanted their own version, starting with Carney Lansford and Tony Phillips. So James started Mimsbandz, and it took off. Soon he had his homeboys from L.A., Eric Davis and Darryl Strawberry, and many of the top Black players and some white ballplayers, too.

For me, wristbands were part of my uniform. They were the first thing I would put on. People always asked why I changed up which wristbands I was wearing. If you look back on what I wore with the A's, a lot of times I would pick colors based on whether we were hot or cold, which I would also do later as a manager—wearing the same color if we were winning and switching up if we lost. The ones I pulled off after we lost were the ones I gave to the kids. When I was managing the Giants, I came into Chicago when we'd lost five or six games in a row and kept changing wristbands. "Johnnie B., I know what you're doing," Billy Williams told me. "You're about out of winning color combinations, aren't you?" I was.

With the A's, I wore wristbands with the Rastafarian colors—green, red, and gold—except I wore green and yellow, the A's colors, along with the red. The red was for the blood that was shed—that's what the Rastamen said.

"Red isn't an A's color," my teammate Steve Henderson said to me. "Why are you wearing those wristbands that color?"

"Those are my Rasta colors," I told him. I started quoting reggae lyrics to him, singing right there on the outfield grass, songs from Steel Pulse, who I caught one time at the Warfield. I'd also caught Bob Marley in Davis back in 1974.

"*Marcus say, 'Red for the blood that flowed like the river,'*" I sang.

I'd been studying Marcus Garvey going back to Sacramento when my mom gave me books on him to read—and later I had the honor of getting to meet Dr. Julius Garvey, one of Marcus Garvey's sons.

"*Marcus say, 'Green for the land Africa,'*" I continued. "*Marcus say, 'Yellow for the gold that they stole.' Marcus say, 'Black for the people it was looted from.'*" I thought of those words every time I put on my wristbands.

"Where is the black, Pork Chop?" Steve asked me, using a nickname he gave me the year before—which I later found out was a nickname given to Hank Aaron as well.

"I'm *wearing* the black," I told Steve. "I'm wearing the black every day."

— — — —

The A's finished ten games under .500 that season, but under La Russa, we were 45–34 and improving. For me, it was a challenging season at the plate. My batting average for the year was .240, just below what it was my first year in L.A. when I was playing on one leg. I only had 271 plate appearances the whole season and never did reach my incentives to earn my money back. But I knew Tony knew what I could do, and I was hoping for a chance to come back the next year.

"Hey, man," Tony told me at the end of that season, "you go home, get in great, great shape, and I'll call you."

I believed him. I went home and got in great, great shape. But I never heard from him—or anyone with the A's. That was the winter they signed Reggie Jackson. The only team that showed any interest in signing me was the Yankees, but they never offered me a contract, which ended up being funny, because for years to come, even after my playing career, George Steinbrenner would write me letters, talking about what a winner I was.

That was the end of my playing career, it turned out. It was hard for me to accept. I wasn't ready to retire. I could still compete. And I had a lot to offer a team, or at least an American League team that needed a DH. My knee was bad and I couldn't really run or play defense anymore, but I knew I could still hit. I'd seen plenty of guys with bad legs stay in the game as designated hitters, like Orlando Cepeda and Rico Carty. I might not have been quite the hitter those two were, but I could hit. Wasn't that what the DH was for? To keep guys around who could still hit?

But I felt like I had landed on baseball's bad boy list. I wasn't the only one dealing with drug rumors. Baseball had launched a league-wide investigation that centered around the Pittsburgh Pirates, and even though a lot of white guys were investigated, it always bothered me that most of the players brought in for questioning were Black or Latino.

In 1985, a grand jury panel convened, then came trials, and at some point my name came up. News reports revealing my name were published on Thanksgiving Day, and my dad showed me the paper.

"Son, did you do this?" my dad asked me.

"For a brief period," I told him.

"Are you still doing it?" he asked.

"Dad, no," I said. "That's way behind me."

"Son, if they really had something on you, they wouldn't even bother to question you, they'd just come get you," my dad told me.

My dad made a good point. I was taught in the Marines to just give name, rank, and serial number. After talking to my dad and legal counsel, we all agreed that I was well within my rights to say nothing, not about myself and not about anyone else.

But when I didn't cooperate, that was when my problems began. Some of the guys who did cooperate paid fines, and a few even got extensions on their contracts. They had to do community service, but they got extensions. I never had to do community service or pay any fines, because it was determined there was "little or no evidence" against me, but I did have to endure years of drug testing, which I got tired of fast, and it did cost me money because I had to accept a reduction in salary.

Years later when talk of a different kind of drug came to dominate, I was questioned by baseball authorities, and the FBI asked whether I believed players I'd managed had used steroids. I stuck to what I knew, which was nothing. I'd heard rumors about some guys, but a rumor is just a rumor. I'd learned that the hard way.

CHAPTER 9

A Giant Tap on the Shoulder

I wasn't watching TV on the night of April 6, 1987. I didn't hear beforehand that Dodgers general manager Al Campanis was going on the ABC late-night show *Nightline* to talk to host Ted Koppel. But his appearance turned out to have a lot to do with my future.

Al had always been cool with me in my time with the Dodgers. He was the man who bet big on me and made the trade that brought me over from the Braves. As a young man, he had played in the same Triple-A infield as Jackie Robinson on the Montreal Royals. The Koppel interview should have been easy for Al, who was on TV just to say a few nice things about Jackie on the fortieth anniversary of his first playing for the Brooklyn Dodgers to break baseball's color barrier.

But as Al talked, he seemed to be saying that Blacks in baseball didn't want to pay their dues.

Koppel pushed back. "But you know in your heart of hearts," he said firmly, "you know that that's a lot of baloney."

Al laughed awkwardly.

"There are a lot of Black players, there are a lot of great Black baseball men who would dearly love to be in managerial positions," Koppel continued, almost pleading with Al to stand up to the moment. "I guess what I'm really asking you is to, you know, peel it away a little bit. Just tell me, why you think it is. Is there still that much prejudice in baseball today?" He was bending over backward to give Al a chance to answer the question.

"No, I don't believe it's prejudice," Al answered. "I truly believe that they may not have some of the necessities to be, let's say, a field manager, or perhaps a general manager."

"Do you really believe that?" Koppel asked him.

"Well, I don't say that all of them, but they certainly are short," Al said that night. "How many quarterbacks do you have? How many pitchers do you have that are Black?"

Koppel rightly enough said that sounded "like garbage." Then Al dug himself deeper by talking about how Black people can't swim because we "don't have the buoyancy." My mom and dad raised all of us to be strong swimmers in part because we didn't want to hear any nonsense about Black people not being able to swim.

Al would never live down saying on national TV that Blacks lacked certain "necessities" to manage in the big leagues or to be a general manager or owner. There was a huge national furor, and he resigned his job. National civil rights leaders spoke out and called for baseball to take meaningful action to hire more qualified minority candidates. It had been a big deal when Frank Robinson took over as manager of the Cleveland Indians for the 1975 season, the first Black man to hold that job. I only wish that Jackie Robinson, who died two years earlier, had still been around. "I think it would have been one of Jackie's biggest thrills," Jackie's widow, Rachel Robinson, told reporters. "He would have been ecstatic. . . . It was such a burning desire of his to see a Black manager. And he felt it was so long overdue."

The first African American to manage a big-league game was actually another Baker, former Negro League infielder Gene Baker. It was September 21, 1963, the Pirates were at Dodger Stadium the year after it opened, and Pirates manager Danny Murtaugh was furious. Bill Virdon came up with the bases loaded in the eighth inning and was called out on a close play at first that ended the inning. Umpire Doug Harvey ejected Murtaugh, so Baker, a Pirates coach, managed the last inning.

Larry Doby, who was second after Jackie to integrate Major League Baseball as a player, was also second after Frank, getting a shot in 1978 to manage the White Sox, but only for eighty-seven games. Hank used to always talk to me about Mr. Doby, what a good all-around ballplayer he was, how he was well-spoken and didn't take any shit from people. I met Mr. Doby when I was a player on the Braves and he was a coach on the Indians. He gave me advice on the importance of training throughout the offseason, after taking a couple weeks off. He said you had to keep at it even on those cold winter days when you don't feel like working out. That's how you get ready for those days during the long season when you don't feel like playing.

Since then, though, there had been no more Black managers, and a consensus had formed that we needed to make sure we were not forgotten. Baseball Commissioner Peter Ueberroth had been talking about wanting to hire more Blacks in the game even before Al Campanis made his comments on *Nightline.* Once the controversy exploded, Ueberroth hired Dr. Harry Edwards of California, a former two-sport athlete at San Jose State (track and basketball) who had been the one advising John Carlos and Tommie Smith when they took the podium at the Mexico City Olympics in 1968 and raised their fists in the "Black Power" salute. Dr. Edwards was a respected figure, and had no background in baseball, but he knew people.

— — — —

April 1987 was my first spring not playing baseball in what felt like forever. I was keeping myself busy organizing my annual Dusty Baker School of Baseball, which took place every July in Sacramento. The work I did at there was all about pure love of the game. It was especially cool for me to see my dad in his element out there coaching young kids, along with a lot of my friends in the game. My dad was hip, and he was respected by all. The kids loved him. The school was mostly being run by my dad with Gene Frechette and Bruce Carmichael and Bruce's dad.

Tosh with Tommy Lasorda.

Harriet, Tosh, and me at spring training, Dodgertown.

Me, Harriet, and Tosh in Dodger Stadium.

Dave Stewart, Pedro Guerrero, Mr. Hardy (Kerry's dad), Kenny Landreaux, and me (*left to right*) at dinner at Mr. and Mrs. Hardy's home in Cincy.

Family photo: Me, Taria, Vic (*seated, left to right*); Rob, Mom, and Tonya (*standing, left to right*). My hand bandaged after one of many hand surgeries while with the Dodgers.

Me, acting composite.

Me leaving the Dodgers' office after signing my big contract.
Anne Knudsen, Herald Examiner Collection / Los Angeles Public Library

Howard Cosell interviewing me prior to the World Series.
Focus on Sport / Getty

They say Glenn Burke and I did the first high five, I guess it caught on.
Rob Brown, Herald Examiner Collection / Los Angeles Public Library

Me and Harriet upon arrival at the airport in LA after winning the 1981 World Series. *AP Images / Lennox Mclendon*

Me, Fernando, and Spanish-language broadcaster Jaime Jarrín at the start of the 1982 season. *Harry Adams / Tom and Ethel Bradley Center at California State University, Northridge*

Tosh and me, 1984, first day back in Dodger Stadium with the Giants. The Dodgers honored me at the game. *Jayne Kamin-Oncea*

My last days as a Dodger, and as I said in the article this photo ran with, "I'm gonna scald for somebody"—I just didn't know for whom. *Mike Sergieff, Herald Examiner Collection / Los Angeles Public Library*

Bob Lurie and Al Rosen.
Courtesy of the San Francisco Giants

Me and Roger Craig.
Courtesy of the San Francisco Giants

Me and Al Rosen.
Courtesy of the San Francisco Giants

Me and James Mims.
Wearing the first wristband he made with my face on it.
Courtesy of the San Francisco Giants

Me and Tosh while with the A's, Oakland Coliseum.
Michael Zagaris

Bobby Bonds, me, and Barry Bonds (*left to right*) figuring things out. *Courtesy of the San Francisco Giants*

Dad and Peter Magowan in San Francisco. *Courtesy of the San Francisco Giants*

Wedding party, surrounded by family.

On my Indian motorcycle, "Rastamobile."

Dad, me, and John Lee Hooker (*left to right*) hanging out in my office in Candlestick Park.

Fishing '93 Giants (*left to right*): Matt Williams, Dave Martinez, Darren Lewis, Royce Clayton, Kirt Manwaring, and me.

Peaceful spot, Kauai.

Clockwise from left: Len Coleman, me, Cito Gaston, Don Baylor, and Buck Leonard.
Courtesy of the San Francisco Giants

Me, Darren, and Dad at hat day, San Francisco.

Me and Melissa, Giants' fashion show, San Francisco.

With Orlando Cepeda.

Me and Mom while with the Giants.

Dad and me in San Francisco.

We were able to bring in a lot of big-leaguers to work with the kids. Some of the coaches I brought in came just once or twice when their team was in the area, like Willie Stargell, Shawon Dunston, and Rick Sutcliffe, and some were regulars, like Bob Oliver, Orlando Cepeda, Jim Barr, Dave Stewart, Shooty Babitt, Leron and Leon Lee, and Rowland Office. We started out at Sac State and then used the field at Rancho Cordova High School, where Jerry Manuel, another one of my coaches, also went to school, and ended up at Capital Christian Center, where Mauricio Dubón, the future Astro, was a student. Guy Anderson, their longtime coach, coached a lot of our kids. Local teacher Clint Brill was also a mainstay, as well as Cliff Rold from Fresno and Hal Steinback, a coach at nearby Del Oro High School. Cordova woodshop teacher Dave DeRosa was there to help the kids feel comfortable in the hotel and scheduled all the activities.

We gave the kids homework and some came just for the day, but most of them were with us for a week at a time. We brought in a lot of kids who went on to big futures in the game, like CC Sabathia, a first-ballot Hall of Famer; Darren Oliver, Bob's son; Derek Lee and Geoff Jenkins; and Steve and Dave Sax, just to name a few. I went on my own PR campaign and got to pay everybody for their time. It was a win for everybody. The kids were happy, and their parents were happy. My dad and all the coaches were happy. A lot of these kids got to see their first major-league game with us, either at Candlestick or the Oakland Coliseum.

My inspiration came from the Squaw Valley Warriors Basketball Camp, where I first met Al Attles and Rick Barry and got my jump shot straightened out. That camp changed my life—and I wanted to make a difference in others' lives, which we did with that camp for more than thirty-five years. Thousands of kids came through. That's a lot of lives to influence. What started out as the Dusty Baker School of Baseball evolved over more than twenty years into the International Baseball Academy with participants from all over the world.

An effort by Black players to organize in the spring of 1987 following the Al Campanis appearance on *Nightline* started with Frank Robinson, Willie Stargell, former pitcher Ray Burris, and former scout Ben Moore. They spoke for a lot of us when they said that whatever MLB might or might actually be trying to change, we needed to organize and make our voices heard as part of the larger discussion. They mailed out letters to 280 of us urging us to get on a plane that November and get ourselves to Texas, where we would be gathering for several days of meetings at a hotel near the Dallas–Fort Worth International Airport. More than fifty Black and Latino players showed up, including Ralph and me, Chris Chambliss, Curt Flood, Al Oliver, Bobby Tolan, and George Foster. Ken Shropshire, a professor at the Wharton School at the University of Pennsylvania, whom I've learned a lot from over the years, was also there.

The organizers really did some work. Among the participants were executives from other fields like Brenda Neal, who at the time was a senior vice president at Drexel Burnham Lambert and then worked for years at Morgan Stanley. She gave us additional legitimacy, along with Ken Shropshire. She was a brilliant lady who was instrumental in keeping everything running smoothly and on time, and she remained my friend in West Palm Beach for a long time.

We met twelve hours that first day and made the decision to form a group called the Baseball Network, which we gave an intentionally ambiguous name but a clear purpose: to work against "the conspicuous absence of Blacks and other minorities in the decision-making process on the field, in the front office, and among umpires." I was asked to join the executive committee and gladly accepted. So did my good friend Don Baylor, Donn Clendenon, Dock Ellis, and Deacon Jones, and Sharon Jones of the Oakland A's front office.

The group's concept was smart, which was to emphasize information and keeping up to date on qualified candidates, and then making that candidate information available to teams looking to hire. Ueberroth immediately agreed to come to Texas and meet with the group's leadership and answer questions.

To me, looking back, the Baseball Network was a reflection of the generation of Blacks who lived through heavy racism, going back to the very beginning when baseball was integrated, and made an impact on the game of baseball by living up to an impossibly high set of standards. For that whole Frank Robinson / Willie Mays / Hank Aaron generation, born in the first half of the 1930s, and for my generation, born in the late 1940s and early 1950s, it was a given that to make it in baseball you had to try to be twice as good in a lot of ways, twice as good a player. You also had to be smart, and here's the key part—you had to be smart without coming across as a threat. You always would rather be underestimated in that sense than overestimated. You were smart because you had to be.

Baseball intelligence is something you know when you see, if you have it. Numbers do not always know better than people. A smart manager, from Vic Harris of the Homestead Grays in the Negro League to Sparky Anderson, Frank Robinson, Bobby Cox, Gene Mauch, and Tony La Russa, has always sought detailed information and numbers to back up their study of the opposition. That's a part of being baseball smart. But another part is about being alive to the game of baseball in all its detail, visual detail and psychological detail and every other detail you can think of. It turns out that when you've lived years in the game, you just see more and feel more, and you learn to trust what you see and feel. Then you make the calls you have to make.

Baseball's 1987 annual winter meetings were held in Dallas, and Frank and Hank asked me to be there, along with other prominent Black players, to keep pressing baseball to do more. A lot of the optimism some had felt just after the Campanis controversy was starting to fade, given the lack of high-level hires in the intervening months. "I am totally disappointed in what has transpired," Hank told one reporter in Dallas. By this point, Hank was a Braves executive, and he and I were in regular contact. He and I were always in regular contact.

The timing ended up being good for some of us. Al's comments were a negative that we turned into a positive, and some of us got jobs. Don Baylor, Hal McRae, and I were all at the end of our playing careers and looking for new opportunities. Don's last year as a player would be 1988 and Hal's was 1987, one year after my last season. We ended up being beneficiaries of Al Campanis, as it turned out, along with Cito Gaston, who would take over as manager of the Blue Jays in May 1989. We were in the right place at the right time, but it would never have happened if we hadn't worked to make sure the Campanis controversy led to meaningful action, including high-level hires.

I was part of a group from the Baseball Network that met with Peter Ueberroth that year at the winter meetings. There was value in serving notice that anytime someone lost a job and there was an opening, we would be supplying names of qualified candidates to the team with the opening. "The man who I think can become an excellent manager is Dusty," Ueberroth said, which I didn't take too seriously, since at the time I didn't even want a job in baseball. I was there in Texas to help other guys get jobs.

As for Harris Edwards and his work within MLB, which was ongoing, he interviewed Al Campanis about his suggestions for Black candidates to manage in the big leagues. Dr. Edwards later explained that my name was the first one Al Campanis gave him.

I had a little trouble keeping up with that. If I was such a bad guy that they were pushing rumors about me just a year or two ago, why was I now being talked up as a possible manager? On the one hand, they want to put handcuffs on me, and on the other, they wanted to give me the keys to the kingdom?

— — — —

In 1987, the first year after I retired as a player, I went back to school and took classes on finance and investing. I got a job as a stockbroker at Conli-Michaels in L.A., but my main focus was trying to save the investment company I'd founded with my brothers Rob and Vic. Our company, Baker Brothers Partnership, had taken a hit in 1986 after some big changes in the tax code that year. President Reagan had been reelected in 1984 vowing to simplify the tax code, which might have sounded good in theory, but the way it went down, the Tax Reform Act of 1986 lowered some tax rates but also switched up a lot of rules relating to allowable tax deductions. What it didn't do was grandfather in the deals that were already underway. Suddenly we had a number of cash calls, phantom income, and legal fees to deal with from past investments that had been carried forward. Most of that fell on me since I was making the most. Banks asked for payment on lines of credit months ahead of when they were due. What had been legal—and smart—a few years ago, when my brother Vic was finding ways to generate us wealth and lessen the tax burden on Baker Brothers' income, was now defined as possibly against the law, though there continued to be a lot of gray area.

That set us back in a big way. Vic took it really hard, blaming himself for giving me and Rob and his other clients bad advice. I don't think he gave us bad advice. He didn't know the Reagan administration was going to change up the whole system. But he still blamed himself. Nothing like regret, especially the regret of having done others wrong, to get a man all twisted up inside. That guilt ate him up and took him to depths that he never recovered from. In my opinion, guilt is the worst of all emotions because it never lets you go. It can do the most harm. It got to where Vic started displaying erratic behavior. He would disappear for days at a time and Rob and I would have to drive around Orange County and L.A. looking for him in different hotels. They were nice hotels, Hilton and Marriotts, and we'd find him in the lobby and he'd be reading *The Wall Street Journal.* One time Rob found him in the Disneyland Hilton, and Vic tried to convince Rob he was the reincarnation of the biblical David.

People from all over town would call us with Vic sightings, and we'd go there, and Vic would be gone. He'd have moved on to another hotel. That was rough, trying to find him, especially fighting that L.A. traffic all the time. We would get calls from different hospitals and mental institutions where they would execute Section 5150—the law that allows them to pick up somebody who is clearly disturbed, talking to himself on the street corner, for example. What made it tough was that Vic was always well dressed and good looking, but he was also six foot six, about 225 pounds at that point, and strong as hell. He looked menacing, but he never harmed anybody.

— — — —

I've always believed I had a guardian angel watching out for me, and it's a belief that has been confirmed again and again. With my back against the wall—finances under pressure, my brother's mental health declining, and my marriage slowly dissolving—someone intervened in my life to help. And unbeknownst to me, he'd already done it once before.

He came up to me at the 1987 winter meetings in Texas, a gray-haired, strong-built man I knew I'd seen before but couldn't place.

"Do you know who I am?" he asked me.

"No, sir," I said.

He told me he was Bob Kennedy, Giants vice president of baseball operations. But that wasn't all. "I recommended the Braves sign you in 1967 based on what I saw at Dodger Stadium," he told me.

"No way," I said. I couldn't believe it. That was the first I'd heard of it. Bob had been a coach with the Braves during my tryout. It turned out he'd gone out of his way to recommend me to Paul Richards, and to convince them to push up my bonus enough that'd I'd sign. Now, twenty years later, he was working as an assistant to Al Rosen with the Giants.

"Al Rosen would like to talk to you about a job," he said.

"I've already got a job," I told Mr. Kennedy. "I'm working as a stockbroker in L.A. I'm not here looking for a job. I'm here to help others get jobs."

"Just listen to him," Bob suggested.

Al Rosen had been president of the Yankees when they beat my Dodger team in the 1978 World Series, and even if you didn't like the Yankees, you had to give him a certain grudging respect. (I always called him Mr. Rosen, even though he told me to call him Al.) This was a man who enlisted in the Navy during World War II and went into Okinawa on an assault boat. The military is like baseball in that it shows you things about who you really are. Mr. Rosen didn't leave the Navy until the year after the war ended, which bit into his baseball career, but he rose to the rank of lieutenant. He was a guy you'd have loved to have as a teammate—tough, a competitor, and he could flat-out hit. As a rookie in 1950,

Rosen hit thirty-seven homers, a record that stood until Mark McGwire hit forty-nine in 1987. After the Yankees, he'd been the GM in Houston until 1985, when the Giants snapped him up.

Mr. Rosen, like me, had also worked as a stockbroker, and that was one thing that came up when we talked at the 1987 winter meetings. Mr. Rosen told me that in his years as Astros GM, he'd had a chance to see me play regularly and had a lot of respect for me.

"If you did accept a job, what job would you want?" he asked me.

I told him I wanted to be his assistant so I could learn the job of general manager. I'd always admired Bill Lucas, who was the first Black general manager in baseball but died suddenly in 1979 at age forty-three. Bill's death left a huge void. There had been no other Black GMs since. Bill was very influential in my career, on and off the field.

"I already have an assistant," Mr. Rosen said. "I think you're better suited for the field."

I must have had a look on my face that said I took to exception to that, because I did.

He replied, almost apologetically, "No, I meant that I think you'd be a fine field manager."

Mr. Rosen and I had more in common than I knew, starting with using our fists. I learned that for him, it wasn't easy being a Jewish ballplayer. He had to fight all the time, like I did, which was maybe part of why he took a liking to me. We had a good talk about that. We had many fights on the Dodgers with his Astros teams, who had taken the place of the Reds as our toughest opponents in the Western Division.

Mr. Rosen said the Giants would hire me as a coach and that if I showed as much promise as he expected, he could see me as a field manager one day. He told me that I'd be ready to manage in about five years, since that was how long it would take to get the player out of me. Until you did that, he said, you could never fully adopt the mindset of a coach or manager.

I called my dad to ask what he thought.

"Go to the mountaintop and pray on it," my dad told me.

I knew I needed to get away to clear my head. Dad said go to the mountaintop, so I went up to the mountaintop. That's what they talked about in biblical times, going up there for clarity and being closer to God. I drove up to Lake Arrowhead in the San Bernardino Mountains with Vic, who was having a better stretch at the time, and our daughters.

It was one of those days you never forget. I always loved pulling into Lake Arrowhead Village, going back to my time as a kid in Riverside. We parked, and I went inside to check in at the Lake Arrowhead Resort. Just then, a whole group came in and I had to wait in line.

As I was standing there, I felt a tap on my shoulder.

"Hey, Dusty!" a friendly familiar voice rang out.

It sounded like Bob Lurie, the owner of the Giants. I turned around, and sure enough, it *was* Bob Lurie. I felt a little like seeing a ghost. I couldn't believe it. What were the odds of running into the Giants owner when I went up to Lake Arrowhead to get away and make a decision about whether or not to join the Giants?

"You gotta come join us," Bob said. "We need you."

I was happy to see him. I always enjoyed talking to him during my year with the Giants. But up until that moment, I was nowhere near ready to take a coaching job.

"Come coach for us!" he said. "The game needs guys like you."

I called my dad from the room. I had to talk to him right away about what happened and what it all meant.

He chuckled in that deep voice of his. My dad had a hearty, heavy laugh that came through the phone. I still hadn't figured it out? "Son, oh my aching back!" he said. "You went up to the mountain to pray and you ain't even prayed yet and the sign walked up and tapped you on the shoulder?" When I drove home to Calabasas, I heard from the Giants again. I kept thinking, *What are the odds?* If I had arrived at Lake Arrowhead Resort a couple minutes earlier or a couple minutes later, I might never have seen Mr. Lurie up there. My whole life might have been totally different. That was a sign to me. I went up looking for a sign, and I was shown a sign.

They flew me to San Francisco to talk with Mr. Rosen, and when I was up there, he suggested I talk to Mr. Lurie again. I also heard from

Willie Mays and Willie Stargell, who both also told me they thought the game needed more guys like me.

I was deciding on more than a job. Harriet didn't want to move to Northern California. That was the last straw. I knew right then the marriage was over. That was the toughest decision at the time, and then it took me six years for the divorce to be final. Tosh would come up on weekends. Almost every Monday, if there was an off day at home, I would fly down to L.A. Sunday night after the game and see Tosh and go to divorce court on Monday, then fly back to San Francisco Tuesday morning.

I packed a small U-Haul truck with all my albums, a few old pots and pans, and my TV and stereo. I drove my Porsche, Juan drove my BMW, which I had bought at Stevens Creek BMW in 1984 as a present to myself when I had to go to the Giants as a player, and Harriet's cousin, John "Jughead" Payton, my good friend, drove the U-Haul. I had never been without a truck, and Harriet was keeping my Bronco, along with her turbo diesel Mercedes, so on the way up to Northern California, I went to see my homeboy Clint Samuels, who grew up with me in Riverside. He had just opened a new Ford dealership in Sonoma. He asked me to come make an appearance to promote his dealership, and he couldn't pay me, but he would let me use a Bronco. So I was never without a truck.

On Monday, January 25, 1988, the Giants announced that I was their new first-base coach, joining manager Roger Craig's staff. The timing was right for me to be back in Northern California. My life was upside down, and going back to Northern California was part of my rebuilding. I took an apartment right under the "South San Francisco" sign, the same way my dad went out and got himself an apartment when my parents broke up. Strange similarities.

It felt great to be in Scottsdale in early February for another spring training, but this whole coaching thing was new to me. I felt more like a rookie than I did when I was a rookie. Mr. Rosen had a point about it taking me awhile to get the player out of me. On the first day of camp, I was supposed to hit grounders, but on my first two tries to first baseman Harry Spilman, I ended up stroking two line drives over his head. I was still wired to hit line drives. "You have to be patient," I hollered out to

Spilman. "I'm new at this!" Weeks later, on March 3, "Hac Man" Jeffrey Leonard, my old Dodger teammate, was still razzing me on my fungo technique: "All he hits is line drives, so we're running ragged."

By February, at least one Bay Area sports columnist was already talking me up as a future manager. That sounded good to me. As I told reporters in early April, "That's why I'm here. I'm not here to be a coach all my life." Mr. Rosen said it would take five years. I knew I could learn a lot about handling pitchers from the Giants manager, Roger Craig, a former pitcher for the Dodgers and Mets, but I was always careful not to come across as too ambitious or as any kind of threat. I had to be patient because I still had a lot to learn.

The best part was that I was excited about baseball again. The year before, when I was working as a broker, I didn't want anything to do with baseball. Many players leave the game with a bad taste in their mouths about how things ended, and many don't leave graciously. But I was coming full circle. Now I was back with the Giants, a team on the move, coming off a ninety-win season and a first-place finish in the National League West. The team had taken the National League Championship Series with the Cardinals to seven games but fell short. You could feel the talent. We had something going and we knew it.

I took to coaching. On Opening Day, I said, "It's like all your life you've wanted to be an astronaut, and now you're standing on the moon." I was starting over and making a living, though on only $45,000 a year, a big drop from when I was a player.

"Is that all you're paying me?" I asked Mr. Rosen. "The more you pay me, the better work I do."

"Buddy boy, you've got it turned around," Mr. Rosen told me, sounding a lot like my dad. "The better work you do, the more you might get paid."

To generate a little more income, I started doing a lot of public speaking. I even worked as a reporter at TV stations in Sacramento and San Francisco. My first interview was on the practice field with George Seifert, who took over from my friend Bill Walsh as head coach of the 49ers in January 1989. George played a joke on me. As an interviewer, the thing you hate most are "yes" and "no" answers. So George gave me a whole bunch of "yes" and "no" answers—and I was lost. Later, I interviewed Reds owner Marge Schott for TV after one of the World Series games in the Oakland Coliseum.

I was once told by a baseball executive, "Anybody can coach." That wasn't what I had seen. For me, and most everyone I knew, some of the most influential people in our lives were coaches—and not everyone can have that kind of influence. For me, coaching was a way of giving back, of paying forward all the wisdom and kindness and perspective that had been passed on to me by so many people in baseball, from Hank Aaron and Satchel Paige to Tommy Lasorda and Sandy Koufax and on and on. A lot of it is about belief. If you get your guys prepared mentally to do what they have to do, then it's a question of putting yourself in the right frame of mind for good things to happen.

— — — —

Living in Northern California again, I reconnected with a lot of good old friends. One of those friends, Melissa, later became my girlfriend. Melissa was working in accounting at the time. She was smart and good looking, a sweet girl who was very good with Tosh. Tosh liked her a lot.

Soon after I moved back to the Bay, I told Melissa, even though she had a boyfriend at the time, "You'll be my girl in a couple years." My mom wasn't going for it because Melissa wasn't African American—and because my mom never liked any girlfriend I introduced her to. My dad loved her from the beginning. For Melissa's Filipino family, there were no issues at all. My homeboys all liked her, too—Stew, Chilli, Kenny, Dennis, and Ralph. My mom later apologized for not giving Melissa a chance and said she was the best thing that ever happened to me. Melissa and I were dating when I was a coach for the Giants, and I told her: "If I ever become a manager, we'll get married." After a divorce, it's tougher to say "I do" a second time.

— — — —

We didn't do enough winning that year. We were 68–57 on August 22 after beating the Expos, eleven games over .500, but went 15–22 the rest of the way to finish at 83–79, all the way back at fourth place. When a team doesn't win, something usually has to give. The Giants decided to part ways with the hitting coach, Jose Morales, my good friend going back to when we were teammates on the Dodgers. Mr. Rosen asked me to take the job.

I was apprehensive to take over as batting coach since Jose Morales was a good friend—and a good coach. Already I was discovering there was a lot about being a player I did not miss, let me tell you. I did not miss icing daily after games or sleepless nights in pain or having my knee drained day after day after day after day, and I did not miss hobbling out to the outfield and having to outthink everybody so I could get an extra jump on that sinking liner to the gap I had to snag, even with my bad knees. I was happy never to play another inning in the outfield with my bad knees or anywhere on defense for that matter, since first base was not my thing. But I knew I would always miss hitting.

That offseason, we had a team meeting with Al Rosen and Bob Kennedy and the staff to talk about acquiring a power hitter to hit behind Will Clark and protect him. We were supposed to come up with ideas, so I called my dad.

"You don't have to go get anyone," my dad told me. "You've got him right under your nose."

"Who, dad?" I asked.

"Kevin Mitchell," he said.

"Dad, the most he's hit is nineteen home runs in a season, and he drops his hands," I said.

That did not faze my dad in the least. If he had an opinion, some thought had gone into it.

I loved Mitch. He was another Californian, born and raised in San Diego. His mother, Alma, was an electrician who worked for the Navy.

Mitch was stocky and strong, built like a running back, and no question he could swing the bat. Before he hit nineteen home runs for the Giants in 1988, he'd hit twenty-two in 1987 for the Padres and Giants, but up to then he hadn't been considered a real power guy.

"Give him a heavy bat," my dad advised me, "and have him sit back on that back leg. And tell him to drop his hands and bring them back up earlier as part of his rhythm."

My dad knew his baseball. I kept thinking about what he said.

In the meeting, Mr. Rosen went around the room asking for names.

"Who do you have?" Mr. Rosen asked me.

"Kevin Mitchell," I said.

Mr. Rosen gave me that cold look we all knew.

"Where'd you get that dumb-ass idea?" he asked.

"My dad," I said.

"What does your dad know?"

"My dad knows a lot."

"Okay, let's see," he said.

Ultimately, the Giants would have had to give up too much to trade for a proven power hitter, so my Kevin Mitchell project moved forward. I talked to Mitch about using a heavy bat, and also sitting back—sitting in the chair, as we called it. Mitch picked it up quickly. He trusted me and wanted to get better.

Mitch started hot in spring training and stayed hot. By late March, he was batting .448 with six home runs. People kept saying, "He'd better save it." I said, "No, he'd better memorize that feeling."

That season, Mitch finished with forty-seven home runs, more than double what he'd ever hit in a year, and 125 RBIs, leading the National League in both categories. He was named National League Most Valuable Player. Thanks to my dad's suggestion and Mitch's work and trust, we'd found our power hitter.

At the end of the 1989 season, when we had another meeting, Mr. Rosen went around the room asking everybody who we should acquire over the winter. I was not going to say a word.

"I know you have something to say, buddy boy," he told me.

"I don't have anything to say, Mr. Rosen," I said. I hated it when he called me "buddy boy." That was when he wanted to get my attention.

"Well, does your dad have any ideas?" Mr. Rosen asked me, and the room erupted in laughter.

Being a batting coach in the big leagues was no easy job. The job has gotten progressively harder since I took it because of all the hours of reviewing film and extra batting practice. About half the guys now have their own personal hitting coaches, but if they don't hit, the batting coach gets all the blame.

To me, batting coaches might have the toughest of all the coaching jobs. You have to learn your players one by one, and trust yourself to find a way to build a bridge, whether with a young player or veteran, to where your relationship is strong enough that you can help. What made it work for me was that it was now my job to talk hitting, and I *loved* to talk hitting. I loved everything about the mechanics of the swing, balance, vision, weight transfer, and a good hand position. I also loved the mental side more than anything, the getting-ready side. I dusted off the books I'd studied as a player—Ted Williams's *The Science of Hitting* and Charlie Lau's *The Art of Hitting .300*—and even wrote my own book with hitting instructor Jeff Mercer and Marv Bittinger, a math textbook author, called *You Can Teach Hitting: A Systematic Approach for Parents, Coaches, and Players,* with forewords by Hank Aaron and Billy Williams.

I worked with everyone, from the best hitters on the team to those who struggled. I remember talking up the catcher Kirt Manwaring to Al Rosen before the 1992 season.

"He can't hit," Al said.

"Give him to me, and I'll work with him," I told Al. I was thinking back to Johnny Roseboro. As a kid, I couldn't figure out why Roseboro was catching for the Dodgers even though he only hit around .235, but later I understood that he was a great defensive catcher who could do it all, and that more than any other player, a catcher is an extension of the manager. I saw those possibilities with Manwaring.

"What do you think he'll hit?" Al asked.

"He can hit .240," I predicted.

Al gave me one of those looks, then he smiled.

"Okay, you're on," he said. "Anything under .240, you owe me five dollars a point, and anything over .240, I'll owe you twenty dollars a point."

"Deal," I said.

We called Manwaring "Money Man," since behind the plate he was money. Nothing got past him, and he would throw out everybody. A pitcher felt comfortable throwing a breaking ball in the dirt with a runner on third base because nothing would get past him. It reminded me of my days on the Dodgers with Steve Yeager, who was the same way.

At the end of the '93 season, Manwaring finished at .244. Al Rosen tried to give me eighty bucks.

"No, keep it," I said.

— — — —

I loved working with Matt Williams, one of the most talented young players on the Giants. He could hit, everyone knew that, but the book on him was that he couldn't hit the breaking ball. That becomes a twofold problem: You have a weakness, and you start thinking too much about that weakness, and you also lose your strength, which in Williams's case was hitting the fastball. Then you're in no-man's-land, which is in between both. You don't want to be in no-man's-land. I had been there. I always had a problem hitting the breaking ball until they sent me to winter ball in Mexico to get better, which I did. I saw nothing but breaking balls down there, then upon my return to Double-A with the Braves, I was watching NBC's *Game of the Week* with Curt Gowdy and he was interviewing Rod Carew about how to hit the breaking ball. Rod said once you identify that it's a breaking ball, you have to hit the breaking ball with imagination. You hit it where it's going and not where you see it. The light came on for me. I never was great hitting the breaking ball, but I got better because I had an idea and a philosophy.

Sometimes your job as a coach is to say something, and sometimes, especially with Matt that spring, your job is to not say too much. I didn't want him to overthink. Matt was a special assignment for me, because Al Rosen was especially hard on him, maybe because he reminded Mr. Rosen of himself, a third baseman who was all business and hit the ball hard.

Spring is about getting ready. It's about working on things, not putting up numbers, unless you're trying to make the team. I was proud of the guys I was coaching. They came to Arizona in the spring of 1989 aiming to prove the team had energy at the plate and could come together as a unit. Guys were hitting home runs. Twelve guys were hitting .300 or better into the second week of March. It was a good start, but spring was spring. We had nothing to celebrate until we'd done a lot more work, but that spring was good for everyone's confidence.

My philosophy was to work up, not down. I worked with players on their mental approach and on their feet, then went from there. You had to look for the little quirks guys had and make the right adjustment, which might be big but also might be a little thing. "One guy might have to crouch more, raise his hands, wiggle his butt," I told a reporter that spring. "Most of hitting is psychological anyway. What I want the players to do is when they have a good day, let their body memorize it. When they have a bad day, don't dwell on it."

We opened the season at Jack Murphy Stadium in San Diego. I liked the top of our order a lot, and that day showed why: Our leadoff hitter, center fielder Brett Butler, spent the day on base—he walked once and had three hits, on his way to scoring three runs. Second baseman Robby Thompson, our number two hitter, had a tough day at the plate but still walked and scored a run. First baseman Will Clark, a classic number three hitter, went 2-for-4 and scored a run, and Mitch, batting cleanup, homered and drove in four runs. We won our first games 5–3 and 8–3 and got off to a good start overall, winning seven of our first ten games. By late June, back in San Diego again, we ran our record to 45–28 with a 3–1 win—and Will Clark drove in three runs with a triple, giving him fifty-one RBIs for the season already.

We won our division by three games over the Padres and were confident going into the National League Championship Series against the

Cubs, but not too confident. Somebody asked me if our power hitters loved hitting in Wrigley Field, and I smiled and said, "Yeah, but the Cubs love it, too."

Game 1 of that series in Chicago was the Will Clark show. The Cubs couldn't get him out. He doubled in the first off Greg Maddux to score our first run, homered in the third, homered in the fourth, singled in the sixth, and walked in the eighth: a six-RBI day. We won 11–3, then won the best-of-seven series in five games and advanced to the World Series against another former team of mine, the Oakland A's. Eight years earlier, I'd won a World Series as a player with the Dodgers. Now I was going back to the World Series, where I always felt I belonged. It was different as a coach than as a player, but just as thrilling.

- - - -

One thing you know about if you grow up in California is earthquake weather. The scientists will tell you there's no such thing and that earthquakes hit in all types of weather, but earthquake weather is still earthquake weather. It stays hot when it should be cooling down, like during an Indian Summer. We didn't lose the 1989 World Series because of movement along the San Andreas Fault, but it didn't help us any.

We opened the series in Oakland facing probably the toughest big-game pitcher of his era, my good friend Dave Stewart. Baseball is a game of focus. There is a next-level kind of higher concentration required to reach historic heights of achievement, the way I'd watched Hank Aaron summon that focus and would later see Barry Bonds do the same as both pursued the career home run record. "Cool Stew," as I nicknamed him, found that kind of higher focus back home in Oakland. His first full season with the A's in 1987, he finished 20–13, tying with Clemens for the league lead in wins, and followed that up with a 21–12 season in 1988 and went 21–9 during the 1989 regular season. (He finished 22–11 in 1990 to make it four straight twenty-win seasons.)

When Stew took the mound at the Oakland Coliseum for Game 1 of the 1989 World Series, I just knew it was going to be tough to beat him. Stew had the glare, of course, cap down over his eyes, but he was especially intimidating because of how he'd learned to focus and get locked in for the entire game. It made him almost unhittable. We didn't get a runner to second base until the sixth inning against Stew in Game 1, and that was when Will Clark doubled and was stranded. Stew pitched a five-hit, complete-game shutout, and the A's won easily, 5–0.

That night, Melissa and I joined Stew to catch some music at Slim's on Eleventh Street in San Francisco, South of Market. That was one of my favorite spots to catch music, opened in 1988 by Boz Scaggs. That night it was Angela Strehli with Derek O'Brien belting out Texas blues and R&B, and it was good to go out and relax. Stew and I, we knew what happened in the game, so there was no sense in talking about it. We didn't talk ball at all. We were out as friends, not competitors. There would be plenty of time for that the next day.

Game 2 turned into almost a replay of Game 1. A's starter Mike Moore held us to four hits in a 5–1 loss. It was a tough way to start the Series, especially for the batting coach, but we were going home, across the bay, to San Franciso, and we were sure it would be different for us there.

It was different, all right. Half an hour before first pitch, I'd done everything I could do to get my guys ready and took a little break to have some banana nut bread in the lunch room. That was when the ground started rumbling. The concrete above me looked like it had almost liquefied. Every earthquake feels a little different, and this one had a slow, syrupy kind of motion to it. It did not so much shake as flow, like Jell-O. It was an earthquake that felt almost gentle, but it had power, 7.0 on the Richter scale, we were soon told. I didn't get afraid until after it was over and I thought about how much steel and concrete was just over us and could have come falling down.

"Earthquake!" I called out right away, keeping my voice calm and controlled. I didn't want anyone to panic.

Guys who aren't used to earthquakes are slow to notice what's going on. Our catcher, Terry Kennedy, thought I was joking. No joke: This was a big one.

I thought of Tosh, my ten-year-old daughter. Just a week earlier, she was studying up for a book report on earthquakes and we talked on the phone.

"Dad, do you know about earthquakes?" she asked.

"A little," I said.

I let her tell me what she knew. "In case of an earthquake, stand under a doorway."

Now I did just like Tosh said. I found a doorway a few steps away and did my best to stay cool and drink my cup of coffee and eat my banana nut bread until the shaking stopped. The one thing you could not do was panic. In a situation like that, panic leads to more panic, the way it does when fans stampede at a big sporting event. "If everyone had panicked," I told one reporter, "it would have been like an English soccer stampede out there."

When the shaking stopped, I walked out on the field, because that was the safest place to be. Nothing was going to fall on you. All the players and their wives, from both sides, came down onto the field. That was a heavy time for all of us. When I heard that part of the Bay Bridge had fallen down, I didn't believe it at first. Soon we were seeing clips of the damage. When you watch part of the Bay Bridge collapse and think how you could have been driving your car across it at the time, that gets your mind going. You think, *What if that quake had been just a little bigger? What if even more people died? What if teammates of mine died?* I was in a kind of shock. I think we all were. "Baseball means nothing," I told one reporter. "Baseball *is* nothing." I never liked earthquakes. Too much unpredictability. "There's nothing you can do," I said. "It just makes me think how weak we are, how we think we're in control and we're not."

Tosh flew up from L.A. during the break in the World Series, and I went down to the Marina with her to visit Bobby Welch, my former Dodger teammate now with the A's, who had a place down there. That whole area was built on landfill and sustained some of the worst damage in the city. There was a three-story building that had shook and settled down into the mud and became a one-story building. Tosh took a picture of that and turned it in with her book report and got an A on that project.

The earthquake did the most damage in Oakland, where Stew was from. That was where a huge chunk of concrete from a freeway fell down and crushed the people below. It was like a scene from a disaster movie. More than forty people were killed under that concrete at the Cypress Structure in Oakland, but it took time for workers to dig out the wreckage pile and know how many had been lost. It was devastating for all of us, but especially for Stew, coming from Oakland. He visited the cleanup crew at the Cypress Structure every day, not because anyone asked him to go, but because this was his hood. He told a TV interviewer he was visiting the workers "honestly just to see if there is any life in the site" and added, "Maybe I'll serve as a morale booster. Who knows? It might just put a little jump into them and they'll work a little bit harder."

After the quake, the A's made a smart move. Tony La Russa made the call to bring the team down to Arizona for a kind of mini spring training to keep them sharp during what ended up being a ten-day layoff before Game 3 of the World Series was played. For the A's, the extra time was a big break. They could shuffle the deck again and deal in their aces: Stew and Mike Moore. That meant for us, Game 3 was like a whole lot of déjà vu all over again with our hitters looking back out at Dave Stewart. We would come out fighting and see what happened. My guys would put good swings on the ball. But Stew gave you the feeling that whatever it took, he was going to get the job done that day.

By the time he came out for the bottom of the first, the A's had already taken a two-run lead. Carney Lansford singled off our starter, Scott Garrelts, and then Canseco was up and got pissed off when Garrelts twice missed inside, once high and tight. A lot of these guys were former teammates, but if there was going to be a scuffle, I was probably going to be in the middle of it to defend the guys on my team. That A's club looked like a football team with Canseco, McGwire, Parker, Dave Henderson, Stew, and Carney Lansford. I stepped up out of the dugout and took a few steps toward any action that might be about to break out. Everyone settled down, and Canseco kind of rolled his wrists over on a ground ball to the left side that found the hole to put two on base. We got Mark McGwire out, then Dave Henderson doubled in two runs to give them a 2–0 lead.

Stew fell behind our leadoff hitter Brett Butler 2-0, but got him on a lazy little pop fly to left. Then Stew struck out Robby Thompson on a forkball, and struck out Will Clark, one of the best hitters in the game, again on a nasty forkball. Matt Williams got to Stew in the second for a solo shot that made it 2–1, but then the A's went ahead 4–1 on homers by Dave Henderson and Tony Phillips. We got a couple more in the fourth to make it 4–3 A's, but in the fifth, Jose Canseco and Dave Henderson both homered, and the Giants broke the game open. It ended up being a 13–7 rout.

Candlestick could actually turn into a hitter's ballpark when those circling winds died down, which was a rare occurrence. That week, there was no wind at all and the ball was flying. Like I said, earthquake weather. The A's Rickey Henderson worked a 2-0 count against Don Robinson in the first at-bat of the game and then turned on a ball and launched it for a game-opening home run that set the tone. By the fifth, the A's were up on us 7–0 and coasted to a 9–6 win.

I hate to lose. Have I told you that enough times? Always have, always will, and it hurt to lose that 1989 World Series to the A's. We ran into a dominant team playing dominant baseball. They were better than us. They were. Of course we all thought that if not for the earthquake, if not for having to face Stew and Moore twice each, we would have found a way to get back in the Series, but at that point speculation did no good. All we could do was go home and get ready for another shot the next year.

– – – –

We were in New York for a series with the Mets in June or July 1992 when I thought my relationship with Al Rosen and the Giants might be over. The Giants had a disappointing season in 1990, finishing third, and we just got worse after that. In 1991, we went 75–87 to finish fourth, and in 1992, we'd finish in fifth. All those years, ever since I'd been asked to answer questions about my alleged involvement with drugs, I was still being tested, even as a coach. I was getting tired of the hassle. Years and years of being tested, and I'd had enough. They'd found nothing.

That day at Shea Stadium, I was in the stall taking a crap, so I could pee into a cup. The guy doing the drug test kicked the door open, as if I was trying to pull a fast one and switch up the sample or something. I kicked it right back at him, and I was hot. The loud boom of me kicking the door alerted everyone. All the players gathered around. Most of them had no idea I was being tested, until that moment.

Everyone was stunned, but I'd reached my limits. My inner dignity would not allow me to continue feeling humiliated in that way, especially in front of my players who I was coaching. No man was going to watch me taking a crap with the door of the stall open. I didn't know what was going to happen to me. If my time in baseball had come to an end, then so be it.

"I quit," I told Mr. Rosen on the phone. "I quit. Man, I've been going through this shit long enough. They ain't found nothing and they never will."

Mr. Rosen told me he would take care of it. I don't know who he called and what he did, but he did take care of it. They stopped testing me after that.

– – – –

By 1992, you could feel the end of an era coming on in San Francisco. Roger Craig was a great manager who understood the importance of keeping guys upbeat, and most players loved his enthusiasm, summed up by his catchphrase, "Humm Baby!," which fired everyone up. But even positive stuff gets old after a while, and with a 72–90 record that year and talk of Bob Lurie selling the team and the franchise moving to Tampa, that was an uncertain time for us all. I didn't want to leave San Francisco and did not see a place for myself in Tampa if the Giants moved.

That offseason, Al Rosen wanted me to go manage in the newly formed Arizona Fall League. He was preparing me. The league was a great concept. You had three of four organizations making up each team, all sending top prospects. In Arizona, I had players from the Giants, Angels, Orioles, and Red Sox, like Eduardo Pérez, Troy Percival, Damion Easley, Garret Anderson, and Scott Hatteberg back when he was a catcher. Bobby Evans, the future Giants official, was my GM. That was where I met Dick Pole, who ended up being my longtime pitching coach and good friend, and former Giant teammate and good friend Joel Youngblood was my other coach.

In the Arizona Fall League, winning wasn't as important as helping to develop players in your organization and other organizations. As a first-time manager, I called Billy Bavasi, the Angels' farm director, and then Doug Melvin, the farm director of the Orioles, and asked them, "How do you want me to play your players? What do you want them to work on?" I think those calls helped give me a good reputation. They could see I cared not only about developing my own players, but also about developing theirs.

Bob Lurie didn't sell the team to Tampa after the National League voted against it, which opened things up for another group, led by Safeway magnate Peter Magowan, who would keep the team in San Francisco. One thing I always appreciated was the way that Mr. Lurie surprised us all when he sold the team by giving everyone Christmas bonuses. For me, the $10,000 he gave me was the best kind of surprise. That was close to a quarter of my yearly salary, and I could use the money.

Mr. Rosen called and told me I had a good chance to be the next Giants manager. He said he had talked to Magowan about me. Bob Quinn, the new Giants general manager, came down to Arizona to interview me at the end of the Fall League.

"The job is yours," Mr. Rosen told me. "Just don't screw it up trying to show them how smart you are."

I was smart enough to say nothing to that.

My first interview for the job of Giants manager came on December 2, 1992. Four days later, the Giants called a press conference to tell reporters they'd signed Barry Bonds to a six-year, $43 million contract. Our fates would be intertwined for the next decade, as they had been intertwined ever since Barry was born. Bobby Bonds, my childhood idol, was hired before me as batting coach. Not only did we have the Riverside connection in common, we were also part of the new ownership group led by Peter Magowan making a splash in its first week as owners of the Giants.

Barry and Bobby were kept waiting for half an hour—only to find out that at the last minute, the Giants had cancelled the press conference. There was a snag related to timing, since Bob Lurie was in the process of selling the team to the Magowan group and found the Bonds deal too rich for his blood. They got it sorted out a couple days later.

I was announced as the team's new manager on December 16, my sister Tonya's birthday, which was fitting since she'd been praying that I get the job. It was five years and a week since Mr. Rosen had said I would need about five years before I was ready to be a manager.

We had the best player in baseball in our midst in Barry Bonds. He had grown up getting an accelerated course in the game. Imagine being around Willie Mays and all those great Giants players as a young kid and watching everything they did and learning from them, and being around his dad, who was a great athlete and a great ballplayer and smart. Bobby Bonds always knew what he was doing out there. I remember one play early in my career that showcased how smart he was. Every young player wants to gun out their hero on the bases. Bobby was going first to third on a single. I was just sure I could throw him out, and I made a strong throw from center that had him by a few steps. Bobby glanced over his right shoulder at the throw coming in, then moved his body into the throw just enough. The ball bounced off his shoulder and ricocheted down the line. I got an error, and he scored. After the game, Bobby picked me up and drove me back to the hotel.

"I had you out!" I said in the car.

"I learned that from Willie," Bobby told me.

Barry inherited from Bobby and Willie a fierce kind of pride and a commitment to doing what was necessary to be the best. He took his training to another level of discipline off the field. He worked his ass off, man. It's not always easy to manage a superstar player. They're like thoroughbreds. They don't like to be ridden. You have to let them run. But you appreciate how talented they are and how much easier they make your job on the field.

Barry didn't need much help from me. He had spent seven years playing in Pittsburgh for Jim Leyland, who was a great person to start Barry's career off. Jimmy Leyland was one of the best around and had also been instrumental at the start of my career. I knew if I could continue the relationship that Barry had with Leyland, it would pay huge dividends for both of us.

"All managers are born to be fired," Al Rosen told me that year as I stepped into the role.

"Not me," I said.

Five manager jobs later, I can say: You're right, Mr. Rosen.

"And one more thing," Mr. Rosen said. "You need to marry Melissa. You're not going to find anyone better."

Right again, Mr. Rosen!

CHAPTER 10

Manager of the Year

Every manager remembers his first game. For me, it came down to a game-winning Barry Bonds sac fly to center. We were at Busch Stadium in St. Louis to open the season in front of 50,000 Cardinals fans fired up for the return of baseball. John Burkett gave us six innings of one-run ball, and my late-inning guys did the rest. Mike Jackson, Kevin Rogers, and Rod Beck put up three innings of zeroes. Matt Williams had doubled earlier to give us our first run, and it was tied 1–1 going into the seventh. I had two of the best left-handed hitters I've ever seen and on the same team—Barry Bonds and Will Clark. In my first game, Will went the other way with a double to left and moved to third when Matt reached on an error. That brought up Barry with another shot at St. Louis starter Bob Tewksbury, a very crafty and intelligent pitcher. He was a right-hander, but he pitched like a left-hander.

Watching from the dugout, like any new manager, you have in the back of your mind how much you hope to avoid a rough start to the season—if you lose the first one, you might lose a couple more, and the next thing you know losing takes on a life of its own and you're 0–10. It was my first game managing, so it was unlike any other game I'd been a part of. It's totally different when you're the manager. You see the whole game as manager. You have to pay attention to everyone and everything. You don't compartmentalize it the way you do if you're a hitting coach or a pitching coach. And you have ultimate responsibility for everything, so you pay attention even more, because any pitch could decide the ballgame.

Tewksbury got Barry out in the second with a liner to the shortstop and struck him out looking to end the third with a runner at second, which was a rare occurrence. This time, with the game on the line, Tewksbury got him out again, but Barry won the battle. We didn't need a homer, we just needed a sacrifice fly, and Barry did the job. He lofted a fly ball to left that was deep enough to score Will from third, and we won 2–1. Just one game, just one win, but it was a good way to start the season, and for me as a rookie manager, it was a relief to get my first win out of the way.

The job of manager is at heart a communication job. For me as a first-time manager, I was glad I had relationships with my players going back years and had worked with most of them closely as their batting coach. That made the transition easier for me, but more important, easier for them. If you don't get to know your players as a manager, and they don't get to know you, then you can't communicate with them to earn their trust. That's how it was for me as a player. As a manager, I tried not to forget what I needed as a player to put me in the right frame of mind to perform at my best daily. Really it all comes down to loving your players. As Bill Russell once told me at a banquet early in my managing career, the secret to the success of those great Boston Celtics teams he played on was love. They loved each other, he told me, and that helped them win. I've tried to use that philosophy throughout my managerial career. My approach to managing always started with loving my players. That came natural to me, because coming up I had managers and especially coaches who loved me.

This is what I think a lot of people might miss. Yes, the in-game strategic choices of managing are very important. Fans and media focus on what they can see with their own eyes, like the timing of a pitching change or giving a runner at first the green light to steal second. But ask any veteran baseball manager, and he'll agree that what's far more important to helping your team win are all the facets of good communication, including showing your players you know what you're doing, through the way you manage the game. That's even more true when you're a rookie manager getting your first shot.

That first win turned out to be the highlight of a rough first few games for us. The Cardinals jumped all over us the next day, 6–2, and then won again, 2–1, to take the three-game series. We flew on to Pittsburgh to face the Pirates at Three Rivers Stadium and lost another game, this time 6–5—but I liked how we came back. We were down 4–2 going into the eighth but put together a three-run rally on doubles from Darren Lewis and Barry and Robby Thompson, and a single by shortstop Royce Clayton. My closer, Rod Beck, made a mistake to Kevin Young in the bottom of the inning, and his two-run homer beat us, but my guys had shown me they had plenty of fight in them. With the talent we had and the vibe around the club, our future looked extremely bright. By May 21, we were 29–14. That was a pace I liked, winning two games for every one we lost, which was in tune with my philosophy about the importance of winning series—and always trying to win on getaway day when guys' focus can tend to wander a little when they're about to fly home. Wins on getaway day create sweeps, prevent getting swept, and win series.

Just after I'd been hired as Giants manager, I got some good advice from Joe Morgan, a confidante going all the way back to when I was a young player with the Braves. Joe told me he thought I should bat Barry third and move Will Clark to cleanup. He made a good point. There was always a thing where your best hitter batted third, like Willie Mays, Roberto Clemente, Hank Aaron, and Mickey Mantle, and your most powerful batter hit cleanup. Barry was the best hitter in that lineup and the most powerful. From a purely baseball standpoint, Barry should have hit third. But I called upon my past to think about how it was when I was the new guy in a new high school taking the quarterback's job. Barry was the new dude in school. Giving him the third spot in the order right then would have been like taking the quarterback's job at the new school and taking his girlfriend, too! Will had always batted third. I figured Barry could handle batting behind Will, rather than Will hitting behind Barry.

So Will stayed in the three slot that season, which turned out to be his last with the Giants.

I decided to bat Barry fifth so that we could have a three-four-five of Will, Matt Williams, and Barry. That choice of mine was about all anyone was talking about in the Bay at the start of the season. "Turn on any talk show, pick up the paper: Somebody is wondering why the Giants manager put Williams in the cleanup spot ahead of the $43 million man, Barry Bonds," the *San Francisco Examiner* wrote. I knew Matty would see more fastballs hitting in front of Barry. I wanted to break up the two lefties, which mattered more back then before Major League Baseball adopted a new rule in 2020 requiring relief pitchers to face a minimum of three batters. My thinking was I wanted to crowd the bases before Barry came up. They would pitch to Will and Matt before they would pitch to Barry. If they got on ahead of him, he'd see better pitches—and have more chances to drive in runs. Most of Barry's career, he protected somebody. Whoever was batting ahead of him had ultimate protection in the lineup.

We didn't have many holes. That was an era of some good-ass baseball. Bob Quinn and then Brian Sabean put together some good Giants teams. We had everything on that team. We had Barry, we had speed, we had power. We had the best defense in the world. At the end of the year, Kirt Manwaring, Robby Thompson, Matt, and Barry were all Gold Glove winners. Will Clark had already won one Gold Glove, and Willie McGee had three. Our shortstop, Royce Clayton, and center fielder Darren Lewis were in the running to win one, and a year later DLew did.

I loved Kevin Mitchell, one of my top pupils in my time as Giants hitting coach, and I wasn't real pleased by the December 1991 trade that sent him to Seattle for Dave Burba, Mike Jackson, and Bill Swift, but that trade made our bullpen. Burba won ten games for me in '93 as a long man. When he came in, usually the game was close or we were behind, but we just knew we were going to win. I had Dave Righetti and Jeff Brantley in the sixth and seventh, then in the eighth Mike Jackson or Kevin Rogers, and then in the ninth Rod Beck, who we called the

Shooter. If we had the lead in the sixth inning, we thought the game was almost over. I loved the Shooter.

Leaders are anointed by their teammates, not appointed by me. That's why I never had a captain. I would just see who they gravitated toward. Rod Beck was our closer, but Mike Jackson was the leader in the bullpen. In my first few weeks as manager, I saw guys gravitate toward Robby Thompson and Willie McGee as leaders. My time as a player helped me as a manager to pay attention to the likes and dislikes of players and see what motivated individuals.

When I was the batting coach, I would go down and talk to the guys in the back of the team charter flight, but I stopped doing that when I was manager, because I knew I needed to have a little separation, all part of a batting coach being like an uncle and the manager being like a dad. As a player, I succeeded and failed. I knew the feeling of being the hero and of being the goat. As a manager, I always kept in mind how hard this game is to play, even though the players make it look easy.

The trade from Seattle did a lot of good for Billy Swift and for us. Until then, he'd never won more than eight games in a season, even though in his last two years with the Mariners, he had earned run averages of 2.39 and then 1.99. With the Giants in '92, he led the National League with a 2.08 and also won ten games for the first time, finishing 10–4, mostly as a starter but also coming out of the bullpen. I didn't know whether to start Billy or use him out of the bullpen. He was potentially my best reliever or my best starter because he had that turbo sinker, but in the past, he'd had arm trouble. In the organization, that was a point of contention, because some wanted him to start and some wanted him to relieve. My pitching coach Dick Pole and I agreed that we'd make him a starter but limit his pitch count. This guy could hit, he could run, he could field his position—he was a good all-around athlete. I figured Billy would be my Opening Day starter, and I knew John Burkett would be trying to keep up with him. I'd been told by the organization that Burky didn't have enough fastball to be effective in the big leagues, even though he kept winning in the minor leagues. This guy won ten or more games in the minors four years in a row. Charlie Hayes, his teammate all through the minors, was the one who convinced me Burky could pitch at the big-league level.

Burky always insisted he was a better bowler than he was a baseball player, and he bowled professionally after he retired from baseball—he even won a PBA Regional Tournament in Houston in 2019. Back at the start of the '92 season, when I was still the batting coach, Burky liked a nice bowling shirt I had with embroidery. He asked me for it.

"How many games you think you're going to win?"

"Fifteen," he said.

"You win fifteen games, and you'll get the shirt," I told him.

I put the shirt in the closet and never wore it again. When he won thirteen that year, he asked me for the shirt.

"You didn't win fifteen!" I told him.

He appeared to be upset. I asked him how many games he thought he could win in 1993.

"Twenty, dammit!" he told me.

With his win on Opening Day, Burky was on his way to earning that bowling shirt, which he did that year. By the end of May, Burky was 7–1, Swifty was 6–2, and Shooter had thirteen saves. Barry at that point was hitting .394 with fourteen home runs and had already driven in forty-one RBIs. Matt Williams had even better power numbers, stroking fifteen home runs to that point with forty-three RBIs. We were playing as a unit. My approach was to just let my players be themselves and play freely.

- - - -

Spring training is all about optimism. All about fresh starts. So even when deep down you know a season might head south in a hurry, you try to lean into your natural sense of optimism. We didn't know if we were going to be good or not. The year before, we'd finished 72–90, and you never know if your talent is going to mesh. Our first week together as a team in spring 1993, I knew I didn't need to work too hard to feel optimistic: I liked what I saw. I remember standing there at Indian School

Park in Scottsdale, Arizona, that February, and just being amazed that we had this talented of a team and I was the one managing it.

I was always someone who liked giving orders more than taking them. I was the oldest in my family, and the captain of every team I ever played on, the role I was always thrust into. But it felt new and different to let it sink in that I now had the freedom to say whatever was on my mind to any player at any time.

One of the toughest decisions I had to make was when I made Darren Lewis the starting center fielder over Dave Martinez. Dave had the edge coming in to camp, but he hurt his elbow, and that opened up more playing time for DLew, who made the most of it. DLew was hustling and running hard on the bases and showing the kind of talent in center field you want to develop. A year earlier, he earned the starting job in center, but he wasn't ready and was sent back down to Triple-A Phoenix. In 1993, he wanted to stick. We called it a platoon going into the start of the season, but DLew was soon our center fielder and started 120 games out there. It was hard to disappoint Dave Martinez, a good player, easy to like, but I needed DLew's defense in center. His skill was better for the club, and even though he was young, I thought he was ready. I was once a young center fielder, too. I told DLew, "I don't think I'll ever be a dad again, but if I ever have a son, I'm going to name him Darren, because I think you're a fine young man."

I wanted my players to lean into the sense of pride they felt playing for the Giants. Our rivals were always the Dodgers, a tradition that moved from New York when the two teams came west, but I took a page from what I'd seen as a player in L.A. That team always celebrated its tradition. They would bring in Roy Campanella to talk catching with Steve Yeager and Mike Scioscia. Carl Erskine would give pitchers advice on throwing a changeup. Sandy Koufax would talk about fastballs and curves—and life. Tommy Davis, my idol growing up, would talk hitting with us. So that spring with the Giants, we had our own Hall of Famers and future Hall of Famers out there passing on what they could. Orlando Cepeda—who would be inducted in 1999—hit fungos to our infielders.

Willie Mays played catch and talked ball with anyone who wanted to learn from one of the greatest players ever. Joe Morgan, briefly a Giant at the end of his career, came out and talked to the guys. Then, as now, baseball could do a much better job of passing on its history and knowledge to young players.

I'd only fallen in love with baseball when I was in danger of losing it, after I blew out my knee playing basketball just after I was traded to the Dodgers, and it was like that for fans in the San Francisco Bay Area that year when they were in danger of losing their team. Peter Magowan and his new ownership group bought the team and kept them in San Francisco and decided to spend on building a stronger team. Relief turned to excitement. What had been lost was not lost—and fans were fired up. We were almost on a kind of mission to show that the Giants could start a new chapter that was about the fans and baseball and what happened on the field.

That spring, my friend Big Dave Donati came to Arizona to hang out. Dave, a veteran of the wine business, had developed a tradition of visiting me everywhere I went in baseball, and we were out at the Biltmore in Scottsdale one night having a nightcap. One thing I have always been very careful about is not taking the wheel if I've had too much to drink. I never wanted to be one of those guys who gets pulled over and winds up with a DUI arrest, especially in Arizona, known as the toughest state in the country on drunk drivers. Maricopa County was overseen by Joe Arpaio, a guy who called himself the Toughest Sheriff in America and was famous for his extreme measures. I didn't want to end up sleeping in a tent and wearing pink underwear, the way some who were arrested for drunk driving were forced to do, including professional athletes I knew. They especially wanted to go after professional athletes and were really on the lookout during spring training.

That night with Big Dave and my brother Vic and some other friends, I was probably pushing my luck a little getting behind the wheel. I can't say if I was over the legal limit or not, but let's say I was close enough to wonder. Vic and Big Dave left just before me, and I drove down Camelback Road, following a few minutes behind. Later when I rejoined them, they told me, "Man, some poor guy just behind us got pulled over by the cops." They had that right. The poor guy behind them was me!

There was a spot on 68th Street, near the canal, just after you turned off Camelback, with these big oleander bushes along the side of the road, ten feet high or so, and the cops would hide themselves there waiting for you. I never saw the cop until he was behind me on his motorcycle with his lights flashing. I was probably driving ten or twenty miles an hour over the speed limit, trying to catch Vic and Dave. I pulled over and rolled down my window and tried not to picture the headlines if I was snagged for speeding and drunk driving before I ever managed my first game. That would have been ugly. That would have been tough. In Arizona, they didn't mess around when it came to coming down hard on drunk drivers. I tried to stay as cool as I could as the cop walked up to my window and looked me over.

"Can I see your license?" he asked me. "Where are you going in such a hurry?"

"I was trying to catch up with my brother," I explained, and told him my brother was in town visiting.

"Well, I've got to give you a ticket," he said. "Give me your license."

Inside, all I could think was *Oh, shit!* But I stayed low-key.

"You been drinking?" he asked.

"Yeah, I had a couple drinks," I told him.

"Well, I've got to test you for drunk driving."

I kept quiet. My thoughts were racing. The cop was kind of staring at my driver's license. I'd always just had "Johnnie B. Baker Jr." on my license, but I'd just added "Dusty" for purposes of cashing checks, since some were made out to "Dusty Baker," so my license now read "Johnnie B. (Dusty) Baker Jr."

"Are you Dusty Baker that used to play for the Dodgers?" he asked me.

"Yes, I played for the Dodgers," I said.

"Well, you know something?" he said. "This is your lucky day."

"Why?" I asked him.

"I'm from L.A.," he said. "I just got transferred from LAPD to Phoenix PD. When I was a kid, you gave me a ball at Dodger Stadium."

I couldn't believe it.

"You were so nice to me," he said. "I'm going to let you go this time, but man, when you're coming down this street, we hide right here in these bushes and try to stop people."

I swear, that was what he told me. After that, I was always extra careful behind the wheel. I knew I'd been lucky that night in Scottsdale, and I was not going to put myself in that position again. I guess you could call it karma, or what goes around comes around, since years earlier I'd been kind to this future cop when he was just another L.A. kid looking to me as a Dodgers star to live up to his hopes and dreams. I always went out of my way to sign that extra autograph or give that extra smile or just hear what someone was trying to tell me, because I never forgot being a kid looking up to my baseball heroes like Tommy Davis.

- - - -

One thing I learned early in my time managing the Giants that stayed with me for years to come was the importance of having a group of coaches that were both great coaches and great people. You're only as good as your players, but you're also only as good as your coaches, since they're the ones who do most of the day-to-day work of keeping your players right and getting them prepared. You want a group of coaches who can hang with each other and help one another, but that's almost a bonus. The main thing that they are going to feel comfortable in the workplace through the grind of a long season, since you and your coaches set the tone for the team in a lot of ways.

I was lucky to have Dick Pole as my first pitching coach. I'd worked with Dick in the Arizona Fall League the year before. He was the Cubs pitching coach from 1988 to 1991, so he had the experience, but what I liked about Dick the most was he thought like a left-handed pitcher. He'd been a right-handed power pitcher, but he *thought* like a left-hander and he taught his pitchers as if he were left-handed. Most left-handers are not power pitchers. They need to use their heads to get people out. It's more about finesse than power. If you can have that mindset, all your pitchers are going to get better. They're going to be pitchers, not just throwers. Subsequent to that, I always liked left-handed pitching coaches, like Ron Perranoski, Dave Righetti, and Bryan Price, and I also had Mike Maddux, Greg Maddux's older brother, who kind of thought and pitched left-handed.

For my bench coach, I kept Bob Lillis, aka the Flea, the former Astros manager who had been my predecessor Roger Craig's bench coach as well. That might have been my best move. Bob taught me many lessons and never told me what to do or not to do, citing his experience with the Astros. He would only say, "Did you ever consider?" and make me think that possibly I had a better option. I also carried over third-base coach Wendell Kim, who would be at my side for years to come, and Bob Brenly, who would later win a World Series as the Diamondbacks manager, as my bullpen coach.

That first year managing the Giants was like Riverside reunited. We had Bobby Bonds as our hitting coach and Barry Bonds as our star player, and my dad came over from Sacramento for a lot of games. Bobby was a knowledgeable guy on and off the field, really smart, who kept everybody loose with his humor. He made you laugh. My dad loved Bobby, who always called him "Mr. Baker." My dad would sit in the dugout and watch batting practice and then go watch the game from the stands. He usually brought along one of my nephews or my brother Vic. Even when my dad didn't say much to me, he was still talking—with his eyes. He would show me with his eyes if he was pleased or displeased, but he wouldn't talk much. My dad was never a man to waste words.

A player like Barry Bonds makes your job as manager easier most of the time. I understood how much Barry wanted to win and how much coming back to the Bay Area was all about having a shot to be on a team he thought could win the World Series. Barry remained distant from most everyone, except a few. He didn't want people to know how smart he was. I probably had as good a shot at understanding Barry as anyone, given that we had Riverside in common and how much it meant to both of us.

Riverside was a whole sports philosophy, passed down to us by many great athletes, mostly led by the Bondses, Robert, David, Rosie, and Bobby. Our families were always close. I held Barry the week he was born. I remember thinking that I hoped I didn't drop him. That was July 1964, a month after I turned fifteen, and in Riverside, the Bonds family was sports royalty. Bobby Bonds was my role model even then. In Riverside, we were about speed. If you couldn't run, you couldn't play. No one ran the way Bobby Bonds did—except his sister Rosie.

Bobby called me and a couple other guys to come and shag for him when he was taking batting practice for his tryout for a San Francisco Giants scout. It was right before dark, and I asked the scout if I could hit for him, too. He said it was too dark and he had to go.

Bobby signed with the Giants shortly after Barry's birth, and by the next year, he was already making a splash in A-ball, hitting .323 with thirty-three stolen bases and twenty-five homers for Lexington in the Western Carolinas League. Bobby was playing in San Francisco by 1968, the year Barry turned four, and he grew up in the Bay Area. When Barry was ten, playing for the San Carlos Yankees, the Giants traded his dad to the New York Yankees, and a reporter asked Barry his reaction. "I don't want to go anywhere, because I'm playing Little League baseball," ten-year-old Barry said. The Giants could have had Barry out of high school, when he hit .467 at Junipero Serra High in San Mateo, but their offer was too low and instead Barry went to Arizona State University. Bobby used to tell me what a good player Barry was going to be, so I followed his progress. Here's an interesting fact about Barry at ASU. He graduated in 1986 with a degree in criminology.

Pittsburgh took Barry sixth overall in the 1985 draft, behind Will Clark (second), and by his fifth season with the Pirates, in 1990, he came into his own, hitting thirty homers for the first time (thirty-three) and batting over .300 for the first time. In San Francisco, Barry was ready to build on what he had done so far. He was hungry to win. By his first

All-Star break with the Giants, he had already hit twenty-four home runs, on pace to hit more than forty for the first time, and had seventy-one RBIs. We wrapped up the first half of the season with the best record ever for a San Francisco Giants team at the break and a healthy lead in the National League West.

Al Rosen had been right that I needed five years to get the player out of me before I would truly be ready to manage in the big leagues. But I still had enough of the player in me that I could think like a player. I never wanted to lose the outlook of a player, which I had inside me, seeing the game and feeling the game the way a player did. That helped when it came time to tell players things they didn't necessarily want to hear. I figured trying to be a good manager had a lot in common with trying to be a good person. Not because you wanted to live up to someone else's idea of how to be, but because you wanted to live up to your *own* standards. You showed people the respect to say what you had to say and not lie to them. "Why doesn't every person in society do it?" I wondered, talking to *The Sacramento Bee.* "If I've got something to say, I say it. That's one thing I learned from Al Rosen. Al would get mad at you on Monday, but when he saw you on Tuesday, it was over. . . . It ain't that hard, not lying to people."

I loved my players. We all came up together from the time I was a coach and, we were close. On the team plane, it was important for the manager to sit up front and give players their space in the back of the plane, where I was used to sitting my whole career. That was an adjustment for me. Most of my players were unmarried or getting married and didn't have a family yet, so we would hang together. Away from work, that's where you really got to know your players as people. On days off on the road, we'd all go fishing together whenever we could. Ten or eleven of us would rent a couple cars to go fishing on the south shore of New Jersey or north of Miami or wherever we might be. One time when we were in Chicago, Will Clark put a fishing trip together for all of us on Lake Michigan. In San Francisco, my buddy Armand Castagna would pick us up after the game and we would go fish the Bay around Angel

Island and the Brothers and Sisters for striped bass, under the Richmond Bridge for sturgeon, and the Berkeley Flats for halibut. We'd go right out from the Golden Gate Bridge, not too far, for salmon. Those were good days, brother.

It's a humbling experience, getting a shot at managing in the big leagues. I kept thinking how grateful I was for those who preceded me, Jackie and Willie and Hank, but also the guys who preceded me as a manager, Frank Robinson and Larry Doby and Maury Wills and Cito Gaston. They empowered me, even though managing had never been my goal. They kept me going. And there were certain pressures that I felt to excel, being one of seven Black managers in history at that point.

Every time I went into Cincinnati, I was always reminded of Jackie Robinson's last speech. Before Game 2 of the 1972 World Series between the A's and the Reds, a pregame ceremony was held at Riverfront Stadium marking twenty-five years since Jackie's first year with the Brooklyn Dodgers. At Riverfront Stadium that day, joined by his wife Rachel, daughter Sharon, and son David, Jackie said, "I am extremely proud and pleased to be here this afternoon, but I must admit that I am going to be tremendously more pleased and more proud when I look at that third-base coaching line one day and see a black face managing in baseball. Thank you very much." (Jackie made it sound like the manager was managing from third base, the way his Brooklyn Dodgers manager Chuck Dressen did, but Chuck might have been the last one to do that.)

That day in 1972, a reporter approached Jackie after he spoke and asked him some more questions. "It's a shame baseball does not have a Black manager," he said. "Frank Robinson has had managerial experience in the Caribbean. Jim Gilliam would make an ideal manager. There are Elston Howard and others."

Nine days later, Jackie had died. His words haunted me. Every time I visited Cincinnati, I remembered Jackie's prediction that he would not live to see a Black manager—which he did not. These are things I always thought about, but I never imagined that the Black manager in Cincinnati Jackie was talking about would be me. Later I would read the text of that speech for motivation and strength and as a reminder of what I meant to so many people as one of the first few Black managers ever.

When you grow up with someone as a constant point of reference, the way it was for me with Jackie, it stays with you a lifetime. I saw every movie I could about Jackie, starting with *The Jackie Robinson Story* (1950). Jackie played himself in that one, and he was cool, looking like he belonged right there on the big screen. The more I learned about Jackie, the more I was inspired, especially by the story of what happened in 1944 after Jackie was transferred to the Army's 761st Tank Battalion in Fort Hood, Texas. One night that summer, Jackie got on a bus and was asked by the driver to move to the back. He refused. At the bus station, there was a scene. Jackie had to deal with racist taunts from people crowding in on him. During his court-martial hearing, Jackie repeated that he told one of the soldiers taunting him that if he called him a "nigger" again, he would "break him in two."

"Lieutenant, do you know what a nigger is?" Jackie was asked.

"I looked it up once, but my grandmother gave me a good definition," Jackie said. "She was a slave, and she said the definition of the word was a low, uncouth person and pertains to no one in particular; but I don't consider that I am low and uncouth. . . . I objected to being called a nigger by this private or by anybody else."

Jackie stood up for himself, and he was eloquent in defending his dignity. Eleven years before Rosa Parks refused to go to the back of the bus, Jackie did the same. Later, when he was playing for the Dodgers, Jackie would write, "I had started the season as a lonely man, often feeling like a black Don Quixote tilting at a lot of white windmills." That was an interesting quote for me, considering I had studied *Don Quixote* and Spanish lore.

It got me thinking about the choices Jackie made and how much they mattered to so many others. It helped me see how my decisions—or my lack of decisions—might influence somebody the way Jackie and Hank and Orlando and Martin Luther King and Gandhi influenced mine. It's good to keep in mind that when you have influence on people, that also brings the weight of responsibility. I try to ask myself hard questions about why I am doing what I am doing, to try to make the honorable choice, like Jackie did when he was court-martialed and Muhammad Ali did when he risked jail rather than being sent to fight in Vietnam. It's not always enough to do the right thing. You also want to be doing the right thing for the right reasons.

There were a lot of people pulling for me as Giants manager, and some people pulling against me, but the people pulling for me won out in the end. Every time you get an opportunity in life, it's a chance to remember who you are. A new job brings pressure. It brings responsibility. Do you go back to what you've learned over the years and apply it? Or do you lose sight of the wisdom life has given you along the way? For me, managing in the big leagues was all about pulling together all the lessons I had learned, above all from Hank, but from so many others as well, from former teammates like Don Baylor and Cito Gaston, to guys I played against, like Pete Rose and Billy Williams, to my managers—and the Marines.

Don Baylor, my friend for just about as long as I had been in baseball, was also getting his first shot at managing that year, taking over in 1993 to lead the Colorado Rockies. Don and I had a lot in common. We'd been talking baseball and life forever, it seemed. But as a manager, he was a little more in the school of Frank Robinson, his former teammate. Back when Don was twenty years old, he told a reporter, "If I get into my groove, I'm gonna play every day," even then with established veterans ahead of him. He was just being honest. He knew what he could do. But the Oriole Kangaroo Court, led by Frank Robinson, took action, and he became "Groove." We all called him that. You'd call him on the phone and he'd answer, "Hey, this is Groove."

Don was supposed to be the next Frank. That was why he stood on the plate and never rubbed a bruise when he got hit by a pitch. Just like Frank. By the time he retired, Don had been hit by pitches more than anyone in the modern era, 267 times, having passed Frank at 198. (To this day, Don ranks fourth all time, and Frank tenth.) Groove was strong, man. We were the same kind of player, but he was stronger than me. He hurt his arm, and I didn't hurt mine, so I had a stronger arm. And when we would play basketball, I was better. Don and his wife, Jo, became such close friends that when I went in to buy Harriet's engagement ring when Don and I were teammates in Puerto Rico, Jo helped me pick it out. Groove and I always talked. But now we were managers in the same division, and I was trying to beat him. Managing an expansion team in its first years is always a tough assignment.

I had a lot of people to thank for helping to put me in the position of having the influence I did. Some managers and coaches taught me how to be and also taught me how *not* to be, which is just as important, in baseball and in life. Tommy Lasorda taught me a lot, Frank Robinson taught me some important things in that one year I played for him, and Roger Craig passed on a lot of insight, especially about pitching and handling pitchers. Clyde King, my Triple-A manager, taught me so much, too. He used to take me out all the time and throw me breaking balls. Another was Preston Gómez, one of the smartest guys I've ever been around. Coaches might have taught me the most, like Jim Gilliam, Danny Ozark, and Bob Lillis. A lot of those guys were third-base coaches, including Tommy Lasorda. And I also have to mention Clete Boyer, Billy Williams, and Manny Mota, all great teachers who taught me different facets of the game.

I would have loved to see Jim Gilliam get a shot at managing in the big leagues, the way Jackie had mentioned. Jim was always considered one of the smartest players out there and also one of the most unselfish. I grew up watching him play and loved how he always played for the good of the team. He knew what made a good team tick. One time on the Dodgers, when Jim was our first-base coach, I asked him why he wasn't managing. He gave me a thoughtful look and thought about how to answer. He told me a modern-day manager had to have a mastery of the King's English, whereas he was from the South and it was difficult for some to understand him. Jim was born in Nashville, Tennessee, and I loved the way he spoke. He had tremendous common sense, but he might not conjugate a verb right—and guys would make fun of him. I was always quick to come to his defense. Jim was self-aware enough to realize that, and he told me he probably would never get the opportunity to manage, because the modern-day manager had to be in front of the camera or a pack of reporters daily.

— — — —

The one question I get maybe more than any other is about the toothpicks. Over the years when people saw me on TV managing a game, they noticed I always had a toothpick in my mouth. It was kind of my thing. That all started when I was in San Francisco when I was still a batting coach. We were getting beat one day by a good five or six runs, and Trevor Wilson came over to me in the dugout.

"You've got to get a rally dip going," he said.

Anything for the team. I didn't really want to start with chewing tobacco—I always hated it and tried to avoid it. I used to get on Bob Welch all the time about snuff. But being a batting coach, I had nothing to lose. Wouldn't you know it, I started dipping and got all dizzy, and then we came back from five or six runs behind to win. It was like Flip Wilson used to say: The Devil made me do it! I dipped again the next day, and we came back to win again. So after that, my dipping became a regular thing. My mom hated it. Melissa hated it. Tosh really hated it. I'd go out to my truck and find my can of snuff had been filled up with water. Thanks, Tosh!

I went to see my dentists, Dr. Jim McKenna and his son Dave, at McKenna Family Dentistry in Palo Alto, and Dave's sister Judy was the hygienist. Judy told me to quit dipping. There was growing awareness then of how it could really be bad for your health. It was receding my gum line. And some players developed cancer of the mouth because of smokeless tobacco, including Tony Gwynn. Judy recommended I go to Whole Foods and get Australian tea-tree oil chewing sticks (basically a fancy name for toothpicks), which I immediately did—and which I use to this day. I was doing periodontal work and trying not to dip tobacco.

I'd keep a toothpick in my mouth to distract me from wanting to dip. The only problem was sometimes in a tight game in the eighth or ninth inning, I'd have a toothpick and dip going at the same time. But eventually I gave up snuff and stuck with the toothpicks. It was something I had in common with my dad. If you needed a toothpick, he always had a toothpick. I can't ever remember him not having one, not one single time. When I was batting coach, no one really noticed my toothpicks, but when I was a manager, the TV cameras were always on me. People saw me in the dugout chewing on a toothpick and wondered what it was all about. Asked about it, I said, jokingly, "Toothpicks are an excellent source of protein."

It's hard now in baseball to win 100 games and get shut out of the postseason—almost impossible, really—but in my years as Giants manager it could happen as a rare occurrence. You won your division or you went home. In 1993, we were 59–30 at the All-Star break and had a nine-game lead on the Braves, but there was a lot of baseball left. The week after the All-Star Game, the Braves made a big trade, sending Melvin Nieves, Donnie Elliott, and Vince Moore to the Padres for Fred McGriff, who could help them in a big way. We couldn't worry about that. We just had to keep winning.

According to one headline in Atlanta, the trade had an immediate impact: "MCGRIFF FIRES UP BRAVES." A reporter stopped by for reaction from the Giants and reported the trade was met by "sarcastic applause." I'm not sure about that. But Barry did tell the reporter, "I ain't worried about him." We were thirty-three games above .500 at the time, the best for a Giants team since 1962. I was quoted saying the trade came "too late" to help the Braves, but what I'd actually said was, "I hope they got him two weeks late." I heard the Braves put that "too late" quote from me up in the clubhouse and used it to motivate them.

The race tightened up. On September 6, we beat the Pirates at home 4–1 to move to 89–48, and the second-place Braves lost to the Dodgers, so at that point we were in first place in the National League West by three and a half games. Then we hit a losing streak: four, five, six games in a row, they kept adding up. By the time we let the Cubs rough us up at home to make it seven in a row, my frustration boiled over. One thing I almost never did as a manager was get on my team in public, but this time I did. It was "a very ugly game," I said afterward. "I'm embarrassed for us. It's an embarrassment to go out and get your brains beat out." I regretted saying that and was personally embarrassed about making that statement. I learned a valuable lesson as a young manager.

We'd fallen two and a half games behind the Braves. Unbelievably, the Cubs completed a three-game sweep the next day, running our losing streak to eight games. San Francisco columnists had a field day, talking about what a disaster this was for the city. What could I say? We had to win a game. Sometimes a change of scenery helps, and a day off helps. We flew to Cincinnati to take on the Reds and came out hot. Will Clark worked a two-out walk to get something going in the first inning against Reds starter John Roper, and then Matt Williams let loose with a 480-foot home run that woke everyone up. Billy Swift gave us a complete-game shutout, we rolled to a 13–0 win, and I gave my bullpen a much-needed rest. That win took a big weight off of all our shoulders.

We swept the Reds, outscoring them in the series by a collective 26–4, then took three of four from Houston at the Astrodome, then came home and swept the Padres, making it ten wins in eleven games. The Rockies came in for a quick two-game series, which we split, and then we closed out our season with a four-game series at Dodger Stadium. I assumed going in that we would probably have to sweep to finish in first, but that Dodger team was young and talented and you could see they were going to be good. Tommy Lasorda, still managing, was always more than a worthy rival. Whenever the protégé is facing his old teacher, the old teacher wants to keep him in line. He wants to show he's still the teacher.

We won the opener of the four-game series, getting just enough off knuckleballer Tom Candiotti to win 3–1 behind Billy Swift (21–8). The big play came in the ninth when Mike Piazza led off with a single and then Eric Karros scorched a line drive down the line that had double written all over it. Matty, with that quick first step of his, got over to cut off the shot, gloved it cleanly, and threw to second to start a double play.

Matty was some third baseman. I never saw him make a bad throw. I can't remember him ever throwing the ball away. Most important that day, the Braves lost to the Astros, 10–8, so our win pulled us back into a tie for first place. We'd been up eight games, lost our lead, and now we'd earned our way back into first and done it the hard way. That was one of the most exciting times of my whole career. It was actually fun being in a pennant race like that. You went to bed thinking about it and woke up thinking about it. That year's pennant race was one of the best I've ever been part of and one of the best all time.

The next day, there were more than 51,000 at Dodger Stadium for a Friday night game, and we held on to win 8–7 on two Barry Bonds homers. People come to see the superstars do super things, whether it's Joe Montana with a last-minute touchdown drive or Michael Jordan pulling up in the fourth quarter to take the big shot and sinking it. Everybody in the place knows what you're trying to do, and you still do it. That game by Barry was one of the premiere clutch performances I can remember by anybody. On Saturday, we won 5–3 to make it fourteen wins in sixteen games, but not without a tense few seconds in the eighth inning. Dave Hansen came up with the bases loaded and drilled one to right that felt to me like it might be out. *Lord, please no, please no,* I was praying in the dugout. Dave Martinez made the catch just in front of the fence, and my reliever, Rod Beck, sauntered off the mound like it was all no big deal. We went into the last day of the season tied with the Braves.

I had a tough decision to make. We had acquired Scott Sanderson and Jim Deshaes just before the trade deadline. There had been speculation we'd pick up veteran Dennis Martinez, but the Braves ended up getting him. I had to decide on a starter. That was a major decision for a first-time manager that could define me for years to come. I thought back to when I was on the Dodgers and we all talked to Tommy Lasorda about starting nineteen-year-old Fernando Valenzuela in our one-game playoff against Houston at the end of the season. He went with experience, the safe choice. Like Tommy back then, I had a promising young pitcher, the hard-throwing Salomón Torres. He was only twenty-one, and raw, but I liked his talent. I took him out to dinner the night before the game at a Latin place in L.A., because I still hadn't made up my mind. By the end of the dinner, I'd made my decision: I liked his chances of shutting down the Dodgers, especially with all the right-handed hitters they had. I also chose to put Robby Thompson back in the lineup to play second base, even though he was coming back from a fractured cheek bone after being hit by pitch. Robby trusted me so much that he followed my suggestion to do what my mother had us doing when we were kids with the mumps, which was to put sardine juice on his cheek to make the swelling go down.

I was banking on winning that game because if we went to a one-game playoff with the Braves, I liked our chances. I had Billy Swift ready to go on normal rest.

The Braves won big over the Rockies before our game started. That was how the day went: not our way. Salomón worked two shutout innings but ended up having a rough outing—he walked five and gave up three runs in three and a third innings. Kevin Gross shut us down, and we lost 12–1. It hadn't worked out for us on the Dodgers when Tommy made the safe choice and used Dave Goltz over Fernando, and it didn't work out for us now when I went with Salomón rather than making the safe choice and going with Sanderson or Deshaies. We both lost. Tommy gloated a little that day. He referenced 1982, when Joe Morgan hit a three-run homer off Terry Forster on the last day of the season to eliminate the Dodgers when I was on that team as a player, and 1991, when the Giants beat the Dodgers on the last day of the season to knock them out of the playoffs and I was with the Giants as batting coach. "You can tell those fucking Giants fans this is just how we felt!" Tommy said after they beat us.

It hurt to fall just short, even after winning 103 games. It hurt because I hate losing, and it hurt because I didn't want the season to end. I wanted to go to the World Series my first year managing the way Tommy Lasorda did in 1977 when I was part of that team. And I wanted to keep bringing my guys together for another game and another chance to show our best, another chance to ride out the bounce of the ball and fight through pain and fatigue to be ready to take advantage of any opportunities given us.

We'd been hit hard by injuries in 1993, including to Matty Williams, but we never let it slow us down too much. Our bench players stepped up, especially Steve Scarsone, Mike Benjamin, Paul Faries, and Erik Johnson, which really taught me how a team can pick each other up. I loved those guys and felt like they were a part of me and I was a part of them. "These guys, they played hurt, they played tired," I said back in San Francisco just after the season. "These guys would fight me if I tried to take them out of the lineup."

I was so worn out. After the season ended, I was sleeping ten hours a night and still waking up feeling tired. I would find myself going into my office at Candlestick telling myself I had some chore to do, when I knew I really didn't, but I wasn't ready to let go of the season just yet. I'd go into my office and watch the playoffs on TV with equipment manager Mike Murphy, the same guy who wouldn't let me into the clubhouse as a Braves rookie.

Finally Melissa turned to me, maybe a week or two into that offseason, and asked me, "You're still sad, aren't you?"

She had that right. "Yeah, I am," I told her.

"Quit going to the office," she said. "You can't bring the season back."

I knew I needed a real rest, I hadn't had a vacation in two years, so I decided to take Melissa and Tosh to Hawaii that December.

I was proud of how many of my guys had become better ballplayers that year and how many would be honored when it came time for the Baseball Writers Association of America to vote on postseason awards. One of the highlights of my own playing career was being named Most Valuable Player of the 1977 NLCS. MVP—that to me was always a big deal. You want to be a great teammate above all, a great competitor, the one who is most valuable to your team. After that 1993 season, the BBWAA not only selected Barry Bonds as the National League MVP but also named three other Giants in the top fifteen in that category: Matt Williams (sixth), Rod Beck (twelfth), and Robby Thompson (fifteenth). In the voting for the Cy Young Award, two of our pitchers finished in the top four—Bill Swift, second behind the winner Greg Maddux, and John Burkett in fourth.

Those to me are the awards that mattered. They also voted on a "Manager of the Year," which for me was more consolation prize than anything. I'd have much, much, *much* rather won the division than won any recognition for my managing, which is a job where you're only as good as what your players give you. They gave me a lot that year. "I'm in real good company," I said when I was named Manager of the Year in 1993. I was the second Black man after Frank Robinson to be so honored, which made me think about Jackie Robinson and his final wishes. Cito Gaston won the World Series in 1992 and 1993 and never won the Manager of the Year, and it would have been great if we could have both won it in '93, two Black managers.

Believe me, it wasn't like this went to my head, even for a second. It was the first major award I'd ever won. One thing I noticed was that plenty of guys went from being Manager of the Year to getting fired. I told reporters I hoped to stick around awhile. I had no idea how long I would manage or for how many teams, but I knew what the ultimate goals were. One was winning a World Series. Another was Cooperstown. "I wanted to be in the Hall of Fame as a player, but that's not going to happen," I said that day. "I've changed my goal to be in the Hall of Fame as a player and a manager, and this is the first step."

CHAPTER 11

When Life Throws You Another Curve

One decision I made when my first marriage ended was that I was going to organize my life around my daughter Tosh whenever I could. I've seen plenty of guys go through divorce and tell themselves they would be there for their daughters and sons. Then, along the way, good intentions get lost. Life has a way of getting in the way. People fall short. Relationships suffer. That was never going to be me, just like it had never been the way my dad was. When my parents divorced, even though my dad was working two jobs, he was always there to support us and keep an eye on us. He was there for me in high school and there for my brothers and sisters, going to recitals and sporting events and other activities.

Tosh and I always had a special bond, going back to when she was small. It wasn't just that I didn't want to lose that connection. I wanted to *build* on that connection. I wanted to take it farther, a lot farther. Once I moved back to Northern California full time to start coaching with the Giants, I tried to spend as much time with Tosh as I could. Her visitations from eight to fourteen were weekends and holidays and in the summer. A lot of times she was flying by herself, and the flight attendants would take care of her. If I wasn't able to pick her up at the airport myself, I'd send Melissa's brother James or our batboy, Bill "Red" Hall, who went on to be a major restaurateur with Hall's Chophouse locations in South Carolina, North Carolina, and Tennessee. One year Tosh would do Thanksgiving with me; the next year she'd do Christmas and New Year's. I just tried to spend as much time with her as I could.

When I was a coach, and my first year or two managing the Giants, she was my roommate on the road. It was a joy for me to share that with her. I knew these were times in both our lives we would never get back, and the more we could see together, and soak in together, the stronger our bond would be. We'd get up in the morning, and if we were in Philadelphia, we'd go to the Liberty Bell. Or if it was New York, we'd go see the Statue of Liberty and the Empire State Buiding. Or if it was St. Louis, we'd go up in the Arch. Most of the time I was going to these places for the first time, like when we went up in the Empire State Building and I told Tosh, "Remember King Kong? Can you picture him climbing up that building?" It was all educational for her but also educational for me. We would go to museums if there was time, and sometimes we'd visit a church or the zoo or just walk around and explore the city. Then I'd try to get a little rest before it was time to go to work.

That was when I really started to feel a closeness to men who were raising daughters. For me, it was only for a week or two at a time, because I had Melissa at home. We were living together by this period, but she was still working in accounting, which meant she rarely came on the road and couldn't spend much time with me in spring training when Tosh was with me over Easter break. Tosh would go to the ballpark with me hours before the game. At every stadium we visited, the people knew Tosh and would take care of her. If players' wives were on the road trip, they would babysit Tosh and could bring her to the game. There are some things that a father has no clue about. Harriet was a great mother, but some things happened during the summertime where I didn't know what to do. You start thinking about how hard it would be to be a single parent, especially as a dad with a daughter. There were times when I took her shopping for a bathing suit, and I wanted her to get a turtleneck one-piece and she wanted a bikini. Then Melissa would take her to go get the bikini.

Tosh always wanted to come in the clubhouse and onto the field, the way boys were allowed to do, but she couldn't since she was a girl. She didn't like that. And she knew me so well, she saw me looking at players out there with their sons on the field—like Bob Boone's boys and Buddy Bell's boys, or Ken Griffey and his son Jr., or Manny Mota's many sons, or Tony Pérez and his son Eduardo. I was a little envious of those guys for having sons out there with them. Tosh couldn't understand why she wasn't allowed out there on the field and had to sit around and wait all the time.

All the players knew Tosh. Later, when she was about sixteen or seventeen, I caught one of them checking her out.

"I wasn't looking at her, I promise," he said.

"Yes, you were," I said, and laughed.

Tosh was a big part of keeping me going, even through some tough times. Looking back, I'm so grateful to have shared so much with Tosh in those years and happy to have had a daughter first. A lot of parenting is being there, those moments that don't feel like much at the time, but you both remember them later. Many teams would not have let me have my daughter around the way the Giants did, and I appreciated the organization for letting Tosh come with me on the road all the time, whether it was an authorized family trip or not. For both of us, those are great memories.

Early in 1993, my dad found out he had prostate cancer, and they were able to treat it. I found out at the time that early detection was key, which was especially important for African American men, who for whatever reason were more likely to get prostate cancer—and if they did get it, more likely to die. I started doing public service announcements urging men to get annual blood tests to monitor their PSA (prostate-specific antigen) levels. I found out that in California, more men ended up with prostate cancer than any other kind of cancer—whereas nationally, lung cancer was most prevalent.

Tosh would come with me when I did some of those appearances to raise awareness, and she also came with me when I went door-to-door feeding AIDS patients in their own apartments. This was when I helped Stacey Beck and the Giants start the Until There's a Cure Foundation. It was a first in the major leagues when we hosted an AIDS awareness day at the ballpark at the end of July 1994, my second year as Giants manager. Ticket sales raised money for AIDS research, and the first 30,000 fans received an "Until There's a Cure Foundation" pin with the Giants logo on there as well.

In those years, Melissa and Tosh started to get close. The way they took to each other meant a lot to me. I'd told Melissa we would get married if I was named manager—then I changed that to we'd get married if we got to the playoffs. I was still stalling, in no hurry to get married again, since it's harder to say "I do" the second time, but Melissa was ready. Her family wasn't crazy about us living together out of wedlock, and my dad kept asking me when we'd get married. "You're not going to find a better girl," he told me, just like Al Rosen had told me in December of 1992.

By 1994, Melissa and I started planning a small wedding ceremony for after the season. We had to make some adjustments. For one, our first choice for a date was Saturday, November 26, but that day turned out not to work. My dad and I had a tradition of always hunting the pheasant opener with each other, and I wasn't going to miss that chance to go shoot pheasant with my dad and Kenny and my dad's close hunting partner for years, Mr. Phillips. Next option: Sunday, November 27. That was easy to remember since it's also my brother Rob's birthday.

We planned the wedding for Ancil Hoffman Park in Carmichael, nestled along a curve in the American River, a park named for the local guy who managed boxer Max Baer, a world heavyweight champion. It was the perfect site for our wedding, but not the perfect weather: It rained and we had to go to Plan B, a new hotel next to the American River in Folsom, northeast of Sacramento. We kept it small, about seventy-five mostly family and a few friends, like Kenny and Dennis.

My brother-in-law Eduardo was the one to marry us. Tonya met Eduardo in Colombia during her twelve years there as a missionary. I sent my dad down to give her away at their wedding, but Tonya and Eduardo had to leave Colombia, for fear of their lives, and moved back to Sacramento and started a bilingual church. At our wedding, Eduardo said, "God designed a specific blueprint just for Dusty and Melissa where one was built for the other for a specific purpose."

I had told Darren Lewis I didn't think I'd ever be a dad again, and I didn't, but after Melissa and I were married a few years, we started talking more about having a child together. She wanted a child. I wasn't sure what I wanted. I had a daughter. I went to talk to my dad to see what he thought. I would turn fifty in 1999, and I was thinking that seemed old to have a new baby, but my dad had his second family when he was around that age.

"Give that girl a baby," my dad told me. "You've got a daughter, and maybe you'll get a son."

So I told Melissa, "Okay, if you can guarantee a boy, then we'll do it."

Our baby boy was born in February 1999. My boy has always had good timing. He came on February 11, just before it was time to head off to Scottsdale for another spring training with the Giants. I always went to spring training on February 15, just after Valentine's Day. I always had my players report to spring training camp after February 15, so they could be home for Valentine's Day. The wives appreciated that.

We named the baby Darren John Fiesta Baker—Darren for DLew, just as I'd promised, John for my dad, and Fiesta after Melissa's grandfather, Pedro Fiesta. I told Melissa it was dangerous putting that "Fiesta" in there, because it means "party," but that's not anything we've ever had to worry about with Darren. That was such a joyous day for the family, and Tosh was there to hold Darren only a few hours after he was born.

From the time Darren was a little kid, he had an eye for baseball. He loved all sports, like me. He loved what he was watching, and he understood it. He loved going to the ballpark. As a two-year-old, he'd sit and watch the whole game and never get bored. We'd be at the airport and he'd slide like he was sliding into base and pronounce himself "Safe!" Darren always had great instincts about people. He'd see someone on TV, even when he was just two or three years old, his eyes would get real big, and he'd know right away if he thought it was someone you could trust. Or not. And you know what? His instincts were usually on target.

— — — —

I'd been part of every strike in baseball history, but always as a player, and in 1994, I was stuck in the middle—middle management. It was very difficult living through that. They called it a strike, but really it was owners pushing players until they had no choice. It was a sad time. We had no World Series for the first time in ninety years. That hurt me, down deep, as I think it hurt anyone who loved baseball.

Other than Matt Williams, who really came into his own that year, we had a tough season in '94. By the end of April, Matt already had ten home runs, a Giants record. He hit another nine in May, tying Eric Davis for the National League record of nineteen homers over the first two months of the season. In June, Matt hit another ten bombs to give him twenty-nine and break Willie Stargell's NL record for home runs before July.

The more talk there was of a possible strike disrupting the season, the more Matt seemed to heat up. On the last day of July, he homered twice in our 9–4 win over the Rockies at home to give him forty for the year and put him in some heady company. Roger Maris had forty by the end of July in 1961, the year he set the single-season home run record. Only Babe Ruth (1928) and Jimmie Foxx (1932) had hit more by July 31.

We were at Wrigley Field in Chicago on August 10 for what ended up being the last day of the season. Matt homered that day, giving him forty-three for the season, and we won 5–2 to pull within three games of the Dodgers in the NL West. What could Matt have done in '94 if the season hadn't ground to a halt? Could he have topped the Roger Maris record of sixty-one homers in 1961? I think he would have, I truly do, but I'll never know. Matt will never know. No one will ever know. It's as if the season were rubbed out completely, a record-setting run basically erased from memory.

At the time, I was focused on our place in the standings. We had picked up ground on the Dodgers, and I was sure we could catch them if the strike got settled. We held a team meeting at Wrigley Field the first day of the strike, and I told my players to stay in shape, because you never knew which way these things were going to go—as I learned the hard way back in 1972 when Hank Aaron told me to stay ready during that year's strike and Ralph and I just fooled around.

Anytime I was away from the game, or the game was away from me, the way it was in 1994 when everything shut down, I always tried to pivot to being thankful for the chance to spend my time other ways. It felt surreal, being at home in October, Indian Summer in Northern California, and there wasn't even any baseball to watch on TV. No playoffs. No World Series. No nothing. My coaches and I were obligated to go watch the team's minor-league affiliates. That August, I flew to Shreveport, my first time back since I played there in '69, then flew to Phoenix to watch Triple-A players, then drove to Tucson.

Then at the start of '95, we all showed up in spring training having no idea if there even would be an Opening Day, or when. I was in agony throughout those months. My sympathies were more with the players, since I'd been through so many work stoppages as a player, but that was something I kept to myself. I called up Bill Walsh to get his advice on managing replacement players, which I'd have to do in spring training after the owners decided to bring them in. Eight years earlier, NFL players went on strike and Bill had to coach replacement players for a couple games. His advice to me: Make spring training fun, to try to cut through the heaviness everyone was feeling. Even if my job at that point was to work with replacement players, he said, I could still reach out to all my regular players, just to check in with them and let them know I'd be counting on them once we got this behind us. I did just that, too, calling guys.

I'm not a man who likes to feel uncomfortable in work situations—you know, a sense of being off-kilter, off your game, reacting to events but not fast enough. That was how we all were during that time. There was no right way to be. We showed up in Scottsdale for spring training with the replacement players and Bob Quinn, the general manager, asked me to address the team. That was the last thing I wanted. I was known as a players' manager and I'd been through so many strikes as a player, so I knew there were people who had their eye on me to see where I stood.

I had many sleepless nights, turning it all over in my head and trying to work out the right thing to do. None of us was getting much sleep in those days. I was kind of told or threatened by the organization that if I sided with the players, I was in trouble. But at the same time, it was made very clear to us by the Major League Baseball Players Association that if as coaches we sided with management, our pensions and medical and dental would be taken away. That was the epitome of being caught in the middle as middle management.

I turned to my council of advisors.

"Dad, what am I going to say to try to satisfy both sides?" I said on the phone.

He mulled over my predicament.

"Dad, I'm not going to speak to them at all," I blurted out.

I could feel him shaking his head, slowly, on the other side of the line.

"Son, you have to say something: You're getting paid by management," my dad told me. "My suggestion is: Address the team and don't say nothing."

"How do you that?" I asked him.

"Make is short and sweet," he said.

"I can do that," I said.

I'd learned that from him. I said as little as possible. I stood in front of the players I'd been given as replacements and said, "The coaches and I understand what you're going through, and no matter what you do, we won't hold it against you now or in the future." Then I said, "Thank you," and sat back down. I could tell that upset the people upstairs, because I didn't necessarily go along with the company line. That might have been the worst time in my career as a manager or coach.

- - - -

The 1990s were a time for me of hating to check the mail. I'd done everything right in making investments with my brother Vic as my advisor, and then the law changed, and just like that, I suddenly owed money I hadn't owed a day before. We're talking crazy numbers. I went from owing nothing to getting notices claiming I owed millions! Clearly the

IRS had made some kind of mistake, but I couldn't get any answers. They kept upping the amount they claimed I owed and adding more years to the ledger when they disallowed tax shelters and other write-offs from those years. That pushed it up to more than $800,000 in tax liability. Over the years, with penalties and interest, that amount ballooned to more than $4 million. I refused to give in since I was sure I was right.

I asked my dad for his advice.

"Son, you've got to pay your debts and don't file for bankruptcy, that's not the right thing to do," he told me. "You've got to eat the elephant one bite at a time."

I knew he was right. From the beginning, I tried to get out in front of it, but it felt like they kept moving the goalposts on me. I can't tell you how many notices I received from the Internal Revenue Service, but the worst was when I went to the bank to write a check and the bank manager, who was a friend of mine, apologized and informed me that the California Franchise Tax Board had taken all the money out of my account—even though I was making regular payments. That was when I started stockpiling cash and cashier's checks at home, because I wasn't ever going to let that happen again. Randall Widmann, a longtime friend and teammate on high school basketball teams and now my lawyer, came to my rescue to cover checks I'd written that had bounced, and I paid him back as soon as I could.

It was a brutal time for me. To this day, I have flashbacks whenever I hear one of those ads on TV or radio talking about the IRS garnishing wages or seizing funds. I lived all that. One IRS agent came to my condo and called me the "typical tax evader," which couldn't have been further from the truth. I always paid my taxes, and on time. I took pride in that, since my mom had told me as a kid all about Joe Louis, Jesse Owens, and other high-profile Black athletes and entertainers who had gotten into trouble over tax issues.

I had to make some hard decisions. My first contract managing the Giants was for $225,000. Anyone at all aware of the Bay Area real estate market knows that doesn't buy much.

I'd taken a place in a middle-class neighborhood in San Bruno near

San Francisco Airport, and people always wondered why as manager I didn't live somewhere more high class and expensive.

"You live here?" Robby Thompson asked when he came over.

"Yep," I said.

San Bruno was just fine with me. The IRS said I had too many luxuries, so I had to sell my bass boat, which I sold to my dad, and also my beloved Porsche, the one the cat burglars had tried to steal from me in L.A. the night I signed my big contract with the Dodgers. That car was my pride and joy, but I had to sell that, too—so I sold it to Randall, my lawyer.

Most painful of all for me, looking back, was what all of this did to my brother Vic. He'd been working for years to give me good financial advice, coming up with strategies that were widely used at the time, and then the laws changed. Vic felt crippling guilt. It ate him up. I told him again and again that he didn't need to feel guilty, he hadn't failed me or the other investors, but none of that helped. I learned then that guilt is the worst of all emotions—it takes on a life of its own and can do serious harm, the way it did to Vic. He might have had a tendency toward manic depression and schizoaffective tendencies before that, as the doctors later informed us, but we never knew it. In that period, as the IRS mess got worse, Rob and I went to a number of doctors with Vic, all part of our thirty-year struggle with Vic's mental illness.

This one hurt deeper than anything in my life. It was hard on Vic, hard on his wife and two daughters, one a year older than Tosh and one a year younger, and hard on our family. That time gave me an education in the roots of homelessness. Vic took to living in different hotels, motels, and apartments, always moving around a lot, so we had a hard time knowing where he was. He was smart enough to get a disability policy and had $8,500 a month coming, so he was never homeless, really, but he'd wear out his welcome anywhere he went. It got worse when he moved back to Sacramento. At that point, he got tired of taking the meds and went through a period of psychosis. Local police that knew our family would pick Vic up off the street and take him to whatever hotel or motel he was staying at.

Vic was hearing voices. We would find him on the street, dirty, and he wouldn't let us help him.

"What are you doing?" I would ask him.

"I just got through kicking the Devil's ass," he would tell me after wallowing in the dirt.

Vic was always wrestling with the Devil. He was possessed by the adversary. I had read about that. I had heard about that. But I saw it firsthand in my own brother. When you see a person speaking in different voices, in different tongues, you never forget that. Tonya and Eduardo had seen similar kinds of things in their missionary work in Colombia. We gathered one day at their house with Vic, and Vic knew what we were there for. I thought I was worldly, but I had never seen anything like that before. Bad as it was, that day increased my belief in God even more. They splashed holy water on Vic, water they had blessed in their church, and it was like it burned him. I'm serious. It was awful. We were there together for hours, trying to drive away the evil spirit. If anyone reading this book knows what I'm talking about, then you know. If it sounds hard to believe, trust me, if you were there that day, you would describe it a lot like I am. After that tiresome, grueling day at Tonya and Eduardo's, we went to my dad's, and then Vic and I went and got a hotel room and both of us went to sleep, exhausted.

One time, Vic ended up in jail. He had no business being there, but he'd gone off his meds. He'd been out on the street and maybe because he was big and strong, the decision was made to bring him in, and they instituted California law 5150, which meant they could pick you up and take you in if it looked like you might do harm to yourself or anyone else. That was one of the hardest things for me, going to visit Vic, who had never been in trouble, at the Placer County jail. He was there a couple weeks, and we had to hire a lawyer. It was a challenging time for us all, which is one reason I'm so involved working on behalf of the mentally ill and homeless.

There were good days as well with Vic. I bought my dad season tickets for the Sacramento Kings starting in their first year, 1985, and I still have them to this day, keeping them in honor of my dad. I couldn't afford those season tickets then, with the IRS taking so much of my money, but catching those games meant so much to my family, so much to my dad especially, who needed to get out of the house now that he was retired, that I chose to take care of my parents that way, hard as it was on me financially. I always found a way. It was also my gift to my brother Vic, who usually went with my dad to the games. Vic always loved basketball. No matter what else changed with him, that never did. He was in his element next to the basketball court, and seemed happy there in a way we never saw elsewhere.

My nightmare with the IRS was another crossroads in my life, one that came with a lot of pain and took a lot of years to navigate. You learn about yourself along the way. You learn there are some things you can't do alone. You'll find friends who will step up to help you, but first you have to be able to *accept* that help. People need to know you're open to humbling yourself in that way. Some people are too proud, including me. People fool themselves into thinking that asking for help is a sign of weakness, when it's anything but. What life teaches you is that asking for help when it's hard to do is the ultimate expression of strength. I had to learn all this the hard way. I was that guy. I felt like I couldn't show weakness by needing anyone. My mindset was always: I'll do it myself. But you get to a point where you're so broken down that you'll welcome help when it does come.

So many people were generous. Reynold Victor, my homeboy from Sacramento, who ran Mercedes and BMW dealerships, always made sure Melissa had new demo cars to drive. My accountant, Jim Church, didn't charge me. My divorce attorney, Bill Hulse, saw how many expenses I was running up, so he also stopped charging me. That helped a lot, since on the other hand I had to pay for Harriet's attorney and the rent-a-judge I had to hire for privacy, since every time I went to the regular Superior Court, so many people recognized me.

My friend Walter Shorenstein, the developer who helped build San Francisco and joined the ownership group that saved the Giants, was one of the wisest men I've ever met. I'd go have lunch with him probably three or four times a year in his offices at the top of the Bank of America building, looking out on San Francisco and the Bay behind. Or I would go to dinner at the house of Walter's daughter, Carol, and her husband, Jeff, a lot of times with Larry Baer and Robin Williams, prior to his passing. Robin was real smart, and it was always fun being around him. He was always on.

When we were on the road, Walter would invite Melissa and Pat Bonds, Barry's mom, to his place in Atherton for a Democratic Party fundraiser. Every conversation with Walter was a kind of education, since he might talk about anything from Willie Mays to his friend Mikhail Gorbachev. On my tax issues, Walter gave me some great advice: He told me always to remember that tax hassles can be stressful, and that stress can be bad for your health. Walter was very good and fair to me and my family, and we shared some of the same political views.

Not long after, the IRS notified the Giants that they would be garnishing my wages except for $4,500 a month to live on. I went in for a meeting with Peter Magowan, the owner of the Giants. "What about if I loan you a million, Dusty?" Peter offered. "You can pay me back when they're no longer garnishing your salary."

I had to think about it. The idea was the money would help me be ready to pay the IRS if they started negotiating with me in good faith, which up to then they hadn't been willing to do. I'd never been in a situation like that before, and I didn't like the idea of feeling obligated to anyone. But after thinking about it, praying on it, and sleeping on it, I agreed to accept Peter's generous offer—and vowed to pay him back as soon as I could. I never spent a penny of that money—the IRS refused to negotiate, even with my million-dollar offer—and later I handed Peter a check for $1 million, repayment in full, the day I announced I was leaving the Giants.

I didn't know where to turn or what to do, but a major turning point came when I went to see Mayor Willie Brown, a family friend I'd visited in his Sacramento office from the time I was young, to get his advice—since my mom made me go see him. Willie had been speaker of the California State Assembly and then in 1995 ran for mayor of San Francisco and won, the first African American elected as San Francisco's mayor. He told me I needed to call Karen Hawkins, an Oakland tax attorney, who might be the best in the whole country at what she did. Her clients included Albert Hakim, one of the defendants who testified on live TV during the Iran-Contra hearings in the 1980s.

Karen was no baseball fan. One of the first things she told me when I met with her was that she didn't care about baseball, which she called "the most boring game on earth"—so if I talked about it, I shouldn't expect her to be interested. I told her that was fine with me, but I just might have to bring her out to a game and see about changing her mind. I liked Karen right away. She had that no-nonsense air you see in people who are good at their job and don't have to prove anything to anybody. I knew right away I could trust her—both her parents were in the Marines, where they'd met, and when it came to my case, she was like a woman on a mission.

She had some shocking information for me. There had actually been a national settlement in the law relating to the tax shelters and investment strategies my brother Vic had set up for us. Many professional people had fallen into this same trap when the law changed. Karen was an expert on the legality of tax shelters. There were dozens all under attack by the IRS in those years. What she told me blew my mind: For some reason she found impossible to understand, no one—not the IRS and not California's Franchise Tax Board and not the firm's investment lawyers—had ever told me about this national settlement, so I had missed the window of opportunity to settle the whole thing. I don't even want to think about how much I would have saved if I'd been able to take care of it then. Instead, the IRS sent me notices with outrageously inflated totals, continuing to add penalties and fees and interest.

Karen knew the IRS mentality. "Since you didn't take advantage of the settlement offer, then their attitude is they're going to just go full bore at you and not give you any breaks," she explained to me. "That's the IRS way of doing things: *If you're not going to take our offer, then we're going to throw the book at you.*"

"But the IRS never *told* me any of this!" I told Karen. "They never *made* me a settlement offer. This is the first I'm hearing about it."

"I understand that," she said.

I gave Karen power of attorney, and she went to work trying to dig into what exactly had happened. It took her some time. She reached out to the Appeals Division of the IRS, which she had often worked with before on previous cases and usually found very professional. This time she got a much different vibe. Something was up. Something wasn't right.

Now keep in mind, Karen Hawkins had a great reputation with the IRS. She was always very respectful and had friends at the agency. This was a woman who made a national name for herself defending Albert Hakim during the Iran-Contra scandal. But working on my case, she was getting nowhere. The appeals officer—who should have been quick to help, since that was the job—was stonewalling.

That was when Karen discovered the cover-up. As we always said in the Watergate era, the cover-up is worse than the original offense. When the appeals officer was asked directly about the paperwork pertaining to my case, Karen learned, he realized a mistake had been made—probably by him—and worked to cover his ass. This was how Karen explained it to me: "He figured out something had gone awry, and he started covering up the fact that they had not made you that offer, that they never sent you any notice of the settlement, and never gave you the opportunity to resolve your case almost five years earlier. And instead of just saying, 'Oh, yeah, we screwed up,' and backing it all up and working with you to resolve it, they hid it." The more Karen pushed them for information, the more it occurred to her that "somebody was not playing straight."

Like I said, both Karen's parents were Marines. This was not someone you messed with. As it happened, Karen had a friend, Nina Olson, who served as the United States Taxpayer Advocate and the head of the Office of the Taxpayer Advocate. If the IRS didn't offer answers, Karen was ready to go all the way—she was ready to fill what's called a 911 request and take up my case with the Taxpayer Advocate, which was going to make the IRS look bad, most likely, but might at least bring my long nightmare to an end.

— — — —

Darren and me during batting practice at
Wrigley, my first year in Chicago, 2003.
Phil Velasquez / Chicago Tribune

Me, Darren, and Hank during the national anthem
in Cincy at the Civil Rights Game.
Greg Rust / Courtesy of the Cincinnati Reds

In my vineyard.

Me and Darren
pheasant hunting.

In Alaska.

Left to right:
Dad, Rob, me, and Darren.

Left to right: Hank Aaron,
Tosh, and Melissa.

With Buddy Guy.

Me, Joe Babich, Darren, and Melissa (*left to right*, Tosh taking the picture), after my stroke, on the plane owned by Cincinnati Red's owner Bob Castellini.

My sister Tonya and brother-in-law Eduardo Orzo, Colombian ministers.

With Tosh at her wedding in the backyard under the sycamore tree as she always wanted.

Sandy Koufax and me.

With Cheyenne elder Dennis Limberhands in Montana.

The Baker boys (*left to right*):
Rob, me, Vic, and Millard (youngest).

Me, while manager of the Washington Nationals, and Jerry Kapstein, agent and friend, after Jerry's retirement.

Left to right: Hank Aaron, Ambassador Andrew Young, me, Frank Robinson, and George Santiago.

With President Obama in the Oval Office.

Fishing with Darren in Alaska.

Bryce Harper, Vin Scully, and me (*left to right*) before a game at Dodger Stadium.

Darren Lewis with namesake Darren Baker and me (*left to right*) at a Cal State event. Both Darrens played baseball at and graduated from Cal.

Me and Kenny, my friend from Riverside Elementary School, duck hunting in Sacramento rice fields.

Cardboard cutouts of Darren and my grandson, Nova, during Covid.

Anne M. Drysdale, Bill Russell, actor, Kareem Abdul-Jabbar, me, Matt Kemp, and Hank Aaron (*left to right*) at the Frank Robinson memorial, Dodger Stadium.

Opus One visit: Thomas Moorehead, me (*back row, left to right*); Billye Aaron, Joyce Moorehead, Dr. Max (Billye's nephew) and his wife (*middle row, left to right*); Hank Aaron (*front*).

Me, Melissa, and Snoop (*left to right*) before a concert at Thunder Valley Casino Resort, Sacramento.

Mark Wahlberg, Travis Scott, and me (*left to right*) in the Astros clubhouse.
Courtesy of the Houston Astros

Lil Wayne and me in the Astros locker room.
Courtesy of the Houston Astros

Left to right: Sylvester Jackson, Dave Stewart, me, Rene Lachemann, Huey Lewis, and Bobby McFerrin in San Francisco.

Astros World Series victory parade. Astros owners Jim and Whitney Crane with me and Melissa.
Carmen Mandato / Getty

Astros pennant-clinching night.
Courtesy of the Houston Astros

With Melissa on the All-Star Game red carpet, Seattle.
Mary DeCicco / Getty

All Del Paso Heights brothers and sisters and Dennis Kludt.

Partners in Baker Family Wines: Me with the winemakers, Polly and Chik.

Me and Darren exchanging lineups in spring training.
Courtesy of the Houston Astros

With Oscar Robinson (*third from left*), David Donati (*third from right*), Sam Jones (*second from right*), and friends.

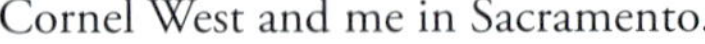

Cornel West and me in Sacramento.

I look back at my life now, past my seventy-fifth birthday, and I ask myself hard questions. Why have I been so fortunate in always having a guardian angel? Why have so many individuals, so many wise men and women of character, gone out of their way not only to help me but to teach me? It's a question that weighs heavier on me as I think about my life left on this planet. I always loved that Bob Marley tune "Stop That Train." Believe me, I've had times where the train felt like it was pulling into the station to pick me up. It didn't stop for me. But it sure has stopped for a lot of people I love. I feel the truth of that Tupac song "Death Around the Corner." My time will come. It won't be too long, as Bob Marley sang, whether I'm right or wrong. True that, but I'd rather be right about more than I'm wrong. And one thing I know is all the people who helped me so much and gave me so much must have done that for some larger reason.

My friend and mentor Bill Walsh told me long ago that you needed to avoid staying in one place, in one job, too long. Bill said that about every five to ten years, it was time for a change. Things can get stale. People come to take you for granted, and maybe you take them for granted, too. A change of scenery does you good. Fresh challenges keep you alive and make you stronger and smarter. I had Bill's words in mind in San Francisco, where in the end I would manage for exactly ten seasons after coaching for five, and even now I think about the wisdom of looking for new ways to make a difference and reach people. Maybe I'm here not only to hit a baseball, and manage baseball teams, but also to show people you can keep your soul strong and joyful into your seventies and eighties and beyond and find a way to connect enough with younger people to let a little life wisdom come through now and then without sounding like some old guy telling stories that no one wants to hear. And in our time of lack of respect for age, with everything being about shoving the old out of the picture, it gives what I'm doing maybe a little more importance. Some of my role models have always been musicians, like my friends John Lee Hooker, Elvin Bishop, Buddy Guy, Ronnie Laws, and Miles Davis. They lived their lives through their music and always wanted to keep playing music as late in life as they could.

Bill Walsh and Al Attles were two heavy dudes who passed so much on to me, I could write a whole book just about them. If I had to distill down the teachings of Bill Walsh, it would probably start with prepare, prepare, prepare, and always think about people as people and find ways to let them teach themselves how to succeed. Bill and I kept in touch regularly over the years. I was the only one from baseball Bill invited to take part in the mentoring sessions he offered to young African Americans in coaching whom he saw as having potential—like Lovie Smith and Marvin Lewis, who would both go on to be NFL head coaches, and Tyrone Willingham.

Even before the Giants hired me as manager, Bill invited me over to his house in Palo Alto and we went through rehearsals of how to handle different questions and situations. He stood next to the grease board and wrote down key words. That was very helpful in helping me prepare to manage. It also taught me about life. Bill told me you have to stay busy, because you can only fish and hunt and play golf so much. Most men get depressed because they get to a certain age and two-thirds of their lives has been filled up with work, and when work is gone and they try to fill up that two-thirds, they can't do it.

Bill earned national fame with his innovative West Coast Offense, and he was known for scripting at least the first ten offensive plays of a game, which he could do because he had spent so much time thinking through every possibility and studying the other team. He was influential on other coaches, and a lot of what he did now seems just like what you expect, since a lot of teams do it, but he was innovative and groundbreaking and always a fresh thinker.

When Bill passed in 2007, it was a big loss. I felt a void, one that was filled a little when I found out Bill had left many of his papers to me—I still have them, notes he took on preparing for meetings, an entire blueprint on how Bill Walsh built the 49ers organization as both head coach and GM. Bill left me the actual cue cards he would use when he was building a culture of winning. He and I would talk about life, and he would write on the grease board to help me think through a problem or situation. Sometimes I pull out those cue cards he left me and read through them like I'm back at school with Bill again.

Here are some my favorites, starting with one from December 1982.

What You're Going to Get

1. Demanding complete concentration at all times
2. Every attention given to detail preparation
3. Continual exchange-communication between players on game plan
4. Complete team involvement in all drills—that make up the practice—special teams—servicing
5. Hard work—complete physical commitment—as the drills dictate
6. Complete study of opponent individuals—team style—personality
7. Commitment to highest standard of play in NFL
8. Out hit—strike quicker—harder—swifter than opponent
9. Continuous sell out effort regardless of score
10. Poise—clear head—concentration on yourself—being a great performer

Loser's Explanations

- Don't find fault with 49ers—use it as reason you are performing
- Don't use teammates as fall guys—they're not performing—why bother?
- Don't distract teammates with your bitches-complaints of coaches, management, etc.
- Coaches failed—stupid direction-decision—why should we put out—they lost it
- Nobody told me
- Coaches don't care—look how they cut players
- It's a business
- The strike and its recriminations—how it has destroyed the season
- Don't go to—can't work with the man—treats me like a dog. Just can't talk to the man.

Standard of Performance

- You have a stake—investment in regard to time spent.
- First minute and last minute must be identical regardless of scoring situation-seasonal circumstances.
- Opponent should be considered as object rather than personality.
- Take pride in execution and victories will follow.
- Prepare decisively and specifically. Must be prepared for all circumstances—have poise and confidence for all game situations.
- Can't let up—be confused—disoriented.
- Don't concern yourself over teammate's failure.
- Don't lose concentration because of previous failures on previous plays. Examples.
- No frustration because of continuing lack of results. Examples.
- Score not a factor—can reverse itself quickly. Examples.

I include these lists of Bill's because they give you the flavor of how his mind worked. They hint at the man's unique thoughtfulness and consideration. But in a way, I'm almost doing an injustice to Bill's brilliance. He used these lists and bullet points to give talks that brought the ideas home—and they stayed home. His focus was so intense. He saw and noticed and could come through with just the right detail to get an idea across. Hank taught me to be smart enough to pay attention and remember so I could figure out later on what a given lesson actually meant. Bill took that forward to looking at football and performance and life as facets of some larger whole that you can keep studying forever because there's always more to see.

Bill for years had been part of what I thought of as my Grand Council of advisors, like a brain trust, guys I could call to talk through a problem or situation: Besides my dad and Bill and Al Attles, the Grand Council included Hank and Willie, Joe Morgan, Orlando Cepeda, and Sandy Koufax, and also Willie Horton, who won a World Series as a left fielder for the Tigers in '68 and coached with the White Sox and Yankees. I would ask certain members of my Grand Council certain questions.

Maybe I would be having a hard time getting through to a player, or might even have had a heated discussion with a player, and I would call Al or Bill and get their advice. I used to call Al when I felt like I was caught in the middle of something with the front office. I had a great situation managing the Giants, but nothing is always cherry. Stuff comes up. Al had a way of putting things into perspective for me.

"Al, how come they don't load me up like they load up some managers, with a shoe-in team?" I asked Attles one time.

"Why would they do that when they know you can win with less?" Al told me. "Why do more? And Dusty, keep in mind, then you can be blamed if they don't win."

For some things, I would go beyond my council of advisors. I might call the writer Leonard Koppett, author of *A Thinking Man's Guide to Baseball.* How's this for a life story? Leonard was born in Moscow in 1923, then Leonid Kopeliovitch, and when he was five his family left the Soviet Union and ended up settling in the Bronx, a block away from Yankee Stadium. Sometimes geography really is destiny. Leonard started a lifelong love affair with baseball and the ways that thinking about baseball taught you about life. He was always a valuable sounding board. Through Leonard, I met Dr. Bill Gould at Stanford, one of the top law professors in the country, a specialist in labor law who worked in the Clinton administration in charge of the National Labor Relations Board. Dr. Gould used to have us all to Stanford to talk to his sports law students, Bill Walsh and Al Attles and me, and sometimes Willie Mays or a sports agent like Bill Duffy. I went with Al and Leonard a number of times, and those students asked some good questions. I always came away feeling like I'd learned as much from them and their inquisitiveness as they ever learned from me.

I needed their help anytime I was at a crossroads. I wasn't always ready to hear what they might have to tell me—or show me. Some of it was forced on me and I learned from it later, as Hank hoped I would. I feel sorry for those who can't retain. Back in the day, if you couldn't accept advice as a young baseball player, they would stop telling you anything. The veterans wouldn't force anything on you, but they would give it to you if you sought it freely. Even guys on other teams, if you were open, if you showed you were listening, they might give you some good advice—but they'd do it after the last game of a series before you left town or they left town, so you couldn't use it against them. I'd go immediately to the phone after the last out of the last game of a series to call over to the other clubhouse before they had time to hit the shower and ask, "What you got?" I can remember getting great tips from Tony Pérez, Willie Stargell, Bob Watson, and Darren Johnson, who had been my teammate when I was starting out with the Braves but was later a hitting coach for the Phillies. They weren't going to give you something to beat them, but maybe you'd beat up on somebody else and it might be one of their rivals.

— — — —

I started getting regular checkups after my dad got cancer, then I was doing PSAs to help other men get screened, but while I was helping other men, I was helping myself in turn without knowing it. One of the most unbelievable moments in a person's life is when you're told you have cancer. It's just total disbelief. After the 2001 season, the Giants doctor noticed in my routine checkup that my PSA (prostate-specific antigens) level had increased, and they sent me to Dr. Reggie Rector, whom I've since recommended to many people.

I'd been tracking my PSAs for years at that point. One thing good about baseball is you know you're going to get a full checkup twice a year, and then you can provide a baseline. I was at 1.5, and then 1.7, and then 2, and then suddenly in 2001, it jumped two more points to 4. Dr. Rector told me I needed to get a biopsy.

I was shocked when the results came back positive and they told me it was an aggressive cancer. I flat-out did not believe it.

"Really, are you serious?" I asked Dr. Rector.

I didn't feel sick. I felt great. I had no symptoms. I didn't have any trouble urinating. I didn't have any trouble doing *anything*.

Dwayne Kurisu, a part-owner of the Giants at the time who is still a friend, organized Hawaii Winter Baseball and flew us to Honolulu for a youth clinic. On the way, Melissa was flipping through the in-flight magazine and reading about how Kauai was not only the Garden Island but also the Healing Island with a spiritual power that can build inside of you. We visited that year, and I knew after that I was going to be all right. We've visited every year since for twenty-four years.

I love Kauai, as green and peaceful a place as you will ever visit. You'll see postcards that say "Garden Isle," but for me, I love the rugged feel of the island, Waimea Canyon and the Na Pali Coast—both just take your breath away with their rugged beauty. It's a place that makes you feel more alive. I visited the Lawai Healing Center and met Lynn Muramoto, the founder of the center and its caretaker, whom I've sent many people to over the years to speed their recovery. The Lawai Healing Center is a special place, a little up from Poipu on the southern coast of the island, next to Kalaheo. It's serene and powerfully spiritual and welcoming, a place where love of nature powers the kind of long, slow smile that starts from deep within. As Lynn likes to say, "This is a place for all people, a sacred place."

That November 2001 visit to Kauai turned into a deeply spiritual experience for me. I walked up a mountain that had a series of cutbacks in the trail as you hiked upward. Each had its own shrine. The switchbacks reminded me of my life, the times when your progress is smooth and straightforward, like my life in L.A. for a period of time, and then parts that are bumpy and your climb is steep. I was walking along a path on that mountain. In Hawaii, especially Kauai, it can be sunny and clear one minute and a few minutes later, suddenly it's raining. That day the rain started falling, only I didn't get wet. I saw the rain coming in the distance, the way you do in Hawaii. I sat down underneath a big tree whose branches formed a canopy above me, and I didn't get a drop of water on me. The big tree was lifting up at just the right angle to block me from the rain, and it gave me the feeling of being sheltered from the storm. The downpour passed me by. It felt like a statement from the universe to me. Then I continued on my journey, walking up one side and then back down the other, and as I looked up the mountain, I saw a bright, massive rainbow. It felt like that big green mountain was smiling down on me, and I was just overcome with this feeling that everything was going to be all right. God was talking to me. He was letting me know that he would protect me.

When we returned to San Francisco, Melissa and I talked over my treatment options. She had lost her mother to cancer the year before. The doctors said I could choose between going through radiation treatment or having surgery to remove my prostate, or doing nothing to wait and see. "Wait and see what?" I asked them. "Wait and see if it's going to kill me?" I also knew from my work with the Prostate Cancer Foundation that African American men are not only more likely to be diagnosed with prostate cancer, but for whatever reason we're also two and a half times as likely to die from it.

"Honey, we have to be aggressive," Melissa told me. "I can't lose you. I just had our child, and I just lost my mother to cancer a year ago."

They operated on me at Stanford Hospital on Monday morning, December 17, 2001, and Dr. Joseph Presti removed my prostate. My surgery lasted about three hours. They biopsied nearby lymph nodes and found no sign of the cancer having spread. I had to take it slow after the surgery. I couldn't even travel and didn't take any trips for more than two months. The first time I got on a plane after the surgery was to go to Las Vegas with Ellis Burks, who invited me to meet him in Vegas to watch the Super Bowl between the Patriots and the Rams in early February 2002. That trip really picked me up, and I'm thankful to Ellis to this day.

I've come to see my cancer as a blessing. It made me a better person and gave me a more grateful outlook on life. I came to find out that both my grandfathers died of prostate cancer. I never knew them. I didn't even know until my auntie told me that was on their death certificates. Two of my uncles, as well, died when they were in their forties. But back then, they didn't have early detection. Coming through prostate cancer put me on a mission to make sure I remind people of the importance of regular monitoring of their PSA levels to establish a baseline. You ask yourself what causes cancer. Is it our diet? Our atmosphere? The water we drink? After my operation, I read that tofu and broccoli are high in antioxidants. Since I wasn't able to do anything, I was cooking every day, and I was putting tofu into everything I cooked, tofu and collard greens, tofu and broccoli, tofu and beans, tofu and everything. I got tired of eating broccoli.

Most of all, I felt much gratitude to God. I felt a fresh love welling up in me for the world around us. If you can pull yourself away from being encompassed with work all the time and refrain from feeling sorry for yourself, you can start to see the world around you again. I saw the stars that I hadn't paid attention to in years. Do you ever do that? Just stand still on a quiet night and stare up at the familiar outline of Orion and its belt, or just check the location of the Big Dipper and follow it to the Little Dipper to see if the North Star is where you thought it was? Or the planets. I love when Venus is rising, bright in the low sky, right next to a big crescent moon. I started paying more attention to birds again, watching them and listening to them. I noticed the different bird sounds the way I did when I was a kid when I listened closely to them. I could mimic every bird sound going. My family was always very important to me, but after that I took every single day as a gift of time with them. I knew I had a lot to live for.

CHAPTER 12

Eight Outs Away

I think it was the music that got me through that night in October 2002. I went back to our team hotel in Anaheim the night after we lost to the Angels in Game 6 of the World Series, as tough a loss as any in my lifetime in sports. I went up to my suite and tried to sleep, but sleep wanted nothing to do with me. I knew I couldn't just lie in bed staring at the wall. So I put my clothes back on and went down to the lobby, just to show myself and to help me think some things through. I ordered myself a single malt Scotch with one big rock and sat alone for a while at a small cocktail table near the little baby grand piano in that Anaheim hotel lobby. There were a lot of people down there, including a lot of sportswriters I knew, but everyone left me alone with my thoughts.

Dave Sheinin of *The Washington Post* was there in hotel lobby that night. Dave, a big, barrel-chested guy, trained as an opera singer, and it got to be a thing where at the winter meetings or All-Star Game or World Series, anytime baseball people were all gathered together, if there was a lobby piano, then Sheinin was going to be tickling the ivories and singing late into the night. That dude has a good voice.

That night in Anaheim, Sheinin started playing, and I could see him giving me little looks, just kind of wondering if I was all right. Then we started talking in music. Or maybe he was talking in music and I was listening. I started moving my shoulders to the beat, clapping a little, even singing along here and there. How can you not sing along to "Love Train"?

I knew Sheinin was talking to me directly, with a friendly wink, when he started playing those haunting, upbeat opening chords to "Midnight Train to Georgia." Then he sang the opening line: "L.A. . . ." And the pause, then: ". . . proved too much for the man." At that point, he definitely had to give a little nod my way, and I nodded back. I love that song, *always* loved that song and Gladys Knight & the Pips, whom I'd seen many times in Atlanta. Music can put the truth out there and do it with beauty: "But he sure found out the hard way / That dreams don't always come true."

Lou Rawls for me was the sound of my childhood, my mom's favorite. That night, Sheinin checked in with a little Lou Rawls, "You'll Never Find Another Love Like Mine"—"Whoa, I'm not braggin' on myself, baby, but I'm the one who loves you," Sheinin sang, "And there's no one else!" And when he sang, "No one else!" again, I sang it with him.

Maybe it was that tune, that night, that brought me back. I knew that teams that lost Game 6 the way we'd lost that night, having a big lead with eight outs to go, often had a hard time bouncing back the next day. We still had one more game to play. We weren't done yet. I stuffed a fifty-dollar bill in the little tip jar they'd put on top of Dave Sheinin's baby grand and thanked him, then went upstairs and fell right asleep.

One thing that always stayed with me about that Game 6 loss was the look on team owner Peter Magowan's face. Peter had a genuine love for baseball and for winning. I can still see his face when I walked off the mound that night after taking Russ Ortiz out of the game. I looked right at him, in the front row, and I could see how much he wanted to win that game. He didn't say anything, but I could see he was thinking: *Did I do the right thing?*

– – – –

I went from winning 103 games in 1993 in my first year as Giants manager to winning fifty-five a year later because of the short season. If not for the strike, I still think we would have found a way to catch the Dodgers in 1994 and win the NL West—we were only 3.5 games back, but the season ended early. We were stuck at 55–60. Then came the replacement-player spring of 1995 and a weird season where we finished ten games under .500. That was when I made the mistake of telling my dad it couldn't get much worse.

"Don't say that, son," he said. "It can always get worse."

I didn't realize how true those words were. In 1996, we finished in last place at 68–94, just trying to avoid losing 100 games, an ordeal of a season. But that was the price of having lost so much talent, which we couldn't keep after the strike cost the organization so much money. If we could have kept that team together, we might have won four or five years in a row. It wasn't to be. Billy Swift and Kirt Manwaring went to Colorado. John Burkett and Will Clark ended up with Texas. Then we traded Robby Thompson and Matt Williams to Cleveland, where Kevin Mitchell also ended up, and we got Jeff Kent back for Robby and Matt. Jeff was a hell of a player and helped us win many games batting behind Barry Bonds. (Jeff Kent and Barry Bonds both deserve to be in the Hall of Fame.) We traded Darren Lewis and Mark Portugal for Deion Sanders, whom we only kept for part of a season. Rod Beck was a Chicago Cub. And Royce Clayton a St. Louis Cardinal. I had players all over the league.

Those were tough times, on and off the field. My tax issues were coming down hard on me, and I was trying to channel what Pete Rose had told me about baseball being your sanctuary, but the baseball was rough. We were so bad that Deion only stayed a third of a season before moving on, even though in San Francisco he could play for both the 49ers and the Giants. For that short time, I loved managing Deion. Not only a great athlete, he was one of the most polite, talented people I'd ever met, and he was very good to everybody. He was no trouble.

I'll never forget one evening when I was at Sweetwater in Mill Valley to catch some music after a Sunday day game. This must have been July or August of 1996. I was hanging out, trying to unwind a little, when a young guy came walking up to me and looked me in the eye, real serious.

"If you don't win this year, we're going to get rid of you," he told me.

Damn! Let me listen to the music! Then in 1997, we were good again. A lot of that had to do with Brian Sabean, who took over as general manager after the '96 season at age forty. Bob Quinn hired Sabean in late 1992 as his assistant general manager, luring him away from a good job as the Yankees' vice president of player development. Those two worked closely together for years. Sabean, first hired by the Yankees in 1985 as a scout, obviously saw potential for the Giants and for himself in moving to San Francisco to rebuild the farm system. Before long, he was a GM-in-waiting.

One thing I did early in my time as Giants manager was ask around about whether the organization had some kind of team handbook. When I joined the Dodgers, they told me about the book they'd put together, *The Dodgers' Way to Play Baseball.* At first, I kind of laughed it off. But when I overthrew the cutoff man one time, I got an earful from Davey Lopes and Bill Russell.

"We don't play like that here," they told me.

"You don't tell me what to do," I told them.

I thought about it and realized I was wrong. That was when I went home and read *The Dodgers' Way.*

Now I wanted something similar with the Giants. Something like that apparently already existed, though no one ever read it, so with the help of Brian Sabean and others, I dusted it off, freshened it up, and shared it with our players. It boiled down to: Play the game right. Good fundamental baseball. And we started implementing that throughout the system.

It was all part of trying to build an identity, a culture of baseball, where guys wanted to do the extra things that win ballgames. We'd finished in second place my first two seasons managing the Giants, then twice in the cellar, but in '97 our ninety-win season was enough to win the division. It was my first postseason managing. We flew to Miami to open our National League Division Series against the Marlins. I couldn't believe all the people who reached out to wish me well, from Don Baylor, Gary Mathews, and Al Rosen to Robby Thompson, Matt Williams, and Royce Clayton.

I wasn't tight—I wouldn't put it that way—but managing in your first postseason, that's a trip. You realize that you played 162 games to get to that moment. It's a step into something you really can't prepare for fully, obviously magnified if you go all the way to the World Series, when all of baseball is focused on everything you do, but as soon as you're in the playoffs, the game comes at you different. It's a little faster. You have to slow it down a little more. I had read where Joe Torre and Don Zimmer talked about how you have to *think* of slowing it down the deeper you get into October games.

I was pleased but not surprised to be there. That's why you play the season, to go to the playoffs. The one thing I didn't like was starting the series in Miami. We had home field advantage, so if it had gone five games, we would have hosted three games at home—but the Marlins got to host the first two games. We knew it wasn't right, the way the series format was set up. You try to put it out of your mind, but it's there somewhere. The rhythm was all wrong. Instead of opening in front of our home fans, we were there in Florida, and lost two one-run games. We were going against a very good manager in Jim Leyland, my confidante and also formerly Barry's manager with the Pirates. By the time the series moved back to San Francisco, we were already down two games. We went up 1–0 in Game 3 on a Jeff Kent home run, and that was where it stood when Devon White came up in the top of the sixth inning with the bases loaded. I could have brought in a right-hander to turn Devon around, but I thought he was a better left-handed hitter than a right-handed hitter, and my starter, Wilson Alvarez, was dealing, so I left him in there. As soon as his drive left the bat, I could tell by the sound it was gone. That took the air out of the building right there. Devon's grand slam to left carried Florida to a 6–2 win and a sweep. After that, we would have to wait three more years to get back to postseason play.

— — — —

When I think back on the night of December 31, 1999, my mind kind of races. In the San Francisco Bay Area and especially Silicon Valley, everyone kept talking about something they were calling the Y2K bug. Sounds like a bad science fiction movie, right? Like worse than *The*

Andromeda Strain? It was supposed to be the end of the world, pretty much. Everything was going to come crashing down, all kinds of experts kept telling us. I never believed it, but I was prepared. I had extra water, extra food, extra cash, and survival equipment.

You do kind of wonder. It was like a pre-panic situation. I was home in San Bruno on New Year's Eve, Darren was a ten-month-old baby, and it was a strange time. You would like to think in your mind that the Y2K panic was nothing, but you couldn't know. I kept asking myself, *How many people have lived to see the turn of a century?* What if you were born in 1901 and died in 1998? A lot of people never see the turn of the century, let alone the end of a millennium. For me, it was a time to pray for the world, to pray for humanity, and ask if we couldn't learn something from our own history to try to live with one another in joy and kindness and peace. Twenty-five years later, I'm still wishing for that.

— — — —

In San Francisco, we knew 2000 was going to be a year of transition, and the whole city was excited. The franchise had moved to the Bay from New York before the 1958 season, and the newly renamed San Francisco Giants shut the Dodgers out 8–0 on their first Opening Day. That was the first of two years at Seals Stadium, where the Giants doubled their average attendance over the last two seasons at the Polo Grounds in New York, which had been less than 8,500 per game in a ballpark with a capacity of 55,000. By 1960, Candlestick Park was ready, and attendance increased again in the big concrete bowl, but by 1995 and 1996, we were averaging less than 18,000 per game in a nearly 44,000 capacity venue. That's how it is when you trade away the nucleus of your team all at the same time and keep losing.

Everything changed for the fans when we started playing at Pac Bell Park, south of Market Street near the heart of the city. Over our first three years in the new ballpark, we would average more than 40,000 fans per game at home. That was something we built up to over time. More than anything else, you build fan excitement by winning. Sure, we did appearances in the community even before we started playing the new ballpark, Barry Bonds and other players and myself, but the way you communicated to the fans that you were building a winning program was to put a competitive team on the field and find a way to win. That started at the end in Candlestick, where we wanted to give the fans winning seasons before we went to the new ballpark. We won ninety-seven games in 1997, and then in 1998 we won eighty-nine, and 1999 we won eighty-six. We did it by developing young talent and making great trades, adding proven veterans like Jason Schmidt and Ellis Birks. At shortstop, we had Brooklyn guys, Shawon Dunston and Rich Aurilia.

To get the ballpark financed, we needed to win and build excitement, and the new ownership group went out on a limb to privately finance the new stadium. That was unheard of then. Fans were seeing what we were doing, and they wanted more.

Our first game in the new ballpark, on April 11, 2000, was filled with speeches and ceremony. Bobby McFerrin sang the National Anthem and McCovey Cove, just beyond the right-field stands, filled up fast with a flotilla of more than eighty boats, everything from yachts to paddleboats and dinghies, with everyone wanting to catch the first homer to splash down out there. It seemed like everyone was there at the ballpark that historic day, from singer Chris Isaak to actor Danny Glover to my old friend Willie Brown and one of my favorite announcers, close friend Chris Berman of ESPN.

Barry Bonds had the first Giant RBI at the new ballpark and the first Giant home run, all on that first day, but we lost to the Dodgers, 6–5. Kevin Elster hit three home runs, and there were six homers total with Barry Bonds, Doug Mirabelli, and J. T. Snow all going deep for us, so suddenly everyone was predicting that Pac Bell was going to be a launching pad. Boy, were they wrong.

That was a magical season in a lot of ways. For a lot of Giants fans, who had loved their team even when suffering in the cold at Candlestick, the new ballpark with its comparatively warm downtown location felt like an unbelievable gift. You could sit up in the right-field stands, looking down on McCovey Cove, with the Bay Bridge and the East Bay looming in the distance across the glassy water of the Bay—and the San Francisco skyline, from the Bank of America building where I used to meet with Walter Shorenstein to newer, sleeker high-rises. Suddenly fans who had turned away at one time or another came back. Will the Thrill Clark had moved on to the Rangers, but in San Francisco there was a definite thrill in the air, a giddy kind of feeling that whatever was going to happen, it was going to be a lot of fun.

We finished the first half of 2000 with a 46–39 record, which was good but not good enough. We were 3.5 games behind the Arizona Diamondbacks at the All-Star break. The season really took off about mid-August. We were in New York taking on the Mets at Shea Stadium, and lost the first game, then the next day we were in a scoreless tie through five. Then my guys lit it up: Billy Mueller led off the sixth with a line-drive single, Barry came up next and singled, then Jeff Kent was hit by a pitch to load up the bases. J. T. Snow brought in one run with a sac fly, and then Ellis Burks and Rich Aurilia, both highly underrated players who came through for us again and again, both singled home runs. We scored five in the sixth and six more in the seventh, and won 11–1 to start what turned into a six-game winning streak.

We had an outstanding second half to surge past a strong Diamondbacks team and won the NL West. Peter Magowan was on the road with us in Arizona at the end of the season when we found out we would be playing the Mets, the wild card winner, in the division series, opening at home. I was thrilled by that, compared to having to go in to Atlanta and play your first two games there.

For Game 1 at home, my starter was Liván Hernández, brother of El Duque Hernández, both Cubans who had been through a lot, and once again, Liván showed he was a big-game pitcher, opening the game with back-to-back strikeouts and giving up just one run. Ellis Burks just kept coming through for us. He'd probably have ended up in the Hall of Fame if not for his bad knees. He lined a three-run homer to left in the third to make it 5–1, the final score.

In Game 2, we fell behind 2–0 early, before Ellis Burks—him again—doubled in the bottom of the second to make it 2–1. That was where it stood in the ninth when I brought in reliever Félix Rodriguez and Edgardo Alfonzo hit a two-run homer to put the Mets up 4–1. It didn't look good, but it's the playoffs, and as long as you've got one out left, you've got a chance. Plus, we had Barry Bonds leading off the ninth for us. He doubled to end Al Leiter's day, then Jeff Kent singled off Mets closer Armando Benítez. That brought up Burks, the tying run, to the plate. He flied out to shallow right, too shallow to score Barry from third. But then J. T. Snow got ahead in the count 2–1 and hit a sharp line drive to right field. I had a great view of the ball from my usual spot in the dugout, right next to the stairs leading up to the field. I was hoping the ball was high enough to clear that tall wall in right field, and it was: a three-run homer. The game was tied.

The intensity ratcheted up a notch going into extra innings. In the top of the tenth, Félix Rodriguez got two quick outs, then Mets manager Bobby Valentine decided to send up Darryl Hamilton to pinch-hit. Darryl was an ex-Giant and one of my favorites, but he was not happy when we traded him for Ellis Burks in July 1998, and when he doubled to left, he was gesturing at me like I'd disrespected him or something. He came around to score on Jay Payton's single, and we lost that one, taking a tied series back to New York.

Game 3 was a heartbreaker—we lost in extra innings again, this time in the thirteenth inning on a Benny Agbayani homer off Aaron Fultz. Our bullpen was running on fumes.

For Game 4, we had Mark Gardner going against the Mets' Bobby Jones, his homeboy from their days playing together at Fresno State. I thought there was no way Bobby Jones was going to shut us out. I was wrong. Jones pitched probably the best game of his life that day. The Mets took an early lead on Robin Ventura's two-run homer in the first, and suddenly we needed runs.

In the top of the fifth, still down 2–0, we loaded the bases on a Jeff Kent double and two walks. Gardner was coming up to bat—Bobby Valentine had intentionally walked our catcher, Doug Mirabelli, to load up the bases, trying to force me to pinch-hit for Mark to get him out of the game. It was a tough call. Jones was dealing for the Mets, but could he keep it going? We'd just lost a thirteen-run game the night before, and I had just one fresh pitcher in Miguel del Toro, who hadn't pitched much for us. I wanted to get all the good innings out of Mark that I could. And Mark was a good hitter. I knew he could handle the bat. I was sure we'd get at least two runs off Jones.

I added up all those considerations and decided to have Mark bat for himself. But he popped up to second, stranding three runners. We lost the game, 4–0, and the Mets advanced, headed for a World Series loss to the Yankees. That's one where if I had to do it again, I would probably not have let Mark hit. I could have pinch-hit and brought in Liván Hernández to pitch. In the moment, I knew he was scheduled to pitch the next day, and I was worried about where that would leave me. I didn't think about that until my pitching coach, Ron Perranoski, brought it to my attention, but by then it was too late—there was not enough time for Liván to get loose anyway. I learned from that one: You've got to win that day. Worry about tomorrow later.

I was surprised when Peter Magowan called a team meeting after Game 4 in New York, but it was almost like nobody heard anything he said, because we were all numb. That was a tough loss, and a tough way to finish the season, but we'd accomplished a lot that year and had nothing to hang our heads about. On the team's charter flight home from New York, Peter avoided talking to me. That stuck with me. Something had changed. My decisions were now being questioned in a way they hadn't been before. We had pulled in more than 3.3 million fans at home that year. We had built a wave that was going to continue to push the team and the city forward—I knew we had built something.

Tosh had turned twenty-one that September, on September 29. She and my lifetime friend Dennis Kludt have the same birthday. I was talking to Tosh about how to celebrate and she said she wanted a trip to New York.

"New York?" I said. "You used to want to go to Chuck E. Cheese."

New York it was. So in November 2000, we flew to New York and my good friend of forty years, George Santiago, showed us around town. We sat down at the first bar and Tosh pretended she was having her first drink ever, but I noticed she knew the name of every vodka drink on the menu. After that we danced all night, and as we walked back to our hotel Tosh hooked my arm. She would always be my little girl Tosh, but now she was legally a woman.

In 2001, we won ninety games and battled the Arizona Diamondbacks for the NL West, but came up two games short—and the D-backs went all the way to the World Series and won, beating the Yankees. That was the year of the 9/11 attacks on the World Trade Center and the Pentagon. I got a call from one of my coaches, Sonny Jackson, and he told me to turn on the TV, and I saw the second plane hit the World Trade Center. I thought I was watching a replay of what had already happened, but then I found out it was a second plane. It was terrible. I couldn't believe it. I thought of people I knew who worked there in the World Trade Center, and I later found out some of them died that day. All flights were grounded, and we were stuck in Houston for days. When baseball started back up again, it took on a different significance. When President George W. Bush, the former Texas Rangers owner, threw out the first pitch before Game 2 of the World Series at Yankee Stadium, that rallied people's spirits.

The highlight of the 2001 season for the Giants was Barry. All season long, he was chasing history, going after the single-season home run record. Fans all over America loved it, whether they liked Barry or not. People would drop whatever they were doing to watch Barry's at-bats. Pitchers were walking him left and right, so he would get one or two hittable pitches all night and not miss—and they were gone. I had been around Hank Aaron early in my career, but to watch Barry that year was to witness the greatest amount of patience and concentration I had ever seen in a ballplayer. There was a tremendous amount of media scrutiny, but Barry didn't let anyone crowd his space or take away his energy. It took a lot of self-composure. Everything had to be together. Your whole circle had to be complete. I'd never seen that level of focus for such a sustained period of time. Shawon Dunston was pushing Barry every day. Barry didn't know if he was going to get the record, but Shawon did.

We were in Houston for a three-game series in early September 2001 and swept all three games, and that was when Barry hit his historic seventieth home run, a 454-foot drive at Enron Field that tied him with Mark McGwire for the single-season record. In the dugout, I was filled with joy. *This is history,* I thought to myself, a familiar feeling going back to earlier in my career, but now I was witnessing it from the dugout when earlier I'd been part of it. At home on the last day of the season, Barry crushed a knuckleball from Dodger Dennis Springer for his seventy-third home of the season, a record that may never be broken. I was teammates with Aaron and McGwire and managed Barry and later Sammy Sosa and Ken Griffey Jr. I was fortunate to see some of the greatest hitters of all time.

— — — —

Pac Bell had such a great location, right on the water, so of course as a fisherman I was going to take advantage whenever I could. I loved getting a quick game in and heading right out to fish San Francisco Bay for a few hours. After a day game one Thursday, I had plans to take a bunch of my players out with my friend Armand Castagna, a master fisherman who knew all the best fishing spots in the Bay. It was a cool setup. Provided the game didn't go too long, we could handle our postgame responsibilities quickly, get dressed, and walk right out to McCovey Cove to meet Armand in the boat. That Thursday, we had Kirk Rueter pitching, and when Kirk was on, he threw some of the quickest games ever, sometimes less than two hours. The game was zipping along. We were on pace for a two-hour game, which would have had us on the water not much after two P.M. At least five players were coming along with Armand and me, and we exchanged quick looks. It was like during a no-hitter. No one wanted to say a word. You never wanted to provoke the baseball gods. Everyone knew that, except the rookie going with us.

"Man," said the rookie, "this sure is a quick game."

We couldn't believe it. You *never* commented on a quick game.

We ended up playing eighteen innings that day. By the time we wrapped up, it was too late to go out. We never let that rookie hear the end of that one.

Armand was one of my best fishing buddies. He was inducted into the California Outdoors Hall of Fame in 2015, ten years before I myself was inducted, thanks in part to the efforts of my friend Tom Stienstra, master outdoors writer with the *San Francisco Chronicle* and another fishing friend. Elvin Bishop, another of my go-to fishing buddies, is in another Hall of Fame, the Rock & Roll Hall of Fame. Elvin grew up in Oklahoma, and he was so smart in high school, he earned a National Merit Scholarship to go to college anywhere he wanted, so he chose Chicago and went there and listened to a lot of blues guitar. He met Paul Butterfield there and started playing with him, and I guess the rest is pretty much history.

I loved all my time on the water, especially with my best fishing buddies Brett Leber, a Pro Bass Fisherman, and Gizzy Galli, a hunter and fisherman whom I hunted and fished with a lot. Also with Paul Raquel, fishing and hunting buddy with the Fish and Game Department, former 49er Eric Wright, and former A's second baseman Shooty Babitt, and all the farmers and landowners up and down the Valley who would let us go pheasant and duck hunting. That was my refuge out there. Out on the water, I could get away from my thoughts and just be. I could feel the beauty and power of nature all around me and just feel like part of something bigger. I could let my mind go quiet, or I could focus if I had something that needed working through.

All through the nineties and into the 2000s, going out on the Bay or in the Sacramento River Delta or up the San Joaquin Valley for a day or a weekend trip was always something I looked forward to. I needed that time, also out duck hunting with my dad and partners, to take my mind off my troubles. One time in 1999, I went out on San Francisco Bay with Tom Stienstra on a dark, rainy day where we might have been the only ones out there fishing. It made me think about hope and about opportunity. "Back on the Braves, Luke Appling took me aside and told me, 'To be lucky, you've got to think lucky,'" I told Tom that day, maybe not for the first time. "That goes for anything. If you don't think lucky in fishing, you don't catch any fish. Am I lucky? It's true, I'm lucky. If you think you're lucky, that's what you get." My son Darren is the perfect example: He always catches fish because he always thinks lucky.

In 2002, we won ninety-five games to finish second in the West, three games behind the Diamondbacks, but this time we squeaked into the playoffs as the wild card team and then came out on top over the Braves in a five-game Division Series. Then we won four of five against the Cardinals in the NLCS to reach the World Series. I'd wanted for years to get back. That's what you always set your sights on, and we were going to win, that was my attitude. I not only wanted to win for us, I wanted to win for the city. I wanted to win for Peter Magowan. I wanted to win for Willie Mays, Orlando Cepeda, and Willie McCovey, and for the memory of Game 7 of the 1962 World Series when that last ball, hit by McCovey, was caught by Bobby Richardson.

I wanted to win knowing full well this might be my last year managing the Giants. Before the World Series, Rich Aurilia and Shawon Dunston had a feeling I might be leaving and asked me straight out: "If we win the whole thing, are you still leaving?"

Yes, I told them. I was noticing how relationships that were once strong had weakened, and I thought about what Bill Walsh told me about being in one place too long.

The first two games of the series were in Anaheim, and I had my Game 1 starter ready in Jason Schmidt, whom we'd acquired one year earlier. After that game, I would have some decisions to make on when and how to use my three other starters—Liván Hernández, Russ Ortiz, and Kirk Rueter. I noticed before Game 1 that Barry was extra quiet. He had waited sixteen years to play in a World Series, and before Game 1 he was really, really focused. I just let him be. He knew what he needed to do to get mentally ready. It was the first World Series game ever in Anaheim, and that crowd of 44,000 was loud, clanging thunder sticks together. Sure enough, Barry got us started in Game 1 when he turned on a high inside fastball for a solo shot in the top of the second. Nothing Barry did amazed us anymore. We'd seen him do so much. Reggie Sanders and J.T. added off-field homers to carry us to a 4–3 win, taking back home field advantage.

I liked our chances of grabbing another win in Game 2. I knew we were swinging the bat well and could put up runs, and I felt good about Russ Ortiz, who had been really good for us the last two years, going 17–9 and 14–10. But that was a tough night to pitch. In the bottom of the first, when David Eckstein led off with a single and Darin Erstad brought him home with a line-drive double, I could already tell the ball was carrying well. It was going to be a hitters' night. The first four Angels all had hits, and they ended up scoring five runs that inning, including one when Brad Fullmer stole home. That was not at all a typical World Series game. The Angels were up 7–4 by the second, but we came back. We showed a tremendous amount of determination and fight. That was how we put together rallies. In the fifth, Rich Aurilia led off with a double and then four different guys singled, giving us a 9–7 lead. It was all tied up at 9 in the eighth, and the game came down to two home runs—Tim Salmon homered for them and Barry Bonds for us, but Salmon had a runner on and Barry hit a solo shot, so we lost 11–10. Barry was having a great series. I would have loved to pull that one out, but we were going home to San Francisco for three games.

One thing I loved about my job was that I could bring my son to work. I'd done that with my daughter for years; she was my roommate on the road. Now it was my son Darren's turn. He turned three in early February 2002, we celebrated at home, and when Darren turned three and a half that August 11, we celebrated at the ballpark. That day was the first time I had Darren serve as a Giants batboy. He'd been bugging me about it all year, he wanted to be out there so much. I told him he was too small and couldn't be a batboy until he turned five. That didn't slow him down much. "Am I five yet?" he'd ask me every week or so. He wore me down. I kept thinking, as many cancer survivors do, *How much time do I have left?* Every time you go back to the doctor for your three-month checkup or later six-month checkup, you wonder, *Is the cancer back? Or am I still clean?* I was only fifty-two, but I asked myself: How many opportunities will I have to be there with my son, living through unforgettable memories together? I decided that if Darren was ready, and I thought he was, I needed him out there so he and I could share that experience.

I asked Barry Bonds if Darren was ready to be a batboy—he thought he was, and said that he was one of the best batboys we had. So starting August 11, Darren worked some games as batboy, and a lot of people told me the fans loved watching him out there, always alert and active, focused on his job, like when he was trying to pick up Barry's bat and elbow guard without losing his own helmet. I gave him three innings and then said that was enough. He kept looking up at the scoreboard to see himself there.

He learned real fast. He was a good batboy, and he loved being out there. In Atlanta for the playoffs in October 2002, he gave Kenny Lofton a low five when Kenny scored a run in our win that day, and the picture made the papers—like when Glenn Burke gave me that high five at Dodger Stadium twenty-five years earlier. Darren would always have questions for me. He'd ask me about games and people and whatever was on his mind, and as with his sister, I never talked down to him, just tried to give him the straight truth.

When I was a player, most guys didn't have their sons or daughters around the team very much. Times change. Big Mac, Mark McGwire, had his son Matthew by his side when he was setting a single-season record for home runs. Every time he hit a big one, the cameras would show him lifting up Matthew. Earlier in the year, before I was cleared to go to spring training, I couldn't pick up anything heavier than ten pounds because of my cancer operation, not even my son Darren. I couldn't drive a car, I couldn't do anything. I had to work my way back after the cancer. Walking up the hill in San Bruno at the top of my condo complex was my exercise. I was cleared one week before I went to spring training.

People asked me why I had Darren out there. I was trying to give him all I could, in case my cancer came back. We felt so much joy as a team having many of our sons around as batboys. That was something you'll never see again in baseball because the rules have changed. The kids loved it, the dads loved it, the fans loved it, and we felt like we were family. On our team in 2002, our batboys included Barry's son, Nikolai, who was twelve then, Marvin Bernard's son, Isaac, and Shawon Dunston's son, Shawon Jr., who was nine. We also had nine-year-old Jackie Lopez, son of my bullpen coach, Juan Lopez, who later played for the Angels or Red Sox, and also Joey Telucci, the son of head of security Gene Telucci. Brandon Evans, who worked for Mike Murphy for years, started as a batboy back then, and now he's in charge of the umpires.

I loved having the kids out there. They brought us laughter and smiles of joy. You'd hear them say things like, "It's okay, you'll get him."

After Darren had been around the team a little, he asked me: "What do you do, dad? Everyone else goes up to bat and you just sit around."

By the time we were back home in San Francisco for Game 3 of the 2002 World Series, still in just our third year at the new downtown ballpark, Darren and the other young batboys had become fan favorites. It was wild at game time, a packed house with everyone waving orange rally towels in the air. It was Candlestick weather, damp and cold, but when Tony Bennett sang "I Left My Heart in San Francisco" from the mound before the first pitch, we felt an amazing energy in the dugout.

Our Game 3 starter was Liván Hernández, who at that point was 6–0 in the postseason, an experienced big-game pitcher. He worked a quiet first and then in the bottom of the inning, Kenny Lofton twice tried to bunt for a base hit, including on a 3–1 pitch, but earned a walk on a pitch that sailed way outside. Kenny kept dancing off of first base, trying to mess with Angels starter Ramón Ortiz's concentration, and stole second when Rich Aurilia struck out, then moved to third on Jeff Kent's check-swing infield hit, off Ortiz's glove.

I knew what that meant. Barry was up next. There was no way the Angels manager Mike Scioscia, my former Dodgers teammate and locker partner, was going to give him a chance to swing the bat and break the game open early with a three-run homer. They gave him the intentional pass—Barry's seventy-sixth intentional walk of the year, including six in the postseason. No team had ever issued a free pass in that situation, first and third in the first inning of the World Series, but that was how it was with Barry. The fans were waving rubber chickens in the stands, but I had to admit it was probably smart to be chicken with Barry, given the way he was locked in. Benito Santiago, who had a very good year for us, brought home Kenny with a little check-swing bouncer toward second base, and Kenny came back into the dugout after giving us a 1–0 lead.

We still had that 1–0 lead in the top of the third when Eckstein worked a leadoff walk and ran down to first base, the way Pete Rose used to run to first on a walk, and then Erstad doubled him to third. Liván went right after Tim Salmon, and had him 0-2, but when Salmon fought off a pitch and hit a sharp grounder to third, it handcuffed David Bell, our sure-handed third baseman. He was given an error. That tied the game 1–1, and before we were out of the inning a Scott Spiezio triple put the Angels up 4–1. By the fourth inning, we were down 8–1 and I had to pull Liván out of the game. We lost 10–4. Two games in a row, the Angels rattled off ten or more runs against us. Afterward I could only call it a tough night.

Back the next day for Game 4, we knew we needed to get something going early to get the crowd into the game. In the first inning, Kenny and Rich Aurilia started us off with back-to-back singles. But after Angels starter John Lackey struck Jeff Kent out, they gave Barry another free pass—and Benito Santiago hit into an inning-ending double play, so we came up empty. We had Woody out there for us, Kirk Rueter, and even after a Troy Glaus two-run homer put the Angels up 3–0 in the third, I was sure he'd settle down and get into a groove.

In fact, I was so confident in Woody that when the bottom of the fifth rolled around, with us still down 3–0, and Rueter's spot in the lineup came around to open the inning, I did not hesitate to let him hit for himself. Woody could handle the bat, and he almost bunted for a base hit, then chopped one right in front of the plate for an infield single. Woody could run. Kenny Lofton then dropped down a beautiful bunt down the third-base line that rolled foul then fair again, and we had two on. Rich Aurilia fell behind 1-2 but hung in there and stroked a clean single to right center to bring home one run. Jeff Kent, who had been a clutch man ever since we acquired him, brought home Kenny with a sacrifice fly, and there was a sweet moment behind home plate with Darren coming out to get the bat. Jeff kind of reached down to help him, with Kenny smiling at them on his way back to the dugout. We tied it 3–3 that inning and went on to win 4–3 on a David Bell RBI single in the eighth off Francisco Rodríguez. Darren had not been batboy for our two games in Anaheim, since he was sick with a sinus infection. Darren told his mom, "I've got to go. The team needs me." After our win in Game 4, some papers carried items noting that with Darren as batboy, we were on a 7–0 winning streak.

At that point, everyone was exhausted. We are all operating on fumes. We had one more game at home before the Series shifted back to Anaheim, and I had Jason Schmidt starting. Before the game, I called my mom from my office at the stadium.

"Dusty, I don't think Darren should be the batboy," she told me. "I've got a bad feeling about the game."

"Okay, Mom," I said, and hung up.

We'd tied up the World Series. It was now down to who could win two of the next three games. Barry finally got to see some pitches with men in scoring position in the first, and doubled home Kenny Lofton to start a three-run rally. We scored three again in the second, on our way to a big win.

But it's the seventh inning that everyone remembers from that game. We were already up 8–4, and J. T. Snow led off with a single right back up the middle. David Bell, up next, took a big cut on an inside fastball and shattered his bat, which sent Shawon Dunston Jr. hurrying out from the dugout to go collect a big shard of wood. Then Angels pitcher Ben Weber hit Bell with a pitch to put runners on first and second. I had Tsuyoshi Shinjo, our ninth hitter, bunting, and he moved the runners over for leadoff man Kenny Lofton.

Before Kenny came up, I heard Darren talking to another batboy, a guest batboy that game that none of us knew. This other batboy told Darren he was going to get Kenny's bat.

"No, you're not," Darren said. "That's my bat to get." Darren always got Kenny's bat.

Kenny worked the count to 2-1 and then turned on a fastball, hitting it deep to right center. The ball caromed off the wall.

I saw Darren run out prematurely to beat that other kid to Kenny's bat, and I reached for him, but he was too quick. Right at the same time I tried to grab Darren, so did Brandon, the oldest of the batboys, but Darren was off and running. He darted toward home plate with the play still developing.

J.T. scored easily with David Bell bearing down hard behind him, J.T. made it there as Darren was heading toward home plate, and he reached down and scooped Darren up just before David Bell scored, and carried him back toward our dugout. Darren was cool the whole time. He wasn't scared. He thought it was fun. He patted J.T. on the shoulder, then as soon as J.T. put him down, Darren ran over quickly to get his helmet and put it back on his head, then he practiced his sliding technique with Isaac Bernard, and then Jeff Kent added a two-run homer to bring home Kenny and give us a 12–4 lead. We won 16–4 to put us one win away from a World Series championship.

As soon as I got back to my office, I heard the phone ringing. It was my mom.

"You don't ever listen to me," she said. "I told you that I had a bad feeling and he shouldn't be the batboy tonight."

"Mom, I've gotta go, the press is coming," I told her.

The press was not there yet. She knew it.

"I don't care," she said. "You tell them to wait. You're going to hear this."

– – – –

I felt good about Russ Ortiz as my starter in Game 6 back in Anaheim. He had a rough time in Game 2, giving up seven runs in less than two innings, but I knew he could bounce back. Sometimes you just know. Before the game, Russ was cool, sitting next to me in the dugout before he went out to warm up. Someone asked me about wearing the World Series ring I won with the Dodgers in 1981, even though now I was managing the Giants, and I lifted my arm in the air. I said my daughter used to watch *She-Ra: Princess of Power,* and so I figured, like in that show, I could lift my ring up to feel the power. Russ laughed at that, and I got him to admit that he used to watch the show, too. He was relaxed and ready to go.

Sure enough, he came out in Anaheim for Game 6 and set the Angels down one-two-three in the first and gave up only a walk in the second. The third was another one-two-three inning for him, and in the fourth he gave up an infield single to Tim Salmon but then got an inning-ending double-play ball.

It was tense at Anaheim Stadium—four innings into the game, and still no one had scored. Then in the top of the fifth, we broke through. David Bell singled on a ball up the middle that Eckstein couldn't quite make a play on, and that brought up Shawon Dunston, who I had in the lineup against Kevin Appier, a sinker-baller, because he was a good low-ball hitter. Sure enough, Appier challenged him with a low inside fastball, and Shawon was right on it. He twisted his body like a golfer hitting his tee shot and homered to left to give us a 2–0 lead. As he crossed home plate, his son Shawon Jr. was there to greet him, and Shawon hugged his son and gave him a kiss, right there in the middle of the World Series. Then before he could get to the dugout so I could congratulate him, Darren was in front of me, whooping it up. Later that inning, Kenny Lofton doubled, stole third, and scored on a wild pitch to make it 3–0.

As any manager will tell you, the half inning just after you take the lead in a game like that is huge. We call that the shutdown inning. You want to put them back on defense again as soon as possible and come in on offense. In the bottom of the fourth, Russ came out and once again set the Angels down in order, getting Troy Glaus, Brad Fullmer, and Scott Spiezio. And we had Barry Bonds leading off the top of the sixth. He'd walked twice in the game already, but reliever Francisco Rodríguez threw Barry a high slider that probably wasn't where he wanted to locate it. Barry was all over that pitch. I tell you, listening from the dugout, the sound Barry's bat made striking that ball, it was something you never forget. You instantly knew it was gone. That ball was drilled, we had a 4–0 lead, and at home plate, like Shawon Dunston before him, Barry was met by his son, Nikolai.

I kept a close eye on Russ Ortiz as he came out to start the bottom of the sixth. It's not just what a pitcher has thrown that you watch, it's the at-bats the other team is having against him. You watch the way guys react to the pitch. Russ went after the first Angel batter, Bengie Molina, getting ahead 1-2, before he hit a fly ball to right field that sent Reggie Saunders a few steps back but he hauled it in easily. Facing Adam Kennedy, up next, Russ missed well high with his first pitch, not a bad way to start him off. You had to throw Kennedy up because he was a dead low-ball hitter. Pitching coach Dave Righetti and I were very aware of where we were in the lineup. Russ's next pitch broke Kennedy's bat, sawed off the handle, but the bat barrel went flying out into the infield along with the ball. Jeff Kent came within about six inches of gloving the ball. Instead, a hit. Those are the types of hits that often start rallies.

David Eckstein was up next, and Russ started him out with a good crisp fastball, right in that down-and-in target area, for strike one. Eckstein gave one a good ride, but way into foul territory, and it was 0-2. Eckstein kept fouling off pitches to stay alive, then Russ finally got him on a soft roller to short that moved the runner up to second. It was one of those long, tense at-bats that makes it almost anticlimactic when he's easily retired, and Darin Erstad, up next, was quickly ahead of Russ 2-0. He walked him to bring up Tim Salmon with two runners on, able to make it a one-run game with one swing of the bat.

I sent Dave Righetti out there to huddle with Russ and talk through the moment. I had Félix Rodríguez and Scott Eyre up in the pen, and they'd be good to go if we needed them. We weren't there yet, I was sure of that. Russ started off Salmon with a well-placed fastball away that he fouled off, lulled him with a breaking ball away, then came back in with a high fastball that looked too good for Salmon not to swing—he tried to check his swing but couldn't, and it was 1-2. In the end, the battle continued, but Russ froze Salmon with a fastball for a called strike three, and the inning was over. Russ had given us six innings of shutout ball against a team that had been tearing the cover off of it. As he walked back to the dugout, taking long, confident strides, he pumped his fist in the air. I was keeping cool. We still had a lot of game left.

We strung together another rally in the top of the seventh. Kenny Lofton singled and then scored on a Jeff Kent single, which gave us a 5–0 lead, but it also meant more time for Russ to be sitting. That's kind of the opposite of a shutdown inning. You love scoring runs, but you don't like your pitcher sitting. Russ came back out in the bottom of the seventh, still working a shutout. He'd given up only two hits over six, both infield hits, but I knew he had to be wearing down. Facing Garret Anderson to lead off the bottom of the seventh, Russ was missing and fell behind 2-0 but then got Anderson on an easy ground ball to second. Troy Glaus, up next, ripped the first pitch he saw from Russ for a crisp single to left. Facing Brad Fullmer, Russ first placed a fastball where he wanted for 0-1, but then missed with two breaking balls away. Then he came back in with a fastball, and Fullmer laced a single to right to put two men on base.

I waited a minute and then walked out to the mound. I didn't make the call to the pen as I walked, righty or lefty, but first went to Russ and looked him in the eye. I could have stuck with Russ longer, that would have been an option. That was a big decision for me. Russ had given us a 5–0 lead and my bullpen was strong and rested and very good. I thought it was time to go to my bullpen because the Angels were starting to hit Russ pretty good.

Then I raised my right arm, to signal that Félix Rodríguez was coming into the game, and told Russ how proud I was of him for how he'd come up big. Just before he walked off the mound, I handed Russ the game ball and slapped him on the back. Everybody thought I gave him the ball because I thought the game was over. People said that's how it looked. To me, that makes no sense. You don't make it one year in baseball, let alone thirty-four years, without learning: *Man, the game ain't* ever *over till it's over,* to quote Yogi Berra. I was not counting any chickens before they were hatched. I was not assuming anything about how the game would end up. We still had to get eight more outs, and even a 5–0 lead could evaporate in a hurry against a team like the Angels. I gave that ball to Russ because he had given heart and soul to pitch his ass off for us that night.

The one weird part of that was that I did end up kind of jinxing Félix or messing him up, which I only came to understand later. Guys all have their own ways of getting mentally ready, and they all have their own routines, some of them very elaborate. Félix had a routine where whenever he came into a game, he would take the ball from the manager and fling the ball into our dugout. Then he got a new ball from the umpire. The ritual would get the funk off the ball and he would start fresh with a clean slate. That night in Anaheim for Game 6 of the World Series, he had to ask for a new ball right away, and couldn't throw one to the dugout the way he usually did. It may or may not have thrown him off, but it's the kind of thing that's important to players.

Scott Spiezio was up next, and he was swinging the bat well, we knew that. One thing about Spiezio to remember was that he was the son of a big-leaguer, Ed Spiezio, and he was a smart player. Joe Morgan later pointed out I could have brought in the lefty Scott Eyre to face Spiezio instead of Félix and turn him around, but the reason I didn't bring in Scott was because I had done my own scouting. A couple weeks earlier, I had seen Spiezio on TV hit a homer off a similar lefty.

Félix got ahead of him 1-2, but you could see Spiezio was picking up the ball pretty well. He was fouling off good fastballs. That was some at-bat. The Angels fans had their thunder sticks going, and the place was loud. At one point Félix stepped off the rubber just to collect himself. And Spiezio in turn, after fouling off yet another live fastball, stepped out of the box to reset.

With a full count, Félix threw a low inside fastball. That's most left-handers' sweet spot. Spiezio dropped the head of the bat on it, launching what looked at first like a lazy fly ball to right, but it kept carrying. Watching Reggie Sanders move back on the ball, I thought he had a play, but the ball just cleared his glove and bounced off the hands of a fan in the first row of the right-field bleachers for a three-run homer. It was a stunning turnaround. Even Spiezio and the Angels seemed stunned. Suddenly our lead was cut to 5–3. The thunder sticks were pounding in Anaheim, but that didn't bother me as much as that Rally Monkey they had going, which the Anaheim fans believed in. I couldn't stand that Rally Monkey.

We came up in the top of the eighth looking to build that lead back up, but Brendan Donnelly had it going and made things tough. He struck out Reggie Sanders and David Bell back to back to end the inning. Tim Worrell, who had been so good all year, gave up a home run to Erstad to make it a one-run lead, and then against my closer, Robb Nen, Troy Glaus doubled in two more runs to give the Angels the lead—and the game. Robb, Tim, and Félix had done the job for us all season long, but that just wasn't their day. Troy Percival came out in the top of the ninth and struck out both Tom Goodwin and Rich Aurilia to finish us out. If we could have got two of the guys on, it would have brought up Barry with a chance to win it. Instead, Angels Stadium was roaring, and Game 6 was in the books.

We still had Game 7 to play. We still had twenty-seven outs, twenty-seven chances at the plate to put up runs. My nemesis during my whole playoff career was Game 6. Now I was past that, thinking about Game 7. I had a choice to make. Did I want to give Kirk Rueter the start, which some of my players wanted, the same way that my Dodgers teammates and I had wanted Fernando to start in 1980? Or did I choose to go with Liván Hernández, who had pitched a lot of big games and come through? In 1997, Liván had won a World Series with the Marlins and was Most Valuable Player of both the National League Championship Series and the World Series. He'd started and won both Game 1 and Game 5 of that World Series. It was a tough call, but I went with Liván over Woody.

We scored first, taking a 1–0 lead on Reggie Sanders's sac fly in the top of the second, but then Bengie Molina tied it up with a double in the second, and one inning later Garret Anderson came up with the bases loaded and doubled home all three runs. That 4–1 score held, and we had to watch the Angels celebrate winning it all.

I'll never forget the feeling after that last out. Darren was crying profusely. He kept saying he didn't want the Angels to win, and I tried to comfort him, along with LeRoy Hendricks, who was in charge of security in our dugout for Major League Baseball at the time. Darren's favorite TV shows at the time were *SpongeBob SquarePants* and *The Bernie Mac Show,* which we watched together as a family. Darren loved Bernie Mac. Seeing Darren on TV crying after the World Series, Bernie Mac said on a late-night talk show that Darren wasn't crying, he was wailing, and that he didn't even know what he was wailing about. Darren knew exactly what he was crying about—and I got in touch with Bernie Mac to tell him that. He sent autographed pictures to me and Darren, and to this day Darren has that picture on his wall, and so do I, and we still watch Bernie Mac anytime he's on TV.

We flew home to San Francisco and the next day had a gathering on the field at Pac Bell. I don't know what they called it, but it was like a wake. More than five thousand fans showed up, and we let them out on the field. I thanked as many as I could, but it was hard for me. I was full of sorrow that we had lost, but I also knew this was a farewell for me. That was the last year of my contract, and the Giants had put no offer on the table. Some fans had brought signs reading things like "Dusty Don't Leave" and "Stay Dusty." The *San Francisco Examiner* summed up the mood by saying the big turnout was in part so fans could "plead for" my return. I didn't want to talk to anybody. Peter Magowan addressed the fans and said, "There are a lot of people I want to thank, starting with our great manager, Dusty Baker." Before he could say more, his words were drowned out by the fans chanting, "Dusty! Dusty! Dusty!" They wanted me to speak next, but I couldn't speak. I remember holding Darren and just feeling so sad, sad for losing and sad for knowing I was leaving. That was the first time I had tears on a baseball field since I dropped that ball for a grand slam in Little League.

You know when it really hit me how bad that World Series loss was? My dad, afterward, told me, "Son, if you didn't win this one, you may never win one."

It was just a few words from my dad, but it was like it struck me to my core, especially after the way we lost Game 6. My dad was tough and he was tough-minded, but he always believed in what my teams could do. My dad also knew me. And he was from a different generation, where negative motivation still had power, not like in today's world.

For years to come, I thought about that night and what my dad said. I loved my dad, I respected my dad, and I also liked proving my dad wrong. That was a real source of motivation to me. It was always very important to me to make my dad proud. I knew that I was going to get another shot at a World Series championship. I would make sure to earn that opportunity, and when I was back in the harsh light of October baseball, I would get a chance to prove my dad wrong.

CHAPTER 13

Chicago, Chicago

I wore the Giants orange and black enough years for it to feel a little weird to show up at Shea Stadium on a cold New York morning in April 2003 wearing blue, taking the field on Opening Day as manager of the Chicago Cubs. Years earlier I had worn blue, Dodger Blue, then for fifteen years the orange and black. As Bill Walsh always told me, change was good, change was necessary. New city, new players, new organization, new ballpark, new fans, new colors.

What I remember most about my first game as Cubs manager was the cold. I'd never been so cold in my life on a baseball field. Technically it was thirty-nine degrees. That was what the mercury said. But given the way the icy wind whipped around that old concrete bowl of a stadium, well, I've been in deep-freezer units that felt warmer than the ballpark that day. The Mets had just signed the former Braves ace Tom Glavine to a big contract, and he was on the mound in his first start for New York. But the ball was so cold, and hard, he couldn't get a decent grip. He walked our leadoff batter, Mark Grudzielanek, then Alex Gonzalez doubled, Sammy Sosa singled, and Moisés Alou, Felipe's son, doubled. Before the inning was out, we were off to a 4–0 start and coasted to a 15–2 win. As a New York *Daily News* headline summed up: "DUSTY GETS TO CHILL OUT." It was just one W, one game of a 162-game marathon, but it was good to be in motion again.

I shocked some people when I left San Francisco after the 2002 season, becoming the first manager in many years to part ways with his team the year after reaching the World Series. I loved so much about managing the Giants, but Bill Walsh was right, things do change. And if you're popular with the fans and maybe the media, that can become a dangerous situation if it starts to give the impression that you're bigger than the organization. In the minds of the organization, no one is bigger than the organization.

I had a good relationship with Peter Magowan for a lot of years. He gave me my chance to manage and get a new start in life. We did good things together in San Francisco, but over time we started having more difficult conversations. I knew how much he wanted to win. Peter really loved baseball, and he had his own ideas about players. Over time, we started having differences over personnel.

I always liked Rich Aurilia, a tough kid out of Brooklyn. I liked Brooklyn guys. You knew they had to be tough, and tough-minded. Richie played baseball at St. John's, where Warriors star Chris Mullin had played basketball, and he had a blue-collar attitude. I heard Richie even worked as a stagehand at the Metropolitan Opera. The Rangers drafted him in the twenty-fourth round in 1992. I knew something about going in the late rounds of the draft and having people overlook the qualities that made you a winner. Richie was a winner, a great teammate who made everyone around him better, and I knew he was ready to be our everyday shortstop, but Peter wasn't sold—and the team kept going out and getting other shortstops. We'd traded everyday regular shortstop Royce Clayton at the end of the 1995 season, and in January 1996, the Giants signed former Cubs shortstop Shawon Dunston, another Brooklyn guy, who I liked a lot. Shawon turned thirty-three that year, which is a lot of wear and tear on a shortstop. At the end of that season, we picked up another veteran shortstop in José Vizcaino from Cleveland as part of the Matt Williams trade that brought Jeff Kent and Julián Tavárez to the Giants. Then in January 1998, the team signed Rey Sánchez, another veteran option at short. After trying three shortstops because that was what Peter wanted, Rich Aurilia became our regular everyday shortstop, and by 2001 he was hitting thirty-seven homers and batting .324.

Another disagreement centered on first baseman J. T. Snow, who I wanted to continue to play. J.T. won six straight Gold Gloves starting in 1995. But it wasn't just his defense I wanted, it was his overall game, which I thought complemented my team. Peter wanted to go another direction. We had Damon Minor in the minors and went out and traded for Andrés Galarraga in July 2001, a month after his fortieth birthday. Peter wanted them at first, but I continued to play J.T. because I knew how important he was in all departments.

Guys complain about being a lame-duck manager. I've been a lame-duck manager everywhere I've been. My contract expired everywhere I went except Cincinnati, where I was fired with one year left. There had been speculation in the papers all through 2002 about how much the Giants wanted to keep me, but on the Giants' side there was basically a loud silence. On my side, I wasn't putting a lot of pressure on them to keep me. I saw Walter Alston and Tommy Lasorda manage year after year with one-year contracts. I learned in L.A. that you can overstay your welcome. I did that at the end of my time with the Dodgers, and I did not want to do it with the Giants. I met with Peter two days after the World Series, and I knew what I wanted to do before I went into that meeting. I wanted to win in the worst way, but I knew it was time to go. Sometimes long enough is simply long enough.

I'd been friends with Tyrone Willingham for years. We had in common being two of the younger coaches that Bill Walsh had chosen to mentor. Tyrone succeeded Bill as head coach at Stanford starting in 1995, and in 2000, he took them all the way to the Rose Bowl. Like me, he had a lot of good years in the Bay before it was time to change it up. In late 2001, after my cancer operation, I woke up afterward and I saw Tyrone on TV with a trench coat on and they said he was going to be the next coach at Notre Dame. He had just come to see me at Stanford Hospital and told me he was going to interview but wasn't going to take the job. That day after my operation, I was still on whatever drugs they'd given me, and I couldn't believe what I was seeing on the TV was real.

I told him I would come see Notre Dame play, and finally got a chance to do that just after the 2002 World Series. I carved out a football weekend with my dad and my good friend Shooty Babitt and his dad, Mack Babitt—first the Notre Dame game on Saturday, then we drove to Indianapolis to catch the Colts game on Sunday. I love college football. Basketball was my first true love in sports, and football was second. A part of me always wished that I'd had a chance to go play football at San Jose State or one of the Arizona schools. So I was in my element in South Bend that weekend to see Tyrone's Fighting Irish. The night before the game, I went to the Notre Dame pep rally, and it was unlike anything I'd ever seen. I said as much when I spoke briefly at the rally at Tyrone's request. It was pretty cool for me as a USC fan, seeing Touchdown Jesus, but I don't think I'll be invited back to any Fighting Irish pep rallies, since they were 8–0 at the time, and after I spoke at the rally, they lost to Boston College.

I just wanted to watch football that weekend and have a little fun and get away from baseball. That wasn't going to happen. People kept asking me on that visit if I was going to come manage the Cubs, who had let my friend Don Baylor go the previous season and then finished the year with Bruce Kimm as interim manager. South Bend was a lot closer to Chicago than I thought. "Come to the Cubs," they kept saying, and they made it sound like fun. They were working on me pretty good.

I watched the game in the Irish VIP box along with my dad and Dave Duerson, a former Chicago Bear. At halftime, I ran into a *Chicago Tribune* sportswriter. Just from talking to him, I could tell a lot of people in Chicago were excited about the idea of me coming to manage the Cubs. In fact, the next day, the Sunday *Tribune* had a picture of me on the front page of the whole paper, offering an "in-depth" look at me as maybe the next Cubs manager.

Back home in California, I met with Brian Sabean one last time, just to be sure I wasn't missing anything. I wasn't. I had my eyes on my future, not my past. It was time for me to go. That was one of a handful of major decisions in my life, a major crossroads that I prayed on, the way I'd prayed on the other big choices in my life, all the way back to the decision of whether to sign with the Braves in 1967. I told my dad what I was doing.

"Where you going?" he asked me.

"I don't know," I told him. "But I'm going somewhere."

The week I parted ways with the Giants, I went into Peter Magowan's office and handed him a check for $1 million, repayment in full. He seemed surprised, but didn't say much. My tax case was moving along. Karen Hawkins's friend Nina Olson, the Taxpayer Advocate, gave her a heads-up about my case. After that, Nina Olson took personal responsibility and issued a "911 order," as it's apparently called, which amounted to a "cease and desist" letter to the IRS on my behalf. The IRS was to cease collection efforts until the various missteps could be sorted out and an accurate accounting reached.

Things got funky after that. A lot of powerful people were upset that Olson had done that, when they'd been trying to cover up wrongdoing. Turns out, powerful people in Washington don't always like it when you call them on something. Olson nearly lost her job. The IRS Commissioner was livid. Even Karen Hawkins found the episode eye-opening. She was surprised to learn what some in the IRS were willing to do. Karen was the one who had to deal with sorting it out, and wading through what she diplomatically called "ugly exchanges" with IRS people.

The main breakthrough was when they assigned my case to the San Francisco office. That meant a top-notch office with some of the best people in the IRS, Karen told me, and it also meant Karen had contacts there. It was just a case of painstakingly working our way backward to ascertain where I would have been if I'd been offered the settlement the IRS should have offered me. Karen got the IRS to agree that I couldn't be liable for all the interest I'd accrued in disputed liability, since that liability would not have existed at all if the letter had been sent to me offering the settlement. The IRS hates to give up on interest. It took two years for Karen, going back and forth, to work this out. Every time she met with the appeals officer, his supervisor sat in on the meetings, since they were so worried about this blowing up on them. Gradually, Karen talked them down from saying I owed millions of dollars to a much lower number:

$800,000. Karen had to convince me it was time to accept this option. I was ready to keep fighting, but she said if I fought, the amount they said I owed could triple in a short period of time. I wrote Karen a check for the amount, in full, and she sent it into the IRS, which was painful for me, since by then they'd garnished well over a million dollars in wages from my Giants salary.

"You've saved my life," I told Karen, and I meant it. Having this monkey off my back was huge for me. I was tired of second-guessing myself for choices I'd made, tired of having to look back when all I wanted was a fresh shot. The combination of Karen's help and signing my $3-million-a-year deal with the Cubs finally enabled me to do that.

I was ready for a change, but I would always be proud of my time in San Francisco. For the most part, I was close to Giants ownership for a lot of years, and still am with some. To this day, I think about how much I like Brian Sabean and liked working with him, and later I recommended him to Houston as a good choice for GM.

— — — —

Chicago energized me the way only a fresh start can. It was a new city and a new team with great tradition, and I was reunited with a coaching staff full of old friends, starting with Sarge (Gary Matthews), Gene Clines, and Sonny Jackson, as well as Chris Speier, Wendell Kim, and Dick Pole, now my bench coach. The team had a new general manager, Jim Hendry, who I didn't really know at that point, but we had a mutual friend in Gary Hughes, the scout. Jim had coached Creighton University to the 1991 College World Series and then worked with Dave Dombrowski, who as a farm director with Montreal in 1987 offered me what would have been my first coaching job, in the New York Penn League, but I turned it down. Jim Hendry worked with Dombrosky when he was Florida Marlins general manager, learning the ropes as a future GM. Now he was getting his shot.

Talking to me, Hendry was saying all the right things about wanting to do things right to try to bring a World Series to Wrigley Field. He looked at me and saw the guy who could get that club over the top, taking all the talent I would have to work with and see about going all the way. I loved the idea of going to the World Series two years in a row, with different teams, and winning it that way. It would be a challenge, but I also liked a good challenge.

A week full of twists and turns of emotion came to a close that Friday with nightmare media coverage: Someone had leaked word of my IRS issues to ESPN, and they'd gone big with the story. The Associated Press filed a report out of San Francisco that same day, which was picked up by papers all over the country. I got a heads-up from a friend in media that this was coming, and I called Karen Hawkins to tell her. She explained to the AP that I owed more than $1 million because I'd invested in a number of tax shelters on the advice of my brother Vic and the company where he was working. I was alerted by a source at ESPN that morning before the story broke, so the person I called was Karen to ask her who would do that. "Was it the IRS?" I asked. "No," she told me, "it was not the IRS." It had to be someone else, but I never found out who. The AP also reported: "Hawkins said the situation with the Internal Revenue Service would be resolved by the end of this year." But somehow that last part got lost in the stampede.

I felt a lot of things all at once. I was mad and kind of embarrassed, and I was a little sad to face the cold truth that people would go so low as to leak IRS allegations to the media. That is some cold, cold shit. I didn't want to think about it, but hell, some stuff we tell ourselves not to think twice about we can't quite shake as easy as all that. Someone was trying to stop me from getting work, like Van Morrison sang about in "Big Time Operators."

For all the different emotions I felt at once, the biggest one I felt was gratitude. Jim Hendry and the Cubs were there. They believed in me, and they dismissed the tax stuff out of hand as a non-issue. What did any of that have to do with my chances of coming in and bringing new life to Wrigley Field and to the whole Cubs organization? Not a thing. And Jim well understood that.

Jim had told me I was his first choice, his second choice, and his third choice. I flew to Chicago and met for more than three hours with Hendry and the Cubs team president, Andy MacPhail, whose dad and grandad both went into the Baseball Hall of Fame as executives. Only after we'd talked through some things and done it the right way, as long as it takes, then I brought in my new agent, Jeff Moorad, whom I turned to after my old friend and agent Jerry Kapstein stopped representing players—he had helped represent his in-laws in their sale of the San Diego Padres and was decertified, since that was seen as a conflict of interest.

People always ask about the interviewing process, and I guess it's a little different every time. For me, especially that year, I had a lot of questions about the Cubs I wanted answered before we could get to talking dollars or years. I had been on winning teams as a player and with winning teams as a coach and manager, and I wanted to know why the Cubs hadn't won in a while. I knew their previous manager, Don Baylor, was a winner who came from the Frank Robinson school of how to win. They told me I would be very involved in player decisions, not in making the final call on things but just in being part of the conversation. Jim Hendry and Andy MacPhail lived up to that promise and more. I had done my research on the Cubs organization, and the thing that really jumped out at me about the job was having a young starting rotation of Mark Prior, Kerry Wood, and Carlos Zambrano. I had visions of young Glavine, Smoltz, and Maddux and what they meant to the Atlanta Braves for so long.

The banner headline stripped across the *Chicago Tribune* sports section that November 16 about said it all: "IT'S ALL YOURS, DUSTY." Chicago sports fans were sky high. They felt a big change coming. I became a symbol of the team investing in hope and optimism and respect for its players as both people and competitors. Columnist Phil Rogers, writing under the headline "CUBS' BIGGEST VICTORY IN YEARS," laid it on pretty good. "Put that money back in your pocket, Jim Hendry," he wrote. "You won't need to buy a round for a long time. Not in this town. Not after bringing one of the most highly respected managers to Wrigley Field."

I was out fishing when I got word we had finalized a deal. I went to

Chicago to win the Cubs a World Series—that was my motivation for going, and that was my mission and my mandate. But I knew I was also going to have some fun along the way. As Don Baylor and Ernie Banks and others I talked to had reminded me, Chicago could be a tough town; it could be a small town, in different ways, but Chicago, when it was good, was really good. I loved Chicago through and through.

Wrigley Field, where the Cubs play, is as unique a setting as any in baseball. Fenway Park and Wrigley were the two oldest parks in baseball, built in 1912 and 1914. I've never seen photosynthesis happen so quickly as it did in the Wrigley Field outfield. You'd look out at the outfield wall before a road trip and there would not be a leaf on that ivy, and when you came back from the road trip, it had all grown in.

There was an entire culture around being a Cubs fan. For years, there had been two teams in the country that people could watch every day, the Braves and the Cubs. Braves games were always airing on Ted Turner's TBS network, and you could watch Cubs games all over the world because they were on WGN. And once you're a Cubs fan, you are a Cubs fan for life. Before I lived in Chicago, I didn't fully understand how distinct Cubs fans and White Sox fans were. Back in the Bay, it was different with Giants and A's fans, who kind of overlapped at times. You even saw half-A's/half-Giants hats. Never in Chicago. We're talking about dividing lines going back decades and etched in stone.

Going into my first month as Cubs manager, I knew we needed to get off to a strong start. There was so much hope and excitement around the club, and if only we could feed that, get people excited, we could build on what we started. We were at .500 after ten games, but as April warmed up, so did we. Starting on April 15, we went on a five-game winning streak to lift our record to 12–6, and we won those games by a lot. It was fun, being on a roll, but I also wanted my guys to aim high, so I tried a little California talk on them. "The way I was raised, if you're having a good ride on a surfboard—even though I haven't had one—you just ride the wave all the way to the shore," I said. "If you start thinking about falling off, you're gonna fall off."

I had stars, but Eric Karros kept everything together. He was part of those good Dodgers teams of the nineties, the first of their record five consecutive Rookies of the Year from 1992 to 1996. Karros, picked up by the Cubs in a December 2002 trade, wasn't even playing every day, but he was the glue. You need those glue guys. They're so important. In Kerry Wood, Prior, and Zambrano, I had three of the best young guns around, along with underrated Matt Clement, who the Cubs traded for in March 2002. Zambrano might have been the best of them all, a great all-around athlete who was a switch-hitter and could run. Prior pitched like he was a veteran and could hit himself. I remember one time talking to Jim Thome when Prior was young and Thome was in his prime, and he told me Prior was the toughest one for him to face. Kerry Wood had electric stuff and could also hit. Clement had a nasty sinker and slider. He was a guy nobody talked about, but he went 14–12 for us in 2003. His mom would make me homemade pierogi when we visited Pittsburgh. I'd never had pierogi before, but after that, I couldn't get enough.

I'd wanted to make a statement over the first quarter of the season, and after forty games, we were 24–16. We struggled midseason, dipping under .500, and I knew Jim Hendry was looking to make a deal to help us. One thing I want to make clear is that I always had good relationships with my general managers. I had respect for every GM I played for and worked with as manager, and I hope they all had respect for me. Did we have disagreements? You bet we did. Disagreements, handled in a respectful way, create new thought processes. Disagreements are important and inevitable and good. It was hard for me to agree with myself sometimes.

I give Jim Hendry credit for asking my opinion.

"Dusty, we can get Joe Randa from the Royals," he told me in early July 2003. "What do you think?"

"I really like Joe Randa," I told Jim. "But let's wait. Something else will come along."

"Okay," Jim said, but he said it nervously. He knew we needed help, as soon as we could get it, but he was going to trust me on this.

I was sure it was smart to wait. Like my Aunt Loreena used to tell me, "Be still, nephew."

Sure enough, it worked out. Hendry waited on a major deal, and an epic trade fell into his lap. On July 22 came the announcement: The Cubs traded José Hernández and Matt Bruback and a player to be named later to the Pirates for Aramis Ramírez and Kenny Lofton. That deal changed the season overnight. ESPN was still writing about the swap a decade later as one of "The Most Lopsided Trades in Recent Memory," but really it was a good trade for both. We got two hitters, two starters. Aramis was there eight more years, even after I left, and became a fixture. He was one of the top third basemen and clutch hitters in the game. Kenny was one of the best leadoff hitters and center fielders in the game, and he'd been with me on the Giants the year before, so I knew just what we were getting.

— — — —

Living in Chicago, I spent a lot of time on the South Side. I'd go to the soul food restaurants, and I'd see friends there. I had met Jesse Jackson years earlier when I was playing for the Braves and Hank was going for the record. It was always a pleasure to see Billy Williams at the ballpark. We shared the same birthday, and he always called me Johnnie B. We talked every birthday—he called me or I called him. Billy was a regular at Wrigley, along with Cubs legends Ernie Banks, Ferguson Jenkins, Andre Dawson, Ron Santo, Ryne Sandberg, and Rick Sutcliffe, my former Dodgers teammate.

One of the real pleasant aspects of being in Chicago was the radio play-by-play announcer, Pat Hughes, who went to San Jose State University. Pat had a great voice and great chemistry with his partner in the booth, Ron Santo, and everyone loved his home run call, "That ball's got a chaaaance . . . gone!" He was later enshrined in the Baseball Hall of Fame in Cooperstown. If you were a Cubs fan, you tried not to miss "the Pat and Ron Show." I loved doing my pregame radio show with Ron, one of the regular duties of any manager. That was a highlight every day, his enthusiasm, his positive attitude, and how he loved the Cubs. A beloved Cub, Ron had lost the lower half of both his legs to diabetes, but he had two prosthetic legs with "Cubs" written on them, and he never complained about anything. Every single day he said, "I think the Cubs are going to win today."

Cubs fans can be hard on you, but they are also eternal optimists. For years, the mood of the town changed so fast based on a win or a loss that day. If they won, everybody would fly the W out their cars or outside their homes, everywhere, and everyone was happy. It controlled the mood of the whole town. You felt that walking along Lake Michigan near the Navy Pier or up the Magnificent Mile, just taking it all in. I liked Lincoln Park, where I lived, because it was relatively close to Wrigley and had good restaurants and bars and music spots and a mixture of young and old people, all near the lake.

Up until Chicago, I had always played, coached, or managed in the Western Division. Now I was playing in the NL Central, which felt like a whole different universe. That year, it also included Houston, St. Louis, Pittsburgh, Cincinnati, and Milwaukee in the Midwest. I'd been to all those cities, many times, but now I started thinking more about the Midwest and its history. Chicago was right at the center of that. As a kid, I was into the original TV series *The Untouchables,* set in Prohibition-era Chicago with Robert Stack as Special Agent Elliot Ness going after gangster Al Capone. I was into stories of Chicago gangsters, like the St. Valentine's Day Massacre in 1929, when a bunch of mobsters were lined up against the wall of a parking garage near Lincoln Park and shot by some other gangsters. I kind of enjoyed it when sportswriters started referring to my first two hitters, Mark Grudzielanek and Alex Gonzalez, as "G Men" and even called them "The Untouchables."

Another thing about living in Chicago was that I discovered a lot of new good fishing spots through a couple of new fishing buddies I made. I'd fish Lake Michigan sometimes, but really I fished the inland lakes more, Lake Geneva and the Chain O' Lakes. It was awesome.

You didn't have to be a huge fan of the blues, the way I was, to know that a lot of African Americans decided to leave the South, including many like my dad who had served in World War II. Some went West, but a lot moved to Chicago. I studied up on it because I wanted to understand. More than half a million Blacks, out of the seven million who left the South to move to the Midwest, chose to live in Chicago. By 1970, Blacks were one-third of the Chicago population, compared to 2 percent before World War I. They came to work in the factories and the steel mills and provide for their families. LaTroy Hawkins told me what it was like growing up in Gary, Indiana, a classic Midwest industrial city, which filled in more of the picture.

The more I learned about the Black migration, the more I got even deeper into the blues. I'd been thinking for years about the difference between Mississippi Delta blues and Chicago blues, and now I had chance to soak up a full education. So many of the great bluesmen sang about leaving the South and coming to Chicago and going to the blues clubs on the South Side and on Rush Street. That's what I would do, too, which was how I came to spend a lot of time with Buddy Guy.

Buddy was born in Louisiana, like Ralph Garr. His parents were sharecroppers. His dad picked cotton. Buddy started picking a guitar, learning first on a two-string diddley bow, then playing a Harmony acoustic. By 1957, just twenty-one, he was in Chicago, soaking up as much Muddy Waters as he could. I think I first heard Buddy's music a decade later, the year I caught Hendrix at Monterey, when Buddy released the album *I Left My Blues in San Francisco,* which was a song I could sing myself later on.

One of my favorite things about living in Chicago was getting to hang out with Buddy at his blues club, Buddy Guy's Legends. He'd let me bring Darren in there, young as he was, and I would bring my coaches, too. We all had a good time just being around Buddy. I'd take a sip of VSOP cognac, which was what he drank, and he always had some moonshine on the side. We'd sit with him for hours, and you never knew what was coming next. Buddy was a smart man. He was an entertainer but also a businessman—and always a performer. One night in January 2004, my coaches and I were at his club when he came out in a red suit and black fedora. Buddy was in some ways almost like Satchel Paige: He was always working the room, and he did it with flair. He ripped through "Hoochie Coochie Man," the Willie Dixon tune, and played some of his older songs, like, "Let Me Love You Baby" and "Damn Right, I've Got the Blues." Afterward, back in his dressing room, Buddy said, "I hope that wasn't boring." Never boring, that was Buddy. He was always good to me and my family, and I still call him every once in a while to see how he's doing.

In Chicago, I drove a Chevy truck and had a little Lexus convertible, which Darren loved, and I drove my Indian motorcycle. I called it my Rasta mobile, because I had Bob Marley on the gas tank and Rasta colors on my fenders.

I had never experienced high-rise living before, so I really felt like I was in the city. I rented two apartments and cut a hole in the middle joining them together. Strolling around Lincoln Park, I would run into players who lived nearby. I would see Ryan Dempster, Moisés Alou, and my catcher Michael Barrett all the time, and LaTroy Hawkins and Jacque Jones both later lived in my building. I was still on the mend from my cancer surgery, but life was good, other than being without my family some of the time, which was hard on me and them.

In Chicago, I found my favorite church in the whole country. I was always on the lookout for churches I could visit. A lot of times it would be Catholic churches, since they were open, and I could go inside and sit awhile before I went to the ballpark. There might be homeless people sleeping inside, and I'd give them some money and give the church some money as well. That was my way of tithing to the church, the way I was taught. One of the best compliments I ever got was from a homeless woman sleeping in a church in Chicago. She looked asleep when I slipped some money in her pocket, but she opened her eyes and asked me, "Are you an angel?" I told her: "No, ma'am, I ain't no angel," and she smiled at me. That took me back to when Darren was a kid and he would always ask me to give homeless people money. I'd ask him why, and he'd say, "Because they could be an angel."

The church I found in Chicago was about two doors down from where I lived, the Hermon Baptist Church, a Black church on the North Side with a history going all the way back to 1888. I loved it when we had late starts on the weekend and I could go to church. On the last Sunday of June 2003, I arrived at the game just a little later than normal after taking Darren and Melissa to Hermon Baptist, and I talked to the team about how the sermon inspired me. "Last thing I remember was hearing that there's a man with one leg, complaining about having one leg, until he saw a man with no legs," I told the players. "That's how I look at life." My friends from that church told me they were all praying for me every time the Cubs had a game.

— — — —

That July 2003 trade that brought over Kenny Lofton and Aramis Ramírez gave us an immediate jolt of new life. We all felt it. We were good before that and a lot better after. The team started playing with more confidence and more purpose. In August, Jim Hendry pulled off another trade with the Pirates, picking up first baseman Randall Simon, who became another starter for us and really helped us, because he could hit.

We finished strong over the last month, and the last week of the season we were locked in a battle for first place in the NL Central with the Astros. On September 27, we were at home at Wrigley Field for a doubleheader with the Pirates. The Astros lost that day and we swept the Pirates in both games, helped by Sammy Sosa's fortieth homer of the season. Sammy was one of the best players in the game. When he was younger, he was a five-tool player, and over time he evolved into a slugger. On the field afterward, we celebrated clinching first place with the fans. Sammy was even spraying champagne into the stands, and I just tried to soak up the delirious atmosphere. The fans had come out that season, more than 2.96 million of them, and they wanted more. So did I.

Once again, baseball would have me take a step back into my history. We'd open the best-of-five Division Series with two games in Atlanta, facing Russ Ortiz, my starting pitcher in Game 6 of the World Series the previous year. I was happy for Russ, who went 21–7 in his first season with the Braves, a career best. But I also wanted to beat him. Bobby Cox was going with Russ in Game 1, and I would go with Kerry Wood, who was 14–11 for me, already at twenty-six a very dominating pitcher. You had the feeling with Kerry that every game he went out was a possible no-hitter. There had only been a handful of pitchers to come on the scene and make a splash like Kerry Wood, like Fernando, Doc Gooden, and Vida Blue before him.

Russ shut us out through five innings that night at Turner Field and we were down 1–0, but in the sixth Moisés Alou, Aramis Ramírez, and Eric Karros all singled to load the bases. Paul Bako tied the game with an RBI groundout, and that meant the pitcher's spot was due up. I could have hit for Kerry, but it was 1–1, he was dealing, and we all knew he could hit. He was one of my aces. I didn't hit for my aces, like when I was back on the Dodgers and we didn't hit for Fernando. Kerry had a hitter's mentality—he was the kind of guy who wanted to come up with the bases loaded—he wanted those ribbies, as we called them (RBIs). So I felt very comfortable sending him up there.

Russ threw Kerry a good fastball, and Kerry liked fastballs. He hit the ball hard to left center and just missed a grand slam. The ball bounced off the wall, good enough for a double that scored two to put us ahead 3–1, and we won the game 4–2.

We traded wins from there, setting up a deciding Game 5 back in Atlanta with Kerry back on the mound for us, this time facing left-hander Mike Hampton. The Braves had 101 wins that season, compared to eighty-eight for us, but come the postseason none of that means much. You just want to get to The Dance, which is the playoffs. In Game 5, we got the jump, scoring single runs in the first and second on a Moisés Alou single and an Alex Gonzalez solo shot. Then in the fourth, we added two more on Aramis Ramírez's home run, to make it 4–0, and we won 5–1. It was all unfolding the way I'd hoped. I'd come to the Cubs because I knew we had a good chance to win, especially after the trades, and all of Chicago was excited about trying to win a World Series for the first time since 1908.

The greatest sporting event I ever saw was a Stanley Cup Final in Chicago, when I was with the Reds in 2013. I'd never seen that kind of electricity at a sporting event. Something about Chicago, with its down-to-earth, working-class background—the people care about sports and live and die with their teams in a way they don't other places. That's why Cubs fans, like Red Sox fans, suffered so much and talked about things like the Curse of the Billy Goat, supposedly placed on the Cubs when a goat was kicked out of a Cubs-Tigers World Series game in 1945.

I kept an eye on the other NL Division Series. If the Giants won, we would have played them in the NLCS, and that would have felt real strange for me. You know that old song "I Left My Heart in San Francisco"? That would have been me, no lie. I was still living in San Francisco in the offseason, too. But it was the Marlins who advanced. "Dusty, you'd better be ready, because they're a good team," Richie Aurilia told me after the Giants lost to the Marlins.

We opened the NLCS at home, and Game 1 turned out into a good old-fashioned seesaw battle. We jumped to a 4–0 lead in the first, then in the third the Marlins answered with a five-spot of their own to take a one-run lead. In the sixth, Florida scored one more to extend the lead, and we answered with two more to tie it. Then in the ninth, they scored two to take a lead, and we scored two on a Sammy Sosa home run to send it into extras. But Florida took it in the eleventh inning when Mike Lowell led off with a home run, and the one run held up.

We didn't have long to think about that loss. The next day, we coasted to a 12–3 win. Mark Prior gave us a strong start, and Sammy led our home run assault. In Miami for Game 3, we had a one-run lead going into the bottom of the ninth and couldn't hold it, but we won it in the eleventh when Doug Glanville tripled home Kenny Lofton. We won again the next day to put us one win away from advancing to the World Series. Even after Josh Beckett pitched a pressure-packed gem in Game 5, winning the potential elimination game 4–0, we went home to Chicago with two more chances to finish off the Marlins with Mark Prior and Kerry Wood going for us.

It was electric back in Chicago for Game 6. You always want to win a series at home if you can. I'd had my heart ripped out the year before in Anaheim, and now I was right back, close to another World Series, and I was so happy to have Chicago fans behind us. It felt like a lot of America was behind us, too. I came to realize there were Cubs fans in every city all over the country.

Watching Mark Prior work from the dugout, I could see he had shutout stuff, but they were fighting him. He would get guys down to their last strike and they'd foul off tough pitches and elevate his pitch count. We went ahead in the first on a Sammy Sosa double to score Kenny Lofton and added two more in the sixth to make it 3–0. Prior was shutting out the Marlins through seven innings, and the Wrigley crowd was getting louder and louder. When Mike Mordecai opened the Marlins' half of the eighth by flying out to left, we were five outs away. Then Juan Pierre doubled into the left-field corner for only the fourth Marlins hit of the day.

That brought up Luis Castillo. Prior got ahead 1-2, then ran the count full. Castillo fouled two balls back. At that point, I got Kyle Farnsworth up in the bullpen. Prior was at 112 pitches but was still strong, and I had total faith in him. It was in my mind that I had taken out Russ Ortiz the year before and it didn't work out. Whatever you do, you'll take heat for it. I didn't want to take Prior out.

On the next pitch, again Castillo hit the ball foul, but right down the left-field line, not more than a foot into foul territory before the cement wall. Moisés Alou went over to make a play on it, leaped and extended his glove—and this was when a fan, Steve Bartman, deflected the ball. Moisés threw down his glove in frustration because he felt like he could have made the play. From my spot in the third-base dugout, I couldn't see the play develop in real time. It's an old-time dugout, down in a hole, and the wall down the foul line is right next to it. The Marlins in the first-base dugout had a better view of the play. I went out to argue, but I couldn't really see. They didn't show any replays on the scoreboard, and we didn't have a big screen at Wrigley then to show replays. I didn't see the play at all until after the game on the TV in the clubhouse, where they showed it about a thousand times. There was no guarantee, but I thought Moisés had a good chance of catching the ball if Bartman had not deflected it.

The umpires ruled there was no fan interference, and it was close, but that was the correct call, since Moisés was reaching into the stands, even if just barely. When play resumed, I continued to feel good about our chances. I assumed nothing. You can never assume. But I thought Prior had enough left in the tank to get out of the inning. The strength of my team was my four starters, and you want to win with your strength.

Prior walked Castillo, then got ahead of Pudge Rodríguez 0-2, but Pudge fought off a good pitch to single to left to make it a 3–1 game. Next up was Miguel Cabrera, and I liked Prior's chances against him. Sure enough, watching in the dugout, I was relieved to see Cabrera hit a routine ground ball to shortstop Alex Gonzalez. Alex was the most sure-handed guy I had. He makes that play ninety-nine times out of a hundred, and they would have turned two because Cabrera wasn't that fleet of foot. This time, Alex didn't make the play. All this is baseball. People are always looking for explanations. Sometimes there aren't any. Things happen you can't explain, and you can't plan ahead of time. I've been on both sides of that, occurrences good and bad.

Farnsworth was ready. Next up for the Marlins was none other than my homeboy Leon Lee's son Derrek Lee, nephew of Leron Lee. D-Lee as a kid had attended the Dusty Baker School of Baseball in Sacramento. I had watched him grow up, and I knew he'd be a tough hitter out here, even if he was 0-for-3 that day and 3-for-25 in the series. Up until then, D-Lee never had a hit off Prior. That night he did what his dad had taught him, which was to jump on a first-pitch fastball if it was where he wanted, and he lined a double to left field to tie up the game. Kyle Farnsworth, on in relief, gave up a sac fly to Jeff Conine and a double to Mike Mordecai, and the game went sideways.

I still felt great about our chances. I'd been trying to dispel the superstitions in town about the Curse of the Billy Goat. I wasn't thinking about curses or goats. We would be back the next night in our home park with Kerry Wood on the mound for us. I told reporters I thought we were in "very, very good shape," and I absolutely meant that. Everyone was talking about this fan, Steve Bartman, wanting to blame him for what happened. I felt really bad for him. Here's a guy, a fan, who woke up that morning excited to go to a game and cheer on his Cubs. He couldn't wait to see the game, and had no clue that within a few hours he was going to be the scorn of Cubs Nation. I realized at that moment how quickly things in your life can change. How quickly things in *anyone's* life can change. I really wanted to win Game 7 of the NLCS and then win the World Series and have Bartman sit with me at the ticker-tape parade.

On the way into Wrigley Field for Game 7, I drove by a hamburger place, the Billy Goat Tavern, and saw they had a pretty goat out front, and a news reporter was interviewing the owner. I was wondering, *What's that goat doing out there?* Then at Wrigley, fifteen minutes before the National Anthem, I was sitting in the dugout and noticed the huge sliding door in right field open up. I can't remember ever seeing that sliding door opened before that. Out came a goat, a real pretty goat. I thought it looked like the same goat I saw that morning, and it turned out it was. Sam Sianis, owner of the Billy Goat Tavern, brought in the goat to lift the Curse of the Billy Goat. Someone told me it was the great-great-grandson of the original goat.

I called upstairs to Andy MacPhail from the dugout phone.

"Who let that goat in here, man?" I asked him. "I'm trying to *dispel* the goat superstition."

"There was a lot of pressure," Andy told me. "If we don't let in the goat and we lose, in the minds of the people, that would be the goat curse all over again."

That was Chicago. Everyone cared so much, they believed in things like that. I believed in baseball, but I couldn't help but wonder, *Is it true?* It just wasn't to be for us in that series, and I don't think it had anything to do with goats. But who knows? I still don't know. The Marlins were a good team. Every time we did something, they answered back. They wouldn't give in. We didn't either, but they finally outlasted us and beat us. That was some series. They went on to win the World Series that year.

Kerry Wood gave up a three-run homer to Cabrera in the first inning of the NLCS Game 7, then settled down. Wood tied it up himself with a two-run homer in the second, and we went up 5–3 in the third when

Moisés homered to bring in Sammy Sosa. Derrek Lee had another big hit for the Marlins in the fifth, singling in Pudge to put the Marlins up 6–5.

Florida broke the game open in the seventh. The Marlins' Alex Gonzalez—we both had players named Alex Gonzalez—came up with runners at first and second, and I brought in reliever Dave Veres to face him. That was an easy call. Farnsworth had just given up back-to-back singles, and he was a fastball pitcher, and Gonzalez was a good fastball hitter. But against Veres, who threw the split-finger, Gonzalez came in 0-for-10 lifetime. I liked that matchup. Gonzalez hit a little broken-bat flare that landed just in front of Kenny Lofton, running hard and diving to try to make the play, and two more runs came in to make it a four-run Florida lead. We lost 9–6.

I liked that team a lot. One of the saddest days of my life came the next spring training when Jim Hendry called me in the office and told me Prior couldn't pitch because he had a sore arm that was aching. That almost killed me. I really couldn't believe it when he told me that. Especially after Mark had worked with Tom House, my former Braves teammate, who was a professor of kinesiology. I hadn't heard anything all winter. Back then, we kept an eye on pitch counts more as a performance thing, and it was very individualized. If someone thought I was overpitching Prior, someone should have told me. We were trying to win a pennant. To win a pennant, somebody or everybody has to overextend. Even the coaches, the trainers, the manager, you all have to overextend. You have restless nights of sleep, you work long hours, you do what you have to do. Baseball, an every day sport, is mentally and physically grueling. If you're not mentally and physically exhausted by the end of the season, you either haven't played or you're just not that good.

— — — —

Hank Aaron had taught me to listen to what he was teaching me, even when I didn't understand, so that maybe I could figure it out later on my own. I always thought of that as baseball advice, but it was also life advice.

Being with Hank had prepared me to deal with a lot. I'd seen how Hank dealt with the hate mail he received when he was chasing Babe Ruth's home run record, I'd read some of those crumpled-up letters when Hank threw them away or tossed them down, and I'd spend a lifetime trying not to let that burn inside of me, even though it finds a way to churn. In Chicago, I started getting a lot of hate mail, and so did LaTroy Hawkins and Jacque Jones. They weren't playing well, they had just signed for a lot of money, and being African American didn't help. The situation got so bad that I was in for an uncomfortable surprise one day going back to my office upstairs after the game.

"There's three suits sitting in your office," the clubhouse guy, Otis Hellmann, told me. "They look like Men in Black."

Sure enough, there were three guys in my office with black suits, white shirts, and little skinny ties.

"How do I know you're with the FBI?" I asked the three suits.

They flashed their IDs: "FBI, Hate Crimes Division."

I'd had enough talking to the FBI in years past, answering questions about performance-enhancing drugs, having them ask me about various players and what they might have been doing. I knew nothing and had nothing to tell them. I was tired of seeing the FBI.

Someone had sent in some white powder in a letter addressed to me, and that got out to the press. That was in those years after the 9/11 attacks when anthrax scares would turn up now and then, starting in late 2001 when anthrax-laced letters had been sent to members of the House and Senate. I talked to the FBI, but I was careful about what I said. I gave them the basics. Then I started hearing that some people were accusing me of making up the anthrax and the hate mail in some kind of bid for sympathy. Were they crazy? Whose sympathy was I supposed to want? None of it made a lick of sense.

One of the FBI guys handed me his card on the way out.

"Call me if anything happens," he said.

"I'll handle it myself, thanks," I said.

For the most part, I always liked media people, print and broadcast, men and women, anyone who showed they respected the job and respected you. That does not seem like too much to ask. My parents raised me to give people a chance, before you come to distrust them, and I stuck with that, but I did get more of an education. I remember one time a local TV personality came up to me and tipped me off: "Be careful," she told me, "there are two guys over there who are practicing how to get under your skin, so you'll go off on one of them and they get a story out of it." Sure enough, one guy asked me a question, and the other tried to play off it. They had rehearsed how to arouse my anger. The lady reporter who tipped me off helped me immensely.

I had one great year and one good year in Chicago. In 2004, we were 89–73 but finished third in a tough NL Central behind the Cardinals and Astros and missed the playoffs—and missed out on a chance to get right back to the NLCS and erase some bad memories from 2003. By the third year, I knew it wasn't happening. There was more and more talk of the team being sold. We were 79–83 in 2005, and then 2006 turned into a really rough year. We started off 13–8, then at one point lost eight in a row and twenty of twenty-five. Derrek Lee, a Cub since 2004, broke his wrist, and we missed having him in the lineup.

I met with Dennis FitzSimons, CEO of the Tribune Company that owned the Cubs at the time, and he told me that the company had to spend less money on the team with a possible sale in the works. That brought back thoughts of what happened when I was a player in Atlanta when they traded all of us and then sold the team to Ted Turner. The Cubs just didn't have the team to compete, and as manager, I bore the brunt of fan frustration. It got really bad. The fans at Wrigley would actually boo me when I stepped out of the dugout. Some even had huge signs reading "FIRE DUSTY."

D-Lee, who I've been knowing since he was a kid, came to see me in my office. He wanted to play, even though he was still coming back from his injury, to try to save my job.

"No, man, take care of your hand, thanks anyway," I told him.

That was the period when Melissa didn't want me going out to restaurants and bars in Chicago by myself, and she quit taking Darren to the games. They were booing me so loud all the time, and Darren wanted to fight everybody. Darren was seven years old, but he was ready to take them on. That was also when I started carrying a pocketknife on me at all times, like my dad always did.

Sometimes I felt like I had no fans in the whole town other than the people I'd known for years. I had friends in the Rainbow Coalition going back to meeting Jesse Jackson years earlier. For years my friend Bob Battie, an umpire, would take me out for soul food on the South Side anytime I was in Chicago. He loved to talk baseball. Annette Scales was a friend I'd known since she was thirteen or fourteen. I met her at the ballpark and would leave her tickets to keep her from hanging with the wrong crowd. She later started an organization for victims of domestic violence. Robert Taylor, a good friend to me and also Hank Aaron, was there at the field every day to watch me. Robert would act as if he was my bodyguard. Melissa's Uncle Leno and Auntie Cora were there and cooked for me all the time. It really helped. I was lonely sometimes. My family was there probably no more than a third of the time since Darren was in school.

My first spring as Cubs manager, I'd befriended a seventh-grade kid, Matt Starcevich, who seemed a little lost and in need of a friend. I met him on one of the caravans we did to schools in Illinois and Indiana through a lot of small towns. He wrote me a letter that year seeking guidance, but I didn't get a chance to answer. Then a year later, I saw him at the ballpark again: "I remember you," I told him.

After that, I told him to come talk to me before games. That was what he did for years. I tried to steer him toward making some good choices about his future and made a deal with him that if he took the SAT and went to college and graduated, I'd help get him a job in baseball.

"Everything here is temporary, it's all going away one day," I used to tell him. "Don't worry so much about stuff in the here and now. Keep your faith in Christ, and it'll all work out."

Matt was one of countless young people I tried to help over the years, and I never wanted or expected anything in return. Seeing them make their way through life was its own reward. When everything got so bad in 2006, I was glad to have him in my corner.

"Matty, I ain't lyin'," I told him, "it's almost like you're the only fan I've got *left* in this city."

"Man, you're the only fan I've got in *life*," he told me, and we both laughed.

Jim Hendry came into my office at the end of the season and was very reluctant and apologetic in his tone. He had bad news for me. He told my contract was not being renewed. Then after I left Chicago, the Ricketts family bought the team from the Tribune Company for more than $800 million, hired Lou Piniella, and spent a lot of money. I was always cool with Lou. He was one of the first ones to start asking me, back when I was a coach, when I was going to get a managing job.

— — — —

During my second spring training with the Cubs in 2004, I decided to have some people over to the house I was renting in Scottsdale for a barbecue. I grilled up some ribs and hot links, had some mac and cheese going, collard greens and cornbread and salad, a nice spread. Besides Melissa and Darren and me, I invited Gary Matthews, a good friend and one of my coaches, and a few other people. Gary asked if he could bring some other friends, a state senator he knew from Illinois and his wife. Of course that was cool with me. Any friend of Gary's was a friend of mine. The young state senator from the South Side of Chicago had an unusual name, Barack Obama, and Gary's wife Sandy was close friends with his wife, Michelle.

We had ourselves a nice time. Barack and I talked a lot. He was a White Sox fan, which made sense for a state senator from the South Side, and he joked about that. Barack came across to me as very smooth and smart. We talked about our backgrounds. We talked a lot about Hawaii, where he was from, and my favorite spot, Kauai, which he'd also visited. It was a pleasant enough conversation, covering everything from basketball and baseball to global warming and college accessibility.

One thing I remember from that barbecue was the kids playing together. Darren had just turned five, this was just a year and a half after

J. T. Snow had lifted him up in a sequence practically everybody in the country had seen at one point or another. Barack and Michelle had two daughters—Malia, who was also five years old that spring, and their younger daughter, Sasha, who was not yet three. Gary's daughter Paige was great friends with Malia and Sasha and was the same age as Sasha.

I'm sure I talked with Barack that day about what it was like for me as a young player hanging out with Hank Aaron in Atlanta in the late 1960s and listening in along with Ralph as Hank talked to Maynard Jackson and Andrew Young and Jesse Jackson and other Civil Rights leaders. Later that year, Barack started campaigning for the United States Senate. There had been some speculation that he might run against popular Bears coach Mike Ditka, and when Ditka announced he was not running, a poll was commissioned that found some people wanted *me* to run for Senate. No, thank you! Michael Jordan came out way ahead in that poll anyway. Then in 2007, when he was running for President, I joined him at a campaign event at Civic Center in San Francisco and another one in Sacramento.

I had no idea Barack was going to be President. At that time you didn't think a Black man could be elected President in your lifetime. I try to stay out of politics, but then I would hear my mom's voice in my head, urging me to play my part. Up until that time whenever you asked kids what they wanted to be when they grow up, there weren't very many Black kids out there saying they wanted to be President of the United States one day. And most who said it, people would tell them: "You must be crazy."

On July 27, 2004, Obama gave a big speech at the Democratic National Convention in Boston, and suddenly the whole country seemed to know who this Illinois state senator was. Back in Illinois after the speech, Obama started attracting big crowds as he campaigned for the U.S. Senate. I caught some highlights and noticed some things. One thing you look for in evaluating talent in a ballplayer is a quality of inner calm, like they know they can do this. Obama had that quality of seeming to get more calm even as the crowds at his speeches kept growing. This was a man who looked at home in front of a crowd. He talked about his African father, who herded goats growing up in Kenya, and how the true genius of America lay in the small miracles we see all around us every day if we keep our eyes open. "We can say what we think, write what we think, without hearing a sudden knock on the door," he said, twenty-odd years ago, before those sudden knocks on the door again became louder in this country.

When Barack was elected to the U.S. Senate that November, he became only the third Black person ever elected to that body. Getting to know Barack was one of the best things that happened to me during my time in Chicago.

CHAPTER 14

"I Don't Want My Daddy to Die"

Baseball has lessons to teach you, if you let it, about life. If you've been through enough highs and lows and wild swings, you come to realize that what looks good at first might also be bad. Even bad news might have serious upside. Taking part in more than six thousand games, I've seen that in baseball, anything can happen. A ball can take a strange bounce. Maybe one of your stars goes down with an injury, and you hate to see him hurt, but it's part of the game. While he's on the DL, you get a chance to see how an up-and-comer handles a shot at the job and you find out he's ready, or sometimes you get a pleasant surprise from someone you weren't expecting all that much from. Then maybe the star comes back, and you find a way to have both in the lineup.

I would never have managed twenty-six seasons in the big leagues if I didn't love it, but baseball was never my *purpose* in life. It was always an avenue to my purpose in life. Your life is what you make of it. That's as true on a Sunday at home during the offseason as it is managing under the glare of October baseball. If I was away from baseball between managing jobs, I was always thankful for the time to pursue my other passions, but I'd miss the action and the paychecks. I'd also miss the challenge of it, for you and your players, and the fun of it, getting to know young guys who weren't even born when you were playing in the big leagues. You have some things to show them, but they might have some things to show you as well. I've always been drawn to the action and the heat of competition, but as much as I hated being pulled away from another shot at taking a club all the way, I also made the most of the years I wasn't in baseball. Life always seemed to have something in store for me. That turned out to be a silver lining for me, those years in between managing jobs, which gave me a chance to live life in a different way.

It was very challenging to find myself back home after the 2006 season. I wasn't ready for a break from baseball. I felt like I hadn't finished what I came to Chicago to do. I always wanted to leave a place better than I found it. I was taking a break from baseball because the Cubs terminated my contract and no other team had reached out to me. But if baseball didn't come calling with something new, it wasn't going to slow me down from living my life.

I had always wanted to visit Africa to see where my dad and mom might have been from. Most Black people don't know where exactly their family came from. I wanted to visit the continent of Nelson Mandela and Bishop Desmond Tutu, both inspirations to me. I never got to meet Mandela, but when I was playing with the Dodgers, I was invited to a reception for Bishop Tutu at Senator Tom Hayden's home in Beverly Hills. That was one of the highlights of my life right there. I met Sidney Poitier and Harry Belafonte that same day, and the three of us had a great conversation. They both knew their baseball. I finally got my chance to go to Africa in 2007. Bob Watson, the second Black general manager in baseball after Bill Lucas, was by then an MLB vice president and helped organize a good-will trip to Ghana in spring 2007. Omar Minaya, the Mets GM, spearheaded the planning, working with his close friend George Ntim, who was from Ghana and worked in guest relations at the Times Square Marriott Marquis.

Omar and George both called to ask me to come on the trip. Back in 1970, I gave my mom a trip to Africa as a graduation present when she finished night school, and I knew it was just a matter of time before I visited myself. Now was my time. I made the trip along with my former Dodgers teammate Reggie Smith, Al Jackson, and Dave Winfield, all good friends. Wendy Lewis, another MLB vice president, also joined us. (Later a McDonald's VP, as of 2025 she was CEO of the Chicago

Sinfonietta.) Wendy is very intelligent, strong, and kind. She's someone I've called for advice for years because she always sees one step ahead.

The flight from New York to Accra, the capital of Ghana, had me thinking some heavy thoughts. I always have my books, and on that flight I was reading *Night,* by Elie Wiesel, his first-person account of surviving the Nazi concentration camp Auschwitz during the Second World War, when six million Jews were murdered. "To forget the dead would be akin to killing them a second time," Wiesel wrote.

We arrived on Friday, February 2, and in the small city of Tema we helped launch a four-team Little League, which was really cool in a country where baseball was played rarely if at all. The dusty field where they played reminded me of sandlot baseball, like I played as a kid in Riverside, but our pristine fields back home looked like big-league parks compared to what I saw in Africa. Pamela Bridgewater, U.S. Ambassador to Ghana, was wearing a Mets jersey, and led the hundred or so Ghanaians in singing, "Take Me Out to the Ballgame," which of course no one knew. In a way, it felt like we were all kids again, playing our first baseball games.

Another day we went to the University of Ghana in Accra and gathered on a soccer field with some government ministers to mark the spot to be developed as a baseball field, all the brainchild of George Ntim. I sketched an outline in the dirt to show them how they should configure their field.

I don't understand why people ignore history. If you do, things tend to happen again. Thinking about slaves on ships, thinking about what it would be like if you were really there below deck in the hold of the ship, breathing that air? What if those shackles were on *your* arms and legs? To me, you don't study history to recite facts. You study history to feel in your bones what it might have been like to live in a different time when some big things were different, but sadly enough, an awful lot was the same.

On that visit to Africa, we also took a three-hour trip to tour a castle in a city called Cape Coast. This is where Africans were brought before they were packed into ships and brought to North America as slaves, starting in 1792. Dave Winfield asked how long the passage took, and the answer was one month from Ghana to the Caribbean. Imagine being crammed into the hold of a ship, in chains, tossed all over the place on the high seas, for a whole month.

The more stories I heard of what it was like, the angrier I felt. For example, in the dungeon of that castle, there was more than a foot of human feces piled up wall to wall. I kept thinking of Elie Wiesel and what he wrote about being transported to the Nazi death camps in cattle cars and having to sleep standing up, it was so packed, and pee on themselves and crap their pants because they had no alternative. One woman on the train in Elie Wiesel's book started screaming about visions of flames before the train ever arrived at the camps. It made me think about the Africans being rounded up and taken as slaves. Some of them must have had visions of what was coming for them, given how spiritual Africans were. It would have been impossible for them to know the extent of what was coming. Touring the castle, I asked a tour guide what happened to pregnant women dragged to that terrible place. "If the baby became a nuisance . . ." our guide told me, trailing off. I finished for him: "Baby gone."

Some in our group cried. Some had to step outside. My reaction surprised me. By that point, I had moved beyond anger. I felt more a sense of a deep and collective spiritual sorrow, like you would feel at a wailing wall, where you could feel the moans and the pain and the humiliation of not being able to sleep or use the bathroom. My ancestors were proud people. They probably had never been in a claustrophobic situation like that before in a place like Africa with wide open spaces. It was jarring. You walked through the Door of No Return, as it was called, where slaves were dragged in chains to the boats that would carry them to ships. I stood there for a long time, Omar Minaya at my side, just letting it all settle. Then we went through the door, and suddenly we were outside and it was the present day again. There were a bunch of kids playing in the ocean, no lifeguards or nothing, just playing, and I stared at those kids, thinking that their ancestors could have been my ancestors.

— — — —

I'm not a man to sit around doing nothing. Like I said, when I was a kid, if I told my dad I had nothing to do, he would find something for me to do, which was usually pulling weeds, and I despise weeds to this day. Soon after that trip to Ghana, ESPN made the announcement that I was joining the network as talent. Chris Berman and his agent, Lou Oppenheim, made that happen. Chris and I had been friends for years since he was a huge Giants fan and would come to as many games as he could in San Francisco and on the road. He would always wear his old purple jacket, and over the years it got pretty raggedy, but we believed it brought us good luck. Years later, I bought my own good-luck purple jacket, which I have to this day.

I was kind of a utility man for ESPN, doing *Baseball Tonight* as an analyst or working games on TV or radio. I had a very good time working with Chris, who helped me get my bearings in Bristol, Connecticut, and Jeff Brantley, who had played for me in San Francisco, and Karl Ravech and Joe Morgan. I felt like a rookie all over again, and they gave me a crash course on the industry.

In early May, I was in San Francisco doing ESPN Radio color commentary for a Giants game against the Phillies, pitcher Tim Lincecum's big-league debut. In the sixth inning, they showed me on the big screen at AT&T Park, and I got a nice ovation from the crowd, so I stood up and waved and smiled. I always did feel at home in the Bay. That same month, I flew to Memphis for the Blues Music Awards courtesy of my buddy Elvin Bishop, who invited me to come along with him to help present the Pinetop Perkins Piano Player of the Year Award. That was when Bobby "Blue" Bland was still alive. I met all the famous bluesmen and blueswomen that my dad and I had been listening to together for years, and they all performed a song or two, so it was like twenty or thirty mini-concerts. Elvin and I also went to Morgan Freeman's place in Mississippi to fish, and that was when I got out of the car that same afternoon to kiss the ground at the crossroads where Robert Johnson supposedly dueled the Devil for his soul. In "Cross Road Blues," Johnson sang about that spot, and how he "fell down on my knees" and asked the Lord to save his soul. I imagined what it would have been like to be in that spot on a dark night, without any lights. It was a spiritual feeling, but eerie.

I liked working as a broadcaster, since it kept me close to the game, and I knew it was also a good education for me. That could come in handy when I got back on the field, where my heart and soul always were. Nothing can replicate the adrenaline rush of being on the field, but you can always keep learning. You can always keep redefining yourself, as Bill Walsh always taught me. Bill was my best teacher on how to talk to the media. He taught me from the very beginning to focus on a few fundamentals:

1. Don't try to be coy.
2. Be honest, but you don't have to tell them everything.
3. You don't have to answer every question, just because someone asked it.

I always understood that media people had a job to do in order to feed their family, just like my job was feeding mine. The only thing I took exception to were personal shots that didn't belong in the interview. My ESPN job gave me a chance to think about whether I might want to make a career in broadcasting. I was thinking about what I wanted to do for the next thirty years. You never know if you'll get another managing job, so I took nothing for granted.

Hank, Bill Walsh, and Al Attles taught me to challenge my mind at all times. When I was interviewed by people like Howard Cosell and Al Michaels, I always tried to pick up how they did it and learn from them. I thought Howard Cosell was pretty cool. He had that unmistakable voice and diction. He always knew what he was talking about, and I didn't see him with a whole bunch of notes or anything, so I figured he had to be smart. Being a boxing fan as a kid, I watched every interview Howard Cosell had with Muhammad Ali and Joe Frazier, so when he interviewed me in L.A., I felt like I'd arrived at the top of my profession. Howard Cosell didn't interview everybody. I always found Al Michaels very, very smooth, like Bob Costas, another one who seemed very smart and very polished. I didn't try to copy them, but I would notice their demeanor and how they spoke. They didn't use words that people couldn't understand, but they didn't sound basic and unintelligent either.

Joe Morgan told me to keep my eyes open out there. You had to beware because there were people who would try to trip you up and make you look bad, but the people I worked with at ESPN were all good with me. I enjoyed my time there. Working the other side, I got more of a feel for what broadcast people did, which helped me understand them better in later years when I was managing again.

— — — —

In 2007, I decided it was time to move back to Sacramento to be closer to my family, especially my dad. San Francisco felt too far away. By then, my dad was having serious issues with dementia. My time with the Cubs had helped me dig out from the financial hole I'd been in for years with my tax troubles. I made much more as a manager than I ever did as a player.

By this time, my dad's dementia was getting noticeably worse. We'd first seen symptoms the year before, but now he was in clear decline. My brother Rob was living in Orange County and moved back home. I also came home to Sacramento, and that was about the time Vic came home from L.A. as well. He drove his truck all the way up and stopped right in front of my dad's house, out of oil and out of gas, but he made it. Vic was still having serious issues himself then. We had lost track of him in L.A., but he just showed up at my dad's house.

Even after I left the Giants in 2003, I still lived in the Bay Area in the offseason, and when I built a new house in Sacramento, I kept my modest condo in San Bruno to serve as a reminder, so I never got too bigheaded and always remembered what it was like to struggle. Same with my cars, which I gave myself to remember past struggles and held on to so I remembered the downs and also the ups. Sometimes you have to give yourself a present for a job well done. You know when you've done good work. I also kept the San Bruno place because in 2001 I had promised Melissa's mother that I would take care of Melissa's youngest brother, Ryan, who is hearing impaired. He lives there to this day, a great brother-in-law, as Melissa's other brothers also are, James and Wayne. Her family of Filipino descent always made me feel like one of them.

Building my own home was important to me. I always remembered that in Riverside my dad had built our house and was able to do it just the way he wanted, as much as he could afford. Now I was ready to build my own house in the Sacramento area, where I could live for years to come. I had built a beautiful house in Calabasas when I was down in L.A. playing for the Dodgers, and now I was going to build another beautiful home as part of my comeback from when I was struggling all those years.

I came home to look for property near Sacramento and couldn't find what I wanted. I found houses I wanted but on lots too small. I found properties I wanted but not with a house we liked. I'm pretty particular. Finally I found the right piece of land near Folsom Lake, up near Rocklin, where the 49ers used to hold their training camps and I first met Bill Walsh, and where I fished a lot when I was in high school.

My homey Dennis, a friend forever by that point, had a background in construction and had just lost his job, so he was a perfect fit to be my project manager. He's the most organized man I know, and he did a great job. Dennis is a perfectionist, he keeps immaculate files, and he's very, very frugal. A guy who grew up with no parents in high school, paying his own rent, he knew how to manage cash. I told Dennis, "Whatever you save me, I'll give you a percentage." He ended up saving me quite a bit.

I had a vision of what I wanted, but I needed an architect to put my ideas into practice. What makes a home? To me, it's livable, very comfortable, and not a place where you're afraid to touch anything. Dennis recommended Bernice Nichols, out of Stockton. All her renderings were done by hand and came out perfectly, true to my vision. And I needed my builder, Mark Ures, to follow Bernice's lead. I'm a very good farmer, but I couldn't even build a doghouse. I could see it, I could imagine it, I could visualize it—I just couldn't build anything. I wanted a batting cage for Darren, so I had one put in and equipped it with stadium seats from all the teams I'd played for, because when they imploded the stadiums, they gave me some of the seats. I even have two from Philadelphia, where I hit a ball to the upper deck. I also had to have a basketball half court with lights, the way my dad had put up lights on the driveway in

Riverside, so I could play basketball out there into the night, and now Darren and his friends could play whenever they wanted.

With Bernice and Mark's help, I built an energy-efficient home. I put in solar panels next to my vineyard and had thermal hot-water heaters, instant hot water, and a solar-powered swimming pool. (That's when I got into solar power and later started my own solar company, Baker Energy Team, with my high school and college classmate Brad Johnson.) I even got an elevator like I had always wanted since the childhood days when I saw one in the house of that rich kid whose lawn I used to mow. Plus, I knew I needed to have an elevator if my dad wanted to come over and watch football games upstairs in the game room, since his stiff leg meant he couldn't do stairs.

I had read in the Bible that you get your fields ready before you build your house (Proverbs 24:27), and I actually planted my vineyard before my house was built. All those years working gardening jobs with my dad helped me develop my landscaping abilities, and I put them to work landscaping the property. I planted roses in the front, because my dad loved roses, and I brought in a big rock for my rose garden. I deemed it my *Dobie Gillis* think rock, like the old sitcom with Maynard G. Krebs, a teenage Beatnik.

Moving back home when I did was one of the best decisions I ever made. You never know how much time you have with the ones you love most. My dad's condition went downhill. I came back home after the Reds' 2009 season and went to see him as soon as I could. He told me he wanted to die at home, not in a hospital or care facility. I hired round-the-clock caretakers so he could stay at his house, which got very costly after a couple years. I was grateful that I had a job where I could afford that.

Four or five different times I'd been notified by the hospice care team, whom I really admired, that my dad was going to pass. They'd heard the crackle of death, which is what you hear when the lungs are giving out. "He won't last twenty-four hours," I was told. Each time, he fought death. I went to see him in November 2009 to tell him he didn't have to fight anymore.

"Daddy, you trained me," I told him, with Rob at my side. By then he couldn't talk, but he could listen. "I'm the oldest," I said. "If you're worried about everybody, I can handle this the way you taught me. It's okay, Dad. It's okay to pass. Rob and I got this."

I went up to the mountain after that, the way my dad always taught me, actually the foothills in Auburn, another twenty miles up I-80 toward Truckee. I was up there to sit and think when I felt it. Just like that, I could feel that my dad had passed. I just knew it.

"Dad's gone," Rob told me when I went back to his house, but I already knew.

At the wake and funeral, when everyone gathered for a meal, I asked the catering company who had paid for the meal, and they told me it was my player Scott Rolen, and I thought that was the most generous and heartfelt gesture I could remember from my time in baseball.

— — — —

As the 2007 season ended and fall arrived, I knew the Cincinnati Reds were interested in hiring me as manager. I had played against the Big Red Machine, and Joe Morgan, Pete Rose, Tony Pérez, Johnny Bench, George Foster, Dave Concepción, and Ken Griffey Sr. were some of my favorite ballplayers on opposing teams. I learned from all of them. I liked the idea of sitting in a dugout in a Reds uniform, just like manager Sparky Anderson had for so many years. I had never worn a red uniform in my life until then.

I never formally interviewed for the job. I met Bob Castellini, the new Reds owner as of 2006, and we just talked, and he told me I was his man. He liked my style of managing going back to my days with the Giants. His general manager, Wayne Krivsky—who I didn't know—recommended me to him. Mr. Castellini, as I always called him, was in the fruit and vegetable business, which I liked, and as I came to find out, he was someone whose word you could trust. He had a direct, no-nonsense kind of style.

One rule of managing I never forgot was that you're only as good as your coaches, and the coaches are only as good as the players. As manager, I was kind of like the maestro of the band, conducting. I saw a program once, Miles Davis *Live at Montreux,* and they asked him his philosophy of how he handled his band. Miles said he would give each of them the freedom to play when it was their turn, famous guys like Herbie Hancock and George Duke. But then, Miles said, he always had the right as a leader to come in when he wanted to—but not abruptly. He'd give it a little *toot-toot* on that trumpet, just to let them know it was time to wrap it up. He gave them the autonomy without micro-managing them. That was how I always tried to be with my coaches.

In Cincinnati, once again I had Dick Pole, my longtime friend and pitching coach, at my side, and as my bench coach Chris Speier, whose niece is married to my nephew Jonathan, oldest son of my sister Tonya. Brook Jacoby, another Californian who had been drafted by the Braves, was my batting coach. Billy Hatcher and Mark Berry were our base coaches, and for my bullpen coach I always liked having a catcher. Juan Lopez, a Puerto Rican former catcher, was my bullpen coach from the Giants to the Cubs to the Reds. Juan had been in the minor leagues with the Giants, and Orlando Cepeda was the one who recommended him to me. He was right under my nose. Juan threw the best batting practice of all time and cooked great Puerto Rican food for the whole staff.

For my first spring training as Reds manager, my first day of camp was February 15. I loved just walking around the Reds spring training complex in Sarasota, Florida, seeing fields named for Tony Pérez, Johnny Bench, Joe Morgan, and Pete Rose, all guys I played against and admired. I liked Sarasota and its vibe. It was my favorite town in Florida with its waterways and keys and good fishing spots. And I had only trained on the Atlantic side, never on the Gulf side of Florida. I rented in Siesta Key, right on the Grand Canal, and fished before bed every night, right off my dock, and caught snook and sheepshead. It was beautiful. I liked that whole area.

I knew the Reds were on the bottom, trying to start some kind of new momentum, but I didn't really know their players at all. One I did know was Scott Hatteberg, who was at the end of his career. I had him in Arizona Fall League when he was a catcher for the Red Sox back at the start of his career, before the A's turned him into a first baseman, in my first job as manager. In 2008, he was thirty-eight. I also had pitcher Mike Lincoln on that team—he was from Citrus Heights, close to where I went to high school, and he showed me pictures of himself at eight or nine years old at my baseball academy.

A key choice I had to make at that camp was to decide on a leadoff hitter. I talked to Kenny Lofton to see if we might sign him, but he was forty by then and didn't want to come to camp unless he had a roster spot. He ended up deciding to retire. One talented kid in camp was outfielder Jay Bruce, a Reds' first-round choice in 2005 who climbed the ladder the previous season with stops at Single-A, Double-A, and Triple-A. Jay, who hadn't even turned twenty-one yet, knew I needed a leadoff hitter and wanted to make the team, so he volunteered.

"I can bat leadoff," he told me in spring training.

Make the team first, son! I had nothing against giving Bruce a shot to stick with the team out of camp, but he was going to have to show that he was ready to play in the big leagues. There was talk of easing Bruce in, but I let it be known I didn't see it that way. Was Ken Griffey Jr. eased in? Was *I* eased in? A whole bunch of guys weren't eased in. To me it came down to trusting what your scouts had seen. All I knew about Bruce until then was stats I'd seen, but there's more to being in the big leagues than just stats. Even then everyone had become so stat-conscious, they were getting away from questions like: *Does he know how to run the bases?* and *Does he throw to the right base?* You look at a player's ability to learn and retain and his baseball instincts. *Can he do the little things to play winning baseball?* Bruce ended up playing about a third of the season for Triple-A Louisville, batting .364, and earned his promotion, and played six years for me on those Reds teams.

Joey Votto only had a couple dozen games with the Reds up to then. A former Reds second-round pick in 2002, as a catcher, he was a twenty-four-year-old who didn't talk much but noticed everything. I'd heard about this kid, a power-hitting first baseman, but I didn't see what they were talking about, since all he did in spring training was take pitches. He wouldn't swing the bat. Come on, dude, you're trying to make the club?

I underestimated Votto. I didn't know what I was getting. I came to see that he was mentally way ahead of where he should have been at the time, but I didn't give him credit. I hadn't run across too many guys that were mentally advanced beyond their age that way. I found him intriguing, serious but relaxed, quiet but witty. He was different. I liked Canadians. They see the world a little differently.

I took to Joey Votto quickly and urged the Reds to give him more of a chance, and not trade him away. That was a hard one for me, since Scott Hatteberg was the one guy I knew on the team and I liked him. But I saw promise in Votto, so I started playing him every day, and Scott didn't see much action, getting only about fifty at-bats that season before retiring. It was the right baseball decision, but it was a little dicey for me as a new field manager, since I knew Scott was a fan favorite in Cincinnati. We had a lot of good guys on that team, and one of the most talented was Brandon Phillips, my All-Star second baseman. My son Darren used to wear his number. Brandon was one of the best second basemen around and later helped Darren learn how to play second.

Two years earlier, the Reds had traded Wily Mo Peña to Boston for pitcher Bronson Arroyo, a right-hander out of Florida who had that high leg kick and made it look easy. He was tall and thin but worked hard and was always in great shape, very limber, like a ballet dancer. I loved Bronson. This guy was smart and fearless. He was a big-game guy and a team leader.

Since I did not know a lot of the players, I asked around and found people whose opinions I could trust. The way I was raised in baseball, you built a network of people you trusted, former teammates, coaches, or managers you knew, even some media people, and you turned to them when you needed a take on someone or needed someone new to ask. I talked to former pitcher Tom Brown, now a pitching coach in the minors, whom I didn't know, even though he had been in baseball as long as I had. I asked Tom what he thought about two young Reds pitching prospects from the Dominican Republican, Edinson Vólquez and Johnny Cueto. Vólquez was a twenty-four-year-old right-hander who'd pitched here and there for the Rangers over three seasons without a breakthrough.

Cueto had just turned twenty-two. He was signed by the Reds in 2004 as an undrafted free agent, and was the Reds' Minor League Player of the Year in both 2006 and 2007.

Tom had Johnny in Double-A with the Chattanooga Lookouts and had seen Edinson when he was pitching for the Frisco RoughRiders in the Rangers' organization, so he knew. Tom told me—in that heavy Louisiana accent of his—that they were both ready. About Edinson, he told me you've got to keep him in the strike zone and don't let him fall in love with his changeup. I told Wayne Krivsky I'd heard good things about both of them. He was comfortable enough in his own ability to see that my judgment was hopefully going to make his job easier. It was a big move when the Reds kept both rookies, Edinson and Johnny, rather than sending them to the minors. And it paid off: Edinson went 17–6 for us with a 3.21 ERA and made the All-Star Game that year. Our third game of the season, Johnny made his major-league debut and struck out ten batters in a 3–2 win. He showed he belonged, even though he finished the season 9–14 with a 4.81 ERA. Within a few years, he would be a workhorse starter who gave you thirty-three or thirty-four starts a season and won you nineteen or twenty games. I convinced Johnny to run stairs to stay fit. When he needed someone to run with him, Darren joined if he was in town.

One time, Darren was in the batting cage early with me, hitting, and I felt eyes on us. I looked up and saw Pete Rose at the back of the cage, watching kind of from the shadows, since Major League Baseball had banned him from even coming to the stadium. "Young Baker, can you hit?" Pete asked him. "Hit the ball back up the middle and stay out of the air," he said, which Darren proceeded to do.

Another case where the team trusted my judgement was on Mike Leake, a right-handed pitcher from San Diego the Reds took out of ASU in the first round of the 2009 draft. In spring training, Mike used to sit near me during the games, and never said much of anything, just sat there. He sat and watched the whole game, taking some notes, and did not leave early, like some other players. That was something I noticed. That impressed me. Dick Pole and I talked it over and decided we thought Mike was ready for the big leagues. He was mentally prepared and didn't need seasoning in the minor leagues. He was 8–4 for us that year with a 4.23 ERA and had a lot of good seasons for me before he was traded to the Giants in 2015.

I liked Francisco Cordero as my closer, but some of the others thought he was close to the end. An eleven-year veteran, Cordero saved forty-nine games for the Rangers one year and the year before saved forty-four. I had to insist on him as our closer. I showed faith in him, and he came through many times. Over the next four seasons, he saved 150 games for us. Homer Bailey was a tall Texan from La Grange, the home of ZZ Top. He was a first round draft pick in 2004 who later went on to throw two no-hitters. We were adding pieces. As a rookie in 2012, Zack Cozart was our starting shortstop, which is hard for a rookie on a contending team, but he handled it beautifully. He did a great job (and his mom was a bass pro who gave me lures all the time).

I knew Walt Jocketty going back to my time with the Oakland A's when Walt was assistant general manager. He was the Cardinals general manager starting in 1994, and brought in Tony La Russa and Mark McGwire and a bunch of former A's. The Cardinals won the World Series in 2006 under Walt, but the next year he was fired. The Reds brought him on as an advisor. Then in April 2008, my first spring managing the club, Wayne Krivsky lost his job twenty-one games into the season. I never knew why that happened. Our record at the time was 9–12.

The Reds named Walt their new general manager. When Walt and I reconnected, I reminded him that he'd tried to lure me to St. Louis back before he hired Tony to take that job, but that Orlando Cepeda had always told me that in those years he didn't think the Midwest was ready for a Black manager, especially in St. Louis, even though he liked St. Louis. Now it was ten years later and Walt told me he'd thought about it afterward and decided I was right about my assessment. They wouldn't have been ready for me. I loved working with Walt, a very fair and patient man with a good soul.

My first year with the Reds, we still had Ken Griffey Jr., whose dad I knew. Junior was thirty-eight by then, playing his twentieth season in the big leagues. That was when I knew I was getting older, when I realized I had seen Junior play as a very young kid and now he'd been in the league twenty years. Junior was real close on that team with Adam Dunn, our big Texan first baseman. Adam knew all the fishing spots, including some exotic fishing and hunting spots in Texas that he took us to, and he was one hell of a fisherman. As I've mentioned many times, forming relationship with your players is as important a part of managing as any on-field activities you have. Fishing with a player will in the long run actually help you with the job of managing.

Junior was going for 600 home runs that season and needed only seven more. Only five guys had reached 600, starting with Babe Ruth, then Hank and Willie and Barry, and also Sammy Sosa, who I managed in Chicago. Junior hit his 597th homer at home on April 23, then a month later hit number 598. At home at the end of May, he drilled number 599—and in Miami on June 9, he connected off Mark Hendrickson in the first inning to get home run number 600. How could I be so fortunate? I could never have imagined it, ever. I'd managed the last three guys to reach 600—Barry, Sammy, and now Junior. Both Hank and Willie called Junior to offer congratulations. It was one of those nights when baseball really feels like a family.

We had a good bunch of guys on that team, we just weren't ready to win yet. I'd helped the Reds build up in my first two seasons, finishing 74–88 in 2008 and 78–84 in 2009, but along the way there were some painful adjustments. Dick Pole was my partner, he'd been at my side for years, and he was good at his job. But near the end of my second season, the Reds fired Dick. I never knew why. That was a dark day. The team had three games left for the 2009 season, but Dick packed his bags and was gone. It was an organizational decision to let him go, and I told the team I wanted to be the one to inform Dick. That was a very difficult conversation for me, because we're so close. Naturally, he was hurt. He asked me not to save him.

"If they don't want me, I don't want to be here," he told me, which was about what he had told me when he was let go in San Francisco. "Don't try to save me." The Giants had told Dick Pole they thought he was more loyal to me than he was to the organization, and my answer to that was "What's wrong with that?" After that, I vowed that no one was going to get rid of a member of my staff but me. We had an interview process to replace Dick. I suggested Tom Brown, then pitching coach at High-A Sarasota, and Triple-A Louisville pitching coach Ted Power, my teammate with the Dodgers. Bryan Price, the former Arizona pitching coach, was also interviewed and so was our minor-league pitching instructor, Mack Jenkins. Price had the first interview, and I guess he did pretty well. The organization's mind was made up. Price was the new pitching coach. I didn't know him before that, so I didn't know what to think. Sometimes things are chosen for you.

You build a team slowly and piece by piece, relationship by relationship. I don't think I heard much about Aroldis Chapman when he was leading the Cuban league in strikeouts at nineteen back in 2007 and hitting 99 on the gun. But I did hear about him in July 2009 when he was pitching for the Cuban National Team at the World Port Tournament in Rotterdam and defected. He just walked out of the team hotel and had a friend waiting to drive him away. In January 2010, the Reds signed him to a six-year contract worth more than $30 million. I was his first manager. I remember talking to him in spring training in 2010 and getting to know him a little. The organization wanted him to be a starter. I asked Aroldis what he preferred, and he told me in Spanish that he preferred to pitch out of the bullpen, which I also thought was a better fit for him. At Triple-A Louisville in 2010, he made thirteen starts—in those games, he had an ERA of 4.11, compared to a 2.40 ERA in relief. When he made his major-league debut in late August 2010, it was as a reliever, a point of contention even then. His first pitch hit 98 miles per hour on the gun. That September in San Diego, he threw the fastest pitch ever recorded, 105 miles per hour.

Getting to know Aroldis took my connection to Cuba to another level. Back in my playing days, I'd always been close to Cuban players. I'd even gone to Cuba with San Francisco hotel owner Rick Swig in December 2010 for a Latin jazz festival. We went to a couple ball games and that was the first time I saw Yuli Gurriel, who would be my first baseman on the Astros. I brought a big hockey bag full of equipment, balls, bats, and shoes, which I took all the way from California to Cancún, Mexico, to Havana, with Darren, Tosh, and Melissa. I was hoping I'd get to meet Fidel Castro, as Hank Aaron had done on his trip to Havana. They took my bag of equipment in the middle of the night, but I never met anyone.

Aroldis was a great dude who I kind of took under my wing. He was one of the most talented players I've ever had and one of the best athletes I've ever seen. This guy could fly. He might have been the fastest runner on the team. He was just a mega-athlete. As an NBA official commented to me when he saw him, he looked like an NBA number two guard. By 2012, I had him closing games for us, and he finished that season and the next with thirty-eight saves each year.

By my third year, the Reds were good. In 2010, we finished 91–71 and won the NL Central, but in the Division Series that year, we ran into a very hot Phillies team that swept us. Doc Halladay no-hit us in Game 1, only the second postseason no-hitter in baseball history after Don Larsen's World Series perfect game for the Dodgers in 1956. Halladay was going through our lineup so quickly, I looked up and I couldn't believe we were in the seventh inning already. They had a hell of a team, Jimmy Rollins and Ryan Howard and Chase Utley and a strong pitching staff. That was one of the best teams I'd ever played against.

– – – –

Sometimes I think about life being all about trying to plant little seeds of good will wherever you can and then moving on, not expecting anything in return, but sometimes down the road you get a chance to see those seeds having grown up into big beautiful trees. Back in Cincinnati in 1980, I was in town with the Dodgers when I first met a fifteen-year-old kid in a stocking cap named Kerry Hardy. He was a sophomore in high school at the time. Like a lot of young people I befriended, he seemed a little lost. He just needed someone to believe in him to help him stay out of trouble. I asked if he wanted to be a batboy and decided to help him. I got a call from his mom asking, "Was Kerry with you until two A.M. in the morning?" I was not going to lie for this boy. "No," I told his mom. Then I told Kerry, "Don't ever ask me to lie for you."

I had him ask Tommy Lasorda if he could be a batboy, and Tommy said yes. I told Kerry that Tommy was superstitious, and if the Dodgers won when he was a batboy, Tommy would ask him back. During the game, we were behind and I saw Kerry in the corner of the dugout praying, praying, praying for a win. We won and swept the series. Before long, we were bringing Kerry to spring training during his spring break, and he would stay with me.

I told Kerry that if he got good grades and went to college, he could keep being a batboy—and he did all that. He graduated from the University of Cincinnati, and Tommy got him a job at Anheuser-Busch in St. Louis. He did well, and was later transferred to Houston. He's doing great, and even started his own limousine business, Supreme Luxury Car Service. Back in Cincinnati, I would see his family all the time, along with Big Mo Morgan, who knew Bob Battie. Big Mo and his crew of ten or eleven brothers were my family away from home. Darren was in school, so I was really alone there until school was out. We tried having him and Melissa visit, but Cincinnati to Northern California is a long way to go just for a weekend, and hard to find a direct route. Kerry's family used to feed me all the time, and I had Big Mo. They kept me going when everyone was on my ass. Everywhere I've been, I've had either a mama or a family that took me in and fed me and gave me some reinforcement when I needed it, so I try to pass that on to others the way it was passed on to me.

Another important person in my life who I met along the way was Yoni Mernick. I was managing the Giants and we were on the road in Toronto. He was at the game as a fan. I saw him sitting near our dugout keeping score, just a young kid about thirteen or fourteen, but he was really into it. He came over to me after the game and asked for the lineup card and we started talking and then the next day he was at the game again and we talked some more.

Yoni became my little buddy. I met his mom and dad and other family members. He moved to Miami and then moved to New York and we kept in touch. He always kept kosher and sometimes that made it hard to eat together. He came to Cincinnati to see me and we drove all over town looking for somewhere he could eat. We always talked about his future and I told him to work hard and look for opportunity, and he did just that. I always knew he would do well and he has. He's now vice president of social media for Boardroom, founded by Kevin Durant and Rich Kleiman, which helped put out the word on this book when we first announced I was doing it.

— — — —

The baseball life has a way of sneaking up on your health. Before the start of the 2012 season, I saw that in September we had three games in Miami and then three in Chicago. You always scanned the schedule to see where you would be and figure out what you'd be doing. Like if I was in Houston, I would always eat at This Is It Soul Food, which opened in 1959. Ralph and I have been going there for forty years. In Atlanta, it was Busy Bee for soul food, where Ralph and I have been going for *fifty* years. I had spots in every town.

If you were a guy who likes to hang out—and I've always been a guy who likes to hang out some—then having Miami and Chicago back-to-back could be hazardous to your health. Those are two cities where you're going to have some late nights, whether you're hanging or not. I was never one to drink to get drunk—what's the fun in that?—but I always did like to unwind after a game with a glass or two of nice Scotch. We were winning and I was enjoying life. I can say now looking back I was probably enjoying it a little bit too much. I had friends everywhere.

That September, the Reds and I were back at Wrigley Field in Chicago, which still felt almost like home to me. We opened a three-game series with the Cubs on September 18 with a 3–1 win. That pushed our record to 89–59, thirty games over .500, and gave us an eleven-game lead over St. Louis in the NL Central. We were on the verge of clinching. My Sacramento homeboy Joe Babich flew into Chicago to hang with me, the way he often did. We've been friends since I was on the Braves and my homeboys Rowland Office and Jerry Royster introduced us forty years earlier. Joe loved to watch baseball, and he was good to have around because he didn't drink.

Back at Wrigley the next day, Joe and our relief pitcher Sam LeCure were behind me as I was walking up a flight of stairs to get up to the clubhouse. I had a weird feeling. I remember thinking, *What the heck?* Something was off, and I didn't know what it was.

"Are you all right?" Sam asked me.

I didn't know. I felt out of breath in a way I never had. I was huffing and puffing and couldn't even get up the stairs. Once we got into the clubhouse, Sam and Joe took me in to see our trainer, Paul Lessard.

"Hey man," Paul told me, "I'm going to call the doctor."

"Why?" I asked him.

"Dusty, you're out of breath," he said. "You can't even come up the stairs."

Paul called the Cubs physician, Dr. Stephen Adams, and had him come over to take a look at me. Dr. Adams knew me well from my time in Chicago and noticed that my ankles were swollen, a bad sign when you put it together with the shortness of breath.

"Get in the car," Dr. Adams told me.

I didn't know what he was talking about.

"Where are we going?" I asked.

"Northwest Memorial Hospital," he said.

I started walking with him and Joe Babich toward the car.

"Man, we're about to clinch," I complained.

"I don't care," Dr. Adams said. "Get in the car."

I thought Dr. Adams was being way too cautious. Maybe I was in denial, I don't know. One funny thing was, as they were checking me in at the hospital, they asked me who Joe Babich was. I told them he was just an attorney friend. They asked what kind of attorney. Personal injury attorney, I said. After that, I tell you, I got the best service you've ever seen.

"Do you always travel with your own personal injury attorney?" one of the nurses asked.

"Yep," I said.

They gave me a bunch of diuretics and ran a bunch of tests. They told me I had atrial fibrillation, otherwise known as an irregular heartbeat, and was having heart failure, which explained the swollen ankles. Right away I thought back to the hell I went through in high school when that doctor told me I could never play sports again because of my irregular heartbeat. Now here it was again, issues with my heart.

The team had gone back to Cincinnati. It was very thoughtful when two Cubs coaches I knew, bullpen coach Lester Strode and fitness coach Tim Busse, came to the hospital to check on me and see if I was okay. I was still there in the hospital watching the game on Joe's iPad when my team clinched the division title on September 22 and celebrated on our home field. My bench coach, former Giants shortstop Chris Speier, took over for me as interim manager.

After about three days, they told me they were ready to discharge me. I'd already lost more than ten pounds. The diuretics they gave me shed some of the water-weight gain that had shown up in my ankles. I couldn't wait to get back to my team. The Reds owner, Mr. Castellini, had a town car waiting out front of the hospital for me. Then he had a private plane waiting for me at Meigs Field to fly me back to Cincinnati. Melissa, Tosh, and Darren were flying in from California to meet me there. Gary Wahoff, our traveling secretary, arranged for them to land right about the time I was supposed to arrive. Being away from Melissa, Darren, and Tosh in Cincinnati so much was the worst part of that job. I missed them so much, I couldn't wait to see them. I was in a good mood, going through the steps they require to discharge you from the hospital.

"What's your name?" the discharging nurse asked me.

"Lady, you ask me this every hour," I said, and it was true, they did ask you that a lot. They had their reasons, as I was about to find out.

"What's your name?" she repeated gently.

"Dee-ba Da," I said.

She looked at me kind of funny and I looked at her the same way.

"*What's* your name?" she asked me again.

"Da-Da Da," I tried again.

It wasn't coming out right. Something in my head was all scrambled up.

"You're having a stroke," she told me.

"Lady, I've got a plane to—" I tried telling her.

"Take your clothes off," she said. "You're not going anywhere."

A very small blood clot that didn't dissolve, even though they had me on blood thinners, had gone to the top of my brain and caused me to have a mini-stroke. Once again my guardian angel was looking out for me. They had me on a gurney in nothing flat. They wheeled me straight to the section of the hospital where they treated stroke patients, right next to where I'd been before. Imagine if I'd been in the town car? Or on the plane? I was able to get instant care, and that helped minimize the damage. How many people are blessed to already be in a hospital when they have a stroke?

I was in a daze. It was a lot to process. I kept seeing all these different faces around me. Later that afternoon, I looked up to see my son Darren staring at me with a hurt look on his face with Melissa and Tosh right next to him. Gary Wahoff had met Melissa, Tosh, and Darren at the airport and redirected them to Chicago from Cincinnati after learning I had a stroke. Darren was thirteen then. When he came in to see me and saw all these tubes sticking out of me, his face fell. He started crying.

"I don't want my daddy to die," he said.

That was a moment that's imprinted in my brain forever. I'll never forget the wave of determination I instantly felt when I saw Darren crying and looking at me that way. I vowed I was going to take better care of myself. I didn't ever want Melissa or my son or my daughter or my future grandchildren ever to see me like that again. This was my second warning after the prostate cancer, and it's an important lesson to heed the warnings. So that was when I said a prayer. *Lord, you let me come out of this, you ain't got to worry about me. I learned my lesson.*

Melissa, Darren, and Tosh flew with me to Cincinnati before they flew home to California so Darren could go back to school. Tosh stayed in Cincinnati to take care of me. I was going to be okay, they told me. I'd been very fortunate, but I was going to have some issues. I noticed pretty quickly that I couldn't write numbers the right way anymore. They came out backwards. It was like my mental wiring had been scrambled. Tosh had me doing puzzles to get my mind working again. I also had a good physical therapist who came to my apartment five days a week.

It was a slow process. By the end of September, I flew to St. Louis with Tosh to get ready to rejoin my team in time for the last three games of the season. I'd lost more than twenty pounds. I regained a little more strength every day, but I still was not myself. Those first three games back, facing the second-place Cardinals, I had some of the stranger moments I've ever had on a baseball field. I went to make a pitching change for my starter, Bronson Arroyo. I tried to lift up my right arm to signal I wanted a right-hander out of the bullpen, Alfredo Simon, and instead my left hand went up. My brain was working in reverse. I figured out that if I kept one hand in my pocket, it wouldn't lift up. I'd go over to my bench coach, Chris Speier, and make sure I had the correct hand out of my pocket.

I only had a few days to get the cobwebs out of my head before we faced my old team, the Giants, in the 2012 Division Series. We won the first game, and in Game 2, we won 9–0 behind Bronson Arroyo, getting to Madison Bumgarner for four runs in four and a third innings, one of only three games Bumgarner ever lost in the postseason, versus eight wins. I was still feeling kind of spacey, whether I was in the dugout managing or at home. The series turned on Game 3 at home in Cincinnati at the Great American Ball Park. We took an early 1–0 lead on a Jay Bruce RBI single, and in the third the Giants tied it up on Ángel Pagán's sac fly. That was how the game stood all the way through the ninth inning. Even though we had blown them out the day before, in the postseason you go in expecting a close game. I badly wanted to win that game and take the series, especially facing my old team. Then in the tenth, Buster Posey scored the go-ahead run on an error by Scott Rolen, who never missed anything and is now in the Hall of Fame. If we had won that game, we would have advanced—instead, we let the Giants have new life, and they won two in a row to force Game 5 in Cincinnati.

Before that game, I talked to a woman who worked in the hotel where the Giants were staying, and she made it sound like they did some serious partying and celebrating, getting a little too loose, and I thought that might give us an advantage. I learned—it's true—a lesson from that about the importance of keeping your players loose. Neither team had scored through four. Mat Latos and Matt Cain were trading zeroes. Then in the top of the fifth, Brandon Crawford tripled and scored. Buster Posey came up with the bases loaded that inning, and I had a choice to make. I still kick this around in my head to this day. I liked the way Mat Latos was throwing. I thought he had enough to get Buster. But I had Sam LeCure ready in the bullpen, and Sam was my pitcher I always counted on to get us out of trouble. It came down to believing Latos could get us out of that. I stuck with my starter. The minute that ball left Posey's bat, I knew it was a grand slam, and my heart just sank. Later I turned it over in my head and came to the conclusion that I should have brought in LeCure just to give Posey another look. Again the team that beat us in a close series won the World Series.

The toughest thing for me after losing was to go home to Northern California in the offseason and walk around in Giants territory, with all the banners and billboards celebrating being world champions. That was the toughest offseason for me ever. That was the start of the Giants and the city of San Francisco coming to believe they would win every even year, which they did in 2010, 2012, and 2014. Friends in the Bay would tell me in the odd-numbered years, "Don't worry, we'll win it next year," and then they did. The power of belief. For me it was real tough to lose again after being ahead, like with the Giants in Anaheim and then in Chicago. You look back and think how close you came, how if one break had gone your way here or there, one hit, one call, one anything, you could have won three or four World Series.

— — — —

Back in California after the season, I went to UC Davis Medical Center to see Dr. Reggie Low, a cardiologist recommended to me by a University of Cincinnati doctor who was his good friend. He said he was the best cardiologist around and just happened to be from my hometown. I thought I was going to meet a brother. With the name "Reggie," I thought he was probably Black. I was kind of shocked when I met Dr. Low and he turned out to be of Asian descent. He sent me to an overnight sleep analysis center, which led to a recommendation of a sleep apnea machine, which has improved my sleep and my energy level. I've only missed one day in thirteen years. Dr. Low also recommended a defibrillator for me (I'm on my second one now, put in on an off day in August 2023 when I was managing the Astros—I didn't miss one day of action) and three ablations for my heart, two of them at Cleveland Clinic and one at UC San Francisco Medical Center in April 2025. All were recommended by Dr. Low as well as the many necessary medications that have kept me alive. He really saved my life. I could have been dead a dozen years ago. I think about that: *Would my kids have turned out the same? Would Darren have been in trouble?* I've seen kids who lost their dads and then ended up in serious trouble. *Would Tosh's two boys, my grandkids, never know their grandad, like I didn't know mine as a kid?* I had a guardian angel looking out for me, and I had a lot to live for.

- - - -

My sixth year with the Reds, 2013, we needed to add another bat, and Walt Jocketty was able to get South Korean outfielder Shin-Soo Choo from Cleveland as part of a three-team deal. Mr. Choo, as I called him, grew up in South Korea but had already played eight years in the big leagues. He and I hit it off right away. I liked his game and liked the man. He was a hard worker and a gamer who played his butt off for me. I really enjoyed Mr. Choo. We would talk about all kinds of things, and he'd sit there listening to whatever I said. One time I gave him a bag of walnuts that were already shelled, which my boys in Willows, California, mailed to me. He said that would be worth a thousand bucks in Korea. His wife cooked me kimchi and rice for a week straight, they were so thankful. He was one of my favorite guys, and now he's in the Korean Hall of Fame.

We finished the 2013 season in third place, but we had a 90–72 record and earned a one-game wild card playoff with the Pirates. That was the year Johnny Cueto dropped the ball on the mound and they called a balk on him and people said he was nervous. He wasn't nervous a bit. He just dropped the ball. It happens. We lost that game 6–2, a tough way to end the season, but I had a year on my contract and was looking forward to the next season. I always had a good relationship with the owner, Mr. Castellini. He was always honest with me. He said what he felt and he felt what he said, and he did what he said. There was one day in September that year that I thought about later. Mr. Castellini was sitting right next to the dugout where I sat on the high bench, and at one point in the game, I felt eyes on me. I looked up, and Mr. Castellini was staring at me with a deep, cold look in his eyes. I notice these things. I'm big on looks and feelings and reading faces. I thought about it later: *Damn, that was a cold look.*

The day after the season ended, I was in my office in the clubhouse packing up to go home when Walt Jocketty came in.

"Mr. Castellini would like to see you in his office," he told me.

"Okay," I said, as we started walking down the tunnel to the elevator. "About what?"

"You know what this day is?" he asked me as we walked.

I had no idea what he meant.

"This is the same day I lost my job in St. Louis," Walt said.

"So what's that mean?" I asked.

He was done beating around the bush.

"I'm taking you up to Mr. Castellini's office because he's going to fire you."

I was surprised.

"With one year left on my contract?" I asked him.

"Yep," he said, and he walked us up to see Mr. Castellini.

He was friendly, but not as friendly as he had always been, and he was regretful, but not regretful enough.

"Dusty, we gave you six years to try to win the pennant," he said.

"Yeah, well, the first two years we were rebuilding," I said, but really there was no point in telling him things he already knew.

"You got anything else to say?" he asked me.

"No, you already made up your mind."

He could see I was shocked. I had never been fired. I'd had my contract run out, but never been fired. There wasn't much of a difference, but still. I knew I had as good a chance of winning with the Reds as anyone else they were going to bring in to replace me. This was my team and my boys. And they were going to be paying me either way, since I still had another year on my contract. It felt strange to me, the whole thing, but I learned years ago that when a man makes up his mind, his mind is made up. I really wanted to win in Cincinnati, for the fans and for Mr. Castellini, and for Joe Morgan and Eric Davis and Delino DeShields and David Bell, managers in Double-A and Triple-A, and for an exiled Pete Rose. I wanted to win for so many other players and people in the organization like Rob Butcher, the PR guy, and Paul Lessard, the trainer, and Matt Krause, the fitness guy, and all the clubhouse attendants, especially Rick and Mark Stowe, who grew up with the Big Red Machine as kids on the visiting and home side when their dad Bernie Stowe was clubhouse attendant. I wanted it for all of them and for me, but it just wasn't going to happen. I'd been proud that Cincinnati had African Americans for both its top coaching jobs, me with the Reds and Marvin Lewis with the Cincinnati Bengals, who had also taken part in Bill Walsh's coaching seminars.

"Dusty," Mr. Castellini said, his voice a little more friendly, "this game almost killed you."

"Well, I'm doing fine now," I said. I shook his hand, and got out of there and went back to Sacramento to take care of my heart, grateful to be in a position to look after my parents, to be there for Melissa and Darren, and to marry my daughter Tosh that next summer under the sycamore tree in my backyard, where she always wanted to have her ceremony.

CHAPTER 15

In the Nation's Capital

There are times when facing the end in baseball feels like facing your own mortality. That was how it was for me on the night of October 28, 2015. I was in Santa Cruz, California, right across Monterey Bay from where I'd seen Jimi Hendrix play half a century earlier, and Melissa called to give me bad news: ESPN was reporting that the Washington Nationals were offering their vacant managing job to former Giants pitcher Bud Black. I thought that job was going to me, based on the very positive two-hour interview I'd had in D.C. with team owner Ted Lerner and his son Mark. At that point in my life, two years out of the game and sixty-six years old, I knew I might never get another job managing.

As I told some reporters later, fortunately the night I got the bad news, I was in a place that gave me spiritual strength. I was staying in the Zen Suite at the Wellstone Center in the Redwoods, my friend and co-author Steve Kettmann's writer's retreat center, which had published my little book *Kiss the Sky* about my love of music and especially Jimi Hendrix. I had one of those moments where life reaches out and awakens you. I took a little walk on the property, four miles up from the Pacific, breathing in that redwood smell I love, and all of a sudden I heard the beautiful sound of music. Was this in my mind? Or real? That was definitely a real saxophone somebody was playing. I could hear it echoing up out of the small canyon I was looking into. I could still hear the music.

Five days later, the Nationals announced me as their new manager. It was that fast. I came out for the press conference and heard a bunch of cameras clicking and whirring all at once, and said, "I haven't heard *that* in a long time." It had looked like the Nationals were going to hire Bud Black, but then I got a call saying they were still interested in me, and next thing I knew, I had the job. I had a new team to manage, a team that was loaded and gave me a lot to work with, if I could overcome some obstacles. This was the most talented team I'd ever inherited up to then, and I could see us in the World Series.

It's all about winning in October. It really is. Or at least it all starts with the singular goal of winning everything, which validates all the work you and your guys have put in together. Winning isn't all you care about. You care about the relationships and the preparation and the eye for the little detail that will make a difference. You care about loving it all, throwing your arms around it with open heart and open eyes and open mind. But the objective you're working toward always involves going all the way. I was back in baseball to win a World Series in Washington. Full stop. Since the team was clearly talented, the challenge would be to channel all I'd learned in my forty years in baseball to that point. I talked that first day about Bill Walsh and what he taught me, and about NBA great Bill Russell and what I learned from him.

"They told me a team has to be close," I said. "Love is the key." But I also talked about South African leader Nelson Mandela, who had died two years earlier at age ninety-five. Mandela might have given the best advice a baseball manager could receive, as I told people that day: "You have to listen as well as talk."

I had nothing but respect for my predecessor as Nationals manager, Matt Williams, who played for me in San Francisco. Matty and I, we've always gotten along. When I heard he'd been fired, I called him.

"Hey, man," I told Matt. "I need your blessing. Can I put my name in the hat for the Washington job?"

Matt had no problem at all with me going for it. He told me he liked working with the National general manager, Mike Rizzo, a former scout and baseball lifer. This was a guy whose father and grandfather were also scouts. It was the family business for him. Matty told me he found Rizzo honest and direct. What you see is what you get. Sounded good to me.

Before I interviewed for the job, I got a call from Joe Gibbs, the former Washington Redskins coach. I'd reached out to him through Rob McDonald of the Nationals, and Mr. Gibbs needed a day or two since his racing team was busy trying to get pole position at the Daytona 500. He won the Super Bowl three times in Washington, but he also had the experience of stepping away from football for more than a decade, when he founded Joe Gibbs Racing, and then coaching the Redskins again. We had a great call. I asked him, "How do you put your businesses to the side, or don't you?" He gave me some great insight into how to handle my businesses now that I was stepping back into managing. He told me that you've got to have good people working for you that you can trust, since they will have a lot of slack to pick up with you busy elsewhere. Then at the end of the conversation, he said, "Son, let me pray for you." And before I even knew it, he was praying for me on the phone—and I got the job.

There was some hard negotiating on salary. I knew I had to take a pay cut from what I'd been making. I learned from seeing and hearing what Frank Robinson, Jim Riggleman, and Davey Johnson had gone through in past salary disputes with the Lerners, but I also had to up the ante as much as I could. I didn't have much leverage, since I really didn't want to negotiate myself out of a deal. As a minority, it's hard for us to turn down jobs because that might be the only job that you're going to get. I wanted to go back to the World Series and needed this opportunity.

Every day in baseball will find a new way to humble you all over again. Like after my welcome press conference in D.C., *The Baltimore Sun* published an article on my arrival on the D.C. sports scene and ran a big, bold, oversized quote from me: "This is my fourth and final team, and beyond compare this is the best talent," along with the tagline, "RUSTY BAKER, NEW NATIONALS MANAGER." *Rusty* Baker? Who they calling *rusty*?

— — — —

I wasn't rusty—baseball was inside of me, ready to come out, but I liked that my break from baseball had given me time for other things. From 1967 to 2013, I was in baseball nearly every year for forty-six years. I had one year off when I worked as a stockbroker before joining the Giants coaching staff for the 1988 season, and I had one year off in 2007 between managing the Cubs and the Reds. Not until 2014 and 2015 did I have two years in a row off from baseball, the longest break I'd had since my mom and I signed that first contract with the Braves in 1967. A two-year break is only double a one-year break, but it feels like a lot more. You feel you've been to the wilderness and back, and I liked that feeling. I liked that I had made the most of my time away from baseball. Things do happen for a reason.

My daughter Tosh married Tim Smith from New Hampshire in our backyard on a beautiful, hot August day in 2014. My brother-in-law Eduardo once again performed the wedding ceremony, as he had for Melissa and me. Eduardo and Tonya's sons, Jonathan and Daniel, both ministers, were also present, and their older sister, Kette, was in the wedding. During the ceremony, Eduardo said, "The wedding ring is a circle that signifies an unending love." I had to leave for a while to run an errand, and while I was gone Gary Matthews went inside the house looking for more wine. Melissa had told him, "Take anything you want." But he climbed up on the ladder I left there in the wine cellar where I kept my Opus One and helped himself to a few bottles. The bottles that he opened were all emptied by the time I got back.

Working on my own businesses was a good way for me to recharge my batteries for the next time I was back between the lines. I thought it was pretty cool when early on in my time as Nationals manager, the *Washington Business Journal* ran an article on me. It's one thing to be on the sports page, but something else to be written about as a businessman. "DUSTY'S DOUBLE PLAY: THE NATS MANAGER IS BOSS OF MORE THAN JUST THE CLUBHOUSE." I liked that recognition, because in the mold of my mom and dad, I'd always wanted to take on new challenges and learn whole new businesses.

Really the person who first got me into wine was Willie Stargell, the

Pittsburgh Pirates first baseman when I arrived in the big leagues in the 1970s. I'd be taking my lead off of first base, trying not to get picked off, and Willie would distract you by talking to you. You don't want anyone talking to you when you're trying to take your lead. But he would talk about wine. I wasn't listening, but I was listening. I'd go over to his house for dinner and he'd pour me different types of wine, always talking about what he liked and what he didn't like, and about rainy years versus dry years and what it meant for the grapes and the wine. He grew up in Alameda and went to Encinal High, and he often visited Napa to make the rounds of vineyards.

When I was building my house, I wanted to put in a pond on the extra two acres, but my insurance man told me I'd be at risk of flooding my neighbors. So I started thinking about growing wine grapes. My good friend Rodney Williams, who back then worked for Mondavi, introduced me to Chik Brenneman, for years the winemaker for the UC Davis Department of Viticulture and Enology. Chik helped me plant my rootstock and put in poles and wires and a drip watering system. I was ready to plant Cabernet Sauvignon grapes, but Chik talked me out of it. He said with our hot weather in the Sacramento area and close to the Sierra Foothills, we were better off growing Syrah. I planted two acres of that with Chik's help. That was almost twenty years ago, and in 2023 we replanted.

Back in my time with the Giants, one of the team's owners, Phil Greer, introduced me to Michael Mondavi, whose grandparents came from Italy and founded the Mondavi family wine business. Mr. Greer and I went fly-fishing with Michael up in Quebec, Canada, on the Godbout River, as beautiful a place as I've seen. I had been on the advisory board of the Robert Mondavi Winery and gone to dinners with their distributors across America while I was in certain cities for baseball, and I would take along my coaches as part of my commitment. Over a three- to four-year period, Mondavi provided more than 50 percent of what I built up in my wine cellar, which Rodney picked out 100 percent. All my coaches got cases of wine and a check at each appearance. Along the way, I learned about the business. Chik and I were making wine and giving away shiners—bottles that are unmarked and unlabeled, except for what

I wrote on the black glass in silver pen. I gave the shiners to fellow ballplayers and other friends, and everybody told me the wine was really good. Then the question was: Can we make a business with this?

I could never just sit around. I would rather get busy and start a business that spoke to me. As it happened, the businesses I started were in wine and alternative energy, which I became interested in when I applied it to getting solar power in my own home. Those also happened to be businesses where you didn't see a lot of African Americans. I wanted to keep busy and also wanted to show others that I was capable of doing more than baseball. I kept asking Chik to join me in starting a wine business and he kept saying no, but finally we figured out the right way to do it, as partners. We started Baker Family Wines in 2012, which at first we ran out of Chik's house, using grapes I'd grown and others Chik could buy elsewhere. In 2013, we moved the company to Treasure Island, in the middle of San Francisco Bay, as part of a wine co-op, and that was where we did our first bottling, producing 130 cases that first year.

In August 2019, I set up a visit with Hank Aaron to Opus One Winery in the Napa Valley, owned by Mondavi, a real first-class place. Over the years, my relationship with Hank had shifted a little as we both got older. When I met Hank, I was eighteen and he was thirty-three. The fifteen-year difference felt huge. Now he was eighty-five and I was seventy. I still had the same reverence and respect for Hank as always, but I had some of my own experience. Before it was man and kid, now it was more man to man.

Hank brought his wife Billye and her nephew, Dr. Mac Roach, an accomplished radiation oncologist in San Francisco, and Hank's close friend, Tom Moorehead, who had gone to Grambling with Ralph Garr, and his wife Joyce. Mr. Moorehead and Hank had the first two Black-owned BMW dealerships in the country, which was right up my alley. I bought my first BMW in 1976 when I was in L.A. and my second one in 1984 when I got to the Giants, as presents to myself for a job well done. After that, I bought one for my daughter, my son, my mama—a total of six or seven BMWs. I even bought Melissa's X5 directly from Mr. Moorehead.

Hank enjoyed himself so much with us on that visit to Opus One, he told me he wanted to invest in Baker Family Wines. Mr. Moorehead was in as well. I didn't really want the added pressure, but they both insisted on buying a piece of the company.

"Can I name a wine after you?" I asked Hank.

"It would have to be a bold Cabernet Sauvignon," he said.

We were a family business in more ways than one. My daughter Tosh and her husband Tim designed the labels, featuring the red seams of a baseball. Chik works closely with his wife, Polly, "Mrs. Winemaker." And having Hank—who for me was always family—as an investor kind of upped the pressure for me to make sure we kept moving inventory and maintained the high quality of our wine. Our first vintage of Hammerin' Hank Cabernet Sauvignon in 2018 sold out quickly. We have nine varietals, including Dusty's Vineyard Syrah and a rosé at the request of my mom, but she passed before she got to taste it. Another popular one was our Walk Off Red variety. If one of my players hit a walk-off anything to win a game, a walk-off homer or a walk-off walk or a walk-off hit or a walk-off sac fly, they loved to celebrate with some of that red, red wine.

I started my solar company Baker Energy in 2014, and it would never have happened if not for a random encounter in a Chicago hotel bar—no, make that two random encounters in a Chicago hotel bar. This was during my time managing the Cubs. One constant of my life is I've always been open to people. If I meet someone new, I'd always rather see what they're about than just shut them out. If you trust your feelings, you usually know a lot about people right off the bat. I was at a hotel bar in Chicago and was talking hunting. A guy came over and introduced himself as Ted Roth. He said he heard I was a bird hunter and wanted to go hunting with me. That's a lot to ask. You don't hunt with someone unless you feel comfortable with them. But this guy seemed okay. I trusted him enough to take his card and tell him I would call to set something up. Only I never did. The right moment never came. Then a year later, I was back at that same bar at the hotel, and I saw Ted again.

"Man, I thought you were going to call me," he said.

"I am, I am," I told him. "I promise. This time, I'll call you."

When I called him, he was coming back from goose hunting in Maryland. I invited him to Northern California for the weekend to hunt wild pheasant with us in Dixon, outside Sacramento, with my hunting buddies and my hunting dogs. He wanted to get a room, but I didn't want to get up that early to go pick him up, so I told him he could stay at my house. I had a good feeling about him, even though I really didn't know much about him.

"Do you know this man?" Melissa asked when I said he was spending the night.

"Not really," I said.

"You want to have a man we don't even know in the house?" she asked me.

I said I did.

"I don't think anything is going to happen," I said. "I think we have adequate protection."

"I'm going to look him up," Melissa said.

She did a Google search, and her eyes got wide. Ted is a very wealthy and accomplished man. He stayed at the house. We went hunting. We became friends. And Ted opened up a lot of opportunity for me. He and his brother Byron had founded Roth Partners, which did a lot of investing in energy, and he invited me to a conference on solar energy they were having in Las Vegas. There were thousands of people there, only a few of them Black. It was a great learning opportunity, and it taught me what I needed to know to start Baker Energy.

Ted invited me to cool events for years. At energy conferences like the Roth Conference in Laguna Beach, people from all over the world would attend. I would hang out with Bill Walton and Aaron Rodgers, also friends of Ted's. One year, they brought Snoop Dogg to perform, another year Pat Benatar, and another year Nelly. I was shocked how hip Aaron Rodgers was. He knew the words to every song. The group Migos was there, and I didn't know who they were, so I asked my son. He couldn't believe it. "Dad, you get to see the Migos?" I did. And I filmed them to show Darren. And it was all because I'd trusted my feelings and invited Ted on that hunting trip and had him stay at our house.

— — — —

Other than the weather, I felt that Washington, D.C., was more me than anywhere other than San Francisco. There was so much to experience. I got closer to the fans in D.C. probably quicker than in any other spot I've managed besides San Francisco, where I played and lived. I really felt appreciated, and I really wanted to be the first one to win in Washington in almost a century. Back in 1924, the old Washington Senators won the World Series, managed by Bucky Harris. I would pass Bucky on the all-time list of wins by a manager in 2023.

I liked the town. I liked the education level. I liked the diversity. I realized how D.C. ran the country and how influential it was in the world, but I never felt real comfortable there security-wise. I would run into guys on the Taliban Task Force. One time, I got lost at night and was stopped outside the CIA headquarters in the dark. I got a real education in a short period of time living in D.C. It was unbelievable to go to the monuments to see all the people who come from all over the world, even more than come to New York. I'd never experienced anything like the Fourth of July in D.C.

I found a place to live in Old Town Alexandria, across the Potomac River in Virginia. I lived right on the river, and I loved it. In other cities where I managed, I practically lived at the ballpark and at restaurants, hanging with homeboy visitors or local people that I knew, but mostly without family because of school. Usually I would only go out exploring the area on an off day. But in D.C., there was so much to see, like museum exhibits and historic sites, I had to go check out what was there. I met so many brilliant people in D.C. I met the head of Homeland Security, generals, and other high-ranking military people. In 2017, I was inducted into the Marine Corps Sports Hall of Fame and visited Quantico for the day, which gave me a chance to honor a time of my life that taught me a lot. Later that summer, I visited the Naval Academy in Annapolis with Darren and Melissa, and even took pictures next to the statue of Kunta Kinte, the former slave whose story author Alex Haley told in *Roots*. I wanted Darren to see that.

I was leaving my place in Old Town Alexandria one day in August 2017 when I noticed a bunch of press people gathered outside. I thought they might be there for me, but I walked right past, and they didn't even notice me. I was invisible. I got to the ballpark and looked up at a TV and saw my building. The FBI had gone after Paul Manafort, the lobbyist and Republican Party consultant, seizing his laptops and phones and anything they could find. In D.C., you never knew who might be living right next to you.

My high school buddy Dave Corvo, who as an underclassman had been manager of our baseball team and had gone on to become the Senior Executive Producer of Primetime News at NBC News, invited me to a party in Chevy Chase, Maryland, with some of the most influential people in the country. I got to be acquainted with George Will, the *Washington Post* columnist and regular on ABC for years. George loved baseball and could talk about anything. We had some very interesting conversations.

In November 2016, I received a nice two-page letter from Supreme Court Justice Anthony Kennedy, who wrote about how he and his wife, Mary, who both grew up in Sacramento, used to watch the Sacramento Solons play in the Pacific Coast League. "We wanted you to know that you are a hero around our house," Justice Kennedy wrote, and invited me to lunch. I brought my friend Joe Babich, whose father was a judge who knew Kennedy in California. Justice Kennedy was joined by Justice Samuel Alito and Justice Elena Kagan. We had a great discussion at lunch and I was surprised at how into baseball they all were.

On some off days, I'd go fishing on Chesapeake Bay. In July 2016, I went to see the American Holly Tree on Wye Island, Maryland, planted in 1816, and read a plaque explaining it was "one of the oldest on the Eastern Shore." An old dude told me to hug the tree and feel the spirit of the past. If they could talk—think about what they've been through: heat, storms, war, marriages, deaths. Then that August, I spent a night in Virginia exploring its wine country, and stayed in an old two-story house in Berryville made of brick, definitely pre–Civil War. The stairway was so skinny, I could barely get upstairs.

For music, I found a couple places I liked in Georgetown. I remember seeing Ritchie Havens at a jazz place there. I hadn't seen Ritchie Havens since the late '60s in San Francisco. I found some blues places in Alexandria I would go to all the time. Sometimes I'd call up Kevin Anderson, a longtime friend from San Francisco, who was the athletic director at the University of Maryland at the time, and we'd check out whoever was in town.

One of the most emotional visits I can remember was going to Walter Reed Hospital, where so many wounded soldiers were brought after losing a limb in Iraq or Afghanistan. It gave me flashbacks to the Vietnam War era. I was invited to the Pentagon and talked to generals and soldiers. I visited the Lincoln Memorial and started having flashbacks. I have photos at my house of Che Guevara and Fidel Castro at the Lincoln Memorial, trying to gain support when they were young and starting out, and I tried to imagine what that was like, leading up to the time of the Bay of Pigs failed invasion of Cuba when I was in elementary school in Riverside. It made me think back to the early 1960s, Khrushchev and Castro and the Kennedys, Dr. Martin Luther King Jr., it all came pouring back.

- - - -

I picked an interesting year to start living in Washington, D.C., that's for sure. I was living in the political capital of the country—maybe the whole world—when everyone was talking about politics. A lot of good things happened when Barack Obama was elected President in 2008, but so did a lot of bad things. Some people really hated seeing a Black man in the White House, especially a Black man as eloquent and smart and graceful as Barack. What he went through reminded me in a very uncomfortable way about what Hank had been through with his hate mail, and what I'd been through as well. I was honored to attend his inauguration in January 2009, before my second year managing the Reds, and was so moved by what I saw, I thanked God for how far we had come as a country in my short lifetime. It felt like people were coming together, and I felt a tremendous amount of happiness and hope for our future.

I was packing for my first spring training with the Nationals in February 2016 when I watched the news on TV and heard about the Iowa caucuses. On the Democratic side, looking to see who would try to succeed Obama in the White House, former First Lady Hillary Clinton won over Bernie Sanders of Vermont, but just barely. Then about a week later, Bernie crushed Hillary in the New Hampshire primary, winning 60.4 percent of the vote. Hillary had been a U.S. Senator from New York and later Secretary of State, and she and Bill Clinton were close friends with Hank and Billye Aaron.

Bill Walsh had always told his players to steer clear of politics, and that's what I had always done. The only exception to that was my friendship with Barack Obama, whom I'd known going back to his days as a state senator in Illinois. I felt more politically involved that year, living in D.C. with everything going on, than I ever had been before, even though I had helped Barack and contributed to his campaigns. When I helped Barack, I was in my domain in California. Now Hillary was running, and I was in D.C.

I noticed that my Nationals players were divided between Hillary Clinton and Donald Trump. You would notice that split in weird ways at times. One of the ways I get to know my players is through music. Years ago when I was a young player, Orlando Cepeda turned me on to a lot of Latin music that was new to me. I loved that music, and loving it brought me closer to Orlando. Managing the Nationals, I would tell them about Otis Redding, Jimi Hendrix, Al Green, and Fleetwood Mac, and I would get tips on music from my players. I would wonder what music they would put on in the clubhouse when it was their turn to choose. We had a diverse clubhouse, and that meant diverse music: Latin day, rap day, rock day, country day. There were always surprises. Some dude that I wouldn't guess was into rap would put on rap, then some other dude that I had pegged as a rap guy would put on jazz or the blues.

One day I heard a song playing in the clubhouse: "Vote for Trump." I came out, looking around, but didn't see who had put it on. The song was by a Texas comedian named Rodney Carrington. I tried not to talk much about politics with my players. That was for a lot of reasons—for one, just respect. They all had their right to their own views. If they held views different than mine, that was still their right.

If guys asked my advice, I told them to try to be informed. Sometimes I would recommend a book or a movie, the way I used to with Brian Boehringer in San Francisco, who would check books out of my office, like I was running a library. I wanted my players to put together on their own what they thought and what they believed and what their values were. That was part of becoming a better person, which was something I always saw as the job of manager, doing what I could to make my guys better men.

— — — —

You win with your stars. That was an old adage, and it was true. The *Moneyball* gang could talk about increasing their winning percentage during the year with this or that stat-influenced move. There are interesting conversations to have there. But to win in October when it mattered most, you needed your stars, your superstars, your super-duper stars.

I liked Bryce Harper. I liked his dad and his mom. Bryce was sixteen when he first appeared on the cover of *Sports Illustrated* with the headline "BASEBALL'S CHOSEN ONE." Sixteen years old. They were calling him the savior, baseball's version of LeBron. One article told the story of when Bryce was a teenager and he heard another player referred to as the "Next LeBron." Bryce joked, "Hey, they stole that from me!"

Bryce was the most talented player I'd managed since Barry Bonds. He was always very respectful with me. There were a few things we had to get straight at first, but I think he appreciated my straightforward approach. My first spring managing the Nationals, Bryce was coming off an unbelievable season in 2015 at age twenty-two. He hit .330 with forty-two homers and ninety-nine RBIs. No one was surprised when he was a unanimous choice as National League Most Valuable Player in 2015. What really impressed me was when I invited players, coaches, front office, and media people to come with me to the Negro League Hall of

Fame in Kansas City, and Bryce not only got up early that morning to come along, he was more knowledgeable than anyone there. He knew or had heard of almost all the players.

I've always said team leaders are anointed, not appointed. They're the guys others are just naturally drawn to for their experience and perspective and for being that kind of teammate. As a young player, your toughest years are generally years three and four, because the league adjusts to you, and you have to adjust back. The league is not going to let you just keep beating them.

My approach was to let Bryce be Bryce. He was so young, he was continuing to develop. Why put limitations on him? I just wanted to give him the room to continue to grow as a player and also as a man. Bryce wanted to be one of the guys and not stand out, and I respected that.

My job as manager was to understand what I could try to make better and what I'd be best off leaving alone. On a team at any time, you're going to have guys who are in good moods and guys in bad moods, guys who are cocky and guys who are insecure. Anytime you're around someone every day, moods are going to change. That's life. Things are going on. You didn't try to control all that emotion, no one could, but you did try to understand it and to notice how it shifted at different times.

Jayson Werth was one of the leaders on the team because he had come off championship teams in Philadelphia, winning the World Series in 2008. J-Dub was thirty-seven that year and he was in charge of showing guys the way and the attitude and how to win. He took Bryce under his wing the way Hank had me. Jayson was a smart player and we had a good relationship.

My third baseman, Ryan Zimmerman, thirty-one that year, had been with the Nationals since 2005. He'd been through the tough times and played for six different Nationals managers, starting with Frank Robinson in 2005 and 2006, then Manny Acta, then Jim Riggleman, then Davey Johnson, my teammate and partner with the Braves, and then Matt Williams. I wanted to win because of Zim, who I really respected. (In fact, the Rolling Stones guitars I have hung up on the wall of my house came to be because I bought them at a charity fundraiser Zim organized for the foundation he created to fight multiple sclerosis. His mother, Cheryl, was diagnosed with MS in 1995.)

Another player I knew from before was outfielder Chris Heisey, who played for me four seasons in Cincinnati and played for the Nationals both my seasons there. He told me about how I was the favorite player of his grandmother, Granny Hess, and we used to talk about that. Years later, when she was on her deathbed, Heisey called me so I could speak to her, and she told me she was praying for me. Can you imagine that? If anything, I should have been praying for her. She died a couple days later.

At the time, I had an All-Star catcher, the Buffalo, big Wilson Ramos from Venezuela. I loved him—he was an offensive force, and the pitchers loved him as a receiver. He'd already caught three no-hitters, and on May 11, 2016, he caught Max Scherzer when he struck out twenty, tying Roger Clemens and Kerry Wood for the major-league record for a nine-inning game. Scherzer and Stephen Strasburg were the anchors of our rotation, the kind of pitchers who could dominate. Jonathan Papelbon was our closer, and for setup man we had Shawn Kelley, who for some reason I used to run into everywhere I went on the road. Our pitching coach Mike Maddux did a great job working with reliever Blake Treinen, who he said went from a "puppy dog" to a "bulldog" that season. If I needed a double play, I'd bring in Treinen, and he'd throw a sinker and get the GDP. I begged the team not to trade Treinen, but in July 2017, he was traded back to the A's, who had drafted him originally.

We had a lot of young talent on that 2016 Nationals team. Our third baseman, Anthony Rendon, was one of the finest young players I'd been around. He grew up in Houston and played for Rice University, and the Astros took him in the first round in 2011. By my first season in Washington, 2016, he was twenty-six, bouncing back from an off year in 2015, slowed by injuries, and was Comeback Player of the Year.

Trea Turner made his big-league debut the year before I arrived. He was just twenty-two that first spring, a talented player with a bright future. He had a lot of personality for a young player, and he had plenty of skills. He got sent down to Triple-A Syracuse at the end of spring training, and when Zim went on paternity leave in June, we called him up, and he had three hits in his first game with us. The organization wanted me to put Trea in center field because we had Danny Espinosa at shortstop and Daniel Murphy, the former Met, at second base, who could really hit and was a great influence on younger players. One day, I walked into the clubhouse and Trea was sitting at his locker, head down.

"What's wrong?" I asked him.

"Nothin'," he said.

"You want to play shortstop, huh?" I said.

"Yup," he said.

I told him the reputation was he needed to work on arm strength and footwork. I mentioned that Hall of Famer Ozzie Smith didn't have great arm strength, but he had a quick release and was always accurate. I went to Mike Rizzo. The thing I liked about Rizzo was he never told me who to play and who not to play. Because of that, out of respect, I talked over what to do with Turner. I wanted to put Trea back at shortstop, but he would need to have not just speed but also energy, because a shortstop has to have energy.

The 2016 season really clicked for us just before the All-Star break when we took three of four from the Mets to build a six-game lead in the NL East. Give the Nationals credit: They didn't want to lose Stephen Strasburg to free agency, so they signed him to a seven-year deal. So far for me that season, he'd gone 12–0 with a 2.62 ERA. We had the best team ERA in baseball. Daniel Murphy already had seventeen homers for us.

My goal was always to win fifteen games a month, which adds up to ninety wins in a season. That might not get you to the playoffs, but it gave you a really good chance. We won the East that year (95–67) by a comfortable eight-game margin over the Mets, and once again I would be going back to Dodger Stadium for postseason baseball. Unfortunately, we lost catcher Wilson Ramos to a knee injury at the end of September and didn't have him in the playoffs. That was a big blow.

We opened the National League Division Series at home with Max Scherzer going for us in Game 1 against Clayton Kershaw. Max was always well informed. He did his homework. He was a studier. When you study, you study everything, stats and video and charts on where guys hit the ball and what they hit best, fastballs up versus fastballs down. You try to learn as much as you can about the opposition. That's what guys like Verlander and Kershaw do.

One thing about Max is if you don't get him early, you're not going to get him. That day, they got him early. In the first inning, Corey Seager had a good swing on a fastball and lifted it to dead center for a solo homer and a 1–0 Dodger lead. Then in the third, Chase Utley singled home another Dodger run, and Justin Turner hit a curve to left, just over Jason Werth's outstretched glove, for a two-run homer to put us down 4–0, and we lost 4–3. Back at Nationals Park the next day for Game 2, Corey Seager homered in the first again, and Josh Reddick singled in a run in the third to make it 2–0 Dodgers, but we took the lead on a three-run homer in the fourth by Jose Lobatón, playing for the injured Wilson Ramos, and won 5–2 to even the series.

For Game 3, the series moved to L.A. It was always exciting and a little strange to be back at Dodger Stadium, especially in the postseason. It brought back memories of when I was a kid living in Riverside coming to Dodger Stadium and of being there as a Dodger player and then also visiting in the years since in my time as a coach and manager. In Game 3, we fell behind early again but busted out with a four-run rally in the third on hits from Jayson Werth and Bryce Harper and Anthony Rendon's two-run homer. We won, 9–3, to put us one win from advancing. Then came Game 4 and a whole lot of at-bats that ended with "hit by pitch." The game was tied 2–2 when Kershaw, who can hit, led off the bottom of the third for the Dodgers with a double he reached down and sliced toward the left-field corner. Kershaw came into the game with a career 1.99 ERA in playoff games and he could help himself at bat, too. My starter, Joe Ross, struck out Chase Utley and got Corey Seager on an infield pop-up. Then Justin Turner lifted a flare to shallow center that fell in to score Kershaw and make it 3–2. Adrian González and Josh Reddick reached on walks to load them up.

That brought up Joc Pederson. I had Óliver Pérez start getting loose in our bullpen, but I liked Joe Ross in that situation. He was a little amped up, but he needed to work through that and go after Pederson. Joe's 1-0 pitch was a fastball that he crushed foul. Joe threw him a breaking ball 2-2, and it sailed in on him just enough to bounce off Pederson's knee. Hit by pitch. Runner forced home from third. A 4–2 lead for the Dodgers.

The Dodger lead stood at 5–2 through seven. Danny Espinosa started us off that inning with a leadoff single against Kershaw, who then got two quick outs before Trea Turner hit a tough ball toward short and Seager fielded it and tossed to second, but not in time to get Danny. That brought up Bryce Harper as the tying run. That's what you love to see. Strength against strength with the game on the line in the seventh. Cy Young Award winner versus MVP. I think Kershaw thought he had him struck out on a couple of close pitches, but in the end, he walked him to load the bases. Roberts brought in Pedro Baez to face Jayson Werth. His first pitch to Jayson was up, high and tight, and hit him, to force in a run and make it 5–3. We'd both scored runs on hit-by-pitch plays. Of all the good hitters we had on our team, it would be safe to say that most of the guys would want Daniel Murphy up there in a key situation, and sure enough, he singled in two more runs to make it a 5–5 game.

The score stayed tied until the bottom of the eighth. Blake Treinen, one of the finest young relievers in baseball, had two outs. Facing Andrew Toles, his 1-0 pitch bored in on Toles and bounced off his foot to make eleven hit batsmen in the series. That was the most all-time in a postseason series, breaking the previous record.

Then Andre Ethier singled to left, setting up a tough choice for me. Next up was Chase Utley, who had hurt me in the past with Philadelphia. He was a clutch hitter. I could bring in my left-hander, Sammy Solis, which would prompt Dave Roberts to pinch-hit Howie Kendrick, who I knew was also a dangerous hitter. That's what's called being in a crossfire. I chose to face Utley, and he hit a single between first and second, and Toles came around to score to give the Dodgers a 6–5 lead. We couldn't answer, so that was the game.

Baseball isn't like football. You don't give a lot of speeches. That was a tough loss, but you find that sometimes it's best not to say anything. Let guys rest in their own thoughts. Most players have learned how to move on to the next game on their own. You have to let them do it their way. We were going back home for Game 5 with Max Scherzer starting for us. Max shut out the Dodgers through six innings, and we still had a 1–0 lead. We almost added one more in the bottom of the sixth, but Jason Werth, who we had to send in that situation, was thrown out at home trying to score.

Sometimes you have to give the other guy credit. Sometimes the pitcher gets the hitter, and sometimes the hitter gets the pitcher. That's baseball. For me there was no question of pulling Max in the top of the seventh with Joc Pedersen leading off. Max was still under one hundred pitches and he'd just closed out the Dodgers in the sixth by striking out Justin Turner on a good live 98-mile-an-hour fastball. Max's first pitch to Pedersen was a low fastball on the outside corner. It was no mistake pitch, that was just where he wanted to throw the ball. But Pedersen went down and got it and lifted it for a game-tying home run, and I went to my bullpen.

It was a wild game. That inning, I used six different pitchers, Max and then Marc Rzepczynski, Blake Treinen, Sammy Solis, Shawn Kelley, and Óliver Pérez. That's a lot of pitching changes, more than you could ever do now with the minimum-three-batter rule implemented in 2020. Then in the bottom of the seventh, after Chris Heisey's two-run homer cut the Dodger lead to 4–3, Dave Roberts brought out his closer, Kenley Jansen, who loaded the bases but struck out Anthony Rendon to end the inning. Anthony was one of the best clutch hitters we had and hard to strike out, but at that time Kenley Jansen was on top of his game and got him.

That's where it stood in the bottom of the ninth. We were still down a run. Jansen was still on the mound for the Dodgers, but Clayton Kershaw, who pitched in Game 4, was up and throwing in the bullpen. Bryce Harper came up, ready to tie the game with one swing, and the fans at Nationals Park were loudly chanting, "Let's go Harper!" Jansen gave him nothing to hit, and walked him. Roberts held up one finger, showing Jansen he was giving him one more batter. Then he went out to the mound to talk to him. Jansen had thrown forty-five pitches by then, the most he'd ever thrown in a big-league game to that point. He walked Jayson Werth, and out came Kershaw, his first relief appearance in seven years. Daniel Murphy just missed and popped up, and we were down to our last out. Kershaw got ahead of Wilmer Difo with a bunch of cutters and then struck him out with a big breaking ball, and our season was over. It was a good game, full of drama and twists and turns and intensity, but the guys jumping up and down on our infield celebrating were in Dodger blue, not hometown red. I wanted to beat my old team so bad, and I especially dislike it when your opponent gets to celebrate on your field and you can't do anything about it. That hurt me more than anything.

— — — —

I'm surprised I even took the call. I was back in D.C. for baseball's annual winter meetings in December 2016, and my phone showed a strange number.

"This is a call from the White House," a voice said.

Who were they trying to fool?

"Hold, please, for the President of the United States," the voice continued.

"How did you get my phone number? How do I know this is the President?"

"Like I told you, I have the President on the line. He wants to talk to you."

Not until I heard the voice and recognized Barack Obama did I really believe this was legit, not a trick someone was playing on me.

"I'd like you to come over and see me," President Obama said.

So on December 5, 2016, I put on a suit and went to see the President in the Oval Office. I went through so much security just to get in there as a guest, I couldn't believe it. I had to wait awhile, and once I got inside through all the security, I still had to wait. I didn't mind, because I knew he was busy. While I was waiting, I had lunch with a few of his aides. Being President is a busy job. When I was shown into the Oval

Office, the President seemed to me like the same Barack Obama who had been over at my house in Arizona when he was a state senator. We were just talking. I told him what a great job I thought he was doing. I knew there was a lot of pressure. We talked about Hawaii, and how whenever I went over, there was always an Obama sighting somewhere. I was asking him questions. He always followed sports. We talked basketball, which we both loved. We also talked about Chicago and what a unique city it is. He was keeping up with the Nationals and had some questions about the team. He was really hoping we'd win it all that year. So was I.

Before I left, he had a photographer come and take some pictures before we said goodbye, and that was the last time I saw him. We haven't gotten together since then. I've followed him, but I haven't seen him. I think he wanted to see me because he knew me from before, and he was leaving office while I was still going to be there in D.C. We overlapped one year. As he was going out, I was coming in.

- - - -

It's a mixed feeling coming off a ninety-five-win season and knowing you have pretty much the same core group of guys, but that was when the action really started. You have to play the season, and every season is different.

We'd lost our closer, Mark Melancon, and reliever Yusmeiro Petit, but you're always turning it over at least a little, and some change was good. Small changes were always necessary, and you hoped the changes you made helped you instead of hurting you. From the first days of 2017 spring training, we knew we had a team on a trajectory toward a strong showing in October. If we could win ninety-five the year before, let's do better. Some years, you need games to work out some issues or questions you have about your team. Not that season. We'd have loved to skip forward to the playoffs. That was when the action really started. But you have to play out the season and get through many obstacles along the way.

We were totally prepared to come out of the gate quickly that season. That was something I was always very focused on, trying to start the season strong. There was almost a quiet fury to the way we went out and added up wins. In mid-April, we went to Philadelphia and swept the Phillies, capping it off with an 8–1 rout behind Max Scherzer that sent our record to 9–1. We cooled down some but kept winning. We were 21–9 after thirty games and 52–36 at the All-Star break. Bryce Harper had a nice bounceback season—he'd batted .330 in 2015, then .243 in 2016, but in 2017 he hit .319 with twenty-nine homers. We had the bats—Zim led the team in homers (thirty-six) and RBIs (108), second baseman Daniel Murphy led the league in doubles, and third baseman Anthony Rendon had one hundred RBIs with a .301 average.

As a manager, you always love to have a Big Three of dominating pitchers, like the great Bobby Cox Braves teams with Smoltz, Glavine, and Maddux. In Chicago, I had Prior, Wood, and Zambrano. That year in Washington, we had Max at the top of his game, Stephen Strasburg coming back from elbow trouble, and lefty Gio Gonzalez, a very underrated pitcher. All three won at least fifteen games for us that season, and we won the NL East by twenty games.

Our first challenge was the Chicago Cubs. Game 1 of our series was at home, and Strasburg made a statement right away, getting leadoff hitter Ben Zobrist on an infield out and then striking out Kris Bryant and Anthony Rizzo back to back. Through five innings, he was no-hitting the Cubs, but we hadn't been able to score.

In the top of the sixth, Javy Báez swung at the first pitch he saw from Strasburg and hit a bouncer right down the third-base line. It looked at first like Rendon might have gloved the ball in foul territory, but it was very close, and the umpire called it fair. It was a tough play—Rendon bobbled the ball and Báez ended up at first on what was ruled an error. I thought it would have been a hit anyway because of Báez's speed and shouldn't have been called an error. Then with two outs, the Cubs scored two unearned runs, both on singles, and took a 2–0 lead, and we lost Game 1, 3–0.

If that game had gone our way, we might won the series in four. We were down in Game 2 but came back with a five-run rally in the eighth (Bryce and Zim both homered) to win 6–3. The Cubs edged us in

Game 3, 2–1, then we made a statement back at Wrigley Field in Game 4, winning 5–0 behind Stephen Strasburg's seven shutout innings and Michael A. Taylor's grand slam. We were one win away. But so were the Cubs.

At home in Washington for Game 5, I just knew we were going to win. I could feel it. I wanted us to win for the city, which I could feel behind the team. I wanted to win especially for guys like Zim and Jayson Werth, who had worked so hard and been through so much, and this was probably his last year. We had a good team, a real good team, and we had a good bullpen. We took an early 4–1 lead in Game 5 on Daniel Murphy's solo shot and Michael A. Taylor's three-run homer. Gio Gonzalez gave us three innings but struggled some, and then Matt Albers, who pitched well for us, gave us one inning. Our bullpen was taxed. That's when I brought in Max Scherzer in relief the same way that the Dodgers had brought in Kershaw in 2016, and the Giants had brought in Bumgarner in 2014. Max had picked up a win out of the bullpen for the Tigers when he was in Detroit.

As he came running in from the bullpen to work the top of the fifth, our lead down to 4–3, a cheer rippled through the crowd as more people noticed it was Max. You had to love his intensity. The big board in the outfield showed a close-up of Max's eyes—one blue, one brown—each with a *K* inside the iris. Max picked up two quick outs on a groundout and a lazy fly to center, then Willson Contreras bounced a ground ball up the middle that Trea Turner fielded, but with no play at first, and pinch-hitter Ben Zobrist looped a little fly ball to shallow left that dropped, and suddenly the Cubs had two on.

Addison Russell, up next, got a good swing on the first pitch he saw and lined it past Rendon at third and into the left-field corner for a double that put Chicago up 5–4. We gave Jason Heyward a free pass, bringing up Javy Báez. I wasn't happy at the turn of events, Max had his good stuff, and I thought he would probably give me a couple shutout innings, but we were still only one down. We would get our chances to take the lead back.

Max needed only three pitches to strike out Báez, but it was a weird play. Báez struck out on a slider in the dirt that got past catcher Matt Wieters, and Báez's bat hit him in the facemask at the end of his swing. Wieters tracked down the ball and threw to first, but wide, and a run scored on the play. Wieters was in a daze, just standing there. I asked for an interference call, and the umpires got together and talked it over, then ruled: "No interference." That might have been the biggest umpire call of that playoff. It was a big play because it would have been the third out. One batter later, we had a catcher's interference call on Wieters. I thought he was groggy after the bat hit him in the facemask. That loaded the bases and then Jon Jay was hit by a pitch, forcing in one more run to make it 7–4. We kept coming back but in the end lost 9–8. It really hurt to lose like that.

I stayed in Washington for a week after the season to take my time packing and see what was going to happen. I went in to the clubhouse every day for a week to await some word on whether I should take everything home or leave some stuff for next year. Finally I flew home on a Friday, and the next morning, Mike Rizzo called. I could hear the reluctance in his voice. I knew we would have won but for a couple quirky things in the game that happened against us, and I knew we had a team that could win for years to come.

Rizzo had always been straight with me, but he was in a tough spot. He never said it outright, but I knew this wasn't coming from him. Apparently, some members of ownership didn't want me back.

I'd led my team to 192 wins in my two seasons and back-to-back division titles for the first time in franchise history, and did it in probably one of the toughest divisions in baseball. That one really hurt. I wanted back. I knew with that team, we were very close to winning a World Series, and I connected with the people of the town in a very short order of time. You know when you did a good job. It's a bad feeling, kind of like—as *USA Today* put it—being "discarded like a week-old pizza box, despite making the postseason." But like Brian Sabean used to tell me all the time, with ownership comes proprietorship. Businessmen make what they call business decisions. Baseball men go on with their lives.

CHAPTER 16

Champagne Showers in Houston

It really shook baseball when Kenny Rosenthal and Evan Drellich reported in the online sports publication *The Athletic* in late 2019 that the Houston Astros had used cameras in center field to steal signs and relayed accusations that they found ways to pass on to the batter which pitch was coming. For me, it felt like someone else's problem. My life moved on from baseball because baseball moved on from me. I always had a lot going on. I led the Nationals to division titles my two seasons in Washington, and then in the two years since, my phone had been quiet. I had only one job interview for a baseball job, with the Phillies in October 2019. I felt it was a strong interview, but they went with a guy I respected, former Yankee manager Joe Girardi. Darren told me, "Maybe God didn't want you to go to Philly."

A lot had changed in baseball in the years since Al Campanis went on *Nightline* and Black players got organized and pushed for more hires through the Baseball Network—but it wasn't as good as people had wanted, or hoped. We'd had momentum, but less than we thought. In December 2019, *USA Today* published an article taking a hard look at Major League Baseball hiring practices. Of eight openings for managers that 2019–20 offseason, seven of eight hires were white. The only exception was Latino Carlos Beltrán, hired by the Mets, then unhired for his role in the Astros scandal. Dave Roberts was the only Black manager in the majors at that time. "I don't know where it's going," I told *USA Today*, "but we've gone backwards in a lot of ways."

By January, Houston had fired general manager Jeff Luhnow and field manager A. J. Hinch. The Astros needed a new manager from outside their organization. I knew nothing about it, other than what was reported. Enos Cabell and Jeff Bagwell spearheaded an effort to bring me to Houston and suggested I talk to the Astros. I told them I was interested. How often are you going to inherit a championship team? It was in a way similar to the situation that Felipe Alou had when he took over the Giants from me in 2003 and inherited a World Series team.

I knew that managing the Astros was my last and best chance to win. Even before I took that job, I knew Houston as well as any town in the country, and I liked it. I'd been going to Houston for so long, playing for National League teams and also going to visit in the offseason. Ralph Garr and a lot of Harriet's relatives were there. I liked the food, the people, the diversity. Houston might be the most diverse big town in the country.

I knew it would be challenging, but I was sure I could take the Astros to the World Series and win a championship or two. It felt like one of those junctures in life where all of my background and experience had uniquely prepared me to be the right manager for the Astros and for baseball. It felt like I'd been chosen for this. *USA Today* called me "the perfect choice" for the job, "the ideal man to get them through perhaps the most tumultuous time an entire organization will face since the Black Sox scandal in 1919." *USA Today* also predicted the Astros would face "horrendous backlash every time they leave the city limits of Houston. They will be insulted, scorned, and ridiculed. And that's just by the opposing players. Fans will taunt them every time they step to the plate, hearing chants of 'Cheater! Cheater! Cheater!' It will be relentless and vicious."

The Astros hired me two weeks before spring training. A. J. Hinch had a good coaching staff, and it was too late to make any changes anyway, plus all the coaches knew the organization, but I did bring Chris

Speier with me and created a position for him—quality-control coach, which was becoming popular in modern baseball. Once we gathered in West Palm Beach for spring training, third baseman Alex Bregman spoke for many when he made a strong statement that he was really sorry for what happened and knew he and his teammates had work to do to regain the trust of fans. Jose Altuve also talked very sincerely about feeling remorse—for the fans and also for the game of baseball. Carlos Correa was very truthful and honest in also making a statement. All those who spoke up were stand-up guys. I knew them, but I didn't *really* know them until that moment. "Listen, I don't give a shit what happened in the past," I told my players that first spring. "I'm going to stand in here with you guys, and we're going to fight. We've got a great team, and we're going to win a World Series."

I asked the world for forgiveness, which people in the world often have trouble giving, myself included. The foundation of that team was a great group of leaders that kept the team together, Bregman, catcher Martin Maldonado, and Michael Brantley, our DH and left fielder, who was called Uncle Mike by his teammates. Bregman was a smart baseball player who was also a gym rat. The guy just loved baseball and couldn't get enough. We'd have an inter-squad game, and he'd come out in full uniform when other guys wore whatever. If there was a pitcher who wanted to throw some extra on a rehab-type situation, Bregman would always be out there to hit.

I knew the importance of leadership, especially with your catcher. As I've noted, your catcher is really an extension of the manager. I believed in Maldy because I needed him. I needed a catcher who was on par with me as field general, and Maldy was a guy who could call a players-only meeting when it was needed. When I played for the Dodgers, Davey Lopes, Reggie Smith, and I called a couple of those meetings. But then when I got to be a coach with the Giants, Roger Craig, a manager I respected and learned from, told me you should never allow a players-only meeting because that's a sign you've lost the ball club. I totally disagreed, but I didn't say anything because I was a coach and respected Roger. As a manager, I always thought you had to trust your players—but it does depend on who calls a meeting and why. Maldy could be trusted to do it at the right time.

Brantley was in his last years, but he had so much knowledge, I had as much trust in him as almost any player I've had. The game needs more guys like Michael Brantley, who came from a great lineage, son of Mickey Brantley, the former Mariners player and Blue Jays hitting coach. Their relationship helped me tremendously in guiding my own relationship with Darren. I've seen many father-son relationships in this game, and some could be very tenuous. Michael Brantley was a big-time leader and a great player who was playing hurt with many injuries, especially his shoulder, which had already been operated on twice.

Jose Altuve was not only one of my favorites as a player, but also as a person. Pound for pound, he was the baddest dude in the land and a model of perseverance. He summed up the character of that team, built on perseverance, belief, and staying positive. We felt like we knew we were going to get to our destination because Jose believed and set the tone.

We had a combination of veteran and young pitchers. A key guy for me was Framber Valdez, who was twenty-six, but he signed late for a Dominican pitcher and did not have much experience. We also had José Urquidy (twenty-five), Cristian Javier and Luis Garcia (both twenty-three), plus veteran leadership like Zack Greinke and Ryan Pressly. For some reason, I had developed a reputation for not liking young players, but that was not me at all. That was such a bad rap, since I myself had been a very young player at nineteen when I first came up. How crazy would that be if I didn't like young players? I love young players—*if they can play.* As a manager, you love young talent you can bring along and school to play correct, winning, team baseball. Their growth as players can accelerate in the postseason. Our young pitchers had to grow up overnight, especially the young Latinos. I saw Framber grow up before my eyes. Man, he learned how to better control himself and how to control his pitches. I saw all these young players turn into men and into professionals.

Once spring training games started in Florida, we had to deal with some loud boos in other teams' ballparks, but then spring training suddenly went dark. As the COVID-19 global pandemic spread, Major League Baseball announced on March 16, 2020, that the season had been postponed indefinitely. We were all sent home. I was just getting to know my team, and we went our separate ways. Competitive sports shut down. With no live games on TV, a lot of people watched replays of old games, since they missed baseball. People kept calling me up to say they'd just seen me playing for the Dodgers in the 1978 World Series (did we lose again?) or the 1981 World Series (did we win again?).

After I'd been home awhile, my attitude was: *Don't worry about what you have no control over.* I never get bored because if I don't have something to do, I'll always make up something I've got to do. I can always go out in the yard, maybe pinch my grapes or dig up my onions or replant my collard greens and tomatoes. I try to keep ahead on everything. Darren tells me that I always have to be doing something, which is probably true. I never watched CNN so much as I did during the Covid pandemic. I wanted to stay up on the facts. I never went to bed so early, but also never got up so early. I would watch a Western on Starz and be in bed by eight-thirty or nine. After a while, you start to think about how baseball is important, but baseball ain't life. We make it like life sometimes, but it's not life or death in the world of importance. If I was away from live baseball action, I always longed to get back, I always missed it, but the time away gave me some of the life experiences I most cherish.

My breaks between managing jobs left me with a choice. I could sit around wishing I was in the game or I could make the most of the time I had, like during the two years between managing in Washington and taking the Astros job. I had always wanted to see Alaska and finally made the trip in 2019 with Darren and Kenny Tennell, my childhood friend from Riverside. For me as a kid reading those *National Geographic* magazines, the pictures of Alaska always grabbed me. Ice-cold mountain streams, moose, bears—I felt like I'd been there. I wanted to see it all with my own eyes but never could, since I always had baseball in summer. In 2019,

I could do what I wanted. We chose August, since it was a good month for Darren, then twenty years old, when he'd gotten through playing summer ball, and also because that time of year they have those long, long days up there.

We flew to Anchorage, went down to Seward on Resurrection Bay, and visited Talkeetna, where three rivers come together up near Mount McKinley. We wanted to take a plane or helicopter up the mountain, but the weather was bad. One Sunday, we went to a Baptist church, and I was surprised by the turnout. I didn't know there were so many Black people up there! I felt right at home in that church, almost like I was back at Reverend Moss's Park Avenue Baptist Church in Riverside with some great preaching and singing. I learned that a lot of the brothers went up to work on the pipeline and stayed, or they were stationed in the military and never left. In Anchorage, we visited the Alaska Native Heritage Center, and they put on a big show with costumes and dances that had been passed on for generations. They explained their philosophy of loving the land, much in the same way my Cheyenne brothers in Montana had shared with me. They were miles apart but had the same philosophy.

I chartered a private plane to fly Darren, Kenny, and me up over the tundra and land on the water to go fishing. We had fished in Montana, Cape Cod, Hawaii, New Mexico, Mexico, and Canada, and now here we were fishing in Alaska. Even though I wasn't working, and was missing time when I could be adding more career victories as manager and earning power, it was worth it to spend that time with my son. That Alaska trip was one of the best I was ever on. Darren loved it. And now we both had something in common with my dad, since years earlier I'd sent him and his second wife Mary up to Alaska through the Western Passage on a cruise that he loved—which aroused my curiosity and made me feel even more connected to him.

– – – –

We finally started our 2020 Astros season in July. Everything was rushed, once they decided it was time to get back to games, and it felt weird to start the season on July 24, similar to 1981 when we went on strike and started back up in early August. We took three of four from the Mariners at home and then hosted the Dodgers for a two-game series that turned ugly. Dodgers pitcher Joe Kelly threw a ball that came way too close to hitting Alex Bregman in the head, and he also taunted Carlos Correa. It got so tense, both benches cleared. Dave Roberts was suspended for one game and Joe Kelly for eight games—and I was fined, since my players had violated Covid protocol.

I was very careful about wearing a mask and gloves, and people would get on me for that later, but I had no choice. I turned seventy-one in 2020, and with my past history of cancer and my stroke, I couldn't afford to get Covid. I was in multiple high-risk categories. Because of Covid, we played the 2020 season in front of empty stadiums, with no fans, only cutout faces. People were sending in pictures and buying seats and putting their faces out there. Melissa put pictures of Darren, my grandsons, and my dogs on cutouts right there in the front row. I could look at them every day. I was so blessed to get to know my grandsons.

It was a boring environment with no fans, but there was less pressure. We were insulated from some of the harsher reactions to the controversy surrounding the team. Outside the stadium and in the streets, it was different. I felt especially bad for Jose Altuve, who bore the brunt of the unwarranted criticism from the press and some fans. I came to admire him, because all he did was take it. I understood that tempers were running hot. People took their shots. They made their jokes. They celebrated our misfortune. But it had actually been worse back in spring training when the controversy was more fresh, and we had a sample of what we could expect.

Dodgers fans stood outside of Anaheim Stadium and booed when we played there. In August, someone hired a plane to fly overhead in Oakland during batting practice with a banner reading "Houston Asterisks." People couldn't get enough of rooting against us. The saddest part of the whole scenario was that only a few players were left who had even taken part in the sign stealing scheme. I often wondered, once the fans came back, if they were booing the uniform or booing the person.

I enjoyed living in Houston, but I missed Melissa and Darren. I lived in Rice Village, which reminded me of Palo Alto, near Stanford University. The saving grace was going over to Ralph Garr's house, where Ruby would cook for us—turkey wings, chicken, collard greens, hot-water cornbread, mac and cheese, and homemade banana pudding for dessert. It was just like the old days at spring training with the Braves all over again. Sometimes I'd bring along my coaches, like Gary Pettis, our third base coach, or Dan Firova, who was with me in Washington and joined the staff after Chris Speier retired. Ralph and I would still go eat at This Is It Soul Food, owned by Craig Joseph, where we'd been going for forty years, and almost every week I'd do my weekly show in the parking lot before I went in to order food for some of the players, especially oxtails for Mauricio Dubón and Yordan Alvarez, who both swore it helped them hit.

I was fortunate in Houston to be insulated by a lot of old friends, new friends, and family. Ex-Giants Mike Jackson and Charlie Hayes, who played for me, lived there, and I also became good friends with Kelvin Sampson, the University of Houston basketball coach, who told me he was a big Braves fan and had followed me since he was a kid and I was with the Braves. I'd go fishing with Jay Bruce, who came over to see me from Beaumont, Texas. Or I might hang with Ralph Cooper, member of the Texas Radio Hall of Fame, who'd been covering me for fifty years, or "Mr. Baseball," as everyone called sportswriter James Montgomery, or Donald Bond, whose father, big Walt Bond, one of the first Black players for the Houston Colt .45's, died of leukemia when Donald was young. I'd visit Joe Fontenot, who was paralyzed and bedridden since his stroke some years earlier, and who passed away in late December 2025. He was a good friend of mine back in the day. I'd invite him out to games, and he'd sit in a gurney in the handicapped section provided by the Astros. He couldn't talk, but he spoke with his eyes.

Somehow I got to be friends with some Houston rappers, starting with Scarface, one of the Geto Boys, and Paul Wall, one of the early Swishahouse rappers, a cool white guy with a grill. He said he was going to buy me a grill, all of white gold. I told him that sounded good—if I were younger. Then in the clubhouse, we had Lil Wayne and Travis Scott and actor Mark Wahlberg and Trae tha Truth and Bun B. It seemed like every week, we had a rapper coming around, and it was always fun. The fact that I knew most of their music through Darren and my nieces and nephews gave my players the impression that I was semi-hip.

We won eight straight in mid-August. We were at home honoring Jackie Robinson Day in late August soon after Wisconsin police killed Jacob Blake. We all wore number 42 for Jackie. We lined up for the playing of the National Anthem, then walked off the field to protest Blake's death. I had a hollow feeling for Jacob Blake's family and a hollow feeling about what this meant for America. We had forty-two seconds of silence, for Jackie, then I walked back to the dugout, and my team followed. We left a "Black Lives Matter" T-shirt over home plate.

We finished second to the A's in the American League West that season, but made the playoffs as a wild card team. We swept the Twins in our best-of-three Wild Card Series and then needed just four games to get past the A's in the Division Series. That put us in the American League Championship Series against the Tampa Bay Rays, managed by Kevin Cash. The whole series would be played at Petco Park in San Diego because of Covid, and we all stayed at the same hotel in north San Diego, which made it kind of weird. Staying in the same hotel as your competition, that never happens. Usually you never see the opposition like that, since one team is at home, which made that year strange. But they wanted to keep us safe.

We opened the ALCS cold. Their pitching shut us down. We kept stranding runners and lost three straight, one loss from elimination. That was a tough place to be, down 3–0 with fans all over the country rooting against us. To that point in baseball history, the team leading a best-of-seven postseason series 3–0 had won thirty-seven out of thirty-eight series. The only exception was the Red Sox, who came back to shock the Yankees in 2004. After Game 3, our players, led by Maldy, Bregman, Correa, and Gurriel, held a meeting to fire everyone up, emphasizing: *We're not ready to go home.*

That week was a sad time for me. My friend Joe Morgan, so important to me for so long, died at home in California. I was on the team bus when I got the call. Joe was seventy-seven. He combined power and speed and did it all even though everyone told him he was too small for baseball, which was what they also said about Jose Altuve, also a second baseman. And they both started their careers on the Astros.

Jose was having a tough time in the field. I'd been there. These things tend to compound on you. He took losing hard, and it hurt all of us to see him hurting. You could see it in his eyes. I'd seen that look before, including in myself looking in the mirror. Jose was one of the finest people I'd ever managed. As a manager, my job was to give him positive support. I announced he'd be back at second base for Game 4—of course he would—and gave Jose a hug.

In the first inning of Game 4, Jose homered to left center to put us ahead. It reminded me of the confidence Lasorda showed in me my first year with the Dodgers and what that meant to me. Then in the third, he doubled to right to drive in another run and make it 2–0. Randy Arozarena tied it up in the fourth with one swing, but in the bottom of the fifth, Maldy singled and George Springer homered to give us a 4–2 lead. In the top of the sixth, Zack Greinke got a quick out and then ran into trouble, giving up back-to-back singles. He struck out Arozarena, then gave up an infield single to Ji-man Choi to load the bases. I wasn't sure if Greinke had had enough and walked out to the mound ready to make the pitching change. I was about to take him out, but something inside of me said, *No.*

I kept thinking, *Who could I bring in who has gotten out of trouble more times over the years than Greinke?* I thought back to Russ Ortiz in the 2002 World Series. I looked Greinke in the eye, and he looked strong and confident. I turned to Maldy. If he thought a pitcher was losing it, he would look down with his eyes. But if he thought the pitcher still had more in the tank, he would look right at me. Maldy looked right at me. He thought Greinke had more in the tank. I trusted that. I left Greinke in the game, and said a few prayers as I walked back to the dugout, praying I'd made the right choice. I had to sweat it out a little as the count to

Mike Brosseau went full, not what you want to see with the bases loaded. But Greinke struck him out to end the inning, and we won the game, 4–3. One down, three to go to advance to the next round.

In Game 5, it was all tied up 3–3 going into the bottom of the ninth. Carlos Correa, due up second, came over to me in the dugout.

"Walk-off," he told me.

"Go ahead, man," I said.

It reminded me of being in the on-deck circle before Hank went up to bat against Al Downing, and he told me he was going to hit number 715 right there. Alex Bregman started off the inning with a good at-bat against Tampa reliever Nick Anderson, taking good swings before flying out to right on a ball I thought at first might drop for a hit, but was caught. Carlos had that confident look in his eye as he stepped up to the plate. Anderson started him off with a high fastball well out of the zone, and Carlos hopped back, before digging in again and taking a big swing on the 1-0 breaking ball, but not getting it. He was looking fastball. On the next pitch, a fastball away, Carlos extended his arms and got all of it: A walk-off homer to center field.

That put us back in the series. Carlos walked into my office right after the game and asked for his bottle of Baker Family Wines "Walk Off Red," which is now in our lineup of wines.

We were down one game, and still facing elimination. Could we make it all the way back from 3–0? In Game 6, Framber Valdez worked six strong innings, giving up just one run, and we won 7–4. We were not through trying to write history. People might hate us, but they had to respect us and what we had done battling back.

In the end, we fell short in Game 7. An early Randy Arozarena home run paced the Rays to a 4–2 win, and our season was over. We were going home, but something happened in those three games we won. To come back like that, after so tough a year, in so many different ways—this was a group that had a lot of fight and character. I realized how much I loved that Astros team.

— — — —

For me, 2021 got off to a tough start. Hank Aaron died in January 2021, and that one hit me as hard as any death other than my dad's. Hank was the most important influence on my life next to my dad and one of the best people that I ever knew, the truest and most honest. He taught me by example how to be a man and how to be a proud African American.

In 2020, my first year managing the Astros, I'd felt almost like a substitute teacher, like an outsider filling in for A. J. Hinch as manager. I inherited his coaches and they all knew his system. I only knew a couple people in the whole organization. It was a strange year all around, even though we had a good run. Then in 2021, we had fans in the stands again, and we had a strong young team with high expectations. My players and I warmly embraced each other in 2021, and they made me feel like one of them. We won ninety-five games and finished five games ahead of Seattle to win the AL West. Then we had series wins over the White Sox and the Red Sox to advance to a World Series with my former team, the Braves. This was the first World Series to be played since Hank died. His footprints were everywhere. I wasn't the only one Hank had taken under his wing. I wasn't even the only manager in the series who owed a lot to Hank, since Brian Snitker's career as a coach and manager had everything to do with Hank, during his time as Atlanta's farm director, giving Snitker a chance to manage early on. Hank was gone, but not gone. For me, he was always a presence, always there in my thoughts, like my dad. I did feel that Hank wanted the Braves to win that year—and wanted me to come back the next year and win it.

It was Atlanta's year, not ours. José Urquidy won two games for us, and we won big in Game 5, 9–5, to send the series back to Houston, but in Game 7, the Braves rolled to a 7–0 win.

Again I watched the other team celebrate a World Series victory. It hurt. It felt terrible. I was tired of being disappointed. It brought back the many hurts of the past, which I was trying to dispel. But as Eddie Kendricks used to say, you've got to "Keep on Truckin.' " That's what we were going to do. We were going to take this loss and remember it and use it as incentive to come back to the World Series the next year and see a different result.

The baseball highlight of the 2021 season in the Baker family might have come in June when Darren was drafted by the Washington Nationals. He played for the Cal Bears for four years and graduated, as my daughter Tosh did twenty years before—that was important to our family, especially after I promised my mom I would graduate college but never did. Darren was a tenth-round draft pick. (Believe me, he let me know that was a lot better than going in the twenty-sixth round.) For spring 2022, we decided to be roommates. It was Darren's idea, and that was the best spring training I ever had. It was so much fun sharing it with my son, especially after we lost my mom that January after a struggle with dementia. That was really hard to take, but I knew my mom was with us. As with my dad's death, I was so thankful for hospice care, one of the greatest medical practices there is, and for all the doctors and nurses had done to assist us and make my dad and mom's last days as comfortable as possible. It was a tough time for the family. My brother Vic had died three years earlier. The family was getting smaller. The more you lose, the more you learn to make the most of the time you have left with those you love most.

Darren and I didn't cook much that spring, except when Melissa visited for a couple weeks. Mostly it was takeout or eating in restaurants. Having me pay all the time was good for Darren, who could eat as much as he wanted. That was a good way to keep the weight on. Like all the Baker men, Darren was a late bloomer and still needed to fill out. We had our routine: Every night, no dishes in the sink and the garbage had been taken out, we would FaceTime Melissa together. We said the Lord's Prayer together every night before bed.

The walls in the house I'd rented near Juno Beach in Jupiter were thin enough that I could hear the water in the pipes when Darren got up at six-thirty and took a shower. That was good: I knew he was up and not oversleeping. I'd take my pickup and drive off to Astros spring training camp, and he'd get in his Toyota Corolla rental car and go to Nationals spring training camp. We'd arrive at the same complex, which we shared. I'd opened that Nationals complex my second year managing the team. I used to go right, now I went left—and Darren went right.

We'd been looking forward to March 20 when the Nationals played the Astros. I was sitting in the dugout before the game started and saw someone waving to me to come out on the field. I thought, *Who's waving at me?* I stepped out and saw it was my son. Nationals manager Davey Martinez had sent Darren out to deliver the lineup card. We walked to home plate together to shake hands with the umpire crew. Darren and I hugged, then exchanged lineup cards, and hugged again. We were going to hug one more time, but the umpires told us please, no more hugs, even though I could pick up a touch of sentiment from them.

"Dad, you know we're going to beat you," Darren called over his shoulder as he walked back to the dugout, flashing that smile of his.

Darren did his part. He came in at second base in the sixth inning, then in his first big-league at-bat singled to right field on the first pitch he saw. Then in the eighth, he came up again and beat us with a sacrifice fly to give the Nationals a 3–2 win. I've never had a more joyous day in baseball—and to think it happened in the same town where I had my first spring training with the Braves. It was emotional when spring training ended and I dropped Darren off at Palm Beach International Airport so he could fly to Wilmington, Delaware, where he'd be playing A-ball with the Blue Rocks, opening the season in a few days against Brooklyn. I didn't know when I'd see him again. I'd kind of gotten used to having him around.

My first two seasons with the Astros, our shortstop was Carlos Correa, a former first-round pick and AL Rookie of the Year. He signed a big free-agent contract with the Twins after the 2021 season, clearing the way for a talented rookie, Jeremy Peña, a twenty-four-year-old Dominican. When I was a young player, Hank had the Braves send me back to the minor leagues to make sure I was ready. As Braves farm director, Hank always said it was better to have a young player one year over-ready than under-ready, because if you fail, it can be very deflating, and a lot of these kids had never failed before. I followed that advice from Hank, which might be why I'd gotten a rap for not liking to give young players a shot. But if a player was ready, a player was ready, and Peña looked good to me. I liked him even when he was in the minor leagues. I liked his actions. I liked his body. More than anything, Bo Schembechler once told me, it's in the face. Not only was Peña handsome, which shouldn't matter, but he had a kind and attentive face. They say it's hard to win with a rookie catcher or rookie shortstop, but we won that year with a rookie shortstop who was MVP of both the ALCS and the World Series.

We had a good young pitching staff, our Young Gun Latins, with Bryan Abreu now joining Garcia, Javier, Urquidy, and Valdez, held together by Maldy and his veteran leadership behind the plate and the veterans Pressly and Justin Verlander, whom I was glad to have back that year from Tommy John surgery. Framber was really maturing. I had a hell of a lineup, starting with Altuve, then Peña and Alvarez, followed by Bregman batting cleanup, and behind him in the five spot our left fielder, Kyle Tucker, probably the most talented guy on the team. He was tooled up. Besides Altuve and Peña, and the Honduran Mauricio Dubón—who had gone to my camp as a kid in Sacramento—we had Cubans Yuli Gurriel and Yordan Alvarez.

I always liked the Cubans because I had an idea of what they had been through to get there. Those guys had been on international teams in Cuba, where they faced more pressure than anything that could go on here. Alvarez defected from Cuba in 2016 and was a unanimous choice as AL Rookie of the Year in 2019, but he missed most of 2020 with knee troubles and Covid. In 2022, he hit a career-high thirty-seven homers. He didn't say much, not in Spanish or English, but he was smart and didn't miss a thing. Yuli was quiet, but an attentive leader, older, and everyone respected him. His dad had been a hell of a player in Cuba.

The 2022 All-Star Game was at Dodger Stadium, and I was managing the American League team against a National League team managed by Brian Snitker. I called my friend Snoop Dogg and asked him if he'd like to be my honorary coach. He loved the idea, but somehow I could never get approval from the league office. Snoop couldn't wait and had other obligations. Eventually they lined up another popular entertainer, Bad Bunny.

Going into the 2022 postseason, I was more determined than ever to win the championship. We'd come so close the year before, and I could feel it coming. We had a powerhouse team hot off a 106-win season, my first hundred-win season since 1993 when I led the Giants to 103 wins as a rookie manager. I had a tough-minded, confident team who knew who they were. They powered through a Division Series sweep of the Mariners and a four-game sweep of the Yankees in the American League Championship Series.

I made a conscious decision before Game 1 of the 2022 World Series at home in Houston. I had to live with the reality that in 2020s baseball, teams paid big for a baseball operations department that used data to decide how a team should be managed and passed that all on to me. I would think about all that data. I would think about the insights I could glean from it. But I was going to draw some lines. I was seventy-three years old, old enough to have learned to remember what you've learned. Hank taught me that you won in baseball by trusting your feelings. I was going to trust my feelings in this Series. I was going to manage with my mind, my heart, *and* my faith. And we would see how it all turned out. Jim Crane trusted me and trusted my judgment, as well as the baseball minds surrounding me—Jeff Bagwell, Enos Cabell, Craig Biggio, and Reggie Jackson.

There was discussion among some of the front office scouts and sabermetrics people on who should play and who should not play, and who should bat where in the lineup. That's when I went on my faith. I know I should have done some things differently, according to the data, but I didn't feel it. Something told me that wasn't right in this situation, and so I chose to do most of the things exactly how I wanted to do them because I felt that those were the right things. As one example, there were some who didn't think it was smart to bat the rookie Peña second. I just felt that was the right thing to do, batting him in front of Alvarez, much like I did with Rich Aurilia in front of Barry Bonds in San Francisco. Or when I moved Robby Thompson in front of Will Clark and Kevin Mitchell. I remember that one came to me in the middle of the night: Robby was hitting sixth, and I decided to move him up. I get a lot of ideas in the night, so I keep a pen and paper on my nightstand, just in case. That's when some of my best thoughts come to me, and if I don't write them down right away, a lot of times I can't remember them the next morning, and that drives me nuts.

One thing you always have to keep in mind is that regular season wins have nothing to do with the postseason. We'd won 106 games and easily won our division. In the World Series, we would face a Philadelphia Phillies team that finished third in the NL East, fourteen games back with a record of 87–75. The Phillies got hot at the right time. They won two straight in their Wild Card Series with the Cardinals to advance, then made quick work of the Braves in the Division Series (3–1) and the Padres in the NLCS (4–1). It's all about getting to the dance. That was always my thing. I'd rather win my division, but you just wanted to find a way to get there. In my four years with the Astros, we went to the World Series two of the four years and we could easily have gone four years in a row—we were that close, one win away, taking the American League Championship Series to seven games the other two seasons.

I was going to set a record by being the most experienced man ever to manage in the World Series—since I'd be the oldest, in terms of years on the planet. Trader Jack McKeon had been the oldest World Series manager ever when he managed the Florida Marlins against the Yankees in 2003 after first beating my Cubs team that season. Jack was seventy-two years, 329 days. And Jack's team won.

That 2022 Astros club was a throwback team in some ways. Our team philosophy was to put the ball in play and put pressure on the other team's defense. During the regular season, we had the second fewest strikeouts of any team in baseball, thanks to my hitting coaches, Alex Cintrón and Troy Snitker, son of Braves manager Brian Snitker. How many times have you seen that? The dad on one side and the son on the other?

I'd always respected Bryce Harper, and as his former manager, I was very aware of just how talented he'd always been. Now, having gone from the Nats to the Phillies in 2019, he loomed as a major challenge to my leading my team to a World Series championship. We opened the 2022 World Series at home on October 28, and before Game 1, I was in my office at Minute Maid Park when I heard a knock on my back door. Not too many people even knew about that back door. I pulled the latch and opened the door, and there was Bryce, wanting to talk to me. The visiting clubhouse guy Steve Perry, whom I'd known for more than thirty years, had driven Bryce over to pay his respects.

"We're going to have a good Series," Bryce said, and I agreed.

We took an early 5–0 lead in Game 1 on Kyle Tucker's two home runs, and the Phillies came back to tie it 5–5 on J. T. Realmuto's double. Then in the tenth, Realmuto homered, and Philadelphia won, 6–5. In Game 2, we were facing Zack Wheeler, one pitcher I wanted nothing to do with. I remember when I managed Bryce on the Nationals asking him which pitcher was the toughest to face and he told me Zack Wheeler, who had been drafted by the Giants, traded to the Mets, and signed by the Phillies. Wheeler was always nasty, but that night we jumped on him early. The first three hitters he faced—Altuve, Peña, and Alvarez—all doubled, we scored three in the first, and won 5–2. But in Game 3 back in Philadelphia, Bryce hit a two-run homer in the first and the Phillies won 7–0. We were down two games to one with two more games in Philadelphia, where the fans are as tough on visiting teams as anywhere in baseball. After the game, Ralph and Ruby Garr and some of my homies gathered in my hotel suite with their families. It made for more of a positive atmosphere and attitude that really helped.

Almost nothing was better than facing two more hard games in Philly and winning them both. Cristian Javier, Abreu, Montero, and Pressly combined for a shutout in Game 4, and we won 5–0, keeping the fans at Citizens Bank Park quiet. Then in Game 5, Verlander outpitched Noah Syndergaard and we won 3–2, after center fielder Chas McCormick had a game-saving catch with one out in the ninth. Realmuto hit a drive to the wall in right center, and Chas went up and got it, leaping and crashing into the wall, then landing flat on his back—but holding on to the ball. Chas grew up going to games in that same ballpark and caught a lot of flak from the Philly fans for making that catch up against the wall. He had a great all-around series.

We were on our way home to Houston one win away from a World Series championship. I didn't get too high over it, not yet. I would never forget the 2003 NLCS when I was manager of the Cubs going up three-two on the Marlins in Miami and flying home to Chicago with Prior and Wood ready to start. You can never get too high. This game will knock you down in a hurry if you do.

One detail from that World Series I never much talked about was my routine of feeding homeless people every night. We threw away a lot of food at the ballpark, and during the season, I would take four to six meals in to-go containers and drop them off to the homeless living underneath the freeway, right around the corner from the stadium. During the World Series, the city ran off the people I usually fed from their usual spot, so I had to search for them. There was one lady, they called her Mama, who lived in a clean and tidy shelter she made by putting boxes together. I told them I didn't want them to be fighting over the food, so I gave it to Mama, and she would disperse it. I'd pull up in my car and roll down the window and give Mama the food, and I never thought she knew who I was. Then we lost a game, and Mama told me, "The Astros got spanked." I'm thinking, *How does this lady know I'm with the Astros?* Then we won the next night and she said, "Good game, Dusty." Seeing her made me think about my brother Vic. Every time I see a homeless person, I think about my brother.

The morning of Game 6, I kept to my usual routine. Game 6 had been my nemesis in too many postseasons. Not this year, I was determined. I slept until 9:40, which was unlike me, but at that point in the season, you are tired and every extra minute of sleep helps. I stopped off at my favorite coffee place in Rice Village, then ran a couple errands, picking up some dress shoes I had resoled and stopping by the dry cleaners. I always put on music that goes with my mood and when I arrived at my office that day, I put on Big Mama Thornton's "Hound Dog," the original version of the song before Elvis recorded it.

You could feel the energy in the clubhouse and in the stadium when you walked out for batting practice. The stands were already half full. There was a lot of positive energy in the air. The game was scoreless through five innings. Framber Valdez and Zack Wheeler were both putting up nothing but zeroes. Kyle Schwarber led off the top of the sixth with a homer off Framber, and even though we were down, it was like that gave our lineup a jolt. We had some big-game players on our side, and I was confident in what they could do.

Maldy was hit by pitch to open the bottom of the sixth, and Jeremy Peña singled to put runners on for Yordan Alvarez. The Phillies went to their bullpen.

Out came left-handed reliever Jose Alvarado, one of the top left-handed relievers around, a hard thrower. It was a great matchup, Alvarado against Alvarez, a left-hander who hit lefties better than right-handers. Alvarado fell behind, and Alvarez crushed a 2-1 pitch for a no-doubt-about-it home run to deep center field. I was happy, but I knew we had nine of the toughest outs you could ever face in front of us.

Yordan was met near home plate by Jose Altuve, who gave him a hug, then he worked his way through the dugout, high-fiving and slapping hands, then came all the way to the far end of the dugout to wind up and give me a big high five—and that high five might have felt as good as any I can remember going back to that very first high five Glenn Burke threw my way after I hit my thirtieth home run as a Dodger in 1977.

We added one more to make it 4–1 going into the seventh. Now I had it set up to go with Hector Neris in the seventh and Bryan Abreu in the eighth and give the ball to my closer Ryan Pressly in the ninth. By the eighth inning, I was counting the outs—and hearing voices in my head. I could hear my dad talking to me, and my mom and my brother Vic. I could hear Hank talking to me, and Don Baylor. I thought of so many in the game who were in my corner and motivated me—Joe Black and Roy Campanella and Jim Gilliam and Willie Stargell and Al Kaline and so many more.

It was 10:17 P.M. when Kyle Tucker moved into foul territory and gloved Nick Castellanos's fly ball for the final out. The first thing I did was write down on my lineup card who made the last out, like I always did, and then I held on for dear life. We'd won the game. We'd won the World Series. I'd climbed to the top of the mountain and reached my ultimate goal as a manager.

In the dugout, my coaches and players mobbed me, and I held on to the screen. Then we had a heck of a celebration afterward on the field, which I had seen a bunch of other guys do when we lost, and which you really dislike having them do on your field. Now, finally, it was our turn. I don't even like the taste of champagne, but that night it was sweet. I like what it means more than the actual taste.

"Thank you for everything," Kyle Tucker told me. "Thank you—I love you."

The Astros had won the World Series five years earlier, but some saw that one as tainted. Not this one. It was a win that had a purifying, vindicating feel to it. The guys had heard the jeers and the boos, and instead of turning bitter or angry, it just brought them closer together. I was extremely happy for the town, for owner Jim Crane, and for GM James Click, who was later fired, but I tried to save his job, even though we didn't see eye to eye on every subject.

I was on the MLB Network platform being interviewed just after the game and saw my son Darren down below, and I jumped off so I could give him a long hug. Darren had come in after his minor league season to join me for the playoffs and World Series, as he always did since he was a kid.

"How do you like that, son?" I said into his ear. "How do you like that?"

"I told you, Dad!" he said. "I told you! I told you that you were going to do it."

It was an unbelievable feeling. Would it have felt that sweet if I hadn't waited so long before winning one as a manager? I guess I'll never know. I was the oldest manager to win a World Series and only the third African American following Cito Gaston and Dave Roberts. I thought of my dad's comment to me after we had lost in Anaheim with the Giants, about how since we hadn't won that one, maybe I never would win as a manager. I remembered how much it motivated me. He always knew how to motivate me.

An hour after we'd won, back in my office, I could only laugh, and laugh and laugh, letting the good feeling wash over me. Josh Rawitch, president of the Baseball Hall of Fame, stopped by my office, already planning an exhibit in Cooperstown.

"Can we have your wristbands?" he asked me.

No problem. I took both off and handed them over to Josh.

"Okay, and by any chance—I know this is going to sound crazy—a toothpick?"

I dug into my drawer and gave him a toothpick.

"It's been a long time coming," Josh said. "I'm so happy for you."

Jim Crane invited all of us into the back room at his Italian restaurant, Potente, right across from the ballpark. I was happy, sharing the moment with Melissa and Darren, Ralph and Ruby, all my homeys, and I was excited, but most of all I was tired. Anytime you play deep into the postseason, those extra games wear on you mentally and physically. I was relieved, but tired. I'd have time to enjoy this, but what I needed then was rest. I went to bed sometime after two A.M. and slept the best I'd slept in a long, long time. I actually slept until eleven A.M., which I never do, and when I woke up and talked to Darren and Melissa, it truly sank in that we were World Series champions. It had escaped me many times, and now I was feeling what it was like to really get there, a deep feeling of satisfaction.

I checked my phone and I had almost 1,300 texts congratulating me. I didn't know all those people had my number! Everybody was happy for me. I got calls from Snoop Dogg, from President Obama, from Bill Cosby, Elvin Bishop, Willie Brown, on and on and on. So many people told me later they never thought they'd root for the Astros but they were rooting for us that year. A lot of people tuned in that might not have been wanting to tune in. It was good for baseball because it helped some of the young people we were losing get back into the game.

Winning the World Series with the Astros as a manager meant as much to me as winning as a player with the Dodgers forty-one years earlier, but they were such different feelings, you couldn't compare. A lot of life had happened in the interim. A lot of emotions had changed. To me, our win in that World Series was all about giving people hope, especially people feeling low in hope. Sometimes, man, you need something to motivate you that you can do it. I hope we helped in some small way some other people who might have been suffering. You don't always think about the impact the game has on some people or how the game offers a perspective of life. Baseball is more like life than any other sport, with the ups and downs and daily highs and lows you have to deal with. No team had dealt with more ups and downs and highs and lows than that Astros team.

At noon on Monday, a day and a half after we won, the city of Houston gathered for the best parade ever. Back in 1981, when I won with the Dodgers, we might have had a quarter-million people come out in L.A. In Houston in November 2022, we probably had two million, nearly double the size of the parade after the Astros won the World Series in 2017. I'd never seen so many people in one place at one time. I was with Melissa and Darren and my nephew Tyler on one of the platform buses, along with Bregman and his wife Reagan, Verlander and his wife Kate, McCullers and his wife Kara, Altuve and his wife Nina, and team owner Jim Crane and his wife Whitney and other team dignitaries. Some players rode on fire engines. The mood of the crowd was so energetic and full of joy and love, I'll never forget it. It was too hot to wear my good-luck purple jacket, like Chris Berman used to wear, but I'd worn it before one of the games in Philly.

The town was rocking. The town was psyched. It was such a feeling of relief and accomplishment. Everyone took off from work to come celebrate. People were hanging off the light poles. They were hanging off the balconies. They were hanging off of rooftops and garages. I had to catch a couple full cans of beers because people were throwing us beers, and I didn't want one to hit somebody in the face. One of the players gave Darren and Tyler cigars. We never did find out who that was!

I had a definite feeling of gratitude and thankfulness. Up until the

Astros job opened up, there were no signs of me having another chance of managing, and now that we had won it all together, I felt like I was given back everything that was lost. My books were balanced. A lot of people assumed that since we'd won, with me as the oldest manager ever to win a World Series, I'd go home satisfied and announce my retirement, but quite to the contrary, that wasn't my mindset at all. I'd been telling friends and the press that if I won one World Series, I wanted two in a row.

"What are you going to do after you win one?" people kept asking.

"If I win one, I really feel that I'll win two," I always said.

Now I'd won one. I'd reached a major milestone I'd been after for a long time, but I still had the fire burning inside me. I wanted number two, and even during that parade, for all the joy of celebration, for all the joy of a city feeling united behind a sense of accomplishment and vindication, I was thinking like a coach. I was looking ahead at getting ready to do what no team had done since Joe Torre's Yankees won back-to-back World Series in 1999 and 2000 and Cito Gaston won two in a row with the Blue Jays in 1992 and 1993.

For the second and final year, my spring training roommate in 2023 was my son, and our baseball worlds again overlapped—in more ways than one. The first spring, Darren drove a rental car. That spring, he drove in style in Hank Aaron's BMW that I purchased from Billye Aaron, which had just been sitting there in Hank's West Palm Beach vacation home. A lot of people wanted that car. I gave it to Darren to drive at spring training and during the season so he would feel Hank's spirit, but it's still my car.

I think it might have worked too well. On March 17 in West Palm Beach, we were playing the Nationals. Melissa was there in the stands wearing a Nationals cap. Darren singled in the eighth and came up in the ninth inning with the bases loaded. We had a four-run lead at the time. Darren got a fastball and lined the ball to left field, and it carried out of there for a grand slam. For Darren, it was an out-of-body experience, he was so happy. For me, as I said at the time, I love my son but I hate to lose—even in spring training. He was looking at me while rounding the bases, and my players and coaches were all looking at me, but I didn't look back. Only that night, when we were alone, did I let him know how happy I was for him.

I wasn't the only former Giants manager leading a Texas team in 2023. Bruce Bochy, who won three World Series with the Giants, had taken over as Rangers manager. That spring, he told me he regretted having announced before his last season with the Giants that he would be retiring at the end of the year. It became a distraction, he said. That's the last thing a manager wants. It's not fair to your players. I took what Boch said to heart and decided I'd keep quiet on my own plans. Even if we won another one, I was not at all tempted to go for three in a row. I would be turning seventy-five in June 2024, and the job was getting more and more exhausting.

Sometime in the summer of 2023, home in Houston, Melissa heard some beeping in the night. At first I thought it was a smoke detector that needed a new battery, but it was me that needed a new battery. I had to have my pacemaker replaced. I'd been hoping to have that done back home in California, but the doctors said I couldn't wait that long. In August, I had my second pacemaker put in and didn't even miss a game, since I had it done on an off day. For that I have a lot of people to thank, starting with the Astros' team physician, Dr. Jim Muntz, who also worked with the Houston Rockets and Houston Texans and was named NFL Physician of the Year in 2022. Dr. Muntz is truly one of the best, and he and Astros trainer Jeremiah Randall, also one of the best, went out of their way to help me through that time. I couldn't lift anything heavier than ten pounds for a couple of weeks, and clubhouse manager Carl Schneider and his staff and visiting clubhouse guy Steve Perry were always there to carry my stuff to get me through those two weeks. All these people helped me so much, and I'm very thankful for that. I felt better with the new pacemaker, but it was a reminder that I had to think of my health. I had a lot of living left to do when my time with the Astros came to an end.

Even though we had won, general manager James Click couldn't get a multiyear deal done for himself and was dismissed, a little like me with the Giants after the 2002 World Series. Baseball can be a tough business. Jim Crane hired Dana Brown as his new GM for my final season with the Astros. I'd been consulted on the hire and recommended Brown along with two other candidates. Brown was trying to combine sabermetrics and scouting with an old-school approach. When I look back on it, I can see how Dana Brown would want to hire his own manager, because I was in the twilight of my career and his career was more at sunup.

Everybody wanted me to play our hot prospect at catcher, Yainer Diaz, who was twenty-four in 2023 but still green. I resisted. I knew Diaz would be an All-Star one day. In my opinion, it wasn't time. His day had not yet arrived to be the everyday catcher. There's so much to learn to master catching at the big-league level, controlling the tempo of the game, getting all the signs from the manager, knowing when to take a timeout, and not losing focus behind the plate when you just struck out with the bases loaded in the last inning. I don't know if I could make that transition from offense to defense as a catcher. That's one of the hardest things there is to do in baseball. It's a lot for a young catcher to learn all that and to try to win a World Series, and the postseason is not the time to be learning on the job. I remembered how the Braves took their time with us as young players, and with a catcher it's even more important to have experience, because a catcher has so many things to learn. Maldy was an extension of me on the field, and we also had veteran Jason Castro—having two catchers with experience helped us immensely. But I took a lot of grief for sticking with Maldy. People just focused on Diaz's bat versus Maldy's—in 2023, .282 versus .191. I said at the time I knew what I was doing and was hoping that everyone would thank me later for Diaz's progress and maturity.

For the second time in four years, we took the ALCS to seven games but were eliminated. The Rangers won the first two games of the ALCS in Houston, then we won all three in Arlington. Back home, we lost Game 6, 9–2, and in Game 7, the Rangers stayed hot and won 11–4 to advance to the World Series, which they won. In my four years with the

Astros, my teams either went to the World Series (twice) or missed the World Series by one game (twice). That was what it's all about, going all the way, and it's rare to go to the World Series four years in a row the way Joe Torre's Yankees did.

The night we were eliminated, I hung with my friends at the Westin Hotel downtown and went out and grabbed tacos at two A.M. at La Calle. It made it easier for me being with my longtime partners. Melissa told me to hang with them because she was going back to the apartment. I felt a sense of peace in knowing what my future held.

I met with Jim Crane the next day to let him know of my plans, and we parted on a positive note. Jim told me I was one of the only ones who could have quieted the storm around the Astros the way I did. I was completely at peace with my decision. I knew it was right for me. I thought I might have had another year in me, but then I considered what Al Campanis had always said back in L.A., which was that if you were going to trade a guy, better a year too early than a year too late. I could see how maybe that applied to my own situation as manager.

I was the only manager ever to lead five different teams to the postseason, I'd won fifty-seven games in the postseason, the fourth most in history, and at that time I ranked seventh all time in wins by a manager with 2,183, behind only Connie Mack, Tony La Russa, John McGraw, Bobby Cox, Joe Torre, and Sparky Anderson. But more important than any number was the knowledge given to me and what I'd passed on to the teams I managed. I took what was given to me and simply retained it and passed it on, above all to the players. Maldy, asked for a quote on me retiring from managing, said, "People love him. He's a guy that gave everything for the city, a guy that gave everything for the players and is going to be in the Hall of Fame."

I knew I'd miss the guys and the competition, but not necessarily the verbal dodgeball routines that managers in modern baseball are required to go through pregame and postgame. I thought about what Bill Walsh said about reaching this stage and having to replace that 60 to 70 percent of your time that you spent at the job with something else or depression sets in. I could see that happening. You can only play golf and fish so much. I was going to stay busy. And I was going to make the most of the time I now had with Melissa and Darren and Tosh. I could play with my grandsons and think about all of Darren's life that I missed while I was playing ball and managing. It's always the mamas that drive their sons and daughters to their games and catch all the action, especially the sons and daughters of men in baseball, since they're off with their teams. Now, finally, I'd have more time to watch him.

— — — —

We got there just in time. Days earlier, Melissa and I were back East and flew home from Scranton, Pennsylvania, after catching some of Darren's games with Triple-A Rochester. This was August 2024, and Darren was swinging the bat real well and stealing a lot of bases. My phone rang and I saw it was Mike Rizzo, my friend and former GM in Washington. Rizzo drafted Darren two years after my time managing the Nationals, so there was never any hint of nepotism.

I saw "Mike Rizzo" on my phone and figured he was calling just to say hello.

"Hey man," he said, conversationally, like he was just telling me about how his week was going. "We're calling up some kid who's got like thirty-eight stolen bases."

"Really?" I asked.

"And is hitting about .290."

"Sounds like Darren," I said.

"It is," he said. "Darren deserves this, and him being your son has nothing to do with it."

I agreed: Darren had earned the shot. And the last thing he wanted was to think he was getting any special treatment because he was my son. He was the type of player a manager loved, a guy who did the little things that help a team win, alert and baseball smart, a good teammate—and fast. Melissa and I scrambled to get to D.C., arrived late and caught a couple hours sleep, then rushed over to Nationals Park. I had a lot of different feelings running through me as Melissa and I made our way inside the stadium. Most of all, I felt pride and love. Pride and love for my boy—a man by then—and pride and love for baseball. My dad taught me the game, and I taught my son. Now he was getting an opportunity. I always loved D.C. as a city and felt a strong connection with Nationals fans. I'd have liked to win it all with the Nationals, but things happen for a reason.

It did feel good to be in our seats. I'm a people person, but also private at the same time. It takes a lot out of you going through a crowd like that and talking to people at every step along the way. I was sitting close to the Cubs dugout and David Ross, the manager, and third-base coach Willie Harris, both former players of mine, seemed like they were trying to get my attention, but I was tripping off being in the stands and not in the dugout and being there as a proud parent.

I wanted to focus on the game. I could feel in my bones that Darren had a good shot of coming in. It was a lopsided game, the Cubs were winning by a lot, and if you're a manager, you always like to get a kid's feet wet, get that first big-league at-bat out of the way to go from there. That was exactly what Davey Martinez did with Darren.

It was a moment I'll always remember when I heard the familiar voice of the PA announcer at Nationals Park calling out that Darren Baker would now be pinch-hitting in the bottom of the ninth. He stepped up to the plate, looking good, all business, like he felt at home and belonged there. Going back to his time as a kid growing up around the big leagues, he'd seen many pinch-hitters and he knew the good ones are always ready to hit from the opening pitch. Sure enough, the first pitch happened to be a strike, and Darren jumped on it. Line drive. Base knock. Melissa was shaking me, everyone was cheering, and I just sat there watching my boy. I'd let Darren come to his love of baseball on his own. I simply made it available to him. You could see that love in the smile he flashed at first base. I might have been a little biased, but to me it seemed like Darren's smile lit up the whole stadium.

EPILOGUE

Take the Road to the Right

The lessons of life, like the lessons of baseball, have to be learned over and over again. If you think you're done relearning those lessons, maybe you learned less than you thought you did. That's why I start every day by taking some time to read and reread my books, including the Bible, especially Proverbs, to acquire wisdom and reflect and gather myself and gain clarity. I learned this from José Rijo years ago at the end of my playing career when I was with the Oakland A's and have stuck with it ever since. A lot of times I've got stuff to do. Phone calls to return. Plants and trees to water and tend. Errands to run. But I do my half-hour reading each morning because it helps keep me dialed in to what's important. It helps me gather myself to move fresh into a new day alert and open enough to take it as it comes.

Letting go is not easy. You could say that letting go runs counter to human nature in a lot of ways. We live in a culture right now where a lot of influences push people to resent or blame others. You see people turning to resentment and bitterness to fuel some kind of internal fire to make themselves feel powerful. But fueling your resentment and bitterness will exact a toll. It will hollow you out. Over time, it will turn you into a different person. The resentments we hold to our heart block us from seeing the good in the world. The resentments we hold onto block our heart from seeing the good in the world. If we hold enough resentment, we stop seeing the good altogether. That's happened to me, in moments, but it did me no good. That way lies emptiness of the soul. I felt angry, but I felt soulless, and that's not a good feeling. That, to me, is the Devil's work. Like anyone, I have had to work to overcome the occasional impulse to blame others. The toughest thing that people do in life is forgive each other.

When I look back at every trial in my life, Jesus was with me, whether I knew it or not. All things were for the good. Not a day goes by that I don't think about how blessed I am to have had the life I've had. That's part of the reflection that starts every day I live. As I've said, Hank Aaron and Orlando Cepeda taught me the lesson that often you don't understand the important truths of life until much later. It took me a long time to see, for example, that my dad had never been against me, even when he cut me from my Little League team three different years or when he took my contract with the Alanta Braves to court to try to nullify it. He was always on my side, looking out for me, helping me to find the right path. I was blessed to have my dad and my mom, whose lessons and teachings and example molded me into the man I became. I was blessed to have Ralph Garr and Cito Gaston and Bill Walsh and Al Attles and so many others. I was blessed that, when I needed a new opportunity in baseball, it always seemed to arrive right on time, sometimes just when I was thinking about quitting, and I was able to make the most of that opportunity.

At some points in telling my story, I've drawn lines I won't go past. Some people might have wanted to hear more about intimate conversations with my players or coaches or scenes in the private sanctuary of the clubhouse or dugout, but there are sacred places in baseball that need to be respected. Some things need to remain private, out of respect. This is my life, and I've opened the door on as much of it as I can.

I think about all the remarkable people I've been fortunate enough to get to know in my life, often as close friends but sometimes just for a few hours, and think about what they've passed on to me. I visited the crossroads in Mississippi where Robert Johnson dueled the Devil for his soul, along with my friend Elvin Bishop when we were down there to go fishing at Morgan Freeman's farm. Elvin said, "Hey, man, we're at the crossroads," and I said, "Stop the car." Morgan Freeman has always been an inspiration to me, still doing his thing into his eighties, helped inspire me to stay cool and stay passionate and keep doing your thing no matter what age you wake up to find yourself.

Or often you can be inspired by a younger person. You never know when you'll meet someone who might inspire you or help shape your life, even a young man polishing your car. Back in the early 1980s when I was with the Dodgers, I took my Porsche to a place in the San Fernando Valley. That was where I met a likable young man from England with aspirations of being a Hollywood filmmaker. He looked up from polishing my Porsche and told me he was going to make it big. That was Graham King. Thirty years later, I heard from him again. He had gone on to win an Academy Award for producing *The Departed* with Jack Nicholson and Leonardo DiCaprio, and also *Bohemian Rhapsody* about Queen and *Michael,* his big Michael Jackson film due out in 2026.

In New York years ago, I met a young man leaning toward trouble. His name was Joel Ramirez. A lot of his friends were involved in gangs, and he was looking for direction. I befriended him and would leave him tickets to the Mets or Yankees games whenever I was in New York. We didn't talk often, but when we did talk, we made it count. Joel ended up in the New York City police department and retired as a detective. Along the way, he finished his undergraduate degree and started working toward a master's. We're still in touch.

I was on the road in New York as Giants manager one time in the 1990s and spent a night going club to club with John F. Kennedy Jr., introduced by our mutual friend Jeff Gradinger, Kennedy's roommate at Brown and co-owner of Miss Pearl's Jam House in San Francisco. It was just the two of us, and he kept taking me to these speakeasies, places with no name out front I'd have never been to on my own. We had a good time hanging out, but what I remember was how deeply humble the young man was. In the clubhouse earlier, the players' wives all had their husbands asking him for autographs, and he was shy, almost embarrassed. When he died in a small plane crash a year or so after that, I kept thinking about that deep humility of his. If he can be that humble, so can all of us. I've always tried to treat everyone I encounter well along the way. If I've ever fallen short of that mark and mistreated anyone, or if someone was hurt along the way, intentionally or not, I humbly apologize and ask for your forgiveness, and sincerely hope I may have helped many more than I hurt.

Baseball is a teacher. It teaches you to look past the disappointment of an hour ago or a day ago or a year ago. If you carry one at-bat into the next, you've already lost. You have to let it go. No one can let it go all the time, but you live that lesson, every day, for enough months, enough years, enough decades, it starts to settle deep inside. Where you find your wisdom is up to you. But that wisdom is out there, all around you, in your life, in the people you know and the experiences you have. Sometimes, every once in a while, we get to a place where we look for wisdom where wisdom has found us. We let that wisdom shine a light. I'm not talking about a blinding tunnel of light, like that scene in *The Blues Brothers* where Jake and Elwood watch James Brown as a preacher up there singing and dancing and an actual shaft of light shines down on Elwood in revelation. ("The band!" he starts saying.) I'm talking about something more like blinking until your eyes adjust to the mellow, heart-melting beauty of light on a horizon gleaming through a tree line, whether fishing in Mississippi or halfway up the Sierra. A kind of hush comes over you, and you feel all of it a little more, you see it all a little more, and maybe something touches you that you didn't know was going to touch you. Even a speck of light in a dark tunnel gives a ray of hope no matter how small.

To me, life is a wonderful gift. That's how it has been for me. I'm so appreciative of all that has come my way. When I let it all settle in my mind, I see that along the way so much that happened to me was all for a purpose, whether it was something good or bad or great. Things happened for a reason, even if it took me months or years or sometimes decades to look back and put it all together. You can't earn that kind of perspective if you don't let go of the distractions along the way. We're all just human. People are going to annoy us or piss us off or just confuse us, and maybe it's a natural human reaction to get a little caught up in that. We feel a pent-up kind of anger or frustration that we bottle up too long.

If you've read this far into my book, thanks for hanging with me. I hope my stories have brought you a smile here and there. I hope you've heard the music with me. I hope you had the feeling of being right there with me at times, almost like you could hear the crack of the bat and instantly know "home run." I hope my stories have offered a reminder that life has a lot to teach us all, the way it has me. We're all going to fall short at times in learning all that we can. Or in letting life's teachings help turn us into better people. But in life, like in baseball, you always get another at-bat, so long as you're alive and kicking. You always get a new at-bat. A new opportunity, if only you can let go of whatever came before. Then you can grip that bat in your hands, bounce a little on your knees in the box to get comfortable, then put your head down and stay alert to what's coming. Maybe you'll barrel up and drive that ball. Maybe you'll hit it right over the fence. Or maybe you swing through an off-speed pitch and strike out. Whatever happens, you keep learning. You stay alert to new lessons. You tune out so you can tune in.

Hopefully, my life story might help someone now or in the future to have faith and give back. We all have crossroads in our lives. You could say our country is at a crossroads as I write these words in October 2025. We all know the difference between right and wrong until we start ignoring the voice in our head that tells us which is which. My dad always told me, "Son, when you come to a crossroads, take the road to the right." In other words: Do the right thing. Finding the right road, the right way, can be hard. I hope that we can all try to look inside a little more and get through this tumultuous period in our country's history, which in a lot of ways reminds me of the 1960s that I lived through. Maybe we can find a way forward without breaking a lot of what was good about this country. Maybe then we might have a chance of doing something about all the ways this country has fallen short. A man can hope. A man can always hope. As John Lewis said, "Never give up. Never give in. . . . Hate is too big a burden a bear." Or as B.B. King sings, "Everybody wants to know /

Why I sing the blues . . . Well, I've been around a long time / I really have paid my dues."

Writing this book has in a way been the biggest crossroads of all for me. I had no idea that delving into my life to tell my story would feel like such a journey with so many crossroads along the way. You won't find me writing words I don't mean. I've thought about every sentence in this book, mulled it over. I had to really look back on some parts of my life that are painful to reconsider. I wanted to do that with honesty and, I hope, with grace. I've never wanted to come across as an angry man because that is not the truth of who I am. Yes, I have anger in me, and it mostly comes out only if I'm provoked. But I've always been someone a lot more likely to laugh or break out in a big smile. This book has been a crossroads because I'm trying to take a few stories from my life and use them to start a kind of conversation about the crossroads we all come upon, what we do with them, and how they shape us.

There was so much more I could have told, but then the book would have been even longer. It will all be worth it every time one person reads my words and talks to another person about what my book made them think or feel. The circle will in a way be complete. From Hank to me to you. From my mom to me to you. From my dad to me to you. From a lot of people I've been lucky enough to be around to me to you. And from the game of baseball itself—which I only fell in love with later in life—to me to you. A lot of perseverance, character, and hope. I love baseball because baseball is everything. It brings out everything in us, at one time or another, and it can teach us just about anything, if we pay attention long enough. To get that far takes a lot of getting over it. A lot of letting go of baggage. But it feels good to travel light. It feels real good. I think I'm almost there.

One-Love,
Dusty Baker

ACKNOWLEDGMENTS

My life started in Riverside, where I have so many to thank for helping raise me up, from Rosie Bonds (my babysitter) and Mama Bonds, my godparents Mr. and Mrs. Clay, who loved me like the grandparents I never had, and Rev. Moss at Park Avenue Baptist Church and coach Hughes, coach Hammerschmidt, and coach Morales, and my teacher Mrs. Shapiro, who didn't laugh when I told her I was going be a professional athlete one day, and my piano teacher Mrs. Burrell. I looked up to guys like Mike Davis and his younger brother Stan, Bobby Bonds's best friend; Marshall Anderson and Art Gilmore; and the Downs brothers, Bill (my Uncle Floyd's best friend), Emmett, and Larry. Sam Salinas and Richard "Chile" Hernandez taught me about Cinco de Mayo. My buddy Rusty Evans, whose sister kept her horse behind our house, and teammates Billy Baker, Mike Bartee, and Eric Hall, and other family friends like Dale Roberts, Tommy Hall, Alvin Davis, and his parents Bill and Hattie Davis, close friends of my parents, Mr. Matthews and his sons, James and Phil, and the Boykin family.

The first two friends I made when my family moved to Carmichael were Dennis Kludt and Brad Johnson, and Brad's mom Mrs. Johnson was like a second mom to me. I want to thank my neighbor Gary Woodrell, Paula Saed and her family, Dave Coleman, who became a renowned doctor, and family, Sue Ells and family, and the Roysters, all good athletes. I learned so much from friends who were great athletes like Darnell

Hillman, the best basketball player of our time, Bob Oliver, the Bobby Bonds of Sacramento, Joe Kemp, Leon and Curtis Brown and Larry Brown, Bill Crenshaw, Tony Thomas, Leron Lee and his brother Leon, and Pete Earhardt. Our team manager, Dave Corso, went on to be NBC's executive in charge of foreign correspondents. Coach McCullough taught me about basketball and about life, like my American Legion coach Spider Jorgensen. Thanks also to Coach McCormick, my econ teacher Mr. Trodos, my English teachers Mrs. White and Mrs. Thaxton (my biggest fan), coach Kasten and coach Al Baeta. Joe Babich and his wife Monica, Steve Skelly and family, and Sam Lovelace remain close friends. Some of my hunting and fishing friends were Kenny Tennell, my cousin Charles Johnson, Gizzy Galli, Brett Leber, and Paul Raquel. And thanks to Mark Gillam, a close family friend and Vic's business partner.

For my Atlanta years, I thank first of Hank's wife Barbara, who took care of me, and Ruby Garr, Ralph's wife, who cooked for us, and Billye Aaron, Hank's second wife, as well as Bill and Ruby Lucas and Buzz Willis and his sister Jean Cook. Mike and Gary Wise's mom would cook for me, too. It was an honor to get to know Maynard Jackson and Ambassador Andrew Young, both mayors of Atlanta, and Jesse Jackson. Joe Hand was best man at my first wedding. Braves trainer Sam Ayoub and clubhouse man John "Red" Holland and director of travel Donald Davidson always took care of me, and scout Bill Wight, GM Paul Richards, coach Bob Kennedy, and GM Eddie Robinson were all supporters. We lived on Busy Bee soul food and Bruce Friedman of Friedman's Shoes gave us a discount and also carried oversized shoes, which I needed, and platform shoes. We had many good conversations.

Chico Renfroe was a reporter who had played shortstop in the Negro Leagues. Among my many teammates who became friends, have to mention Davey Johnson, Darrell Evans, Marty Perez, Johnny Oates, Leo Foster, Larvell "Sugar Bear" Blanks, Oscar Brown, Tom House, Rowland Office, and Paul Casanova. Orlando Cepeda turned me on to a world of Latin music and so much more. Billy Williams, who had the same birthday as me, taught me about the life of baseball. Willie McCovey, Willie Mays, Joe Morgan, and Willie Stargell welcomed me to the big leagues as a kid. Thanks to my minor-league managers, Clint Courtney, Eddie Haas, and Clyde King, and my Marine Corps drill sergeant, Sgt. Goolesby, for helping make a man out of me. Other lifelong friends from then are Alan Rabinovitch, Alan Lande and Mitchell Gant in Montreal, and Bill Cosby, a big baseball fan, my friend for many years.

Sandy Koufax retired in 1966 at age thirty, but when I joined the Dodgers in 1976 he looked to me like he could probably still pitch a complete-game shutout. He quickly became a lifelong friend and confidant. Other mentors were Jim Gilliam, a brilliant baseball man, and Don Newcombe, Roy Campanella, Joe Black, my boyhood hero Tommy Davis, and Lou Johnson, as good a problem solver as I've met. I also learned from coaches Preston Gómez and Danny Ozark, both great baseball men. Thanks to Dr. Frank Jobe, who saved my knees and saved my career, and tax expert Karen Hawkins, who saved my finances, along with my accountant, Jim Church. I'd listened to the great Vin Scully on a transistor radio as a kid and he became a friend, along with broadcaster Russ Porter. Billy DeLury, Dodger traveling secretary going back to Brooklyn, took care of me. L.A. friends included the sportswriter Lyle Spencer, Mayor Tom Bradley and his wife Ethel, John Payton, Juan Avant, and sportscaster Jim Hill, a longtime friend who helped keep me straight in L.A., and finally Pastor John Werhas, a former big-league third baseman, who was our chapel leader and ministered us on the Dodgers at a time when I needed it badly. I met Brett Crawford in L.A. when he was about twelve and we were so close, he was like a son to me, and I later went to see him in Illinois, him and his sons Dustin and Dalton and wife Angie. And a special shoutout to Bob Nightengale, one of the most knowledgeable sportswriters of all time, and Chris Howe, Steve Howe's younger brother, and I've remained close to Chris and the Howe family.

I may never have landed my coaching and managing jobs in San Francisco if not for the mentorship of Warriors coach Al Attles and 49er coach Bill Walsh, two great men with great minds. The 49ers president Carmen Policy was also good to me and my family. I'll always be thankful to Giants owner Peter Magowan, who first gave me the opportunity to manage and helped me along the way, and Karen Sweeney, Mario Alioto, Russ Stanley, and Mike Murphy. Many others in the Giants' ownership group became generous friends and confidants, especially Walter Shorenstein, Phil Greer, Dick Goldman, Larry Nibbi, and Allan Byer. Thanks also to Giants president Larry Baer and to Bob Quinn, my first GM as manager, and Brian Sabean and Ned Colletti, trainers Mark Letendre and Stan Conte, media relations people Jim Moorehead, Staci Slaughter, Robin Carr Locke, Shana Daum, and traveling secretaries Dirk Smith and Reggie Younger Jr., and Rob McDonald. Bertha Fajardo was always there for both Orlando and me.

San Francisco Mayor Willie Brown was also a longtime mentor and confidant. I learned from Frank Robinson, the first Black manager, and former Giant Gary Matthews ("Sarge"), a friend who later was one of my coaches. I can't give shoutouts to all the cool people in Bay Area sports media, but I have to mention Mark Ibanez of KTVU and Martin Wyatt of KGO, both good men. Giants broadcasters Mike Krukow and Duane Kuiper, Jon Miller, Hank Greenwald, Ted Robinson, Tito Fuentes, Amaury Pi-Gonzalez, John Catchings and his wife Lynn, Howard Bryant, a former newspaper guy who went on to write some heavy books, Monte Poole, Terence Moore, Bruce Jenkins, Ron Thomas, Mark Gonzalez, Vern Glenn, John Shea, Glenn Schwarz, Henry Schulman, and Joan Ryan.

Sylvester Jackson, a radio personality and good friend, went to many music venues with Melissa and me. When he passed in 1992, I promised his wife Marilyn I would help take care of their two young children, Noah and Jolieba. Both are successes in life. Noah was Darren's coach at Cal. Other friends in the Bay Area include legendary blues man John Lee Hooker, auto dealer Reynold Victor, Dr. Bill Gould and Brooks Johnson of Stanford, my dentist Dr. James McKenna, Dr. Dave and Judy, Eric Wright and Kenna Turner, Setrak Soghomonian, Dr. Reggie Rector and Dr. Joseph Presti, Father Jim, Jack Williams, and Terry Heffernan. And finally, thanks to Earl Smith, pastor and chaplain for the Giants and 49ers and at San Quentin, a great man with a great story, and the Reverend Cecil Williams, minister and Civil Rights leader, a good friend who helped me immensely.

In Chicago, GM Jim Hendry was easy to work with and a good baseball man who showed me much respect, along with team president Andy MacPhail, PR director Sharon Pannozzo, clubhouse manager Otis Hellmann, and team physician Dr. Adams who saved my life a few years later. Thanks to all my coaches for all they did, Sarge, Gene Clines, Wendell Kim, Dick Pole, Chris Speier, and Juan Lopez, and to Buddy Guy, Chuck Barksdale of the Dells, Chef Hans, Uncle Lino and Auntie Cora Chavez, Bob Battie, Steve King, Robert Taylor, and Matt Starcevich.

You're only as good as your coaches and players, and in Cincinnati I was fortunate to have a great team leader in Scott Rolen, also a good person, and a great group of players. I was joined once again by coaches Dick Pole, Chris Speier, and Juan Lopez, and also had Brook Jacoby, Billy Hatcher, and Mark Berry, Mack Jenkins and later Bryan Price. Thanks also to Pete Rose, always a generous competitor, and director of travel Gary Wahoff, trainer Paul Lessard, and fitness instructor Matt Krause, all the Stowe family, owner Bob Castellini, GMs Wayne Krivsky and Walt Jocketty, PR man Rob Butcher, team president Dick Williams, and his older brother, Tom Williams, part of the ownership group. Kerry Hardy's parents, Mr. and Mrs. Hardy, and Dr. Reggie Low and his assistant Wendy Foster kept me going in Sacramento, even to this day.

In Washington, I'll start by thanking my friend Barack Obama, who inspired me and motivated me as a leader of men, and Dennis Limberhands, a great spirit, and his son D.J. Limberhands. Nationals GM Mike Rizzo was fair and direct and let me do my job, PR director Amanda Comak and her assistant Kyle Brostowitz were both conscientious and honest with me, and excellent scouts Johnny DiPuglia and De Jon Watson were also good friends. As always, everything depended on my coaches: Chris Speier, Jacque Jones, Rick Schu, Mike Maddux, Dan Firova, Davey Lopes, and Bob Henley.

Thanks to Astros owner Jim Crane for trusting me to step into a difficult situation for us all, and his assistant Paula Harris, and also to Anita Sehgal and Gene Dias, who looked out for me with the media, trainer Jeremiah Randall and Dr. Muntz, team counsel Giles Kibbe, GM Jim Quick, assistant GM Jeff Bagwell, Enos Cabell, Craig Biggio, and Reggie

Jackson, and Mr. Baseball and my coaches: Joe Espada, Alex Cintron, Troy Snitker, Brent Strom, Josh Miller, Omar Lopez, Gary Pettis, and Bill Murphy. Other Houston friends included Jimmy Lee Solomon, a Major League Baseball executive vice president, Mayor Sylvester Turner, Joe Fontenot, Donald Bond, Walter Bond's son, Ralph Cooper, Bob Watson, J. R. Richard, and Jennifer Springs.

My cement man, Mike Homen, became a good friend who cheered us along as we made progress on the book, and is always there, like Kenny and Dennis. Thanks to Michael Zagaris, as great a dude as he is a photographer, for driving all the way from the Bay to take my picture for the cover, and fellow great Bay Area photographer Brad Mangin, and at Crown Kevin Doughten and his assistant Jess Scott for really caring and putting so much into this project from Day One—and for giving me the freedom to really express myself. And thanks to my assistant Nicole Romeo, who is also a writer, for all her hard work and professionalism, and especially for all the extra work it took to get the pictures ready for the book and for her sharp editorial eye in proofreading for needed corrections. My agents Joe Branch and Alex Kane guided me through the process and both have very bright futures. This is the fourth project I've worked on with Steve Kettmann, including doing an essay for his Pedro Gomez book *Remember Who You Are.* Steve, you have my gratitude for all the time, effort, and guidance. This was a major project which brought back many emotions from deep inside. I'm hoping that you feel as good about this project as I do. (And thanks to Coco, Anaïs, and Sarah for lending me your dad and husband, oftentimes away from home, when I know you wanted him with you.) Thank you, Steve, and you've become a good friend.

My wife Melissa read the book and made some corrections and helped me keep going even when this project felt like it would never end. I'm lucky to have her, my son Darren, and my daughter Tosh to remind me of what's most important. When I married Melissa, I added another family, Uncle Alex and Auntie Puring, Wayne, Margaux, Ryan, James, Renee, Tyler and Alexandria, and cousins Butch, Cely, Jonathan, and Andre, also Amador, Imelda, Herb, Ashley, Kiana and Kailey, Vivian,

Lindsay, Eric, Flo, Aaron, Sarah, Jacob, Marc, Virna, Austin, Alaina, and Abigal. I miss my late mother-in-law, Ysabel Violeta, Uncle Tinoy, Uncle Jun, and Carlos.

I only made one All-Star team growing up, so I'm especially thankful for any Hall of Fame that inducts me, and it's a good list:

Little League Hall of Excellence
Baseball Digest Lifetime Achievement Award
Booker T. Washington Lifetime Achievement Award
Jackie Robinson Chairman's Award
13th and 14th NAACP Image Awards
Lou Gehrig Ironman Award
Sacramento City and County Hall of Fame
Riverside Sport Hall of Fame
Sacramento Sports Hall of Fame
National High School Sports Hall of Fame
African American Ethnic Hall of Fame
California Outdoors Hall of Fame
Sac-Joaquin Section Hall of Fame
Sacramento Walk of Stars
Arizona Cactus League Hall of Fame
Arizona Fall League Hall of Fame
Marine Corps Sports Hall of Fame

Last of all, I want to thank you the reader or you the listener.

ABOUT THE AUTHOR

JOHNNIE B. "DUSTY" BAKER JR. is the former manager of the San Francisco Giants, Chicago Cubs, Cincinnati Reds, Washington Nationals, and Houston Astros. Baker was drafted by the Atlanta Braves after graduating high school in 1967 and went on to win the World Series in 1981 with the Los Angeles Dodgers. Baker retired as a player in 1986 and has since become one of the most celebrated managers in MLB history. He was the recipient of *Baseball Digest*'s Lifetime Achievement Award in 2024.